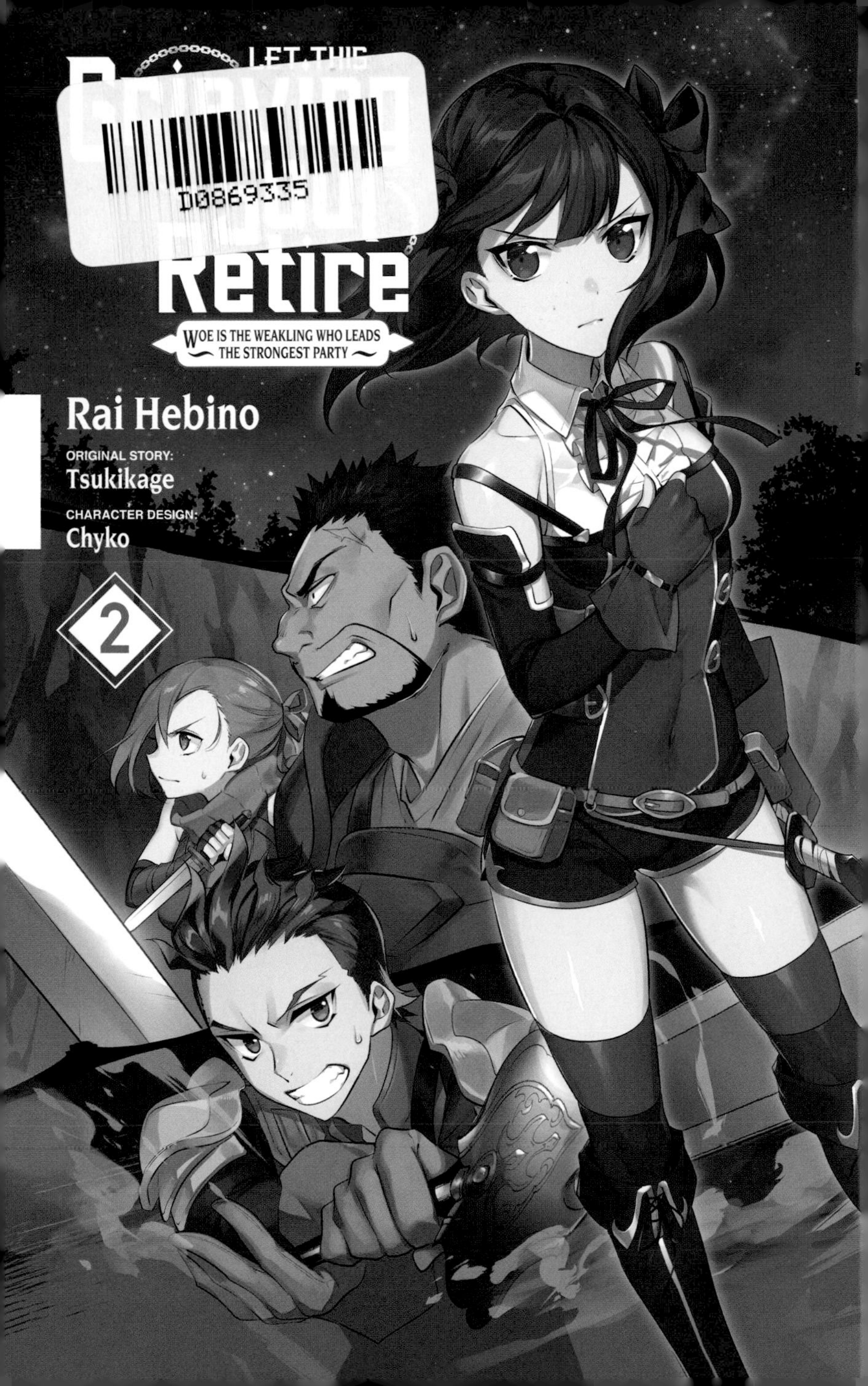

LET THIS

Retire

WOE IS THE WEAKLING WHO LEADS THE STRONGEST PARTY

Rai Hebino

ORIGINAL STORY:
Tsukikage

CHARACTER DESIGN:
Chyko

2

CONTENTS

Let This Grieving Soul Retire
~ Woe Is the Weakling Who
Leads the Strongest Party ~

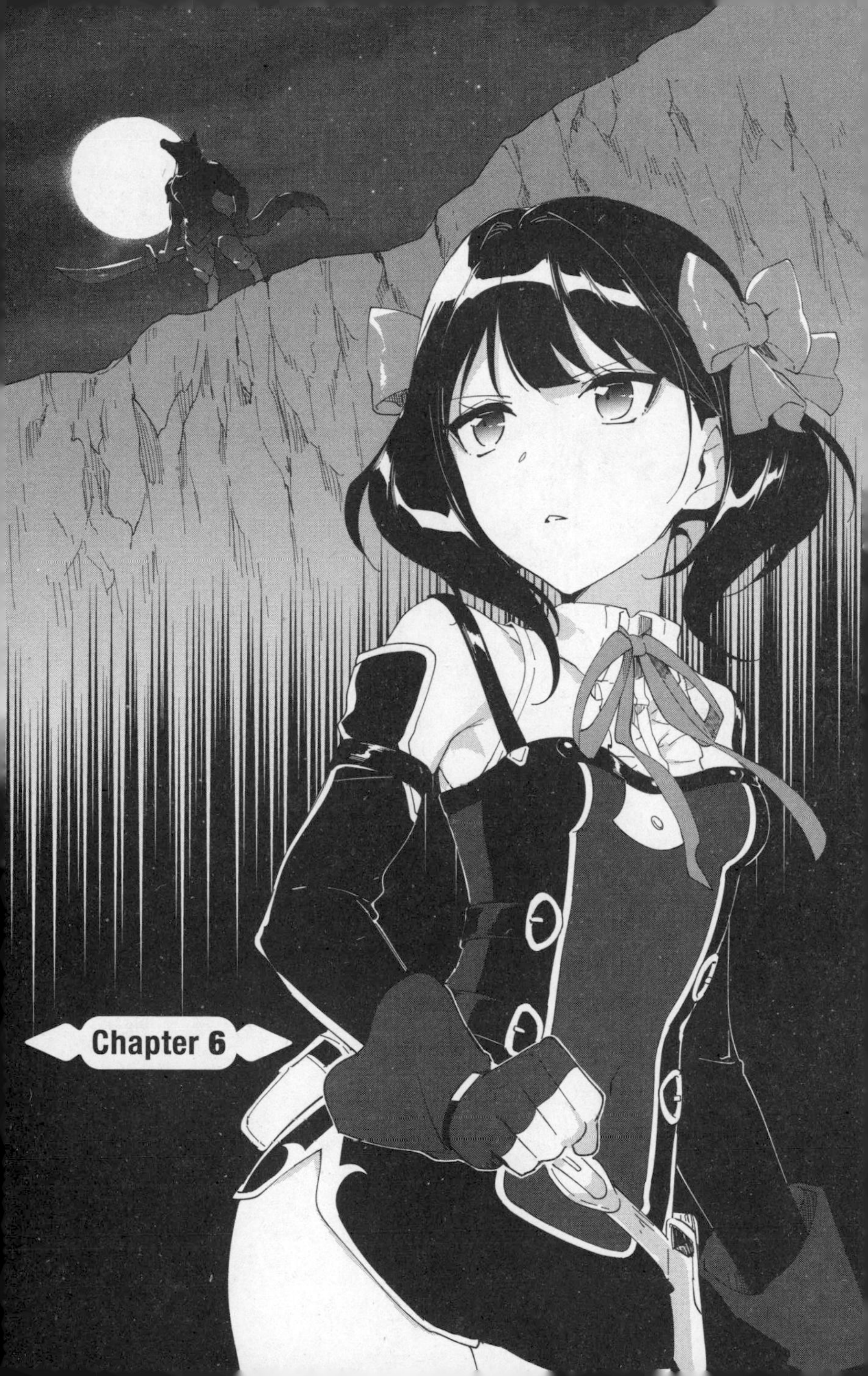
Chapter 6

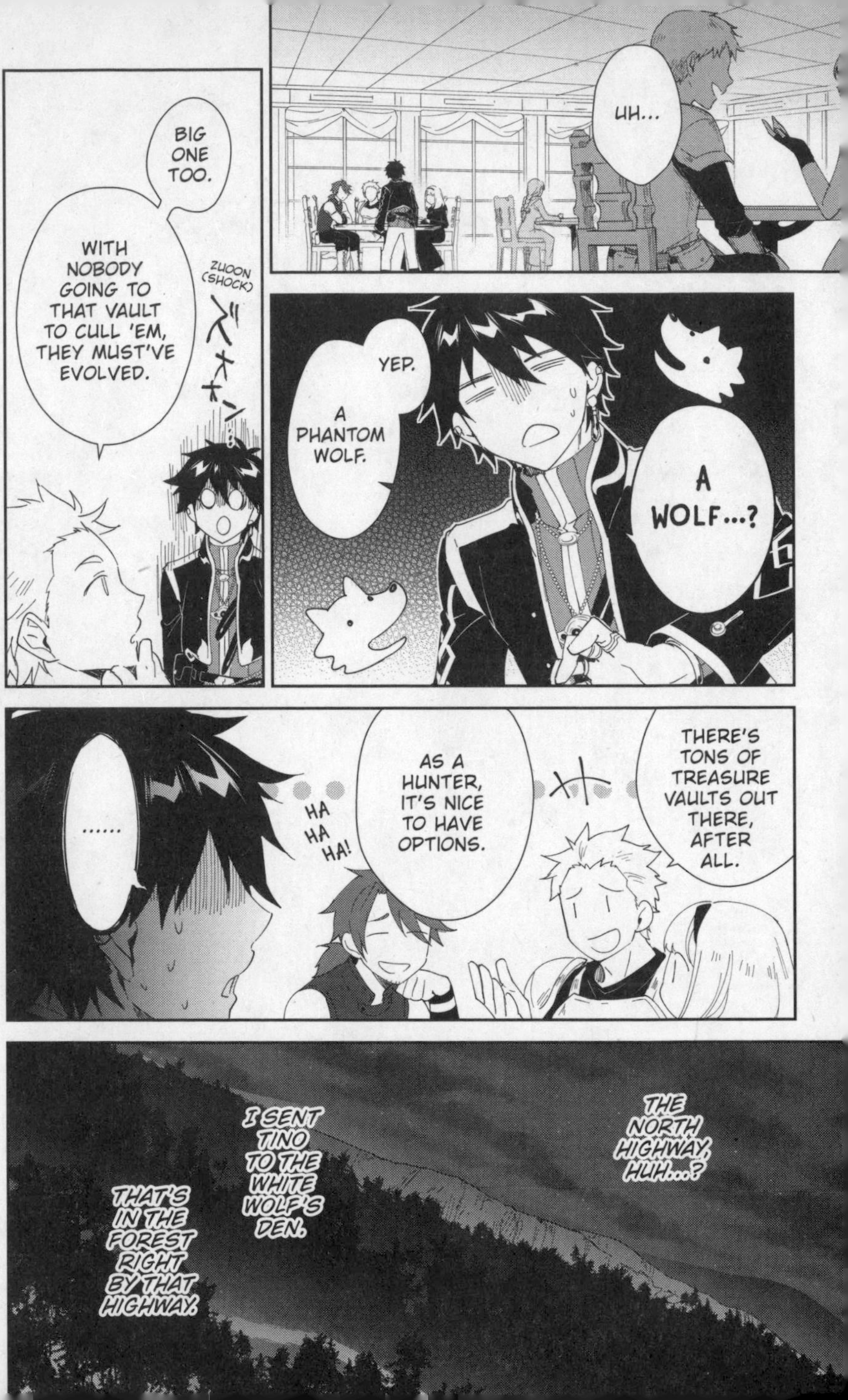
UH...
A WOLF...?
YEP.
A PHANTOM WOLF.
BIG ONE TOO.
WITH NOBODY GOING TO THAT VAULT TO CULL 'EM, THEY MUST'VE EVOLVED.
ZUOON (SHOCK)
THERE'S TONS OF TREASURE VAULTS OUT THERE, AFTER ALL.
AS A HUNTER, IT'S NICE TO HAVE OPTIONS.
HA HA HA!
......
THE NORTH HIGHWAY, HUH...?
I SENT TINO TO THE WHITE WOLF'S DEN.
THAT'S IN THE FOREST RIGHT BY THAT HIGHWAY.

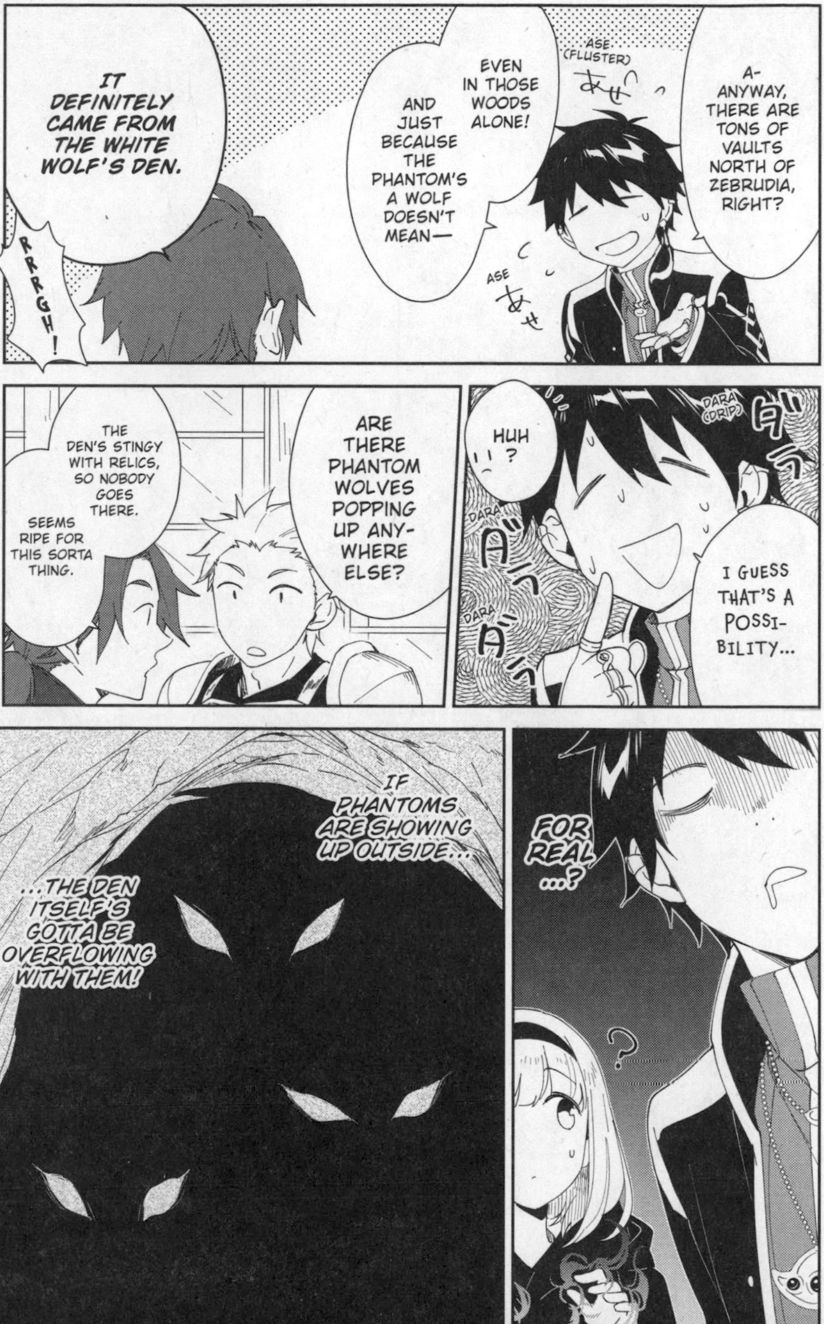
A- ANYWAY, THERE ARE TONS OF VAULTS NORTH OF ZEBRUDIA, RIGHT?
ASE (FLUSTER) あせ
EVEN IN THOSE WOODS ALONE!
AND JUST BECAUSE THE PHANTOM'S A WOLF DOESN'T MEAN—
ASE あせ
IT DEFINITELY CAME FROM THE WHITE WOLF'S DEN.
RRRGH!
DARA (DRIP) ダラ
HUH?
I GUESS THAT'S A POSSIBILITY...
DARA ダラ
DARA ダラ
ARE THERE PHANTOM WOLVES POPPING UP ANYWHERE ELSE?
THE DEN'S STINGY WITH RELICS, SO NOBODY GOES THERE.
SEEMS RIPE FOR THIS SORTA THING.
FOR REAL...?
IF PHANTOMS ARE SHOWING UP OUTSIDE...
...THE DEN ITSELF'S GOTTA BE OVERFLOWING WITH THEM!

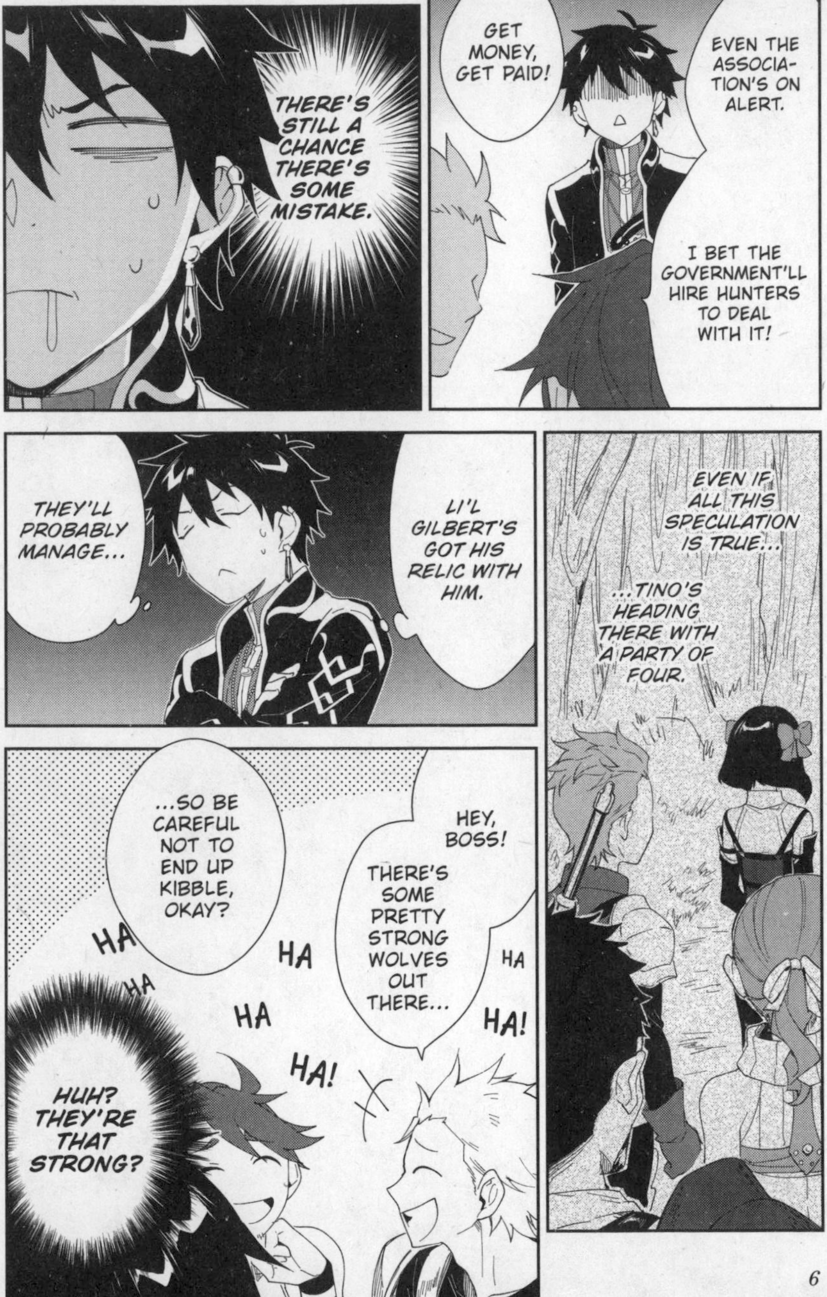
EVEN THE ASSOCIATION'S ON ALERT.
GET MONEY, GET PAID!
I BET THE GOVERNMENT'LL HIRE HUNTERS TO DEAL WITH IT!
THERE'S STILL A CHANCE THERE'S SOME MISTAKE.
EVEN IF ALL THIS SPECULATION IS TRUE...
...TINO'S HEADING THERE WITH A PARTY OF FOUR.
LI'L GILBERT'S GOT HIS RELIC WITH HIM.
THEY'LL PROBABLY MANAGE...
HEY, BOSS!
THERE'S SOME PRETTY STRONG WOLVES OUT THERE...
...SO BE CAREFUL NOT TO END UP KIBBLE, OKAY?
HA
HA!
HA
HA
HA!
HA
HA
HUH? THEY'RE THAT STRONG?

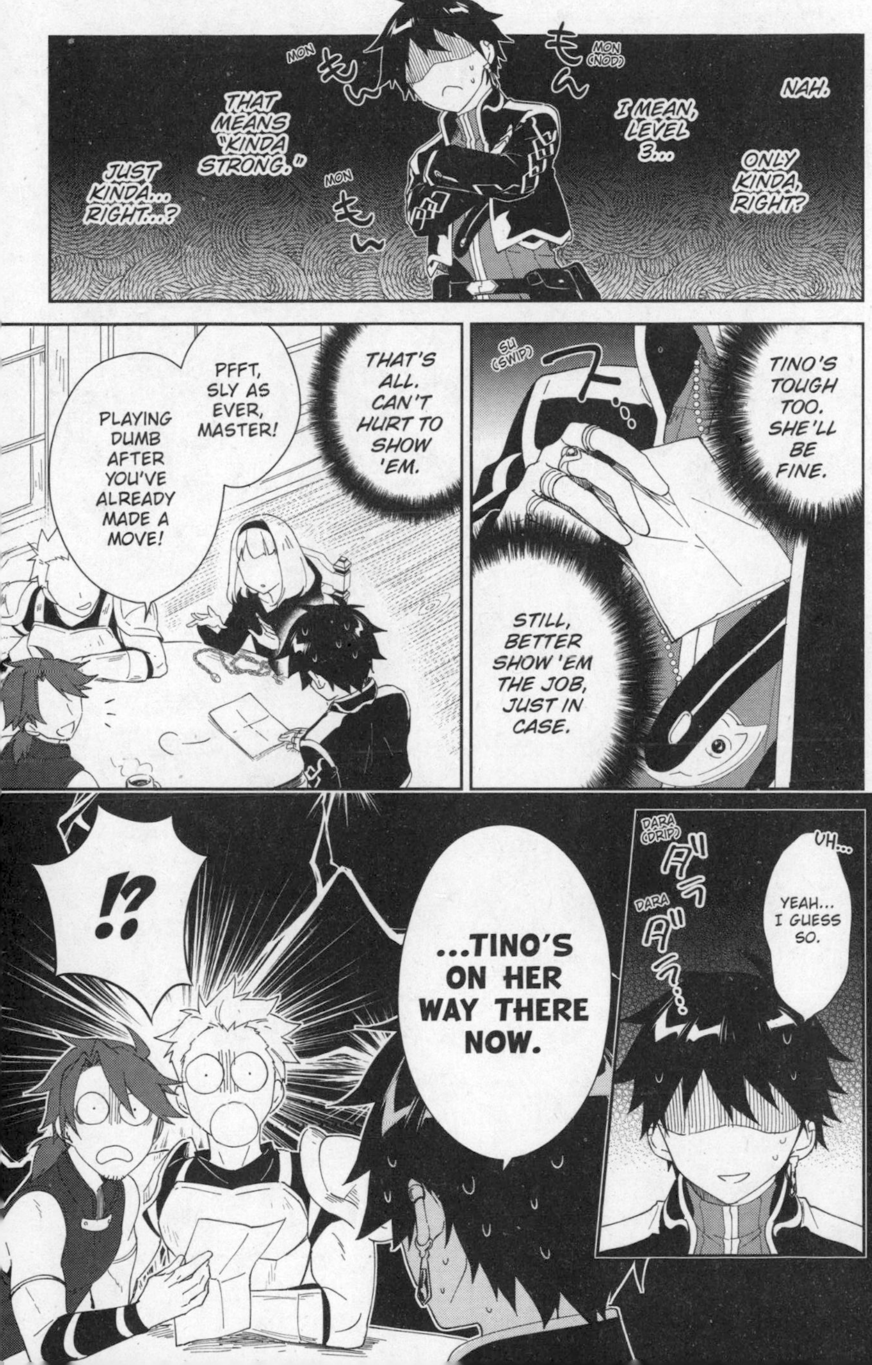
MON (NOD)
もん
NAH.
I MEAN, LEVEL 3...
ONLY KINDA, RIGHT?
MON
もん
THAT MEANS "KINDA STRONG."
MON
もん
JUST KINDA... RIGHT...?
TINO'S TOUGH TOO. SHE'LL BE FINE.
SU (SWIP)
ス…
STILL, BETTER SHOW 'EM THE JOB, JUST IN CASE.
THAT'S ALL. CAN'T HURT TO SHOW 'EM.
PFFT, SLY AS EVER, MASTER!
PLAYING DUMB AFTER YOU'VE ALREADY MADE A MOVE!
UH...
YEAH... I GUESS SO.
DARA (DRIP)
ダラ
DARA
ダラ…
...TINO'S ON HER WAY THERE NOW.
!?

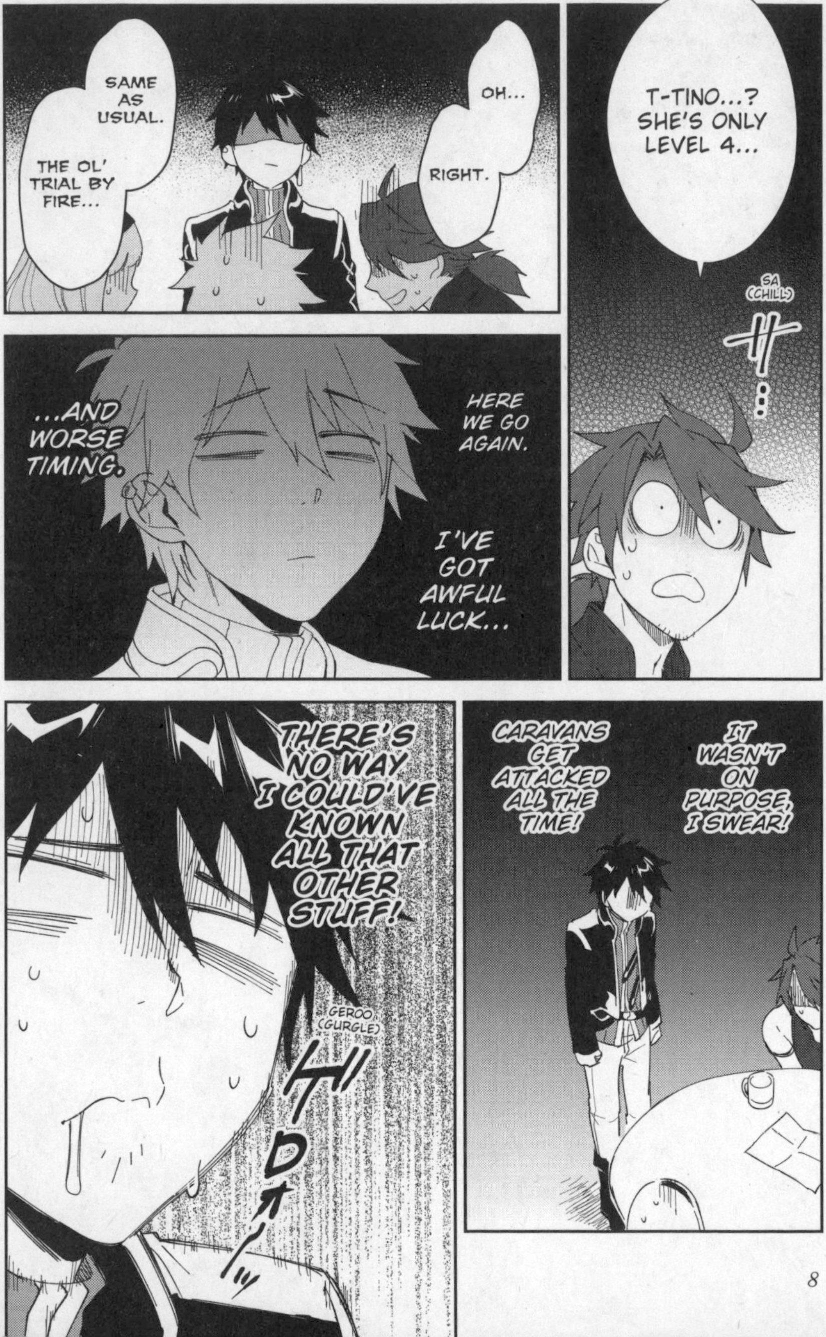
T-TINO...? SHE'S ONLY LEVEL 4...
SA (CHILL)
OH... RIGHT.
SAME AS USUAL.
THE OL' TRIAL BY FIRE...
HERE WE GO AGAIN.
I'VE GOT AWFUL LUCK...
...AND WORSE TIMING.
IT WASN'T ON PURPOSE, I SWEAR!
CARAVANS GET ATTACKED ALL THE TIME!
THERE'S NO WAY I COULD'VE KNOWN ALL THAT OTHER STUFF!
GEROO (GURGLE)

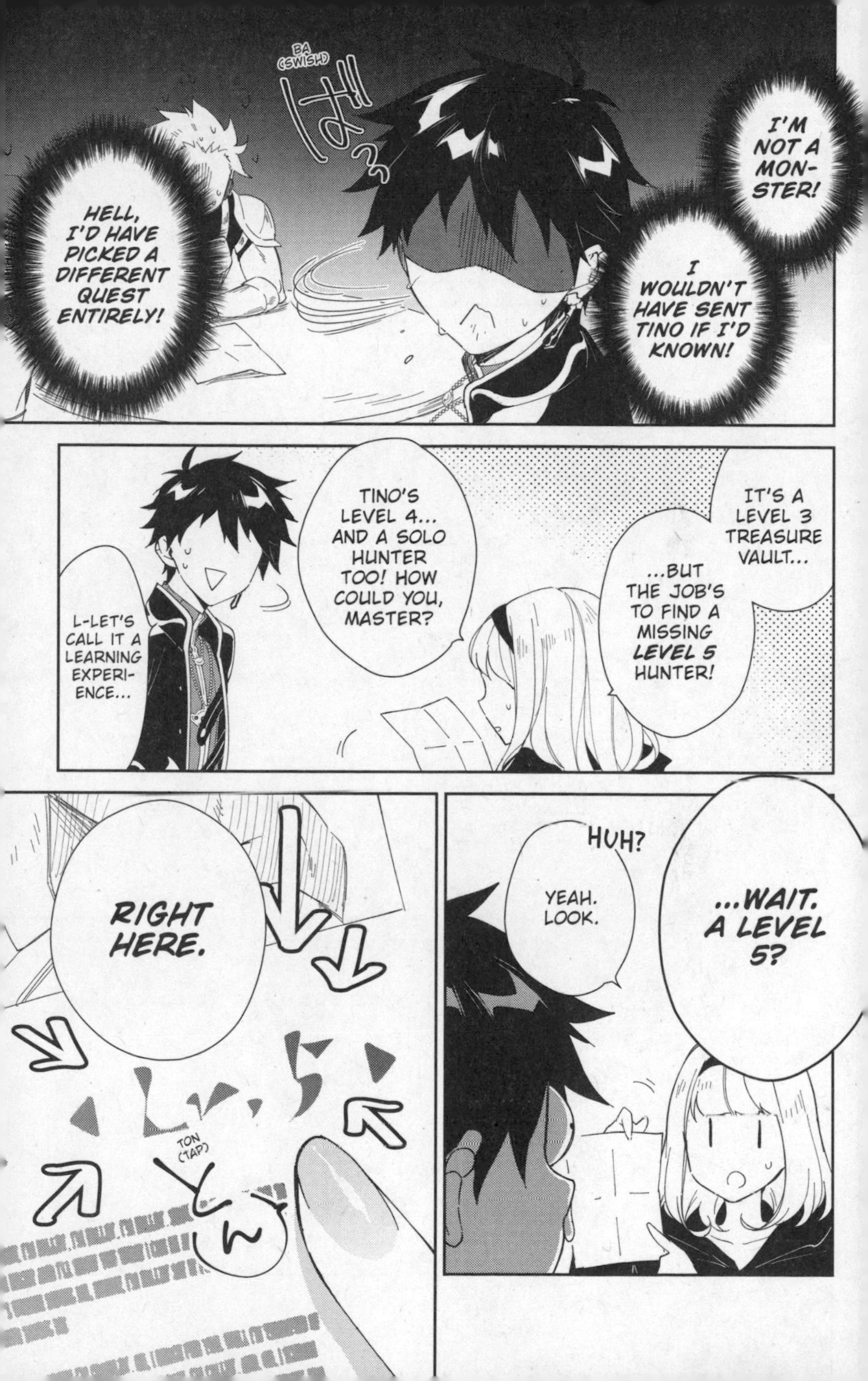
I'M NOT A MON-STER!
I WOULDN'T HAVE SENT TINO IF I'D KNOWN!
BA (SWISH)
HELL, I'D HAVE PICKED A DIFFERENT QUEST ENTIRELY!
IT'S A LEVEL 3 TREASURE VAULT...
...BUT THE JOB'S TO FIND A MISSING LEVEL 5 HUNTER!
TINO'S LEVEL 4... AND A SOLO HUNTER TOO! HOW COULD YOU, MASTER?
L-LET'S CALL IT A LEARNING EXPERI-ENCE...
...WAIT. A LEVEL 5?
HUH?
YEAH. LOOK.
RIGHT HERE.
TON (TAP)

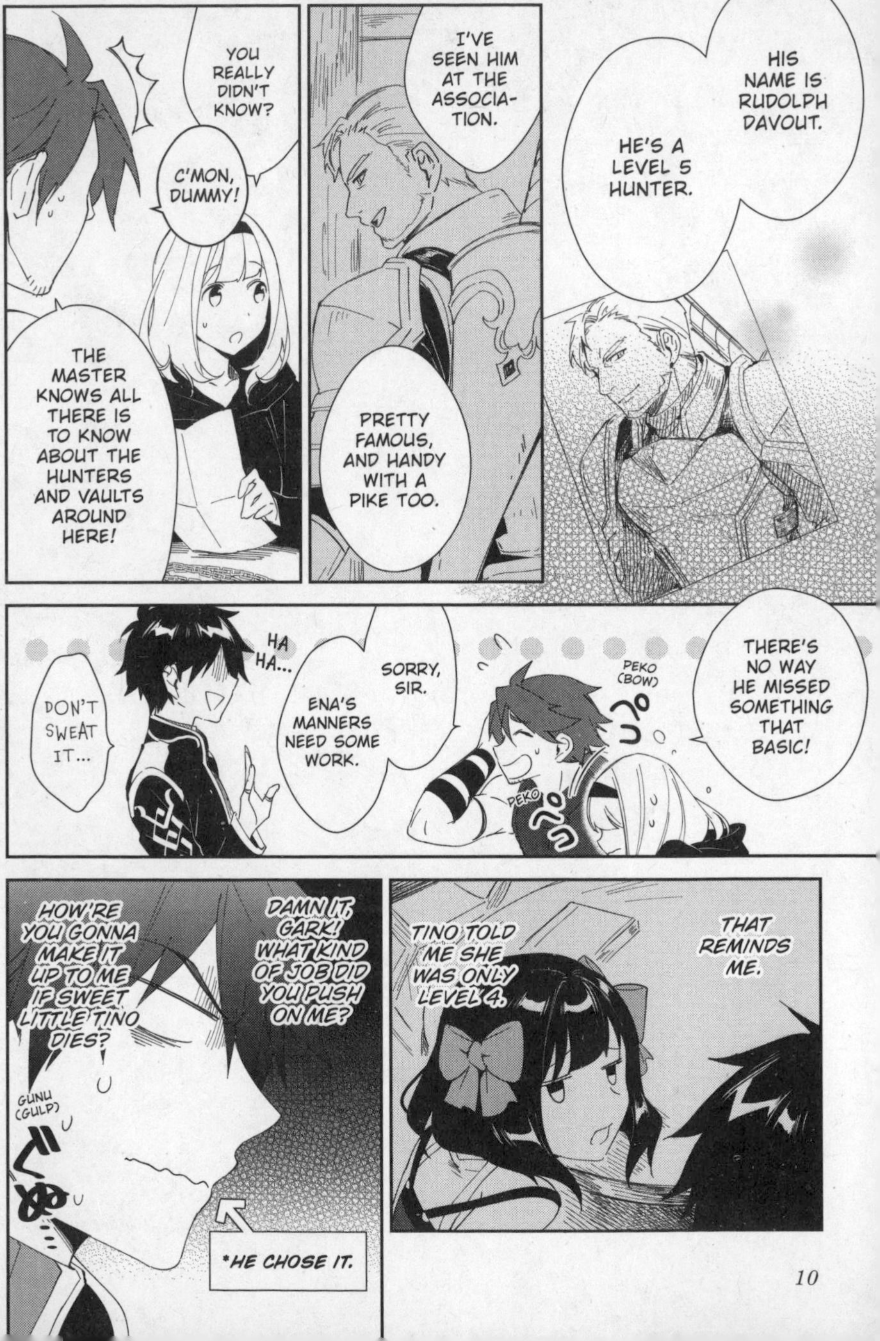
HIS NAME IS RUDOLPH DAVOUT.
HE'S A LEVEL 5 HUNTER.
I'VE SEEN HIM AT THE ASSOCIA-TION.
PRETTY FAMOUS, AND HANDY WITH A PIKE TOO.
YOU REALLY DIDN'T KNOW?
C'MON, DUMMY!
THE MASTER KNOWS ALL THERE IS TO KNOW ABOUT THE HUNTERS AND VAULTS AROUND HERE!
THERE'S NO WAY HE MISSED SOMETHING THAT BASIC!
PEKO (BOW)
PEKO
SORRY, SIR.
ENA'S MANNERS NEED SOME WORK.
HA HA...
DON'T SWEAT IT...
THAT REMINDS ME.
TINO TOLD ME SHE WAS ONLY LEVEL 4.
DAMN IT, GARK! WHAT KIND OF JOB DID YOU PUSH ON ME?
HOW'RE YOU GONNA MAKE IT UP TO ME IF SWEET LITTLE TINO DIES?
GUNU (GULP)
*HE CHOSE IT.

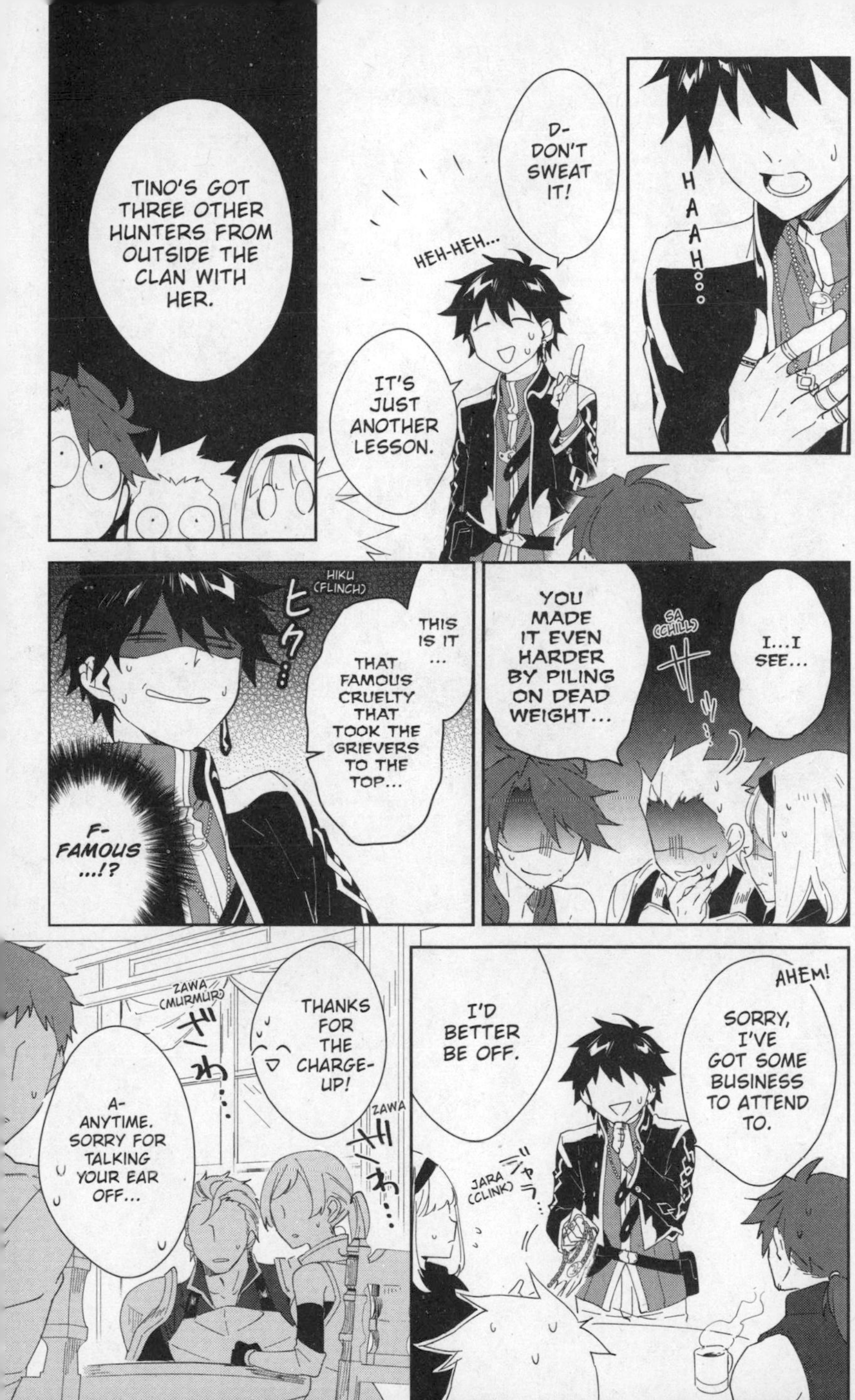
HAAH...
D-DON'T SWEAT IT!
HEH-HEH...
IT'S JUST ANOTHER LESSON.
TINO'S GOT THREE OTHER HUNTERS FROM OUTSIDE THE CLAN WITH HER.
I...I SEE...
SA (CHILL)
YOU MADE IT EVEN HARDER BY PILING ON DEAD WEIGHT...
HIKU (FLINCH)
THIS IS IT ... THAT FAMOUS CRUELTY THAT TOOK THE GRIEVERS TO THE TOP...
F-FAMOUS...!?
AHEM!
SORRY, I'VE GOT SOME BUSINESS TO ATTEND TO.
I'D BETTER BE OFF.
JARA (CLINK)
THANKS FOR THE CHARGE-UP!
ZAWA (MURMUR)
ZAWA
A-ANYTIME. SORRY FOR TALKING YOUR EAR OFF...

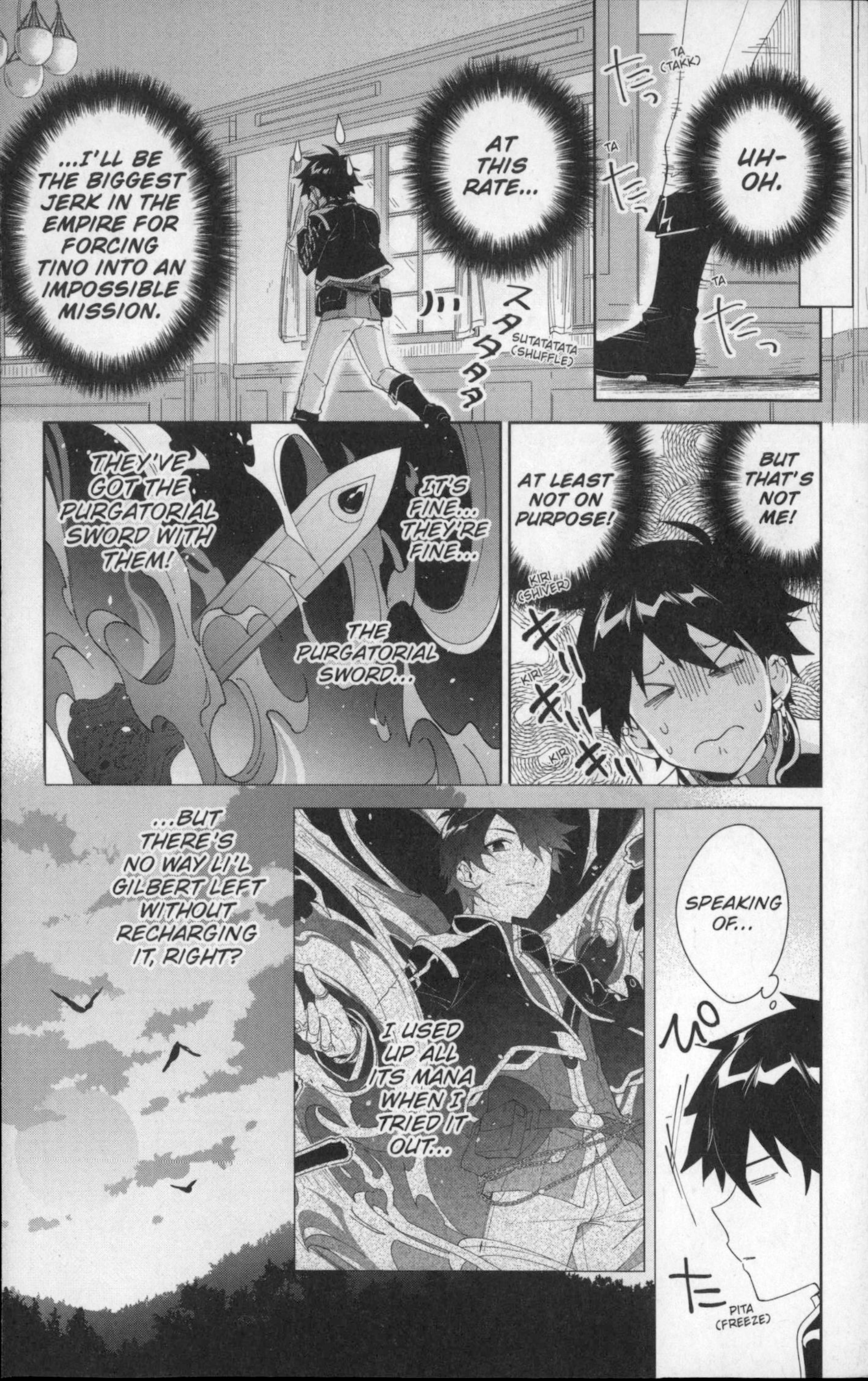

TA (TAKK)
UH-OH.
TA
TA
AT THIS RATE...
...I'LL BE THE BIGGEST JERK IN THE EMPIRE FOR FORCING TINO INTO AN IMPOSSIBLE MISSION.
SUTATATATA (SHUFFLE)
BUT THAT'S NOT ME!
AT LEAST NOT ON PURPOSE!
KIRI (SHIVER)
KIRI
KIRI
IT'S FINE... THEY'RE FINE...
THEY'VE GOT THE PURGATORIAL SWORD WITH THEM!
THE PURGATORIAL SWORD...
SPEAKING OF...
PITA (FREEZE)
I USED UP ALL ITS MANA WHEN I TRIED IT OUT...
...BUT THERE'S NO WAY LI'L GILBERT LEFT WITHOUT RECHARGING IT, RIGHT?

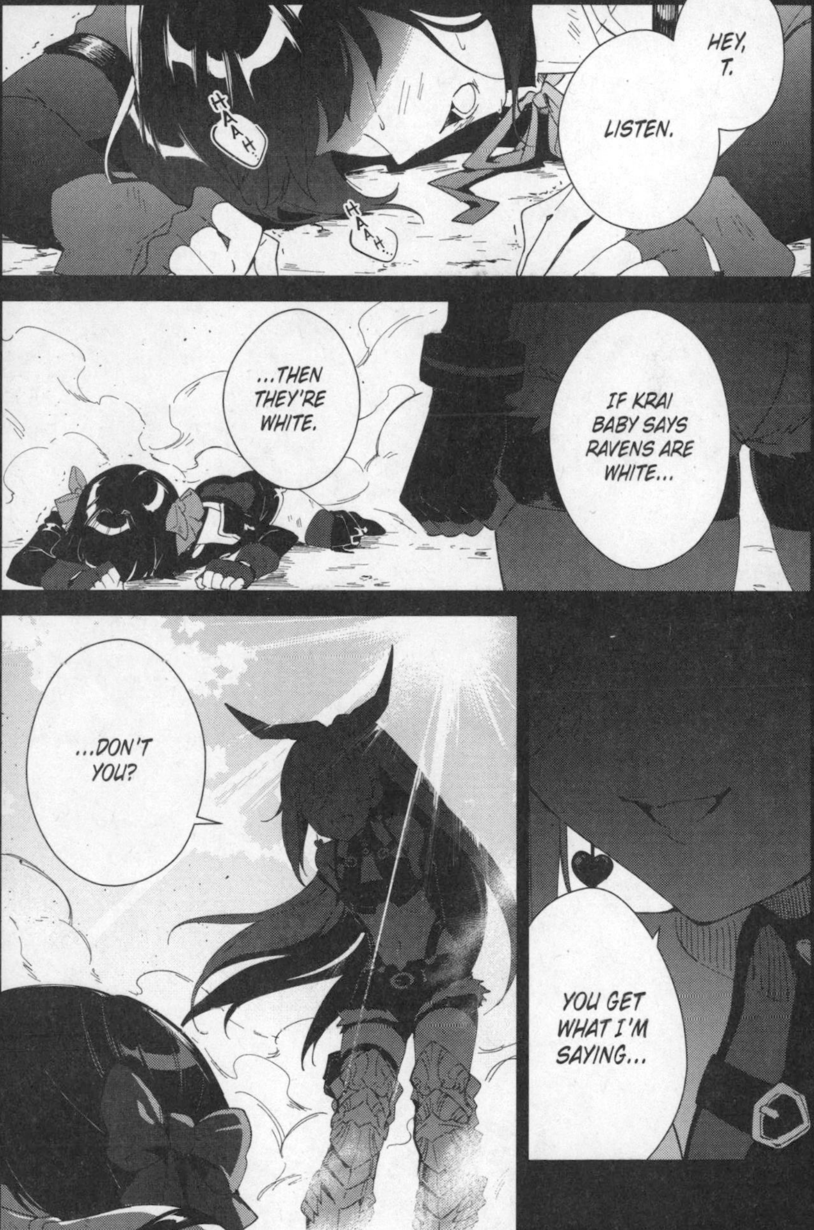
HEY, T.
LISTEN.
HAAH...
HAAH...
IF KRAI BABY SAYS RAVENS ARE WHITE...
...THEN THEY'RE WHITE.
YOU GET WHAT I'M SAYING...
...DON'T YOU?

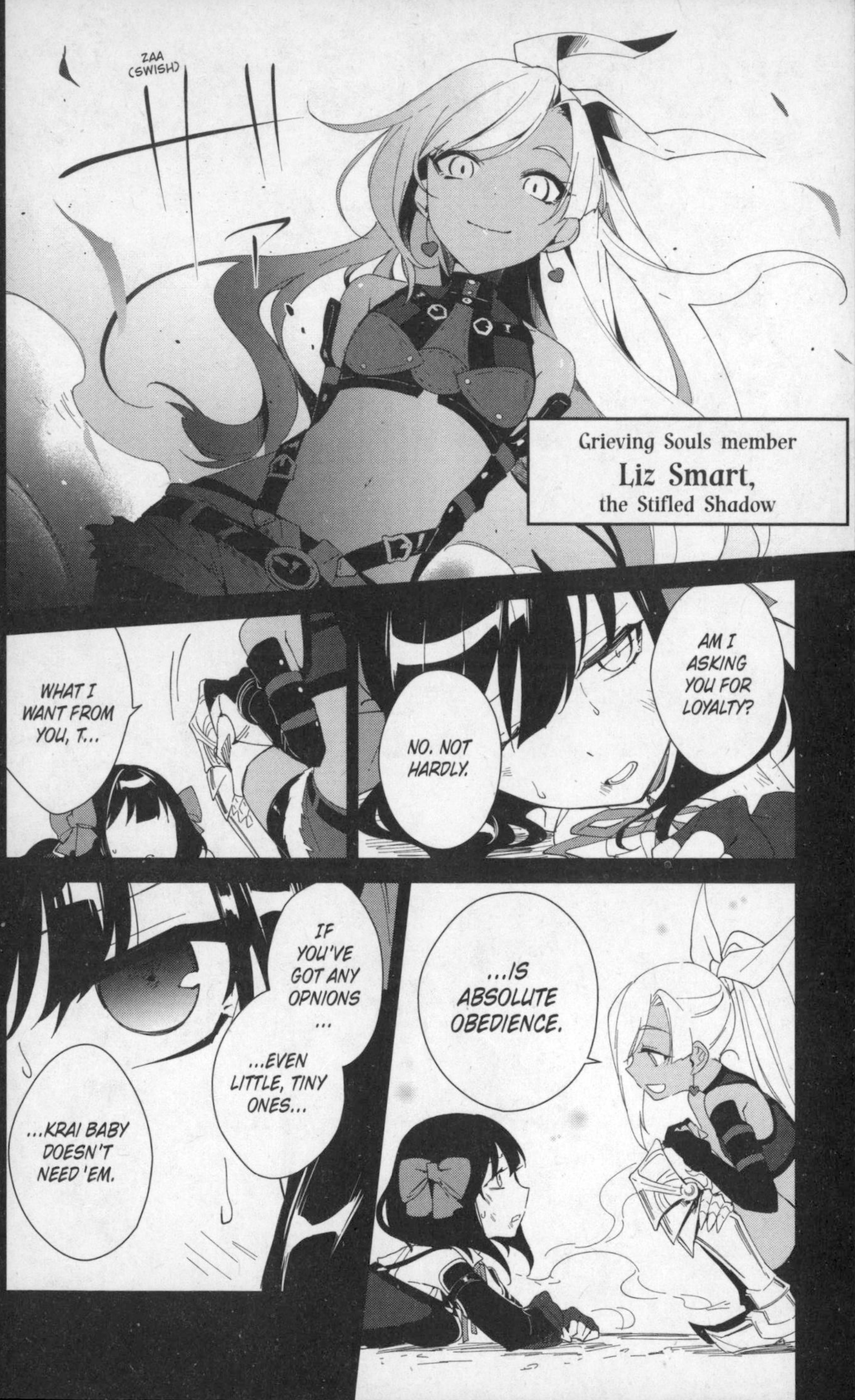
ZAA (SWISH)
Grieving Souls member Liz Smart, the Stifled Shadow
AM I ASKING YOU FOR LOYALTY?
NO. NOT HARDLY.
WHAT I WANT FROM YOU, T...
...IS ABSOLUTE OBEDIENCE.
IF YOU'VE GOT ANY OPNIONS ...
...EVEN LITTLE, TINY ONES...
...KRAI BABY DOESN'T NEED 'EM.

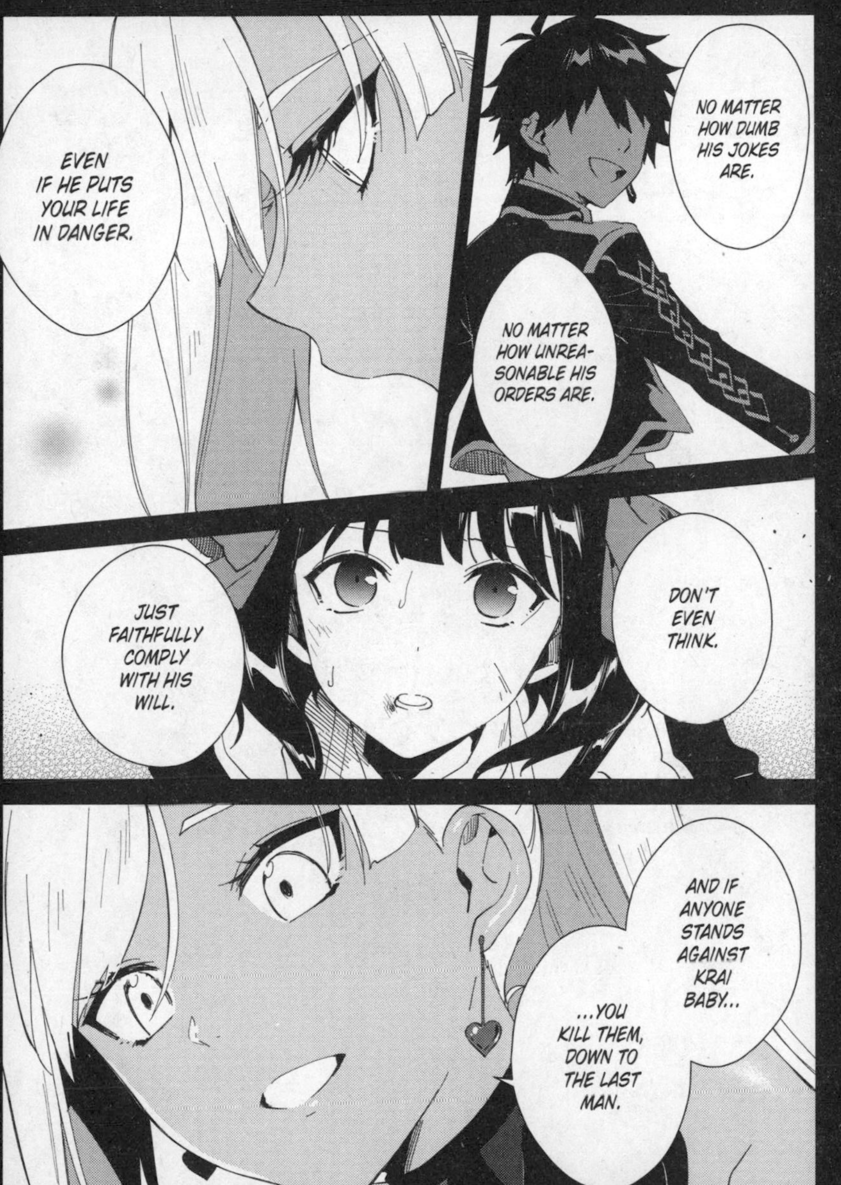
NO MATTER HOW DUMB HIS JOKES ARE.
NO MATTER HOW UNREASONABLE HIS ORDERS ARE.
EVEN IF HE PUTS YOUR LIFE IN DANGER.
DON'T EVEN THINK.
JUST FAITHFULLY COMPLY WITH HIS WILL.
AND IF ANYONE STANDS AGAINST KRAI BABY...
...YOU KILL THEM, DOWN TO THE LAST MAN.

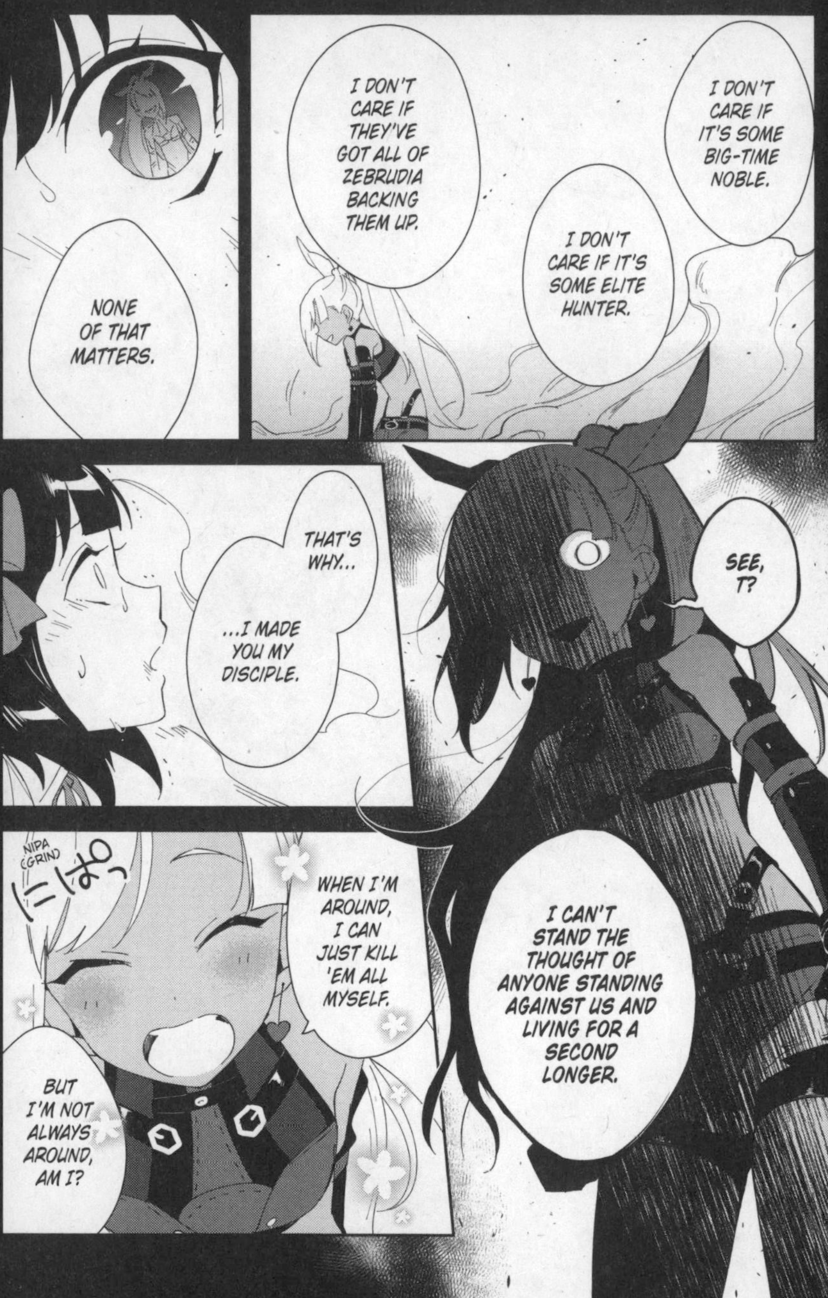
I DON'T CARE IF IT'S SOME BIG-TIME NOBLE.
I DON'T CARE IF IT'S SOME ELITE HUNTER.
I DON'T CARE IF THEY'VE GOT ALL OF ZEBRUDIA BACKING THEM UP.
NONE OF THAT MATTERS.
SEE, T?
I CAN'T STAND THE THOUGHT OF ANYONE STANDING AGAINST US AND LIVING FOR A SECOND LONGER.
THAT'S WHY...
...I MADE YOU MY DISCIPLE.
NIPA (GRIN)
にぱっ
WHEN I'M AROUND, I CAN JUST KILL 'EM ALL MYSELF.
BUT I'M NOT ALWAYS AROUND, AM I?

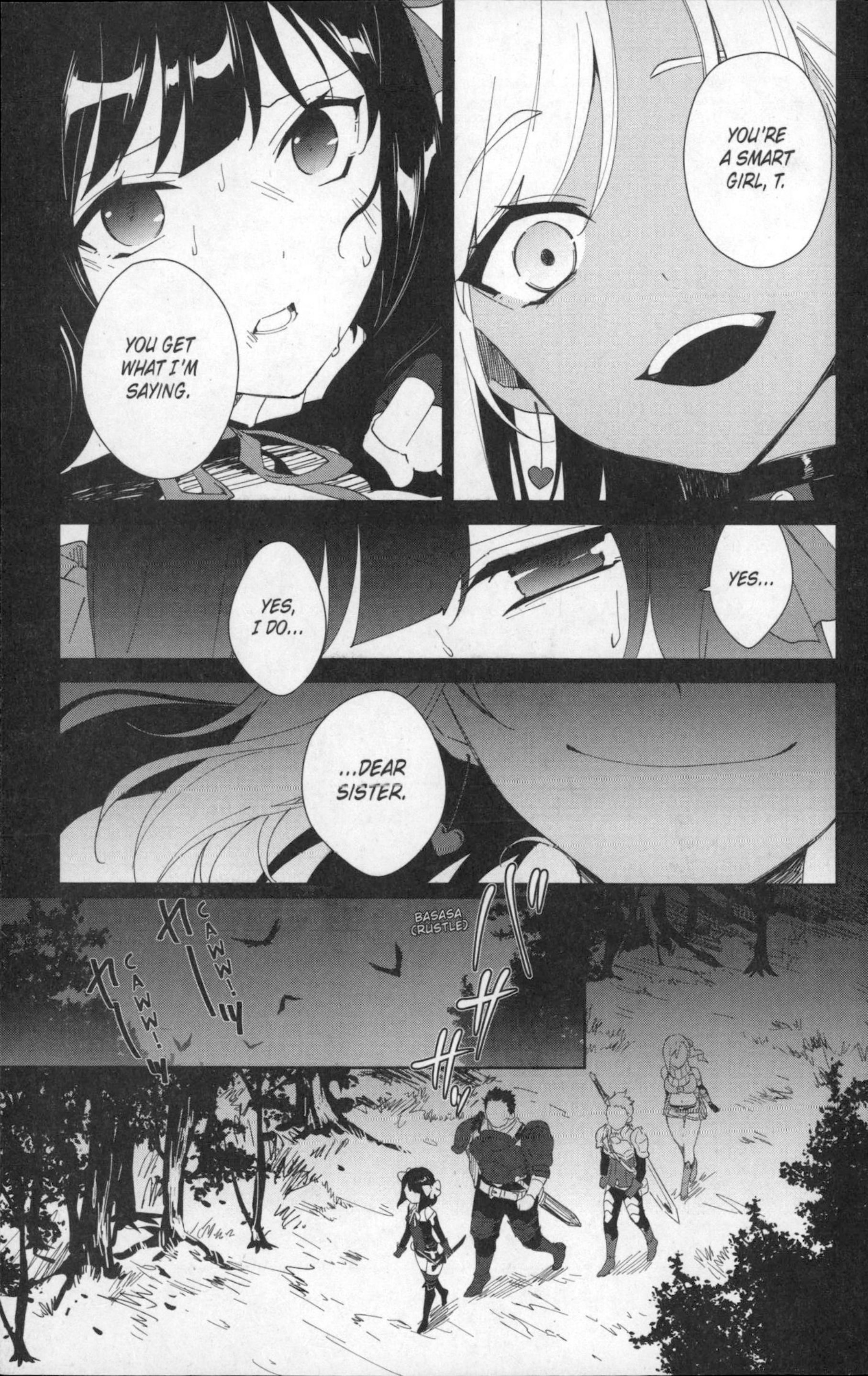
YOU'RE A SMART GIRL, T.
YOU GET WHAT I'M SAYING.
YES...
YES, I DO...
...DEAR SISTER.
BASASA (RUSTLE)
CAWW!
CAWW!

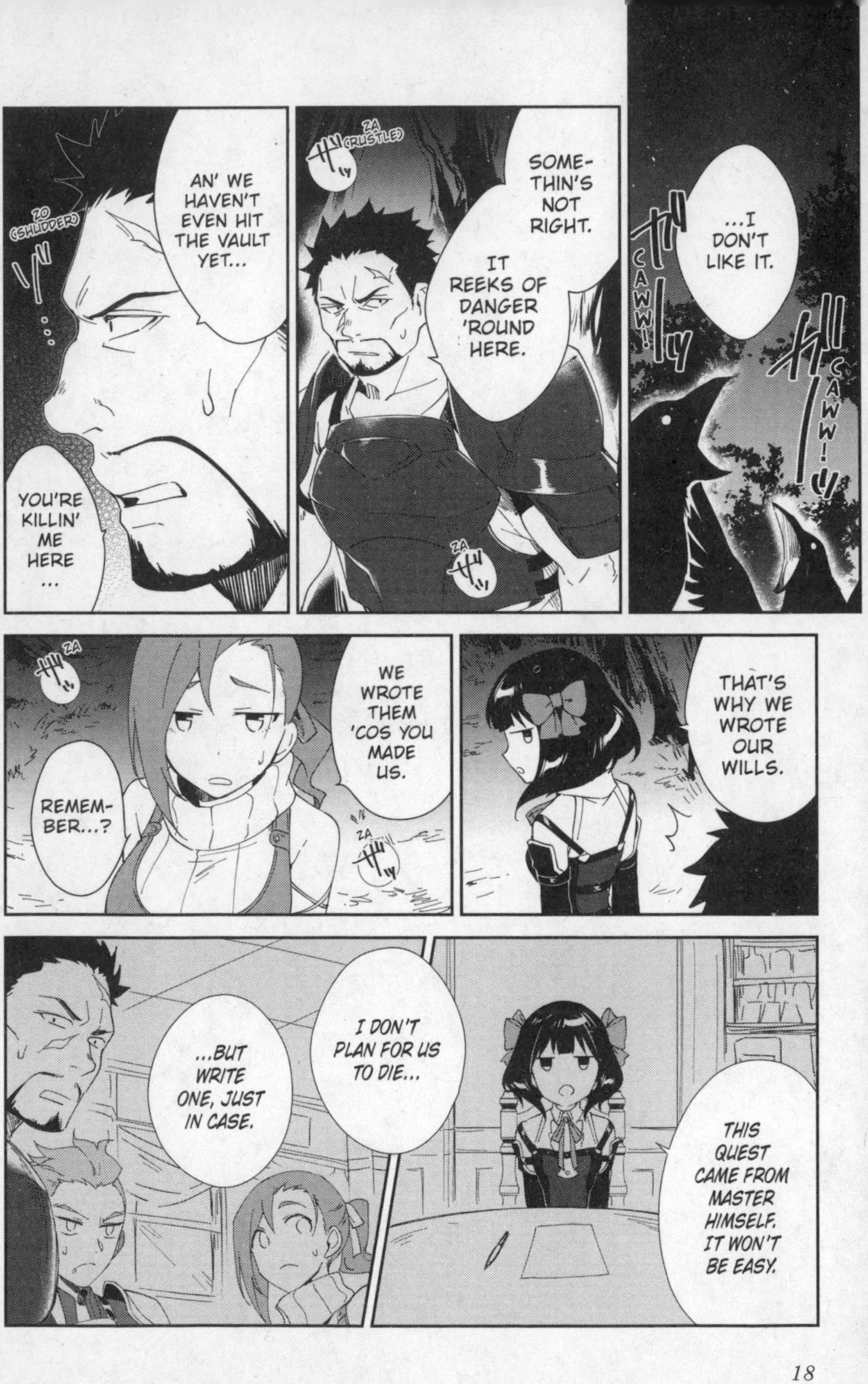

...I DON'T LIKE IT.
CAWW!
CAWW!
ZA (RUSTLE)
SOME-THIN'S NOT RIGHT.
IT REEKS OF DANGER 'ROUND HERE.
ZA
AN' WE HAVEN'T EVEN HIT THE VAULT YET...
ZO (SHUDDER)
YOU'RE KILLIN' ME HERE...
THAT'S WHY WE WROTE OUR WILLS.
ZA
WE WROTE THEM 'COS YOU MADE US.
REMEM-BER...?
ZA
THIS QUEST CAME FROM MASTER HIMSELF. IT WON'T BE EASY.
I DON'T PLAN FOR US TO DIE...
...BUT WRITE ONE, JUST IN CASE.

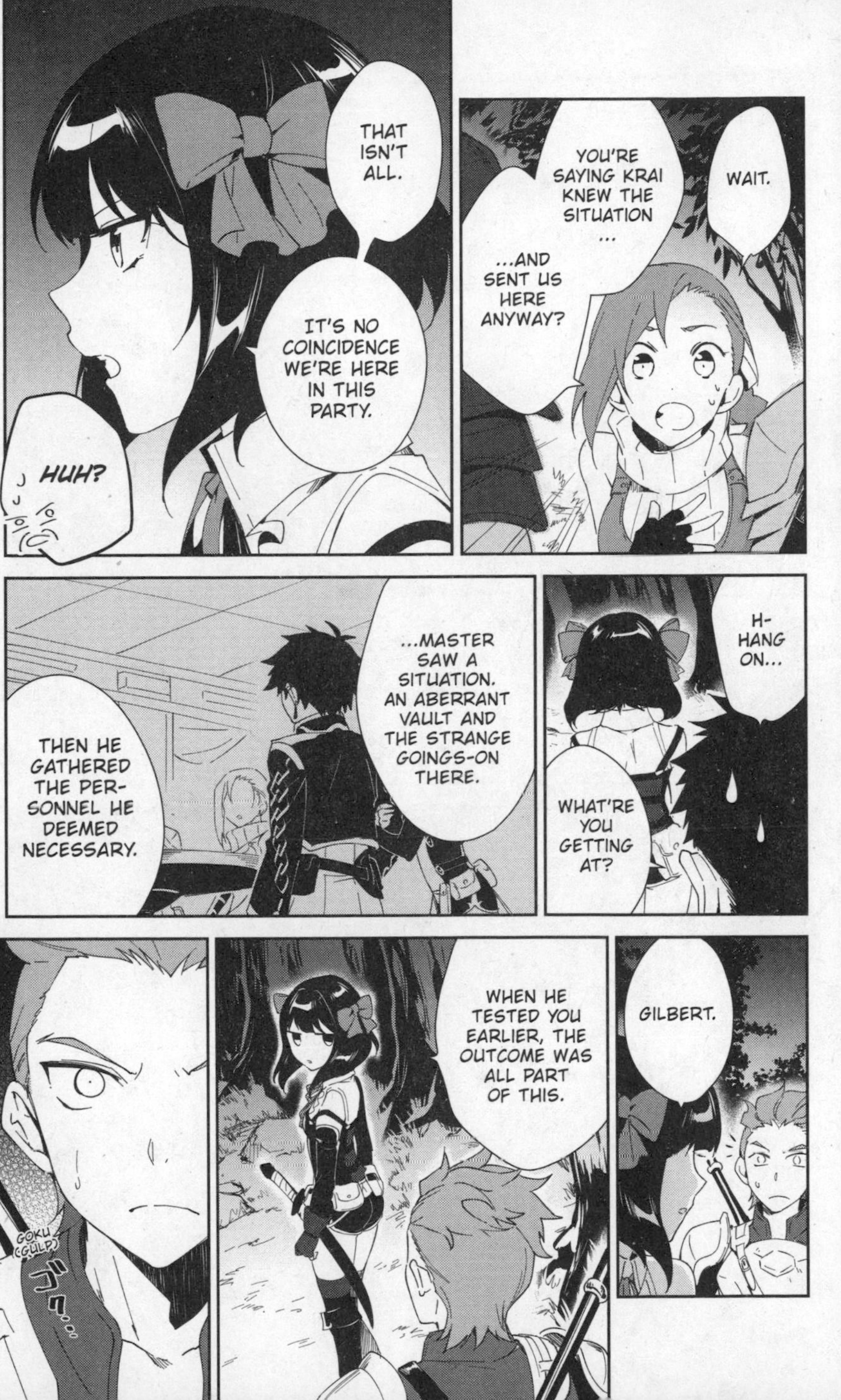
WAIT.
YOU'RE SAYING KRAI KNEW THE SITUATION ...
...AND SENT US HERE ANYWAY?
THAT ISN'T ALL.
IT'S NO COINCIDENCE WE'RE HERE IN THIS PARTY.
HUH?
H- HANG ON...
WHAT'RE YOU GETTING AT?
...MASTER SAW A SITUATION. AN ABERRANT VAULT AND THE STRANGE GOINGS-ON THERE.
THEN HE GATHERED THE PER- SONNEL HE DEEMED NECESSARY.
GILBERT.
WHEN HE TESTED YOU EARLIER, THE OUTCOME WAS ALL PART OF THIS.
GOKU (GULP)
ゴク…

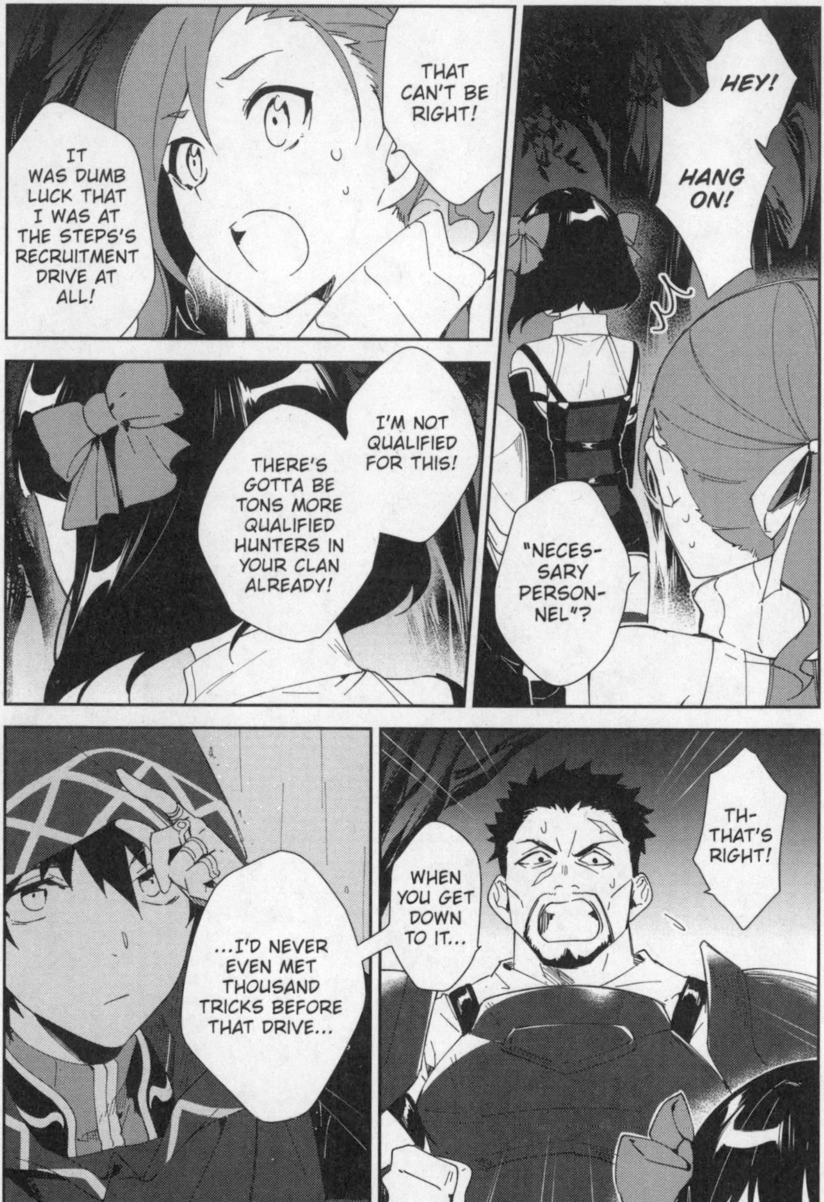
HEY!
HANG ON!
"NECESSARY PERSONNEL"?
THAT CAN'T BE RIGHT!
IT WAS DUMB LUCK THAT I WAS AT THE STEPS'S RECRUITMENT DRIVE AT ALL!
I'M NOT QUALIFIED FOR THIS!
THERE'S GOTTA BE TONS MORE QUALIFIED HUNTERS IN YOUR CLAN ALREADY!
TH-THAT'S RIGHT!
WHEN YOU GET DOWN TO IT...
...I'D NEVER EVEN MET THOUSAND TRICKS BEFORE THAT DRIVE...

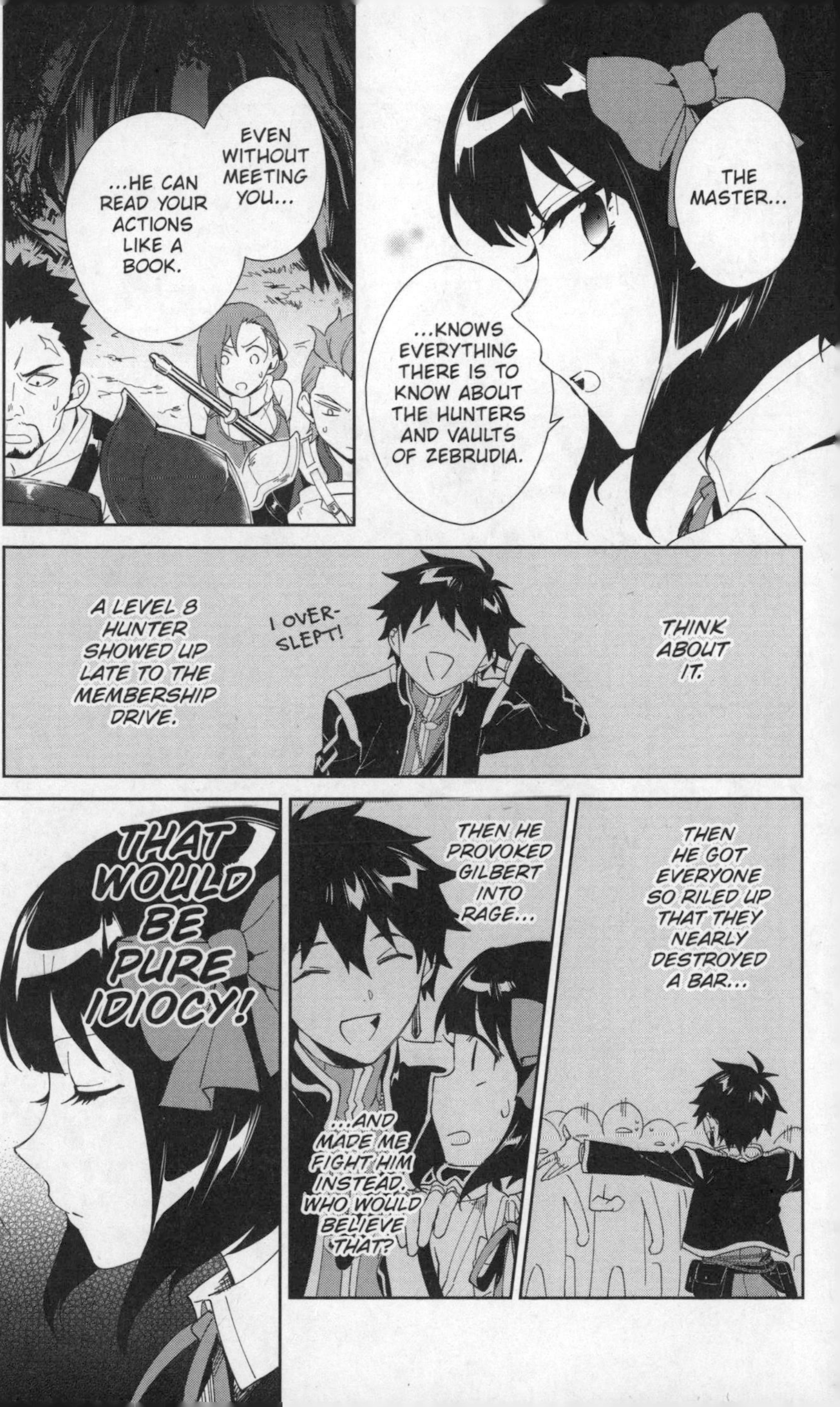
THE MASTER...
...KNOWS EVERYTHING THERE IS TO KNOW ABOUT THE HUNTERS AND VAULTS OF ZEBRUDIA.
EVEN WITHOUT MEETING YOU...
...HE CAN READ YOUR ACTIONS LIKE A BOOK.
THINK ABOUT IT.
I OVER-SLEPT!
A LEVEL 8 HUNTER SHOWED UP LATE TO THE MEMBERSHIP DRIVE.
THEN HE GOT EVERYONE SO RILED UP THAT THEY NEARLY DESTROYED A BAR...
THEN HE PROVOKED GILBERT INTO RAGE...
...AND MADE ME FIGHT HIM INSTEAD. WHO WOULD BELIEVE THAT?
THAT WOULD BE PURE IDIOCY!

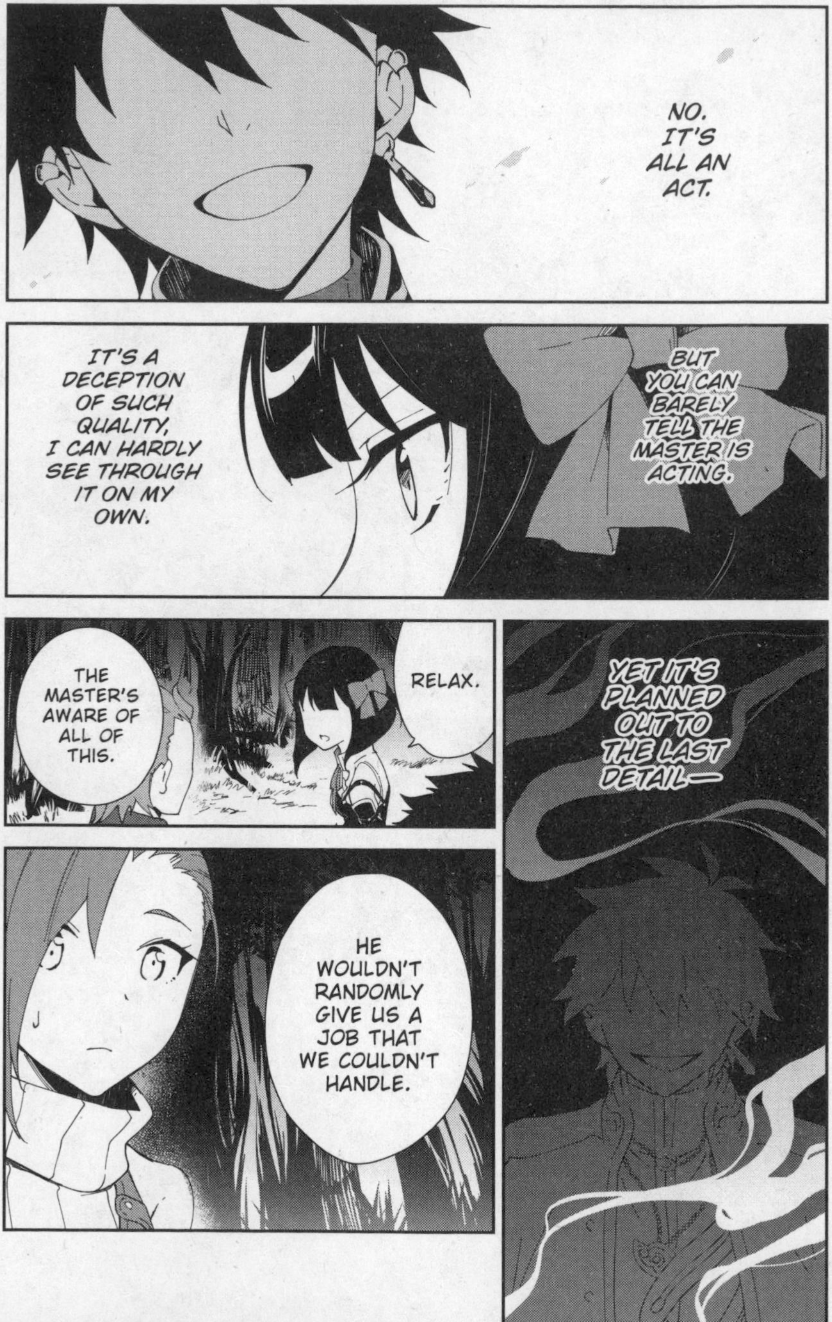
NO. IT'S ALL AN ACT.
BUT YOU CAN BARELY TELL THE MASTER IS ACTING.
IT'S A DECEPTION OF SUCH QUALITY, I CAN HARDLY SEE THROUGH IT ON MY OWN.
YET IT'S PLANNED OUT TO THE LAST DETAIL—
RELAX.
THE MASTER'S AWARE OF ALL OF THIS.
HE WOULDN'T RANDOMLY GIVE US A JOB THAT WE COULDN'T HANDLE.

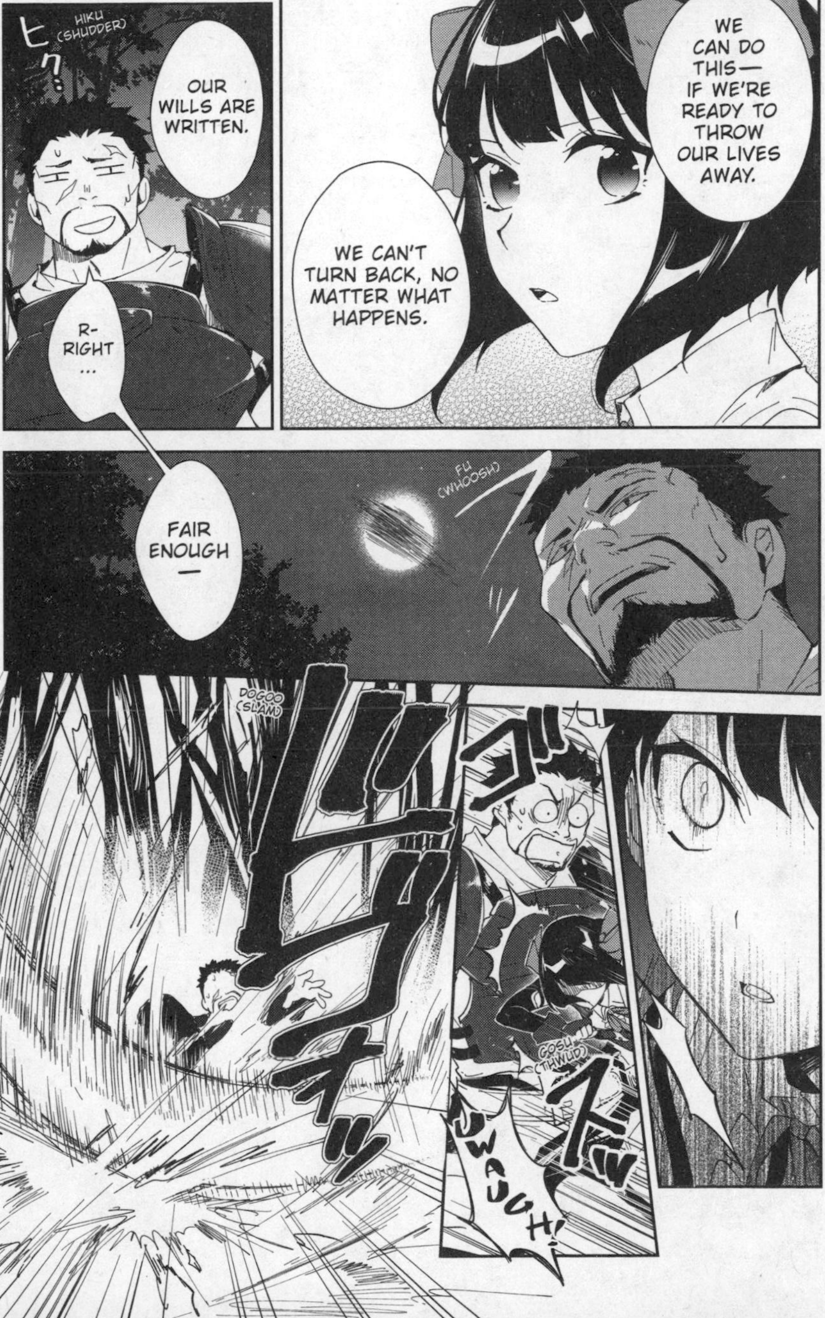
WE CAN DO THIS— IF WE'RE READY TO THROW OUR LIVES AWAY.
WE CAN'T TURN BACK, NO MATTER WHAT HAPPENS.
ヒク
HIKU (SHUDDER)
OUR WILLS ARE WRITTEN.
R-RIGHT...
FU (WHOOSH)
FAIR ENOUGH—
GOSU (THWUD)
UWAUGH!
DOGOO (SLAM)

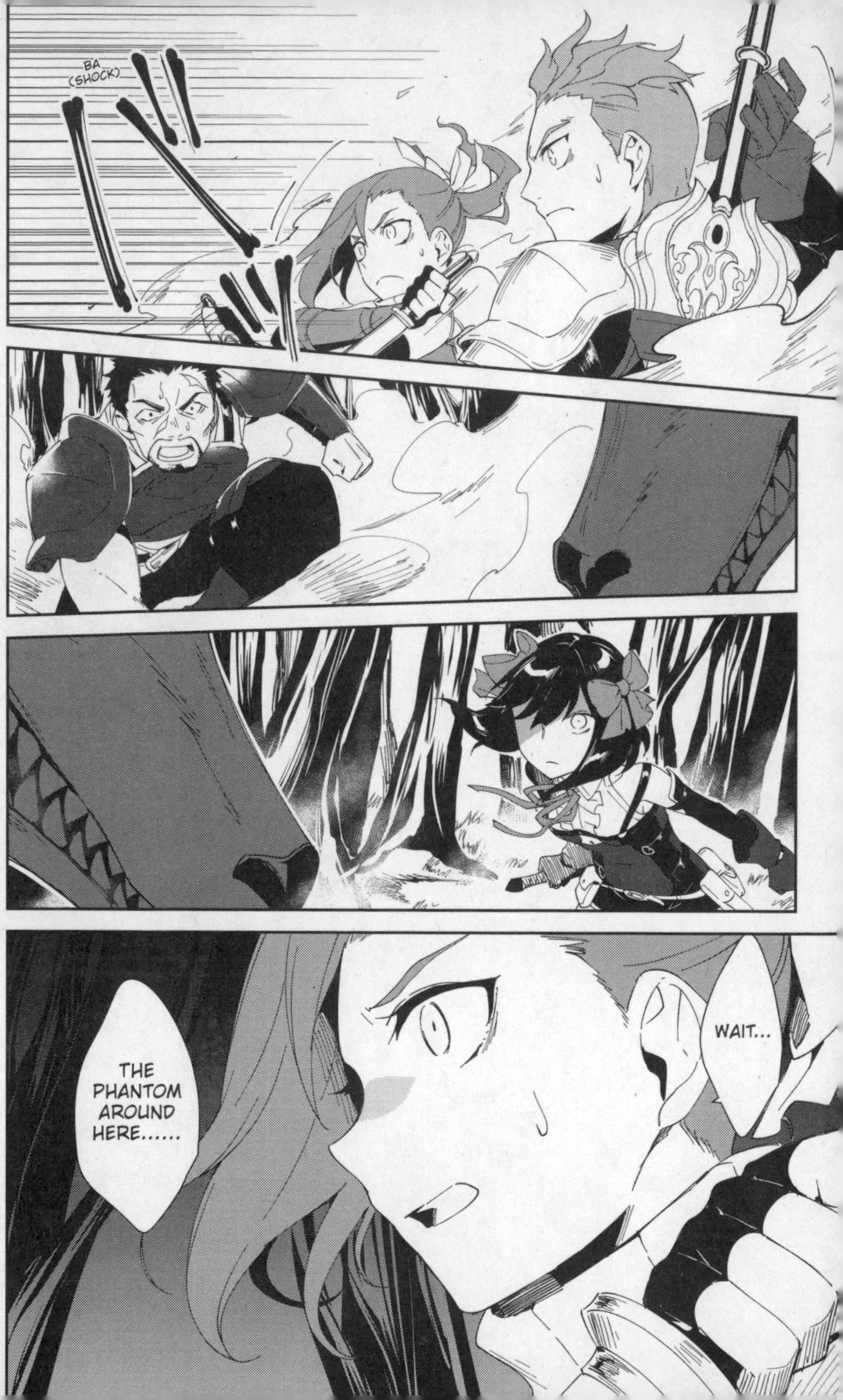
BA (SHOCK)
WAIT...
THE PHANTOM AROUND HERE......

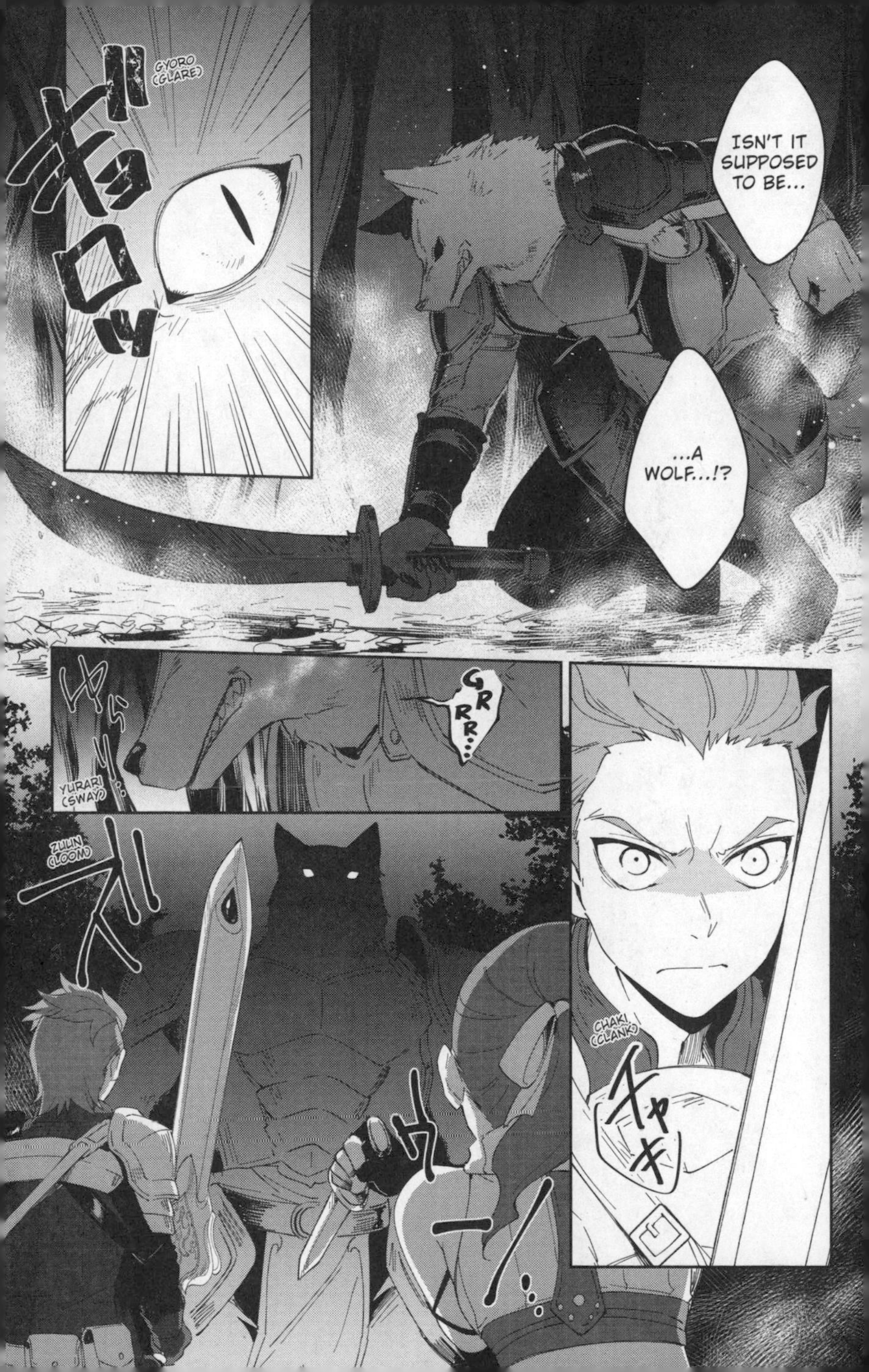
ISN'T IT SUPPOSED TO BE...
...A WOLF...!?
GYORO (GLARE)
CHAKI (CLANK)
GRRR...
YURARI (SWAY)
ZULIN (LOOM)

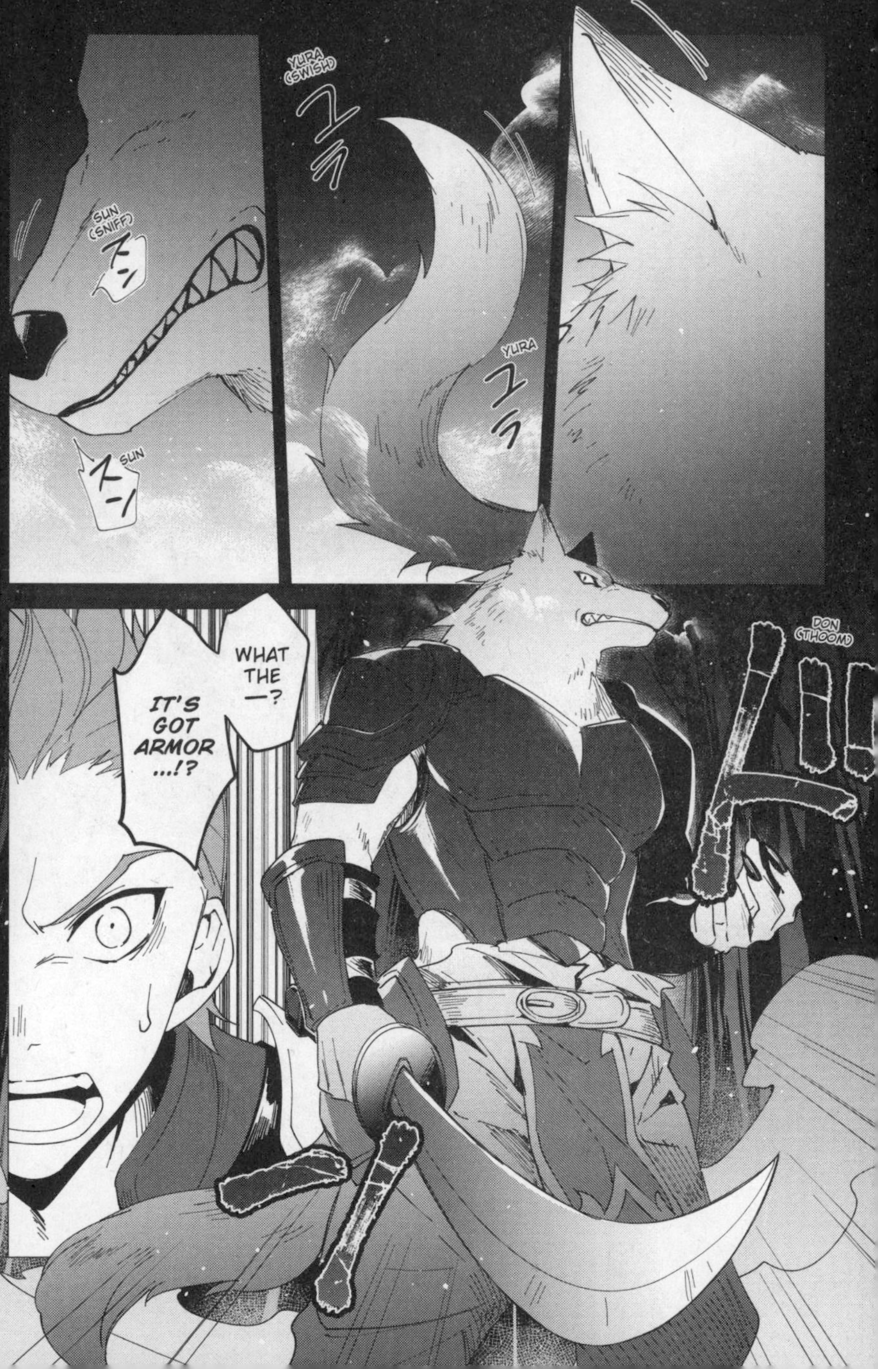
YURA
YURA (SWISH)
SUN (SNIFF)
SUN
DON (THOOM)
WHAT THE—?
IT'S GOT ARMOR ...!?

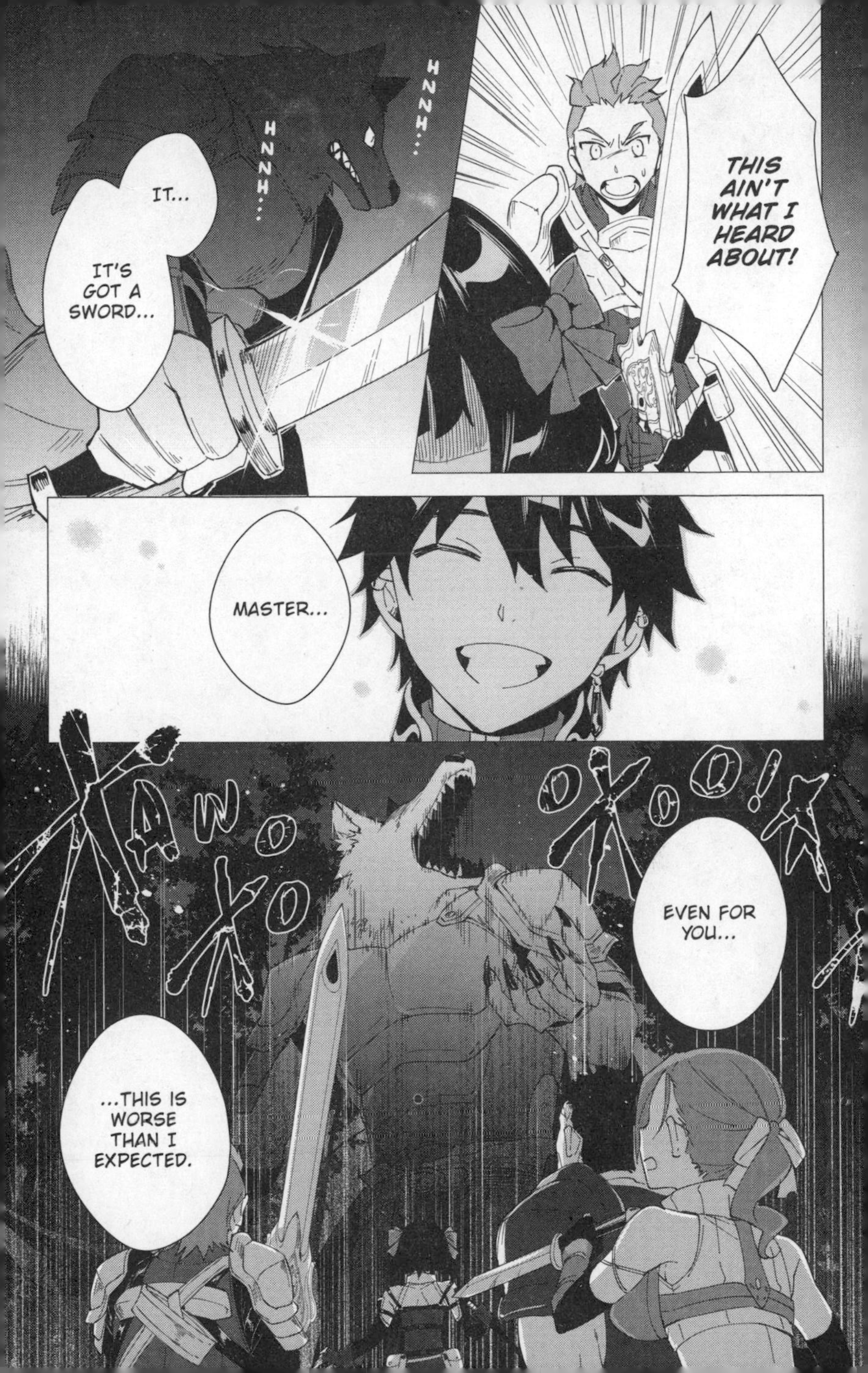
THIS AIN'T WHAT I HEARD ABOUT!
HNNH...
HNNH...
IT...
IT'S GOT A SWORD...
MASTER...
AWOOOOOO!
EVEN FOR YOU...
...THIS IS WORSE THAN I EXPECTED.

LET THIS

Grieving Soul Retire

WOE IS THE WEAKLING WHO LEADS THE STRONGEST PARTY

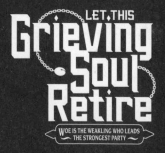

Chapter 7

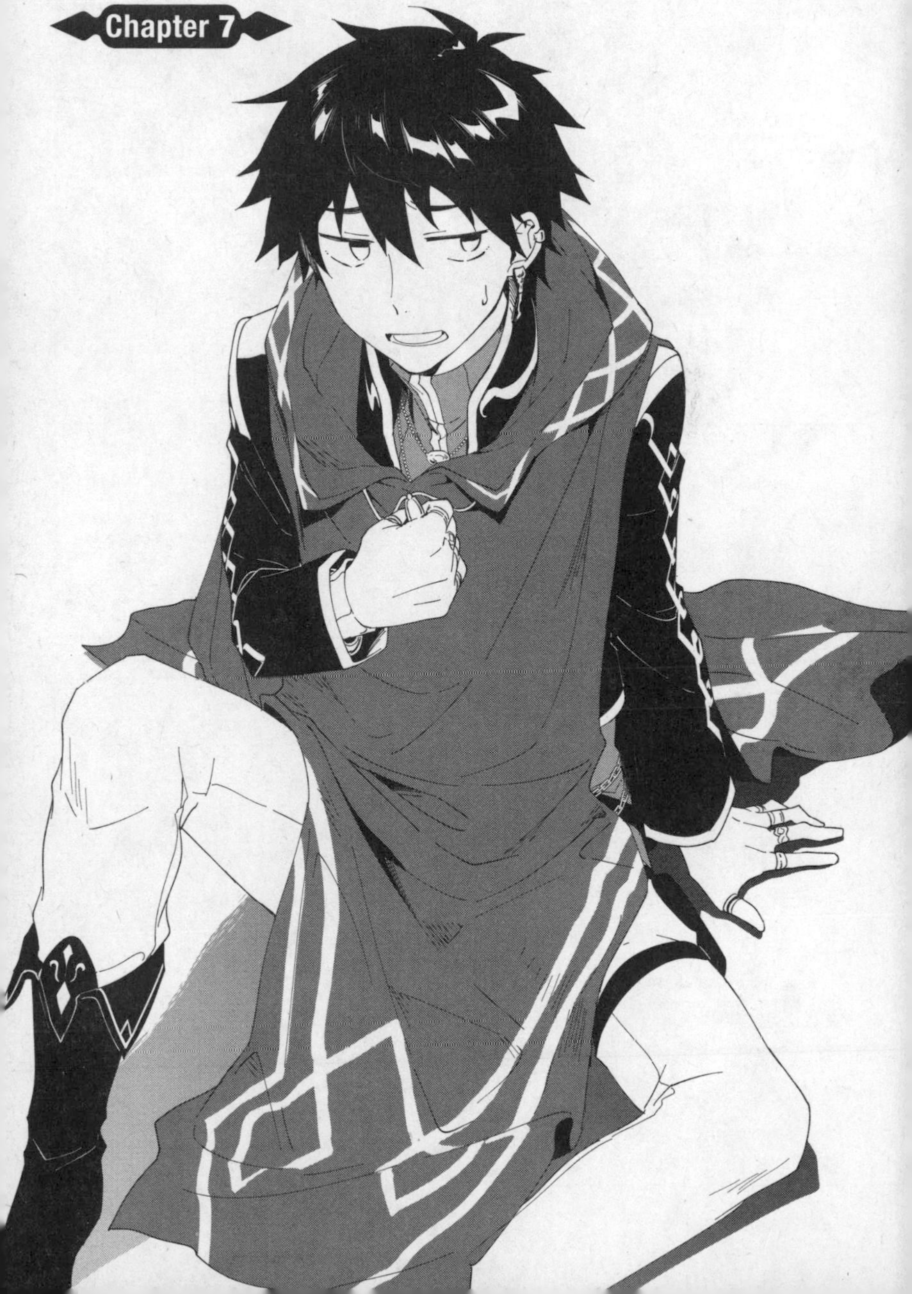

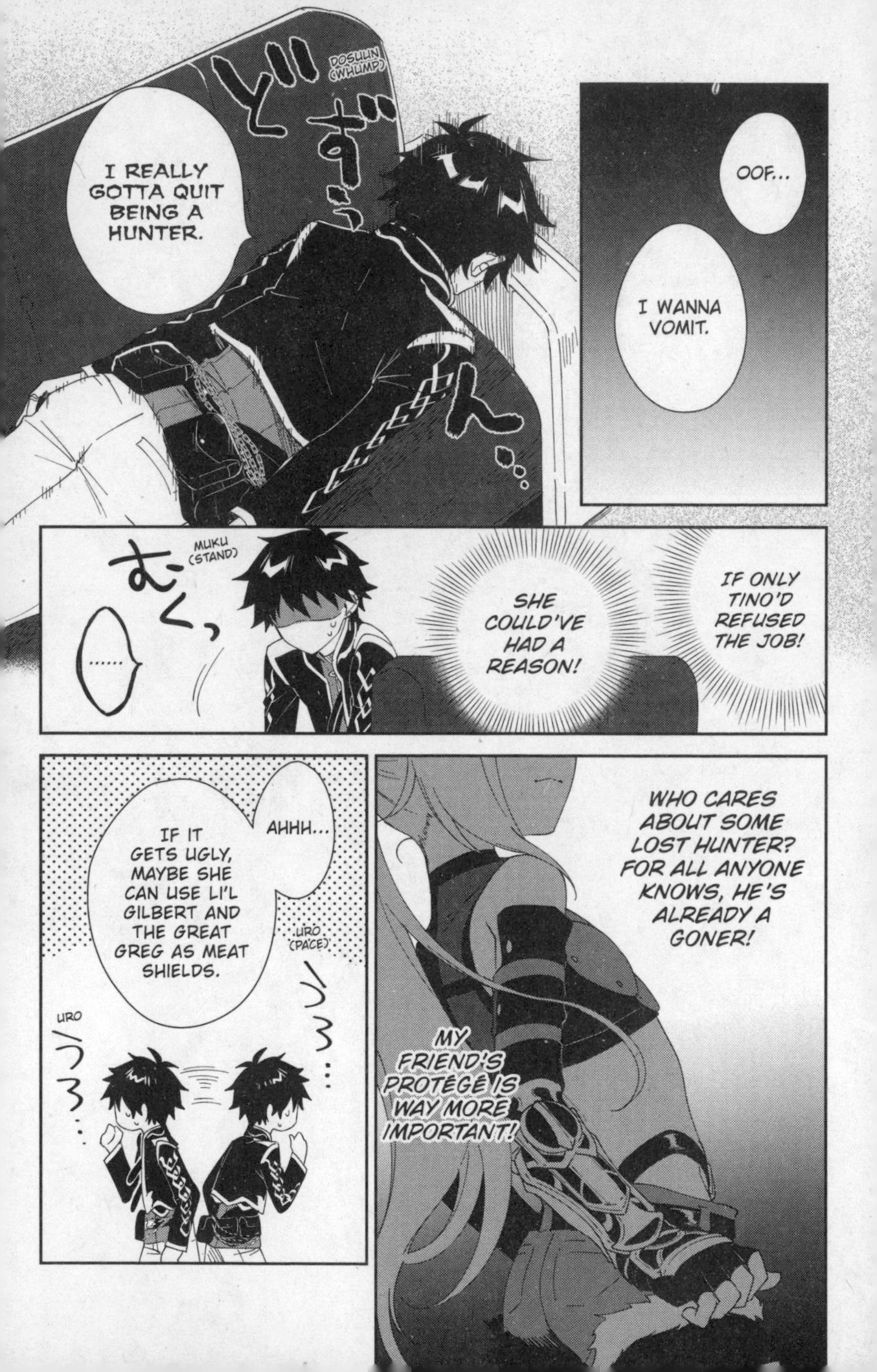
OOF...
I WANNA VOMIT.
DOSUUN (WHUMP)
I REALLY GOTTA QUIT BEING A HUNTER.
IF ONLY TINO'D REFUSED THE JOB!
SHE COULD'VE HAD A REASON!
MUKU (STAND)
......
WHO CARES ABOUT SOME LOST HUNTER? FOR ALL ANYONE KNOWS, HE'S ALREADY A GONER!
MY FRIEND'S PROTÉGÉ IS WAY MORE IMPORTANT!
AHHH...
IF IT GETS UGLY, MAYBE SHE CAN USE LI'L GILBERT AND THE GREAT GREG AS MEAT SHIELDS.
URO (PACE)
URO

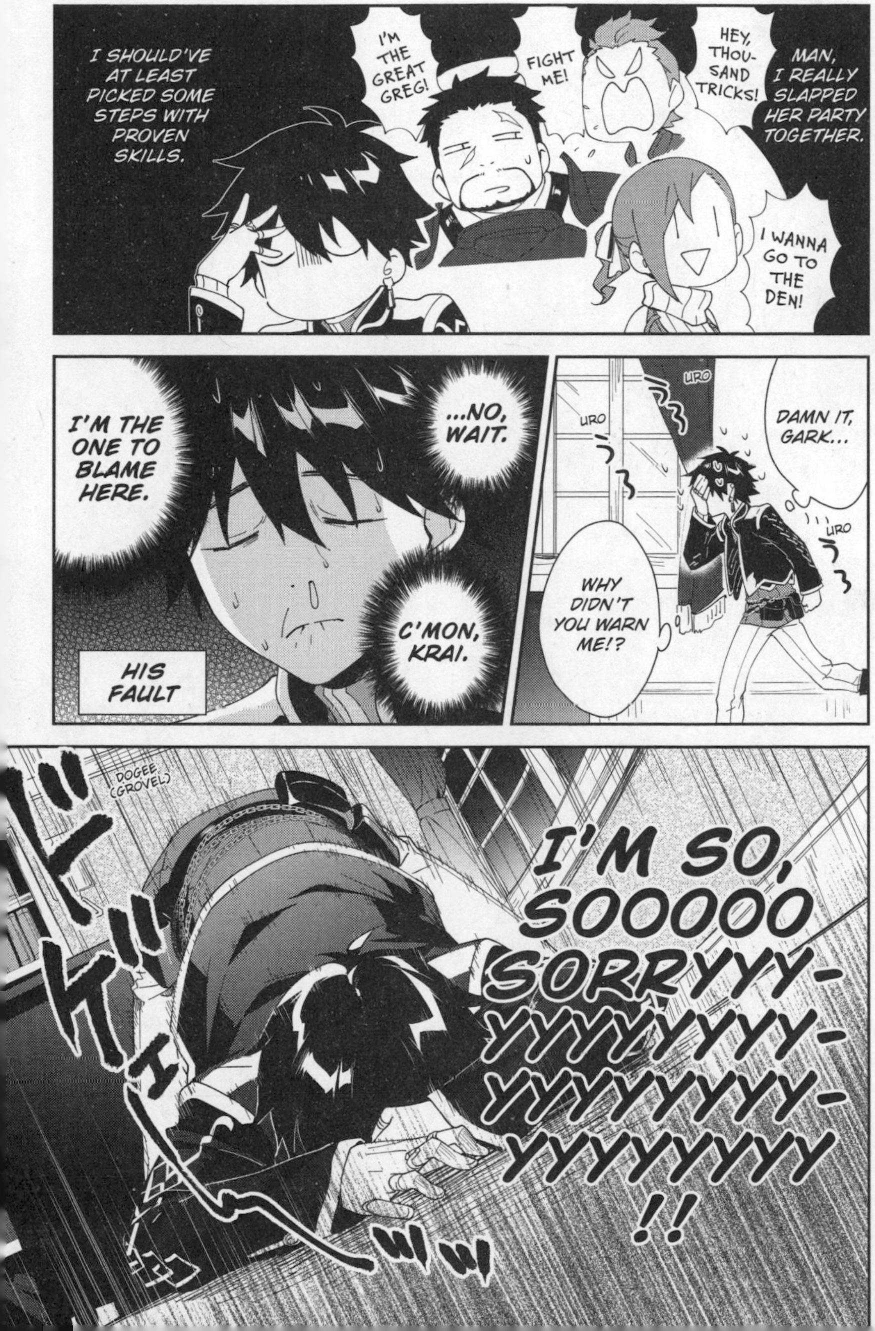
MAN, I REALLY SLAPPED HER PARTY TOGETHER.
I WANNA GO TO THE DEN!
HEY, THOU-SAND TRICKS!
FIGHT ME!
I'M THE GREAT GREG!
I SHOULD'VE AT LEAST PICKED SOME STEPS WITH PROVEN SKILLS.
DAMN IT, GARK...
URO
URO
URO
WHY DIDN'T YOU WARN ME!?
...NO, WAIT.
C'MON, KRAI.
I'M THE ONE TO BLAME HERE.
HIS FAULT
DOGEE (GROVEL)
I'M SO, SOOOOO SORRYYY-YYYYYYYY-YYYYYYYYY-YYYYYYYYY!!

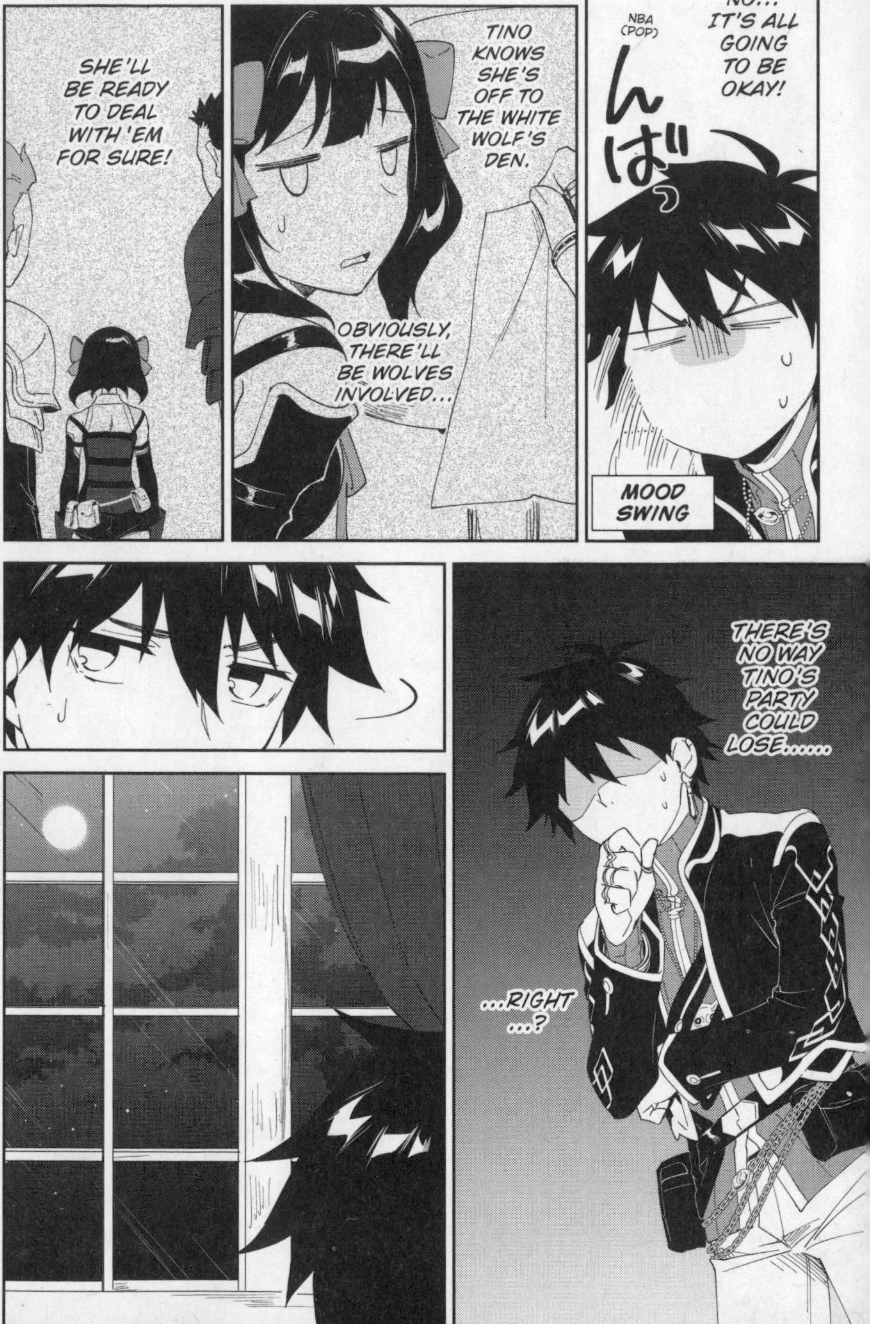
NO... IT'S ALL GOING TO BE OKAY!
NBA (POP)
んばっ
MOOD SWING
TINO KNOWS SHE'S OFF TO THE WHITE WOLF'S DEN.
OBVIOUSLY, THERE'LL BE WOLVES INVOLVED...
SHE'LL BE READY TO DEAL WITH 'EM FOR SURE!
THERE'S NO WAY TINO'S PARTY COULD LOSE.......
...RIGHT...?

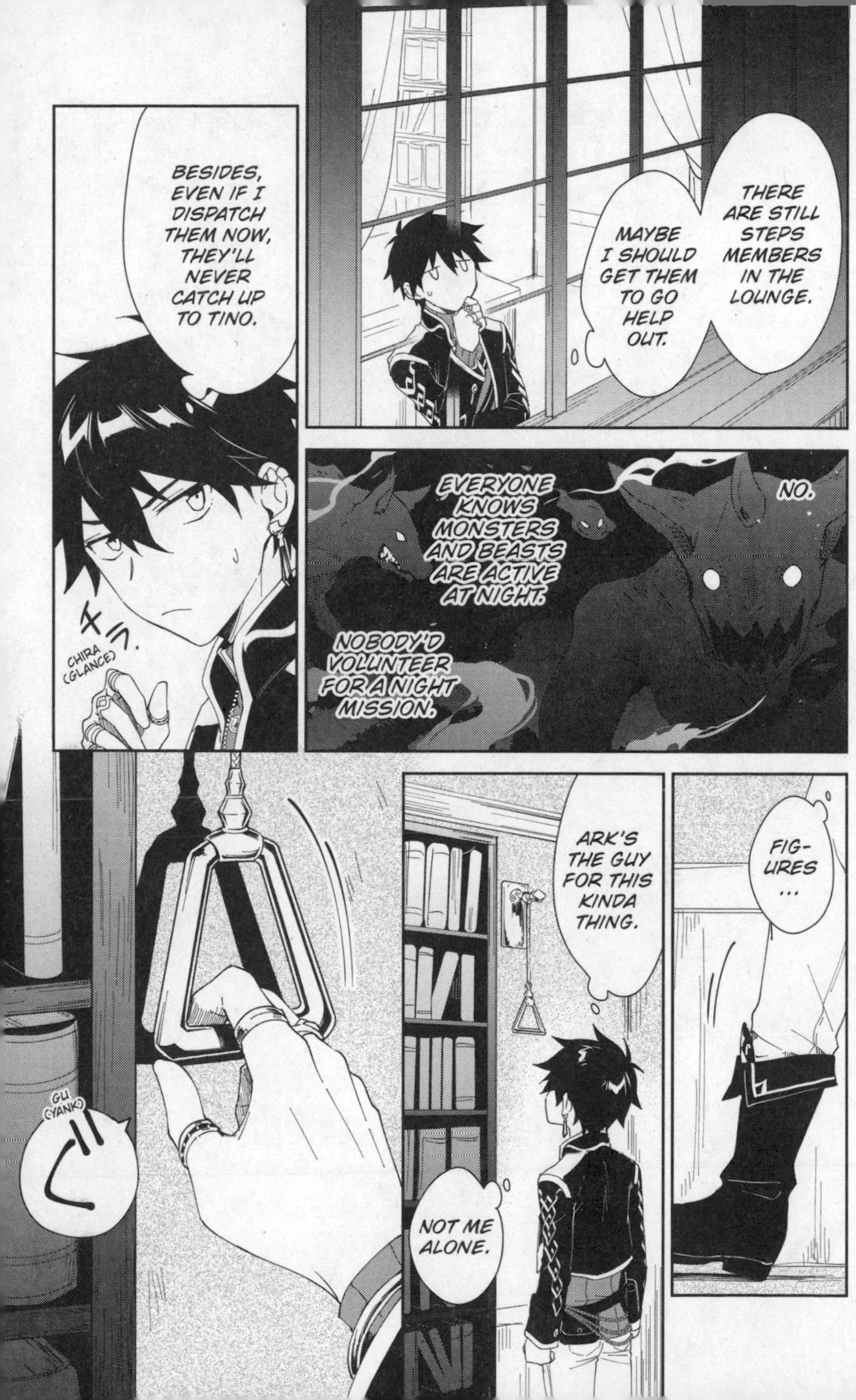
THERE ARE STILL STEPS MEMBERS IN THE LOUNGE.
MAYBE I SHOULD GET THEM TO GO HELP OUT.
NO.
EVERYONE KNOWS MONSTERS AND BEASTS ARE ACTIVE AT NIGHT.
NOBODY'D VOLUNTEER FOR A NIGHT MISSION.
BESIDES, EVEN IF I DISPATCH THEM NOW, THEY'LL NEVER CATCH UP TO TINO.
チラ
CHIRA (GLANCE)
FIG-URES...
ARK'S THE GUY FOR THIS KINDA THING.
NOT ME ALONE.
ぐい
GU (YANK)

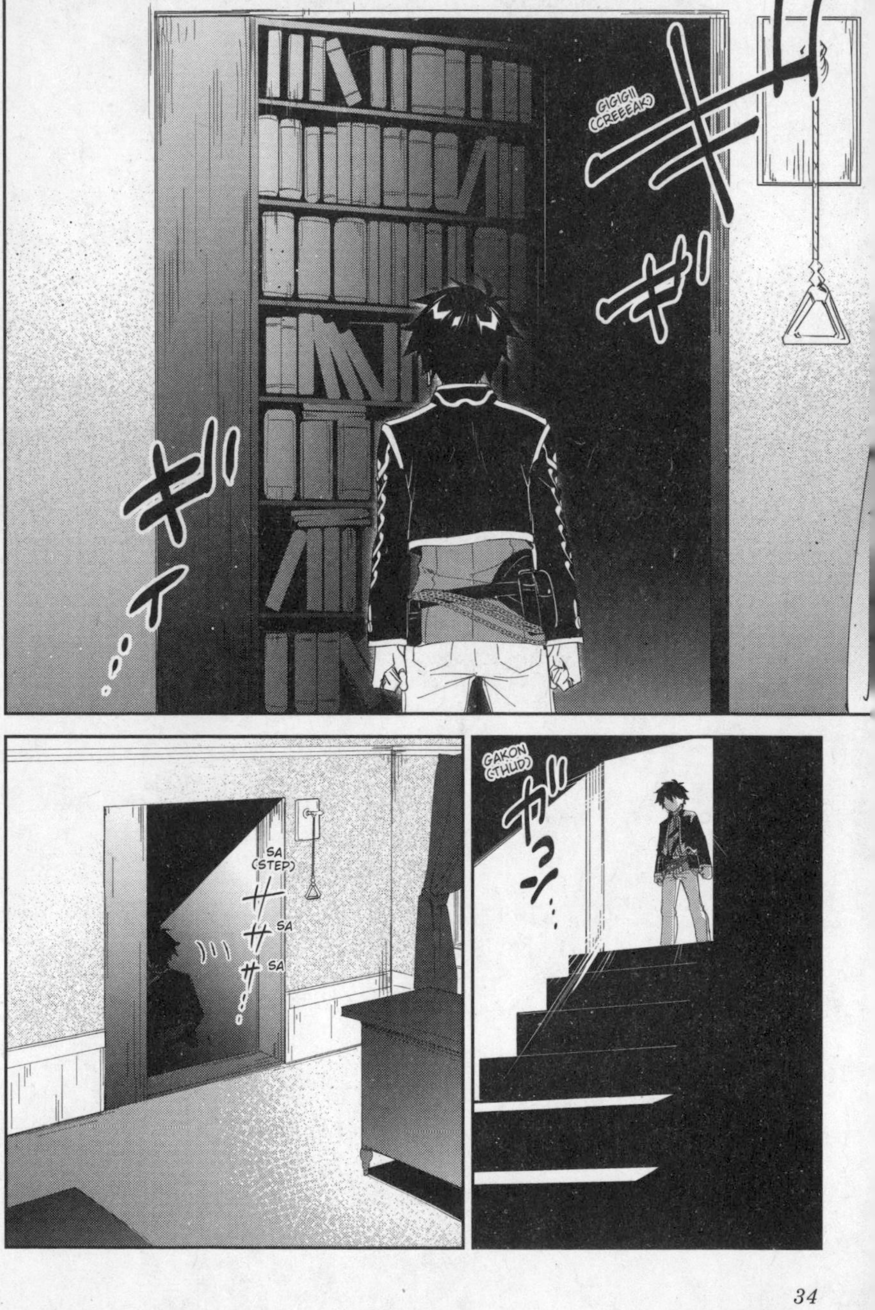
GIGIGII (CREEEAK)
GAKON (THUD)
SA (STEP)
SA
SA

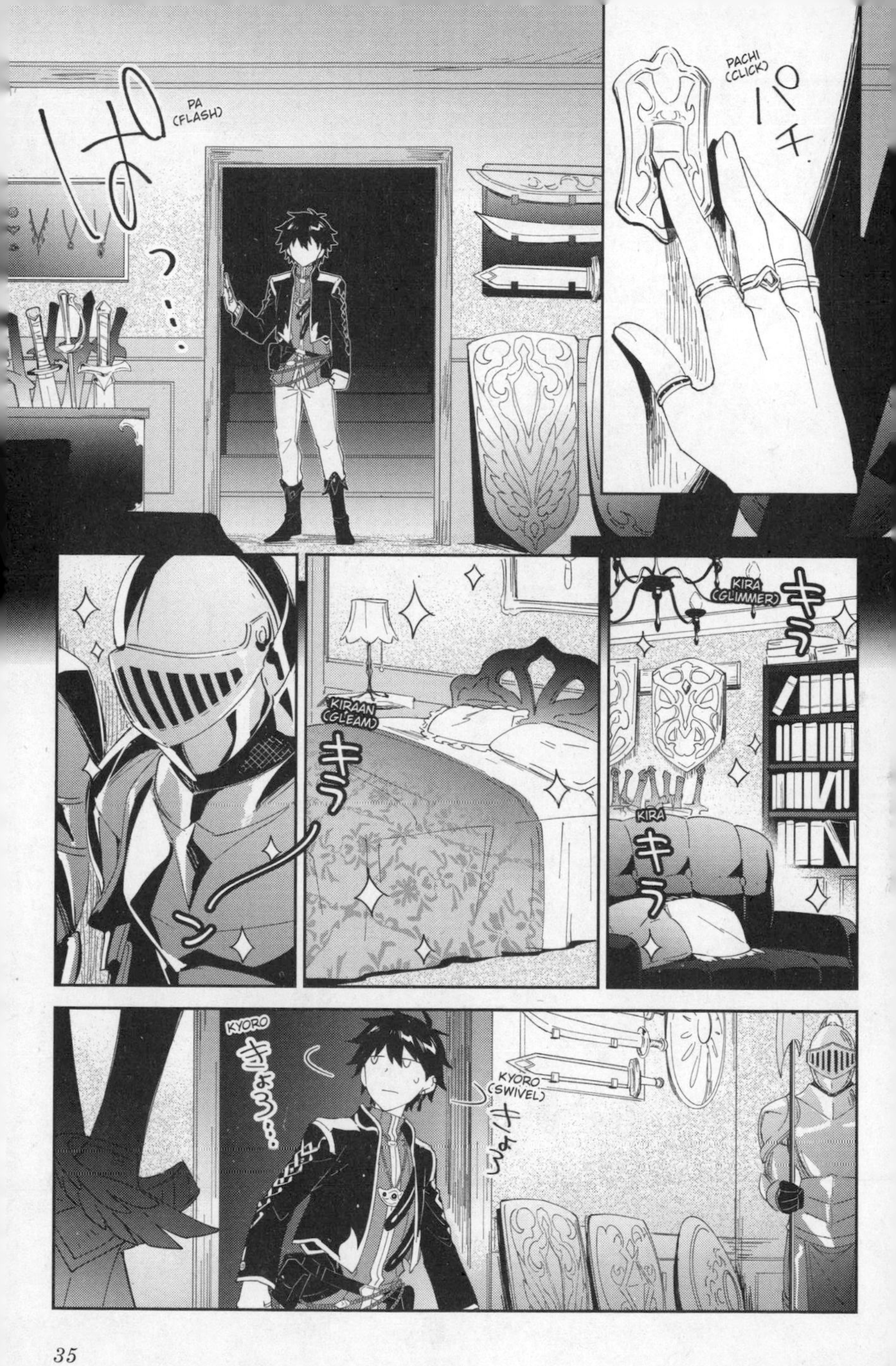
PACHI (CLICK)
パチ
PA (FLASH)
ぱっ…
KIRA (GLIMMER)
キラ
KIRA
キラ
KIRAAN (GLEAM)
キラーン
KYORO (SWIVEL)
きょろ
KYORO
きょろ…

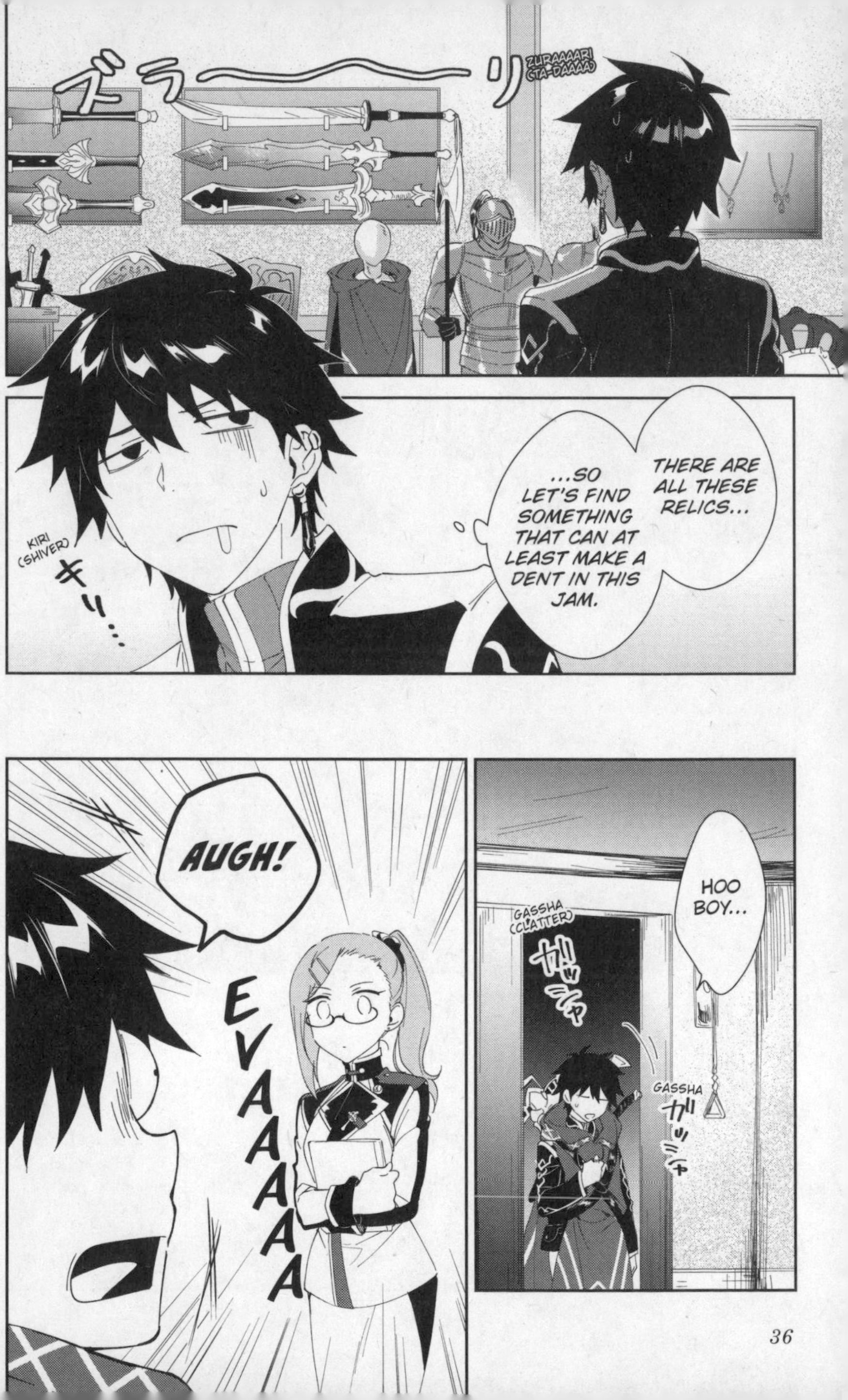

ズラ〜〜〜リ
ZURAAAARI (TA-DAAAA)
THERE ARE ALL THESE RELICS...
...SO LET'S FIND SOMETHING THAT CAN AT LEAST MAKE A DENT IN THIS JAM.
KIRI (SHIVER)
キリ…
GASSHA (CLATTER)
ガシャ
HOO BOY...
GASSHA
ガシャ
AUGH!
EVAAAAAA

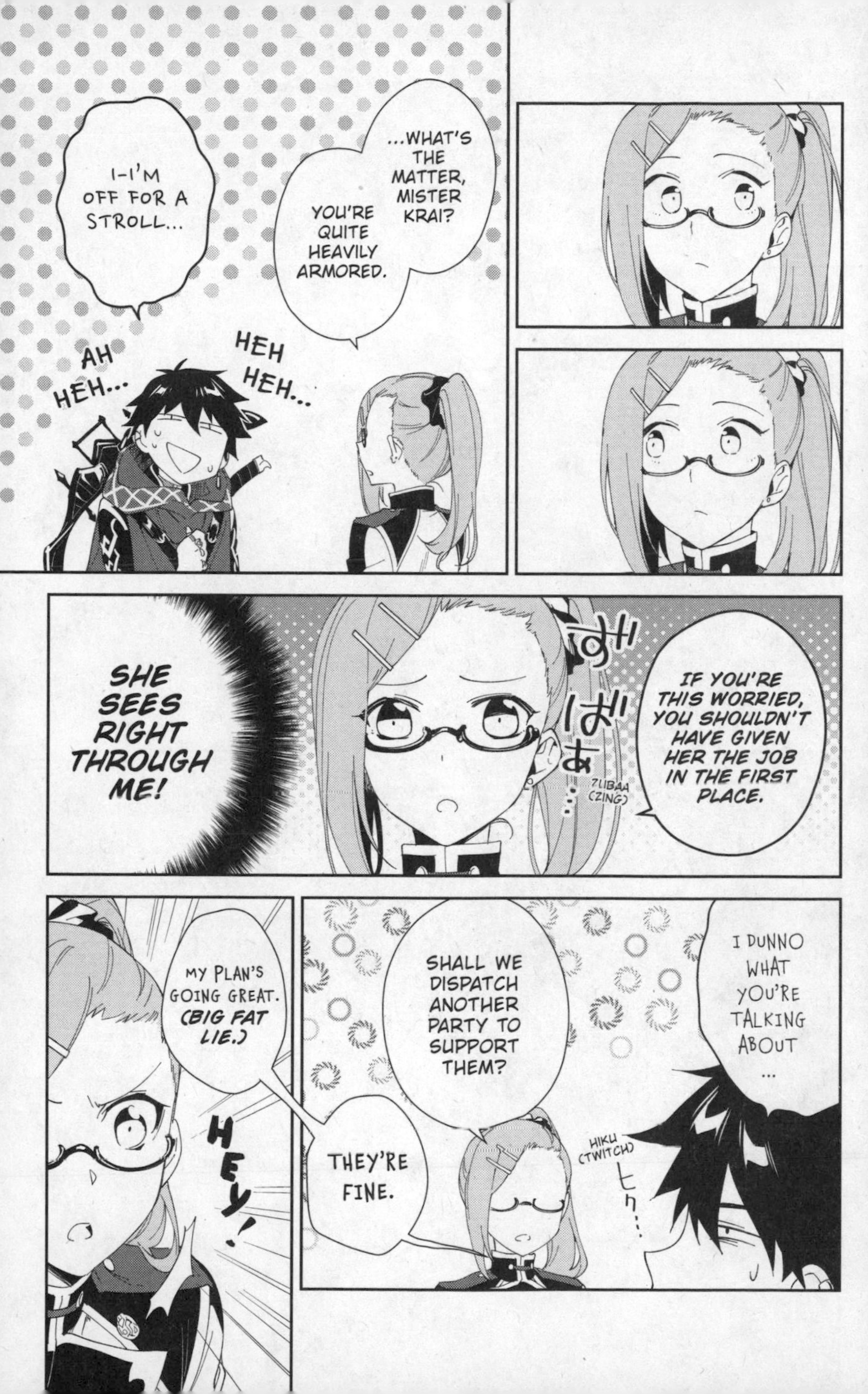
...WHAT'S THE MATTER, MISTER KRAI?
YOU'RE QUITE HEAVILY ARMORED.
I-I'M OFF FOR A STROLL...
HEH HEH...
AH HEH...
IF YOU'RE THIS WORRIED, YOU SHOULDN'T HAVE GIVEN HER THE JOB IN THE FIRST PLACE.
ずばぁ...
ZUBAA (ZING)
SHE SEES RIGHT THROUGH ME!
I DUNNO WHAT YOU'RE TALKING ABOUT...
SHALL WE DISPATCH ANOTHER PARTY TO SUPPORT THEM?
HIKU (TWITCH)
ヒク...
THEY'RE FINE.
MY PLAN'S GOING GREAT. (BIG FAT LIE.)
HEY!

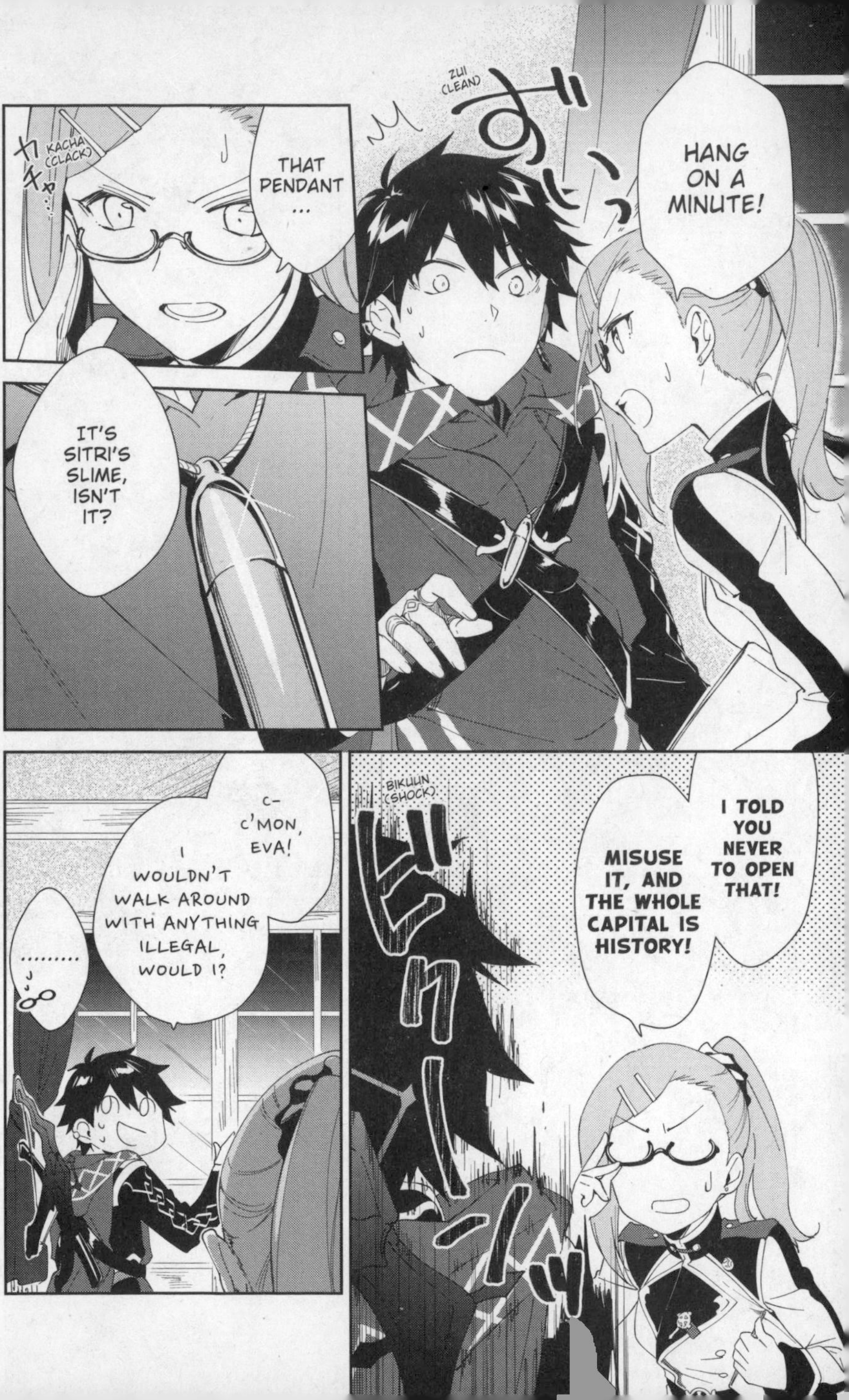
ZUI (LEAN)
HANG ON A MINUTE!
THAT PENDANT ...
KACHA (CLACK)
IT'S SITRI'S SLIME, ISN'T IT?
BIKUUN (SHOCK)
I TOLD YOU NEVER TO OPEN THAT!
MISUSE IT, AND THE WHOLE CAPITAL IS HISTORY!
C-C'MON, EVA!
I WOULDN'T WALK AROUND WITH ANYTHING ILLEGAL, WOULD I?
....

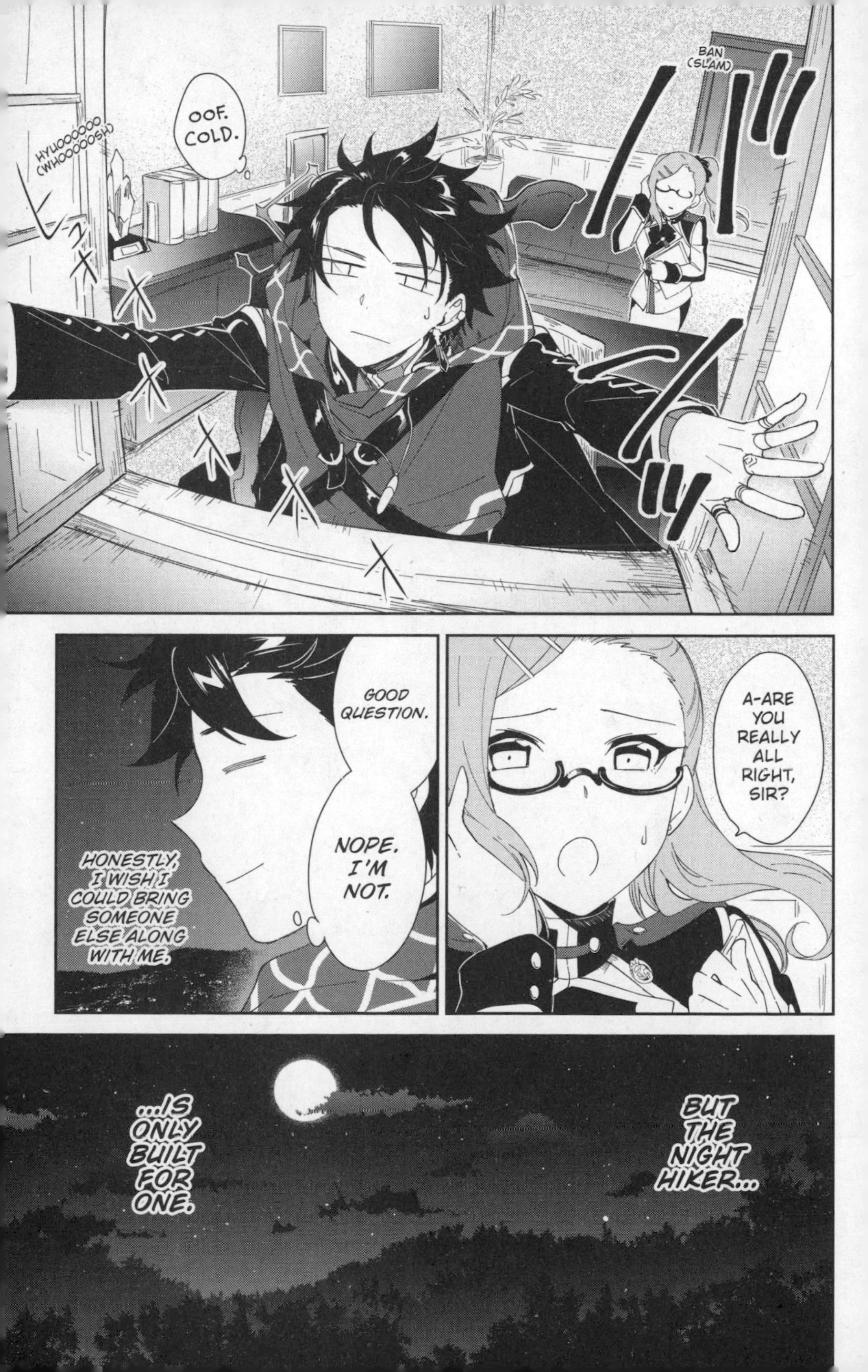
BAN (SLAM)
OOF. COLD.
HYUOOOOOOO (WHOOOOOOSH)
A-ARE YOU REALLY ALL RIGHT, SIR?
GOOD QUESTION.
NOPE. I'M NOT.
HONESTLY, I WISH I COULD BRING SOMEONE ELSE ALONG WITH ME.
BUT THE NIGHT HIKER...
...IS ONLY BUILT FOR ONE.

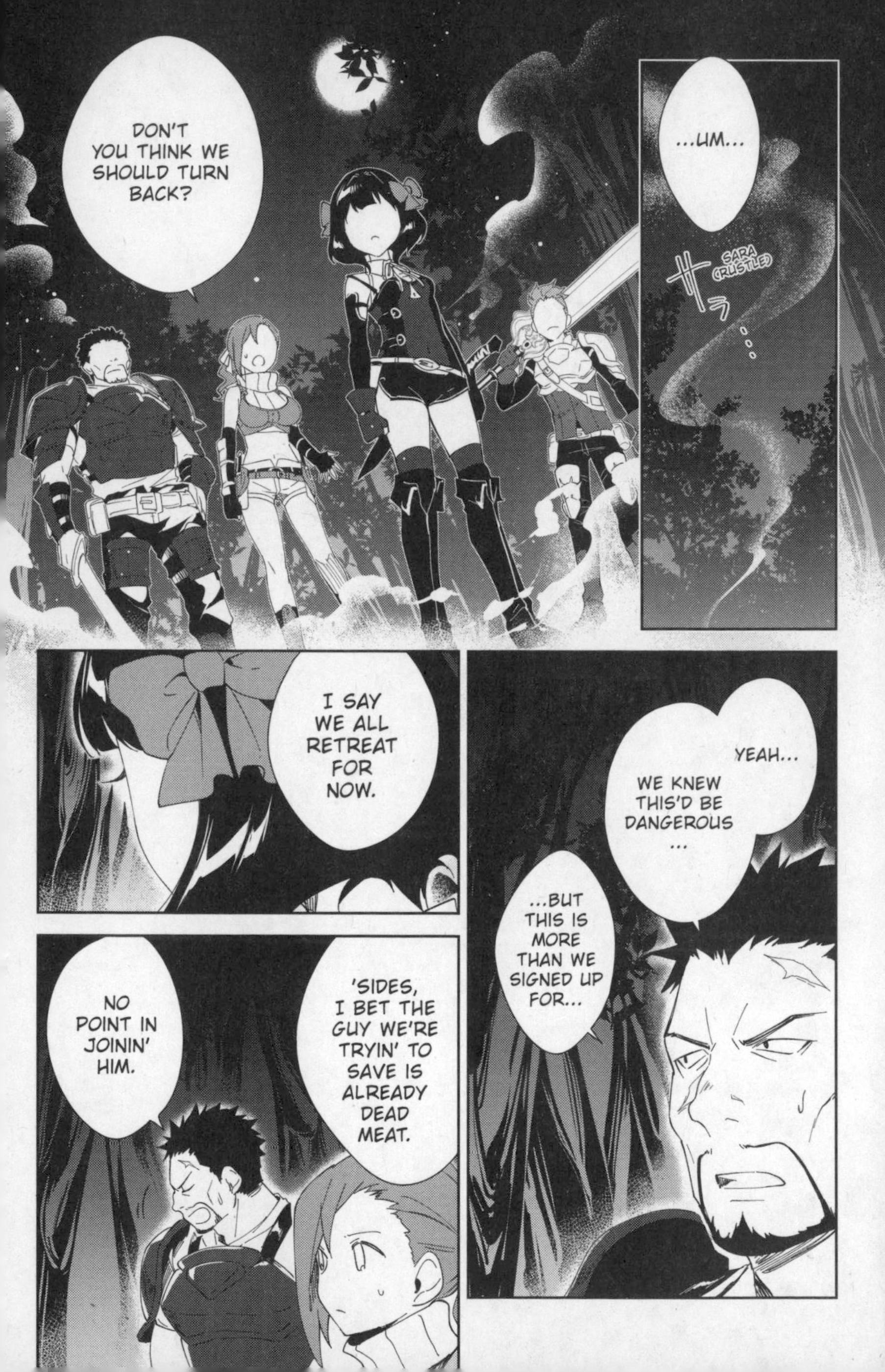
...UM...
SARA (RUSTLE)
DON'T YOU THINK WE SHOULD TURN BACK?
YEAH... WE KNEW THIS'D BE DANGEROUS...
...BUT THIS IS MORE THAN WE SIGNED UP FOR...
I SAY WE ALL RETREAT FOR NOW.
'SIDES, I BET THE GUY WE'RE TRYIN' TO SAVE IS ALREADY DEAD MEAT.
NO POINT IN JOININ' HIM.

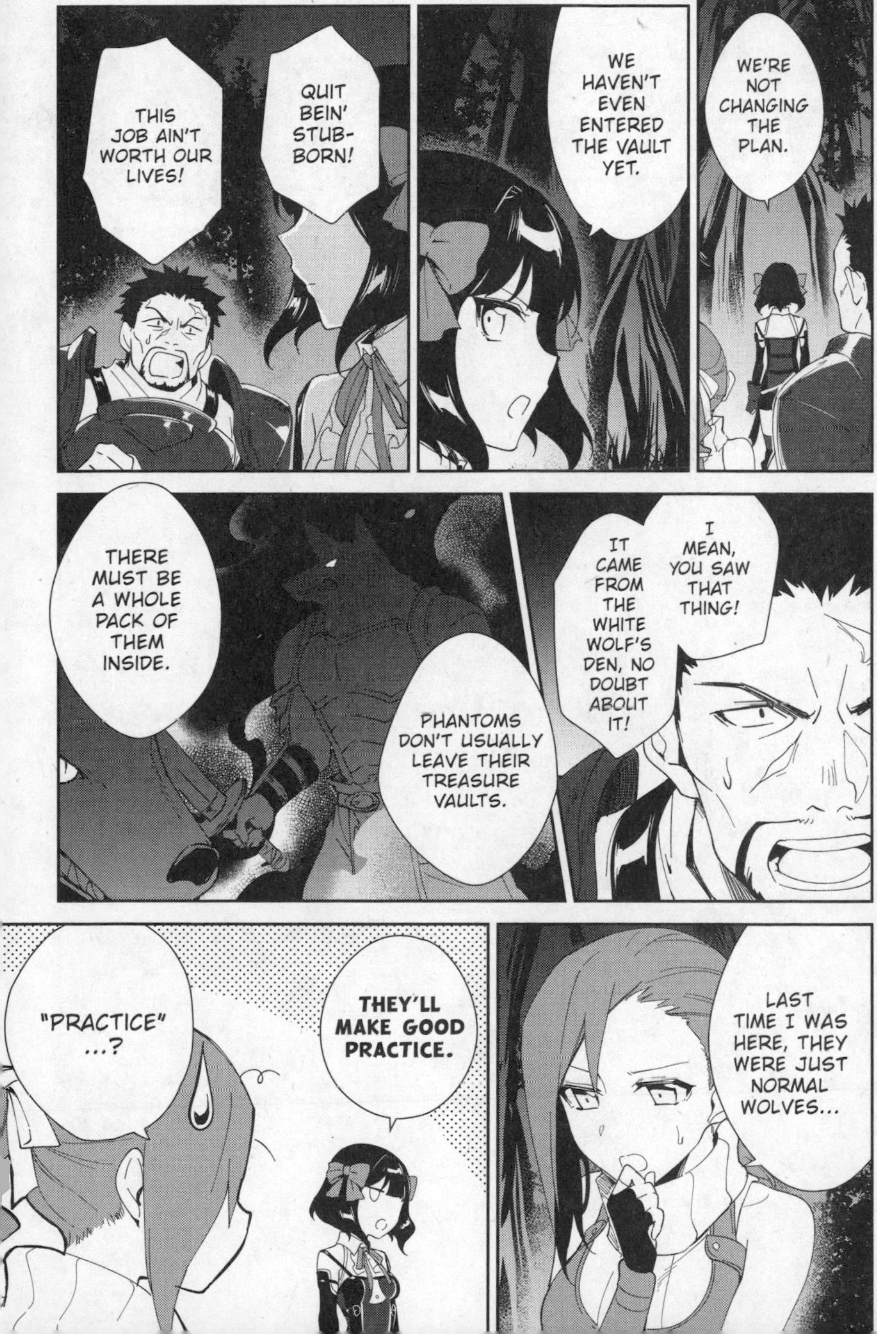
WE'RE NOT CHANGING THE PLAN.
WE HAVEN'T EVEN ENTERED THE VAULT YET.
QUIT BEIN' STUB-BORN!
THIS JOB AIN'T WORTH OUR LIVES!
I MEAN, YOU SAW THAT THING!
IT CAME FROM THE WHITE WOLF'S DEN, NO DOUBT ABOUT IT!
PHANTOMS DON'T USUALLY LEAVE THEIR TREASURE VAULTS.
THERE MUST BE A WHOLE PACK OF THEM INSIDE.
LAST TIME I WAS HERE, THEY WERE JUST NORMAL WOLVES...
THEY'LL MAKE GOOD PRACTICE.
"PRACTICE" ...?

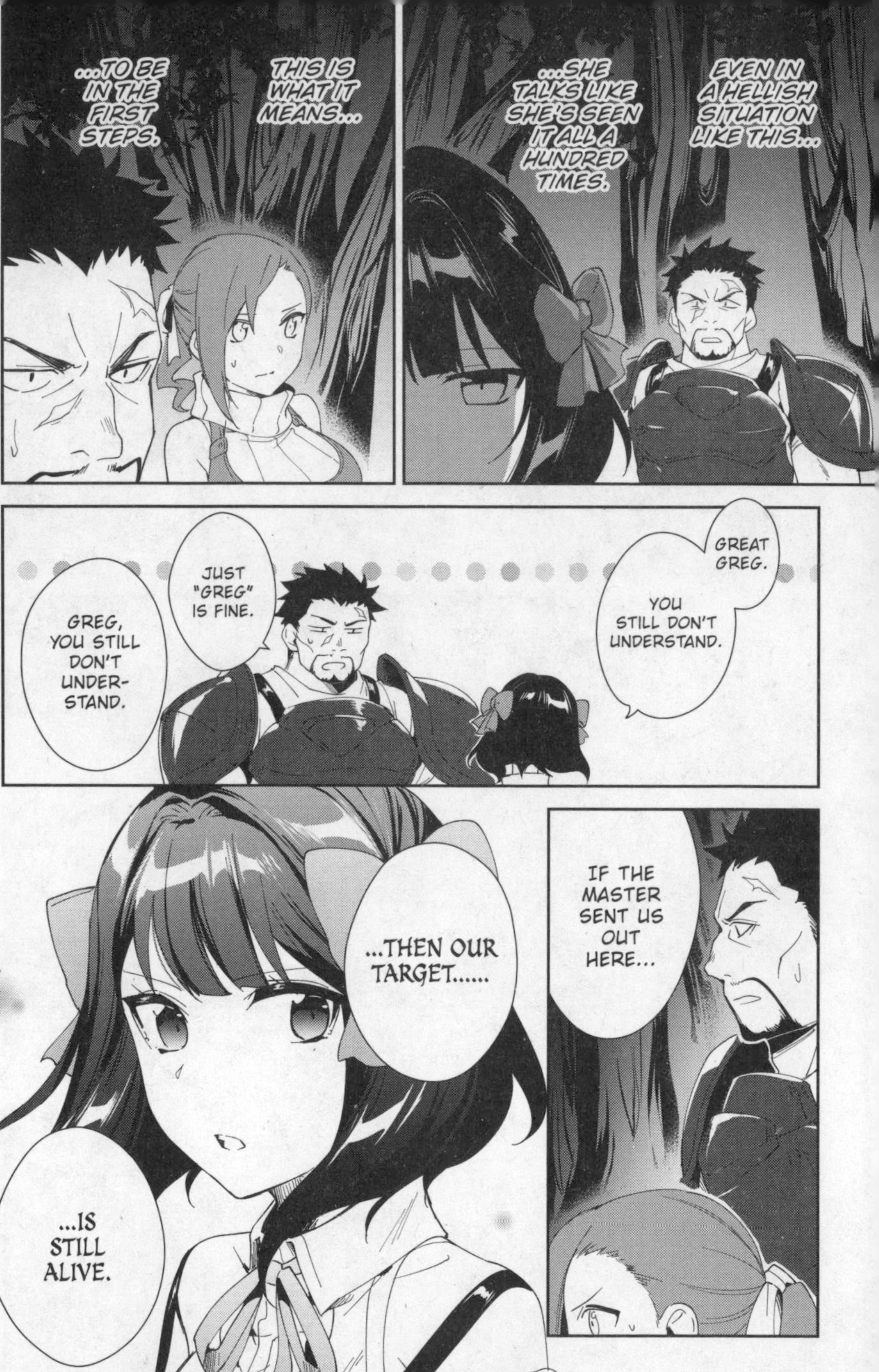
EVEN IN A HELLISH SITUATION LIKE THIS...
...SHE TALKS LIKE SHE'S SEEN IT ALL A HUNDRED TIMES.
THIS IS WHAT IT MEANS...
...TO BE IN THE FIRST STEPS.
GREAT GREG.
YOU STILL DON'T UNDERSTAND.
JUST "GREG" IS FINE.
GREG, YOU STILL DON'T UNDER-STAND.
IF THE MASTER SENT US OUT HERE...
...THEN OUR TARGET......
...IS STILL ALIVE.

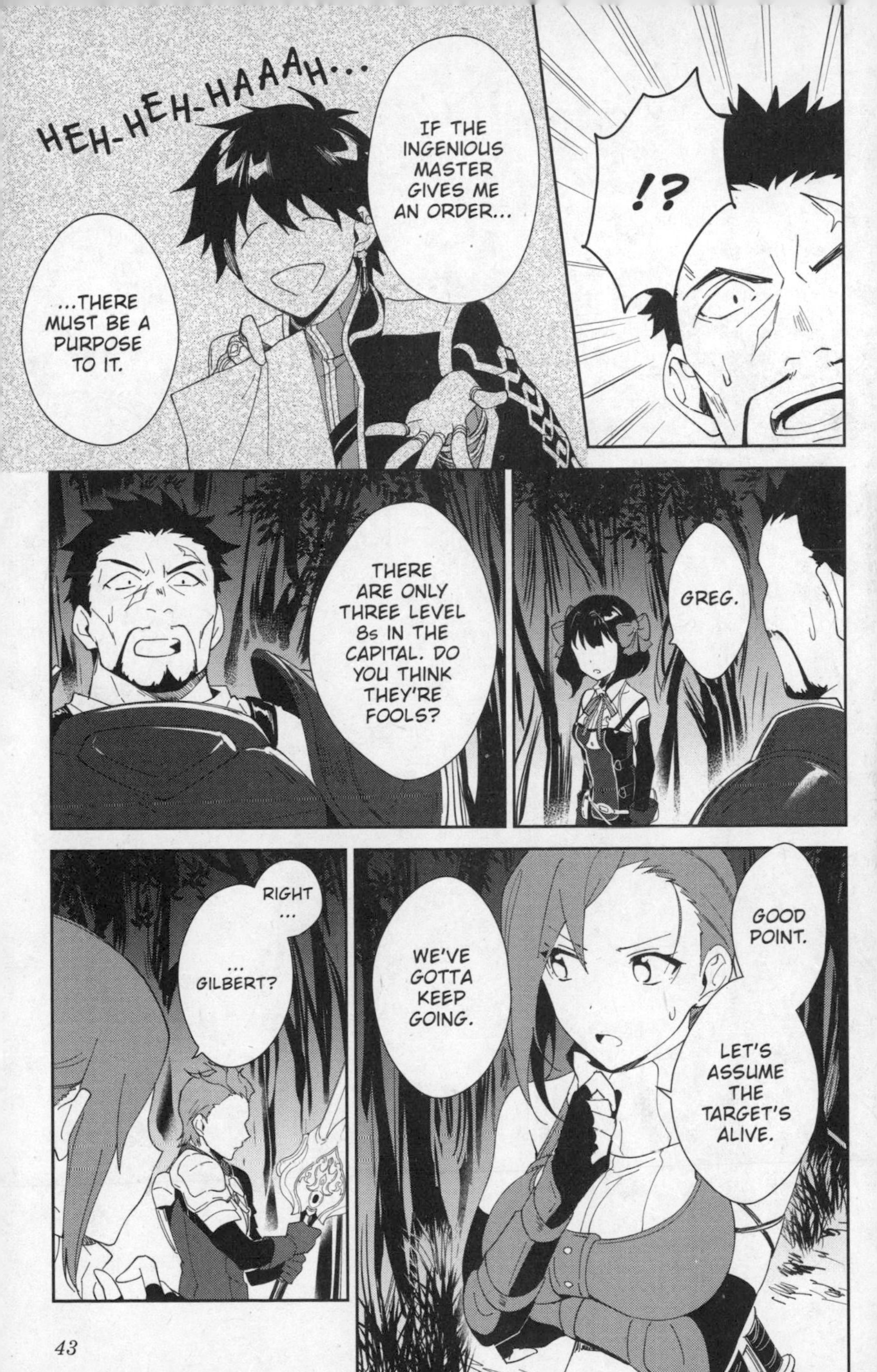
!?
IF THE INGENIOUS MASTER GIVES ME AN ORDER...
HEH-HEH-HAAAAH...
...THERE MUST BE A PURPOSE TO IT.
GREG.
THERE ARE ONLY THREE LEVEL 8s IN THE CAPITAL. DO YOU THINK THEY'RE FOOLS?
GOOD POINT.
LET'S ASSUME THE TARGET'S ALIVE.
WE'VE GOTTA KEEP GOING.
RIGHT...
...GILBERT?

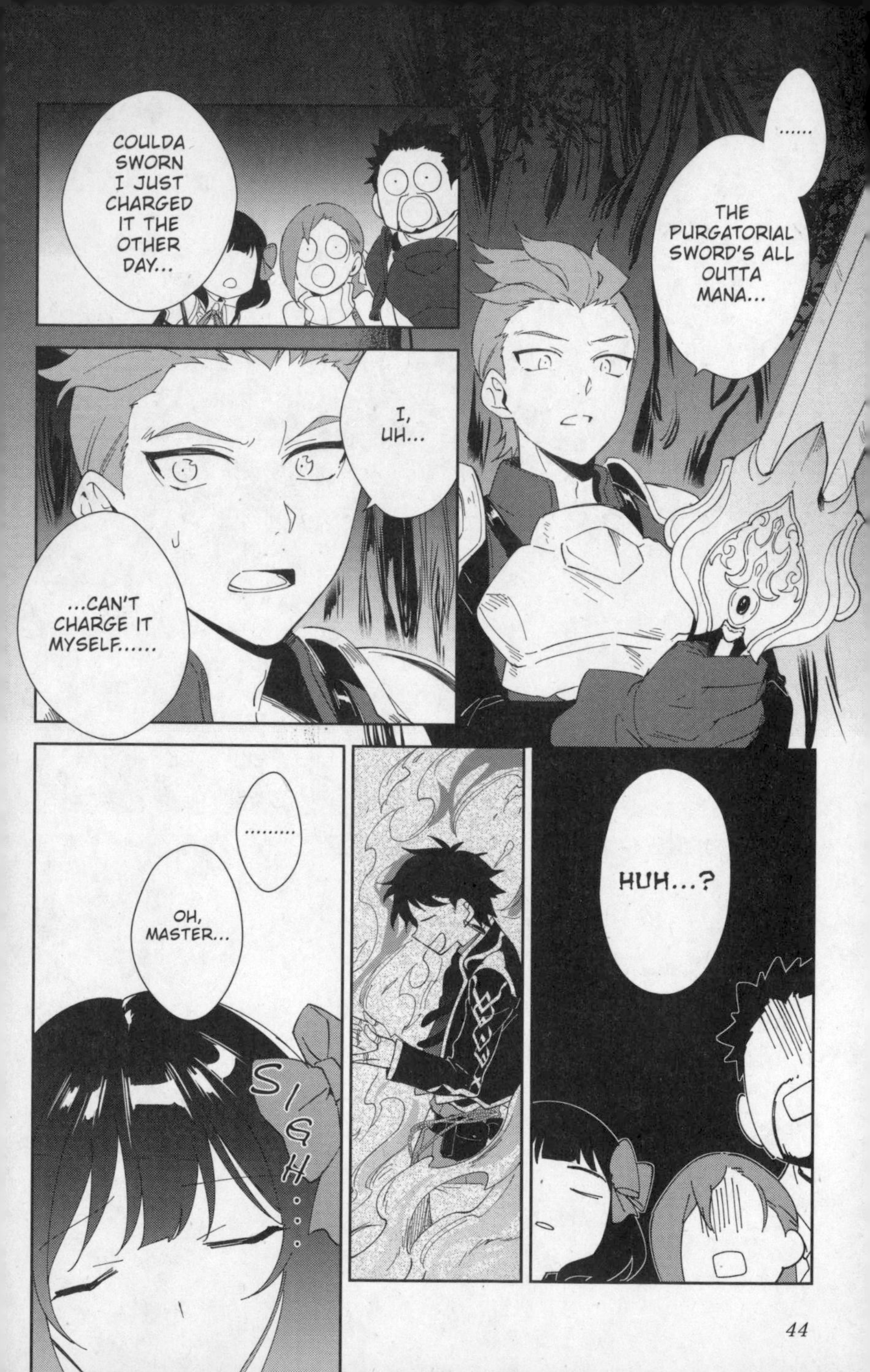
......
THE PURGATORIAL SWORD'S ALL OUTTA MANA...
COULDA SWORN I JUST CHARGED IT THE OTHER DAY...
I, UH...
...CAN'T CHARGE IT MYSELF......
HUH...?
....
OH, MASTER...
SIGH...

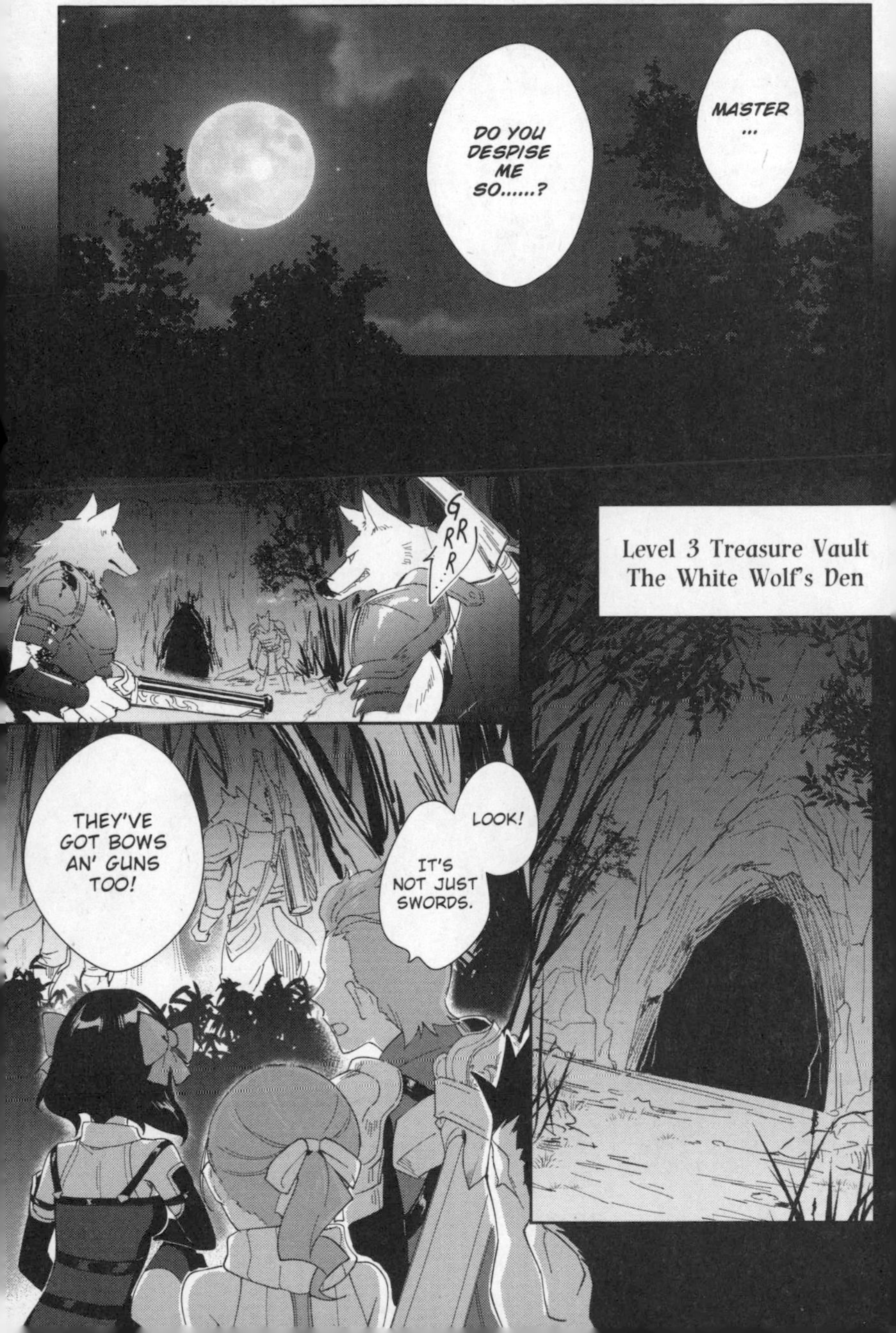
MASTER ...
DO YOU DESPISE ME SO......?
Level 3 Treasure Vault
The White Wolf's Den
GRRR...
LOOK!
IT'S NOT JUST SWORDS.
THEY'VE GOT BOWS AN' GUNS TOO!

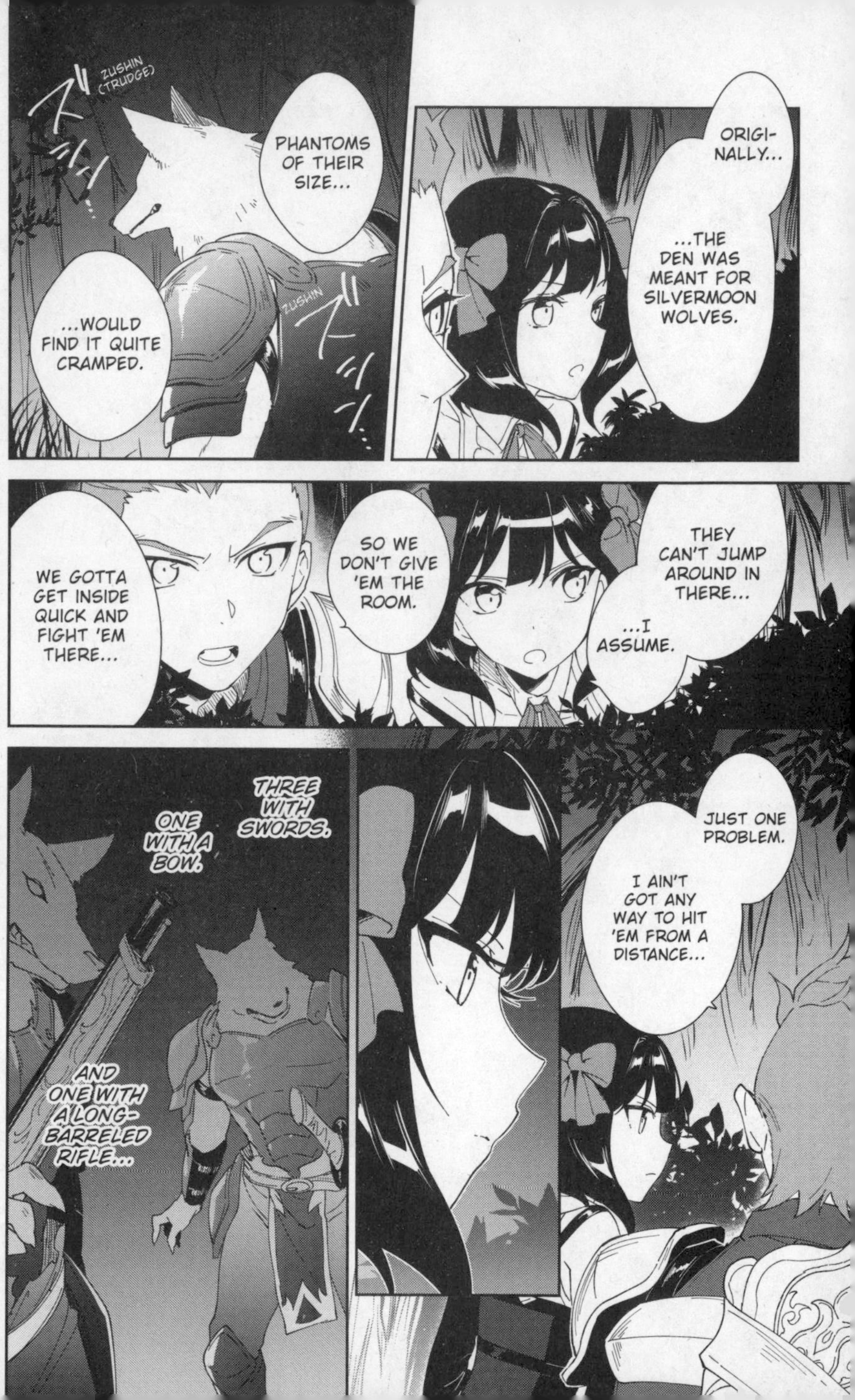
ORIGI-NALLY...
...THE DEN WAS MEANT FOR SILVERMOON WOLVES.
ZUSHIN (TRUDGE)
PHANTOMS OF THEIR SIZE...
ZUSHIN
...WOULD FIND IT QUITE CRAMPED.
THEY CAN'T JUMP AROUND IN THERE...
...I ASSUME.
SO WE DON'T GIVE 'EM THE ROOM.
WE GOTTA GET INSIDE QUICK AND FIGHT 'EM THERE...
JUST ONE PROBLEM.
I AIN'T GOT ANY WAY TO HIT 'EM FROM A DISTANCE...
THREE WITH SWORDS.
ONE WITH A BOW.
AND ONE WITH A LONG-BARRELED RIFLE...

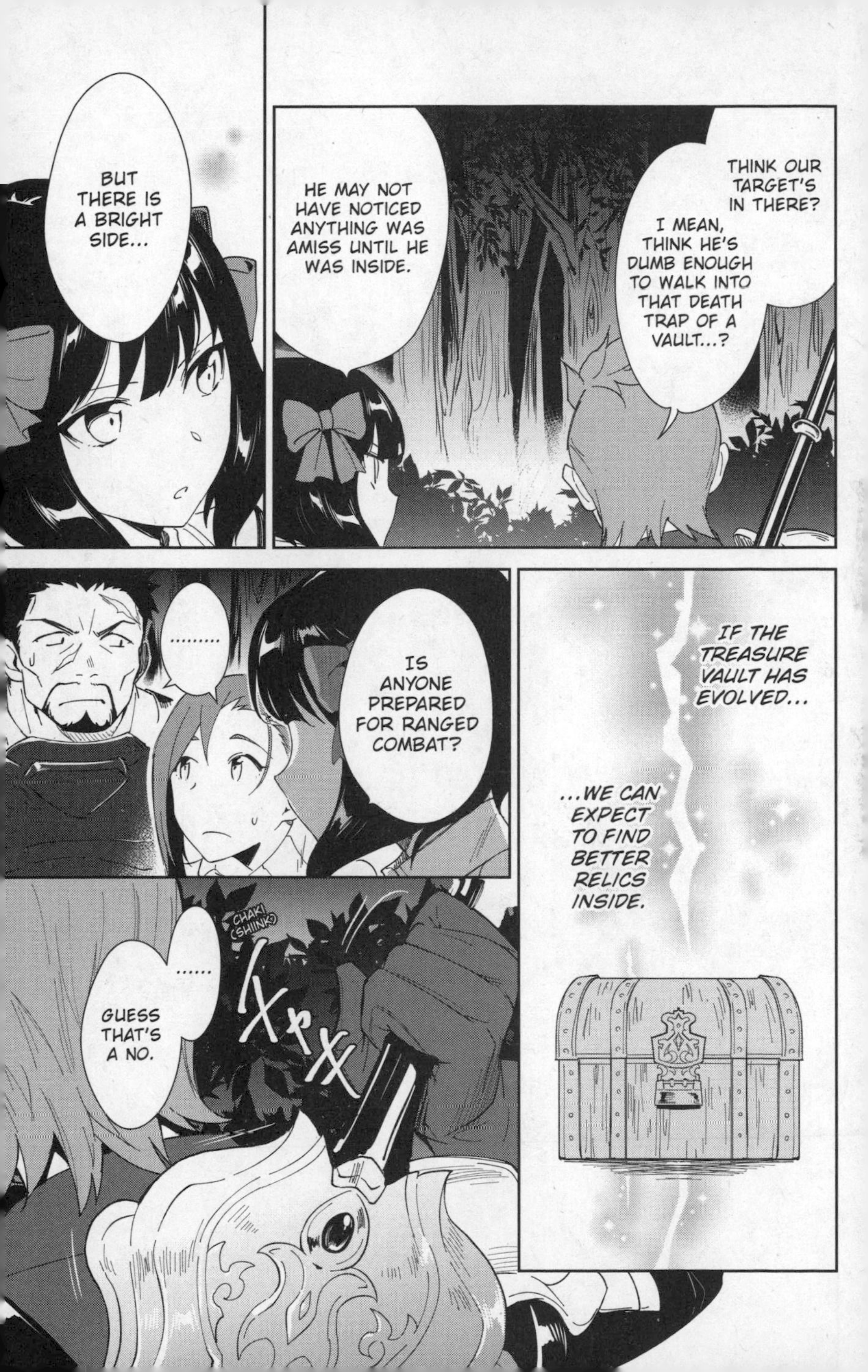
THINK OUR TARGET'S IN THERE?
I MEAN, THINK HE'S DUMB ENOUGH TO WALK INTO THAT DEATH TRAP OF A VAULT...?
HE MAY NOT HAVE NOTICED ANYTHING WAS AMISS UNTIL HE WAS INSIDE.
BUT THERE IS A BRIGHT SIDE...
IF THE TREASURE VAULT HAS EVOLVED...
...WE CAN EXPECT TO FIND BETTER RELICS INSIDE.
IS ANYONE PREPARED FOR RANGED COMBAT?
....
CHAKI (SHINK)
......
GUESS THAT'S A NO.

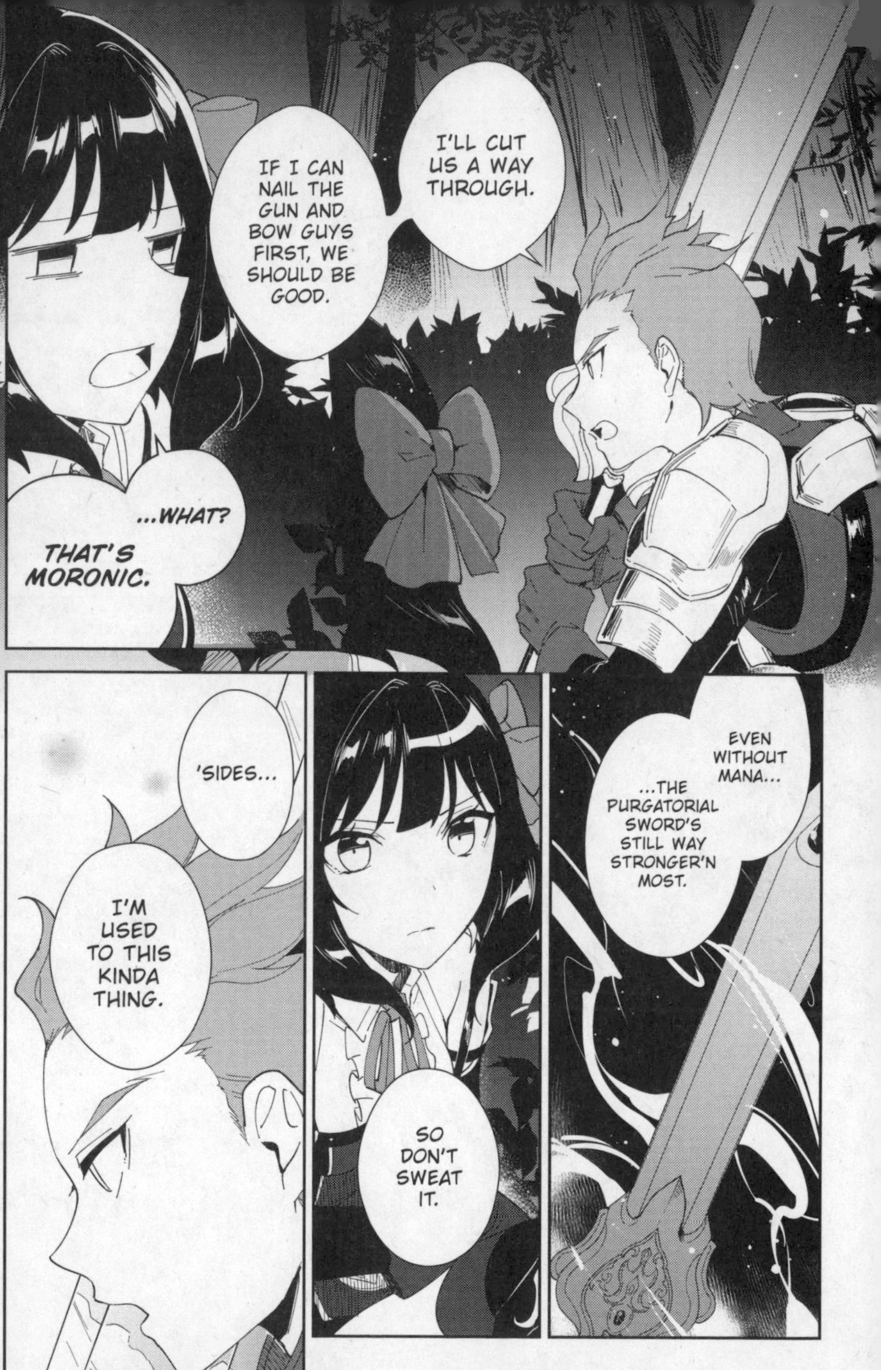
I'LL CUT US A WAY THROUGH.
IF I CAN NAIL THE GUN AND BOW GUYS FIRST, WE SHOULD BE GOOD.
...WHAT?
THAT'S MORONIC.
EVEN WITHOUT MANA...
...THE PURGATORIAL SWORD'S STILL WAY STRONGER'N MOST.
SO DON'T SWEAT IT.
'SIDES...
I'M USED TO THIS KINDA THING.

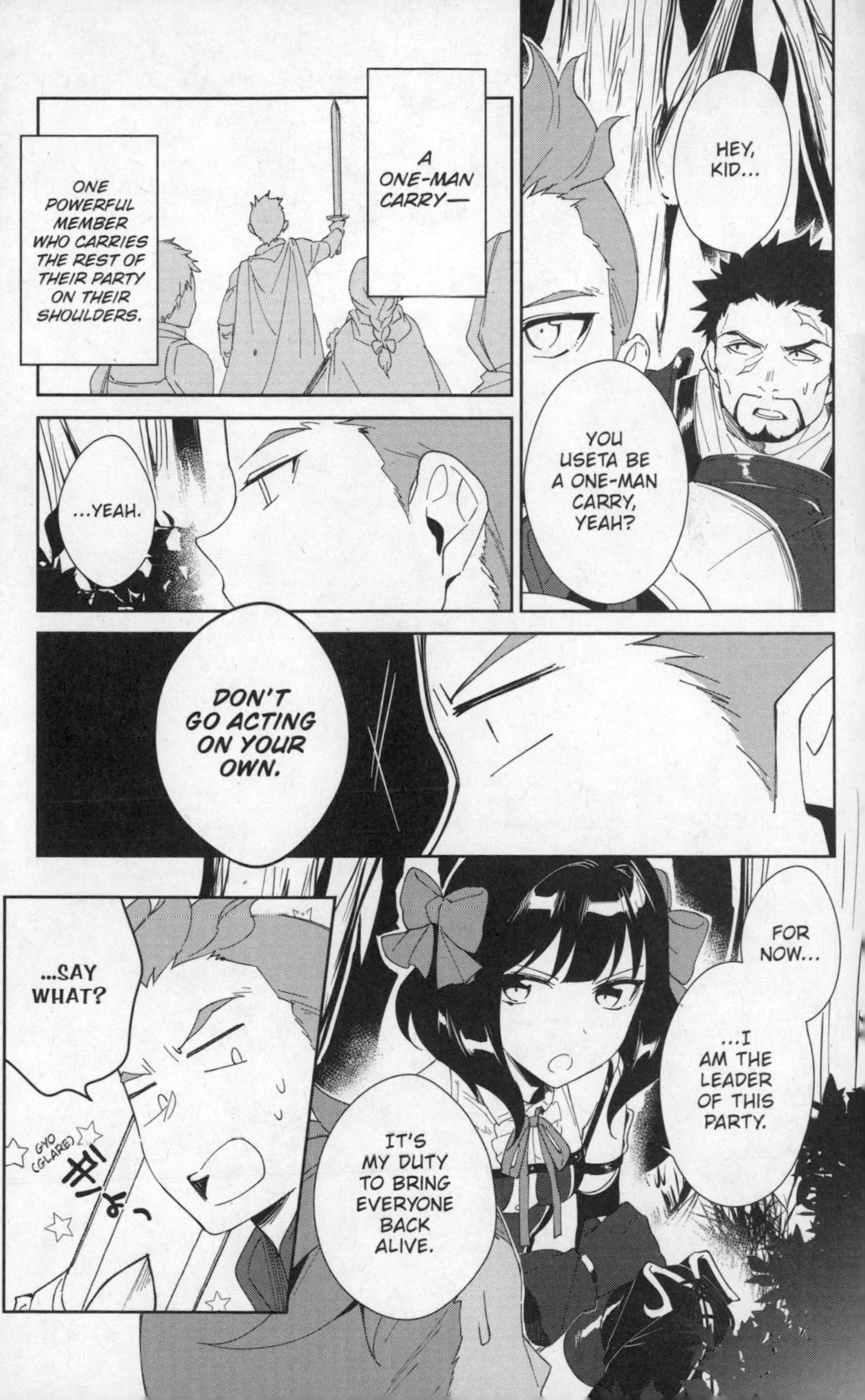
HEY, KID...
YOU USETA BE A ONE-MAN CARRY, YEAH?
A ONE-MAN CARRY—
ONE POWERFUL MEMBER WHO CARRIES THE REST OF THEIR PARTY ON THEIR SHOULDERS.
...YEAH.
DON'T GO ACTING ON YOUR OWN.
FOR NOW...
...I AM THE LEADER OF THIS PARTY.
IT'S MY DUTY TO BRING EVERYONE BACK ALIVE.
...SAY WHAT?
GYO (GLARE)

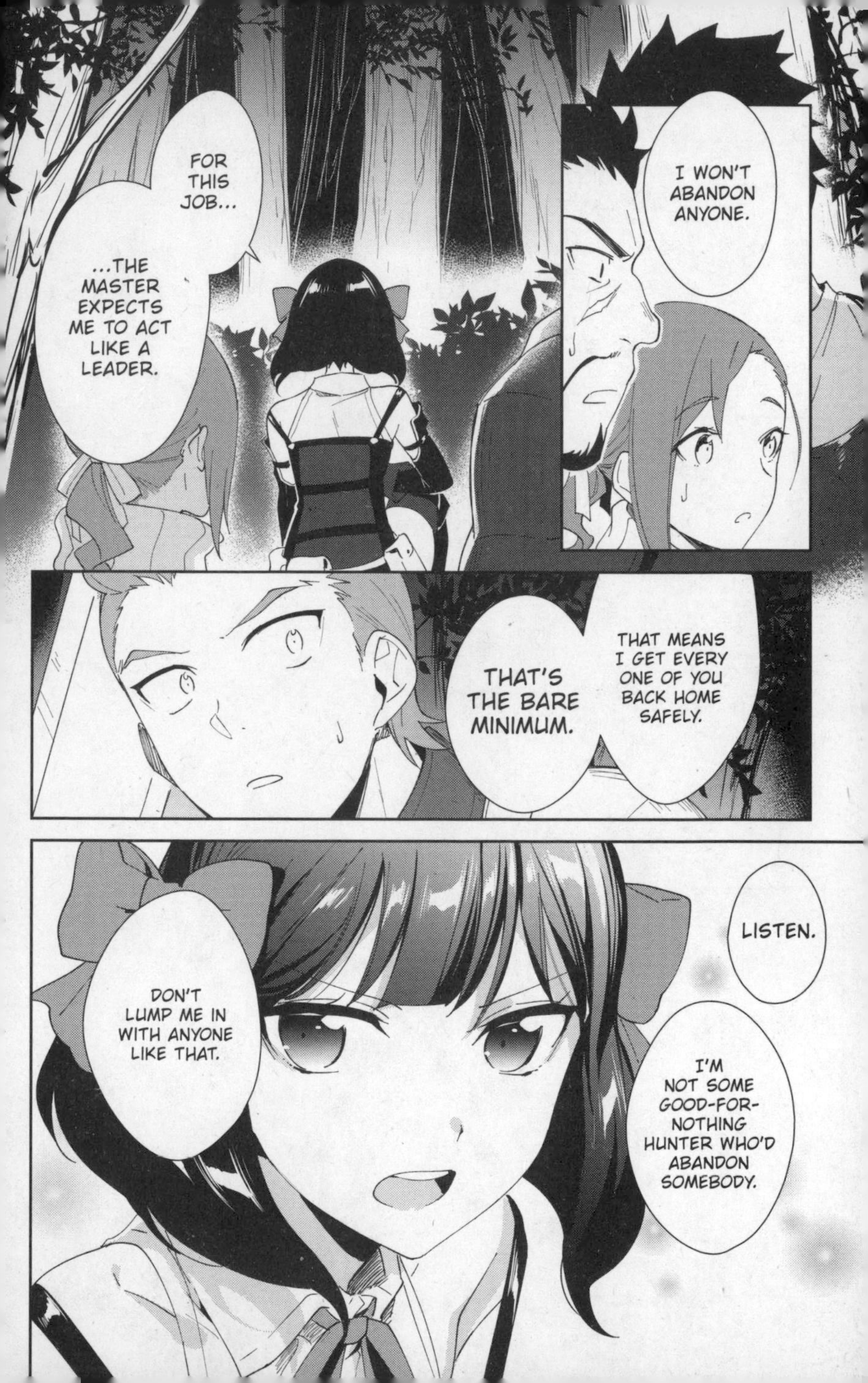
I WON'T ABANDON ANYONE.
FOR THIS JOB...
...THE MASTER EXPECTS ME TO ACT LIKE A LEADER.
THAT MEANS I GET EVERY ONE OF YOU BACK HOME SAFELY.
THAT'S THE BARE MINIMUM.
LISTEN.
I'M NOT SOME GOOD-FOR-NOTHING HUNTER WHO'D ABANDON SOMEBODY.
DON'T LUMP ME IN WITH ANYONE LIKE THAT.

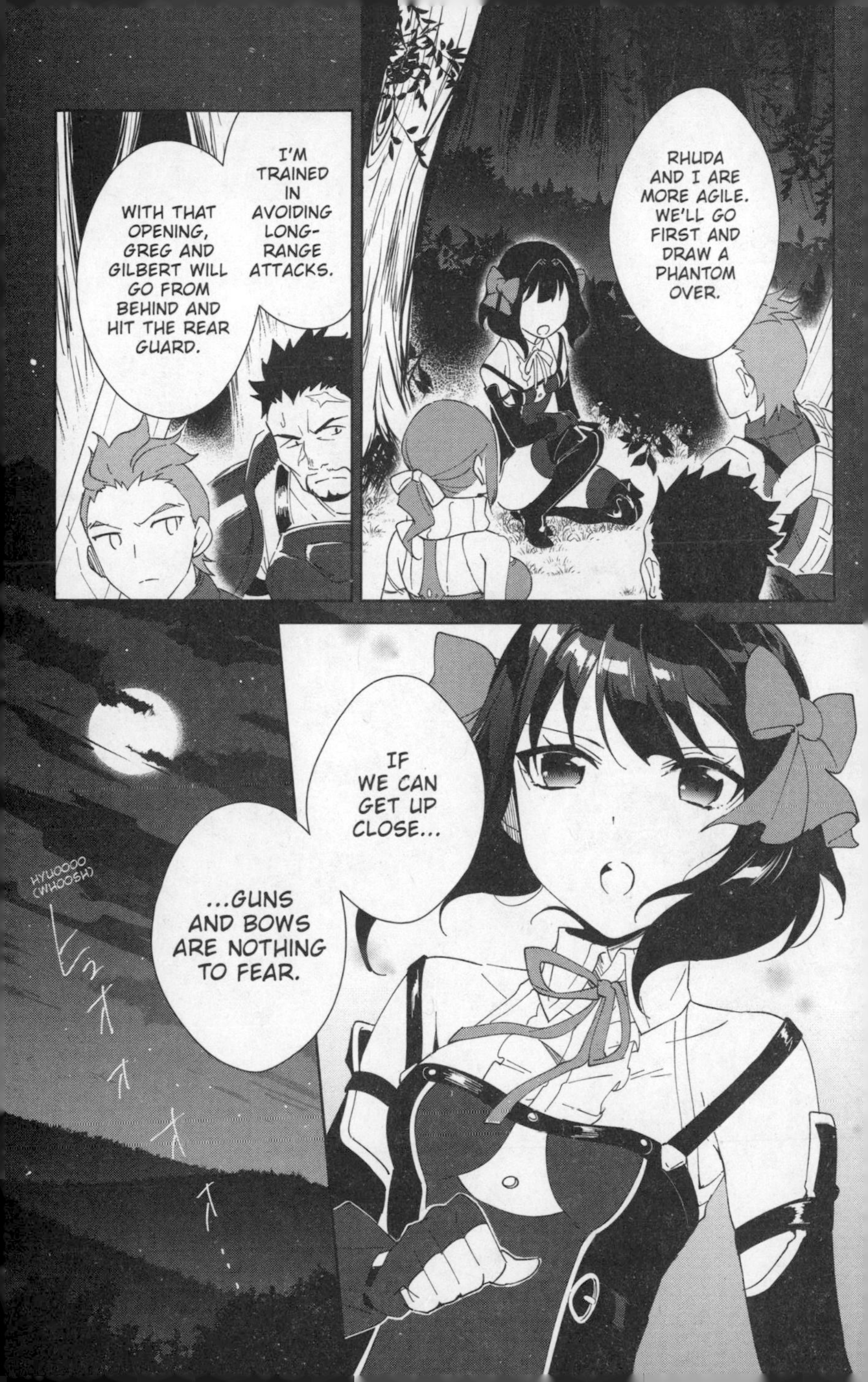
RHUDA AND I ARE MORE AGILE. WE'LL GO FIRST AND DRAW A PHANTOM OVER.
I'M TRAINED IN AVOIDING LONG-RANGE ATTACKS.
WITH THAT OPENING, GREG AND GILBERT WILL GO FROM BEHIND AND HIT THE REAR GUARD.
IF WE CAN GET UP CLOSE...
...GUNS AND BOWS ARE NOTHING TO FEAR.
HYUOOOO (WHOOSH)

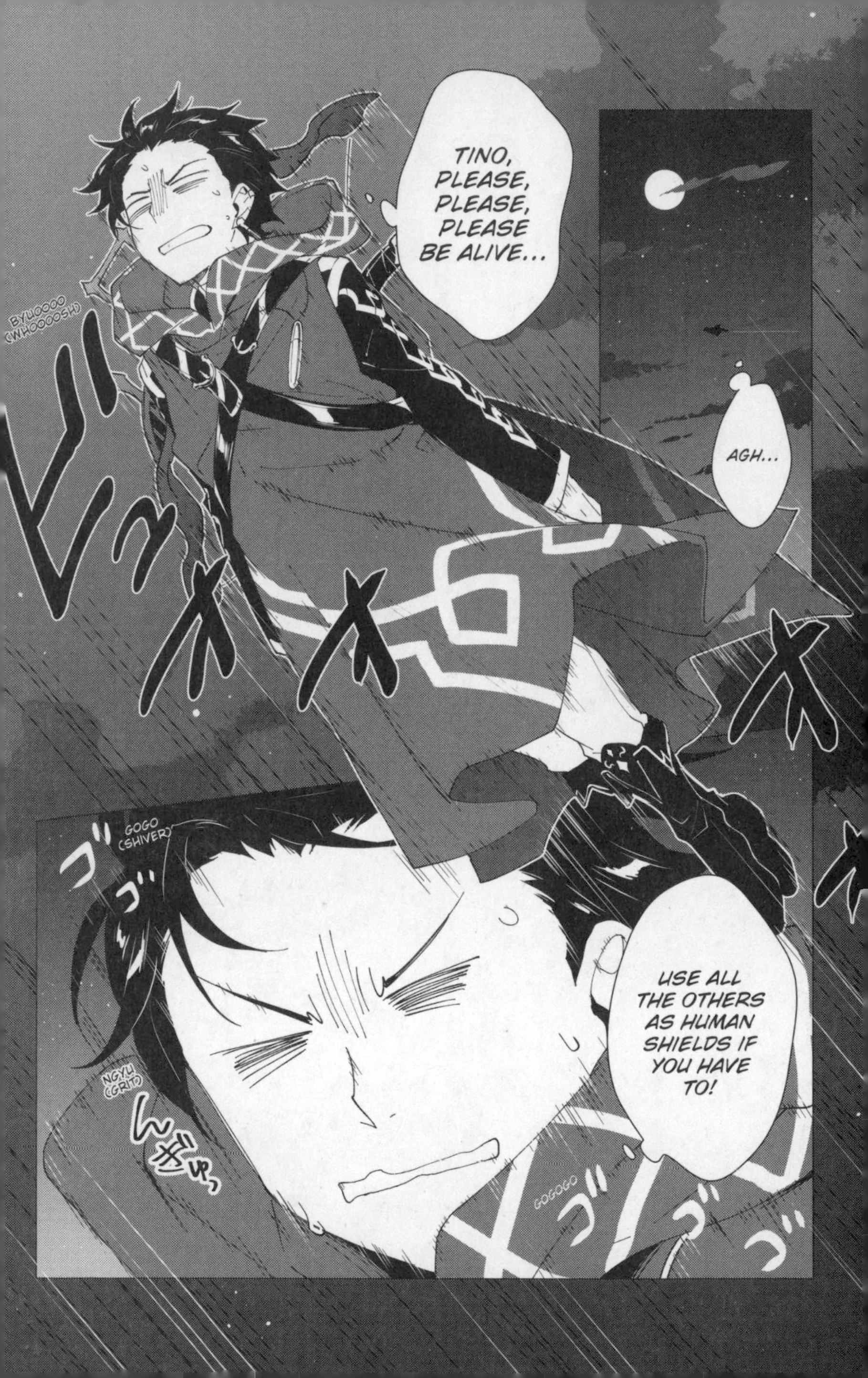

BYUOOOO (WHOOOOSH)
TINO, PLEASE, PLEASE, PLEASE BE ALIVE...
AGH...
GOGO (SHIVER)
NGYU (GRIT)
USE ALL THE OTHERS AS HUMAN SHIELDS IF YOU HAVE TO!
GOGOGO

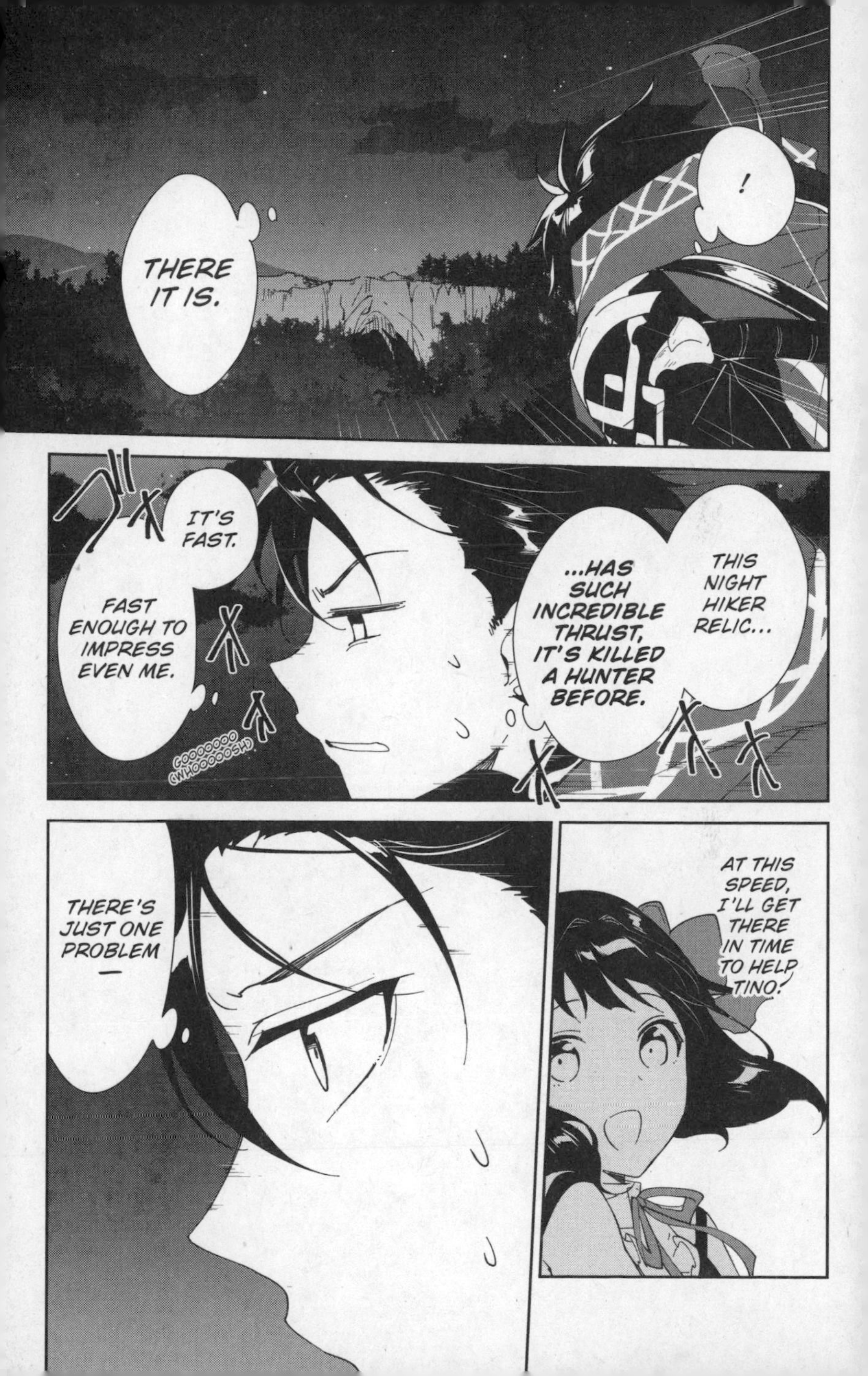
!
THERE IT IS.
THIS NIGHT HIKER RELIC...
...HAS SUCH INCREDIBLE THRUST, IT'S KILLED A HUNTER BEFORE.
IT'S FAST.
FAST ENOUGH TO IMPRESS EVEN ME.
GOOOOOOO (WHOOOOOOSH)
AT THIS SPEED, I'LL GET THERE IN TIME TO HELP TINO!
THERE'S JUST ONE PROBLEM—

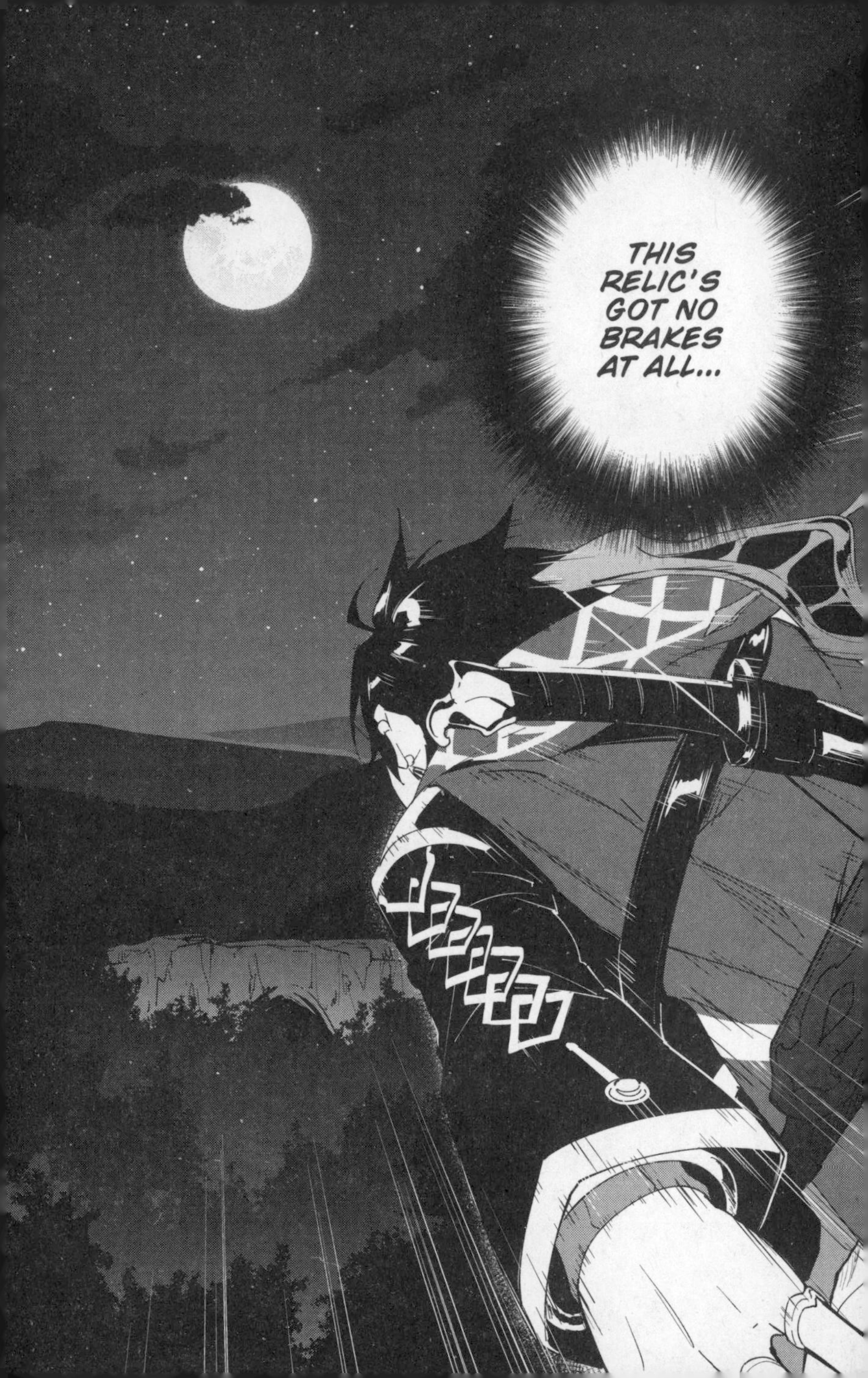
THIS RELIC'S GOT NO BRAKES AT ALL...

LET THIS

Grieving Soul Retire

WOE IS THE WEAKLING WHO LEADS THE STRONGEST PARTY

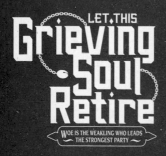

LET THIS
Grieving Soul Retire
~WOE IS THE WEAKLING WHO LEADS THE STRONGEST PARTY~

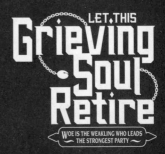

Chapter 8

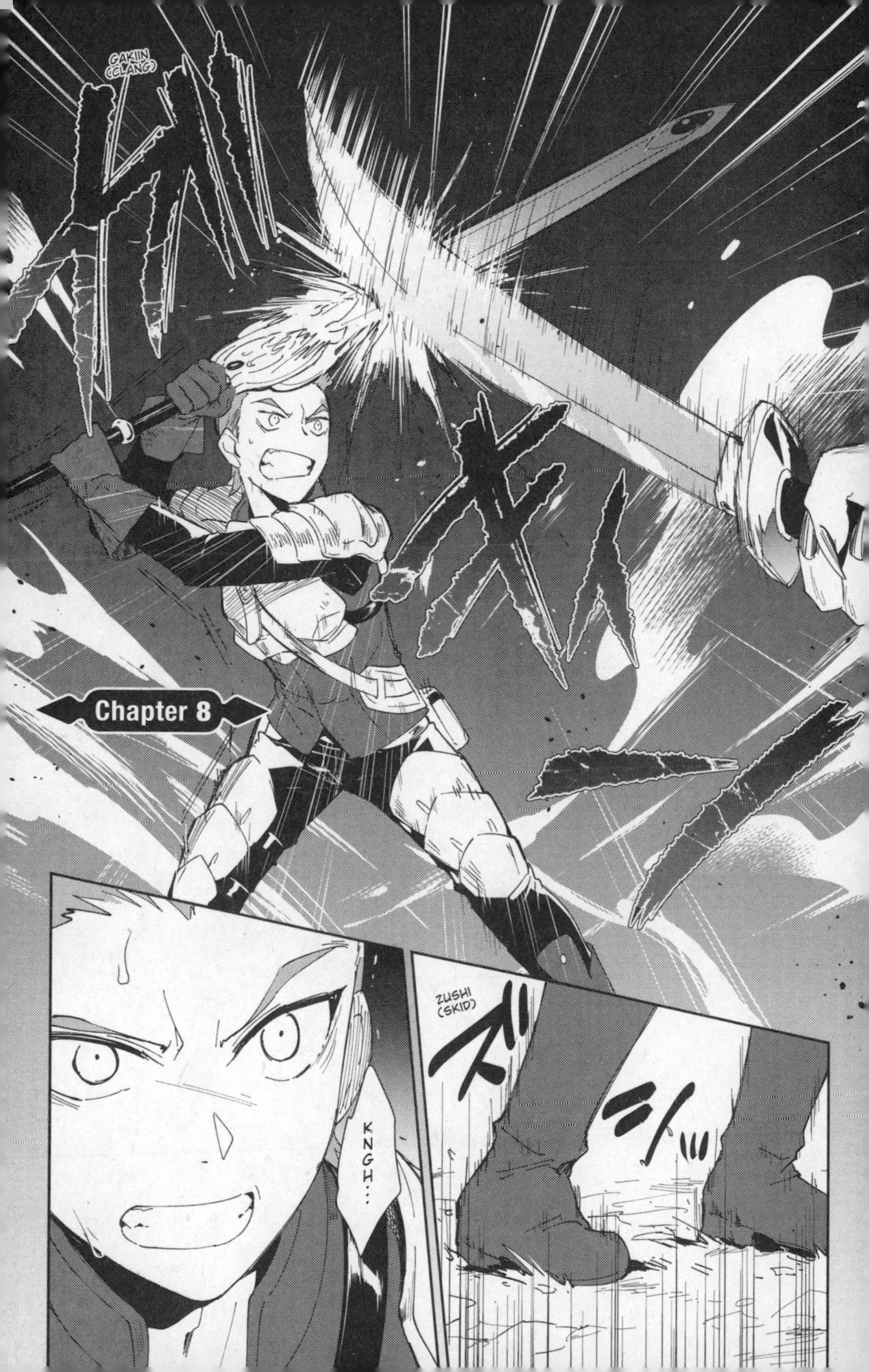
GAKIIN (CLANG)
ZUSHI (SKID)
KNGH...

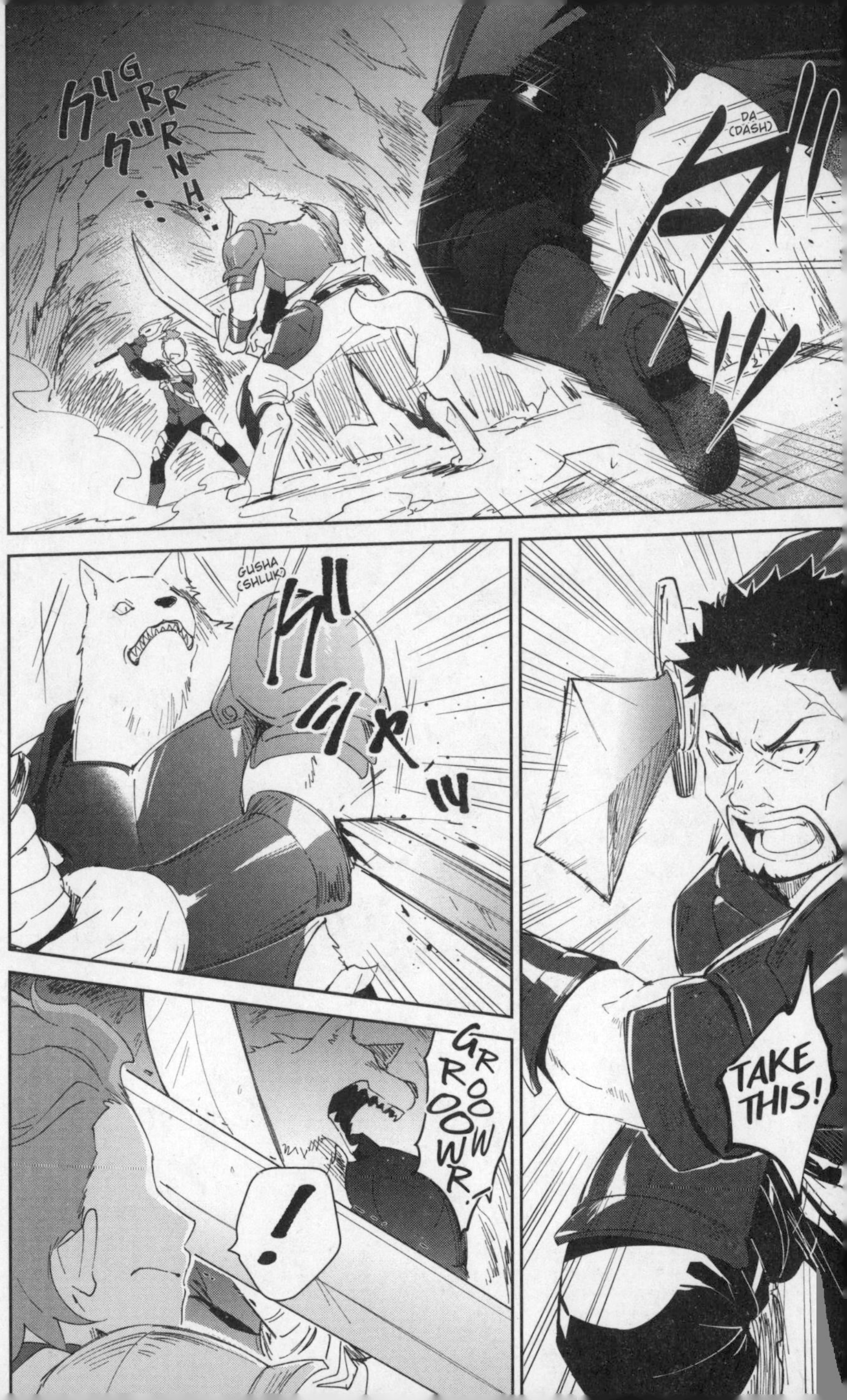
DA (DASH)
GRRRRNH...
TAKE THIS!
GUSHA (SHLUK)
GRROOOOWR!
!

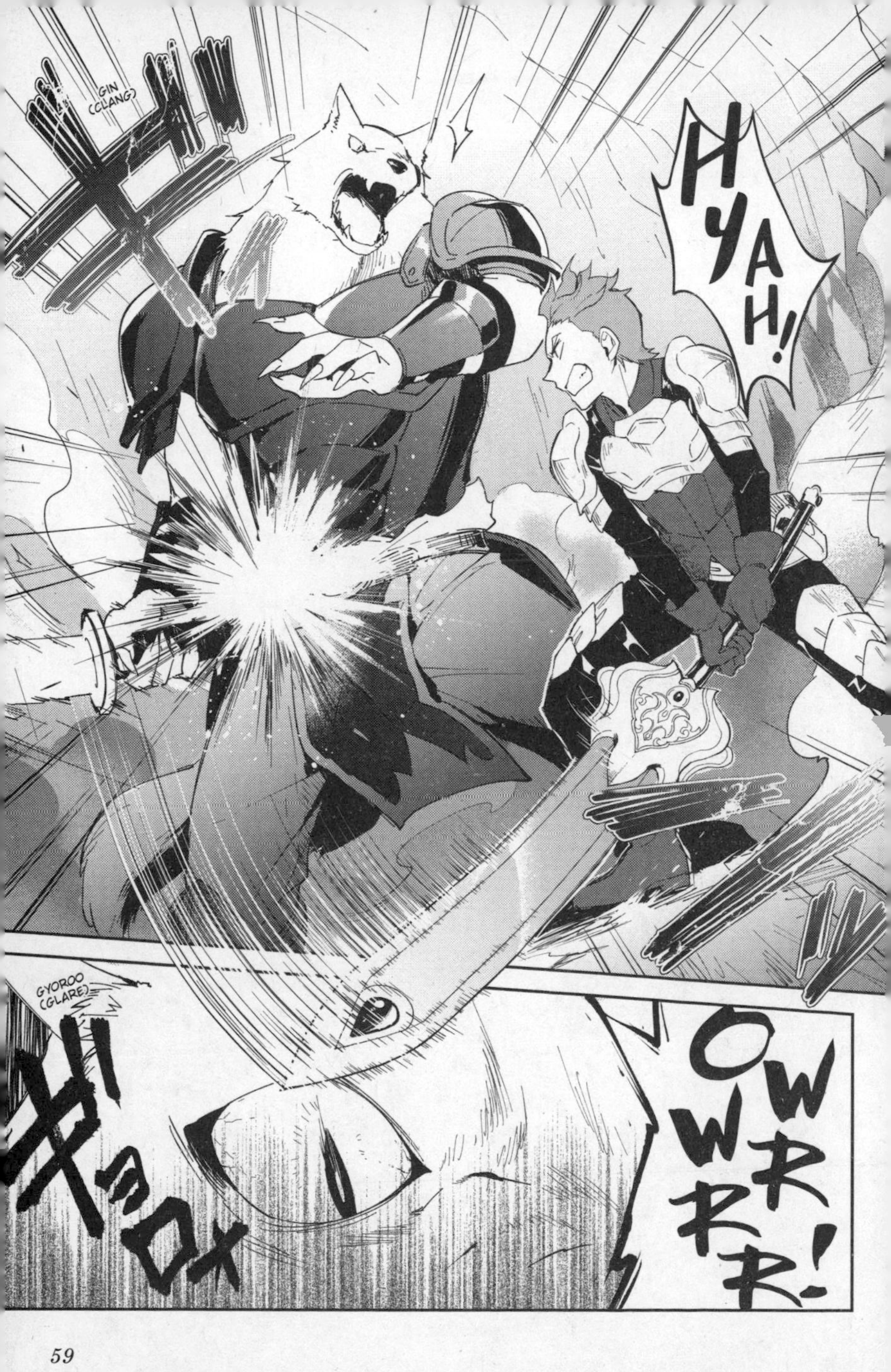
HYAH!
GIN (CLANG)
OWWRRR!
GYOROO (GLARE)

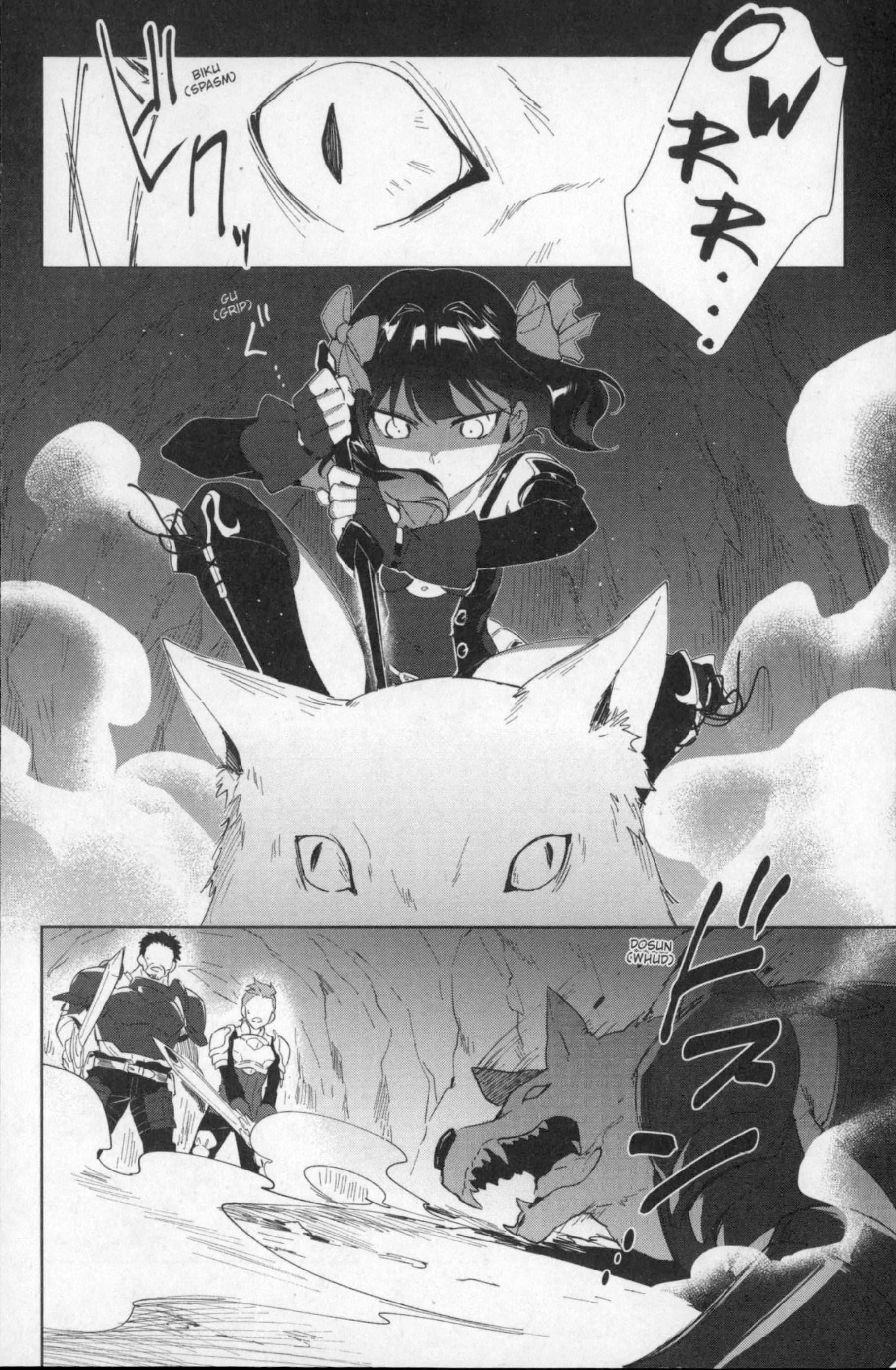
OWRR..
BIKU (SPASM)
GU (GRIP)
DOSUN (WHUD)

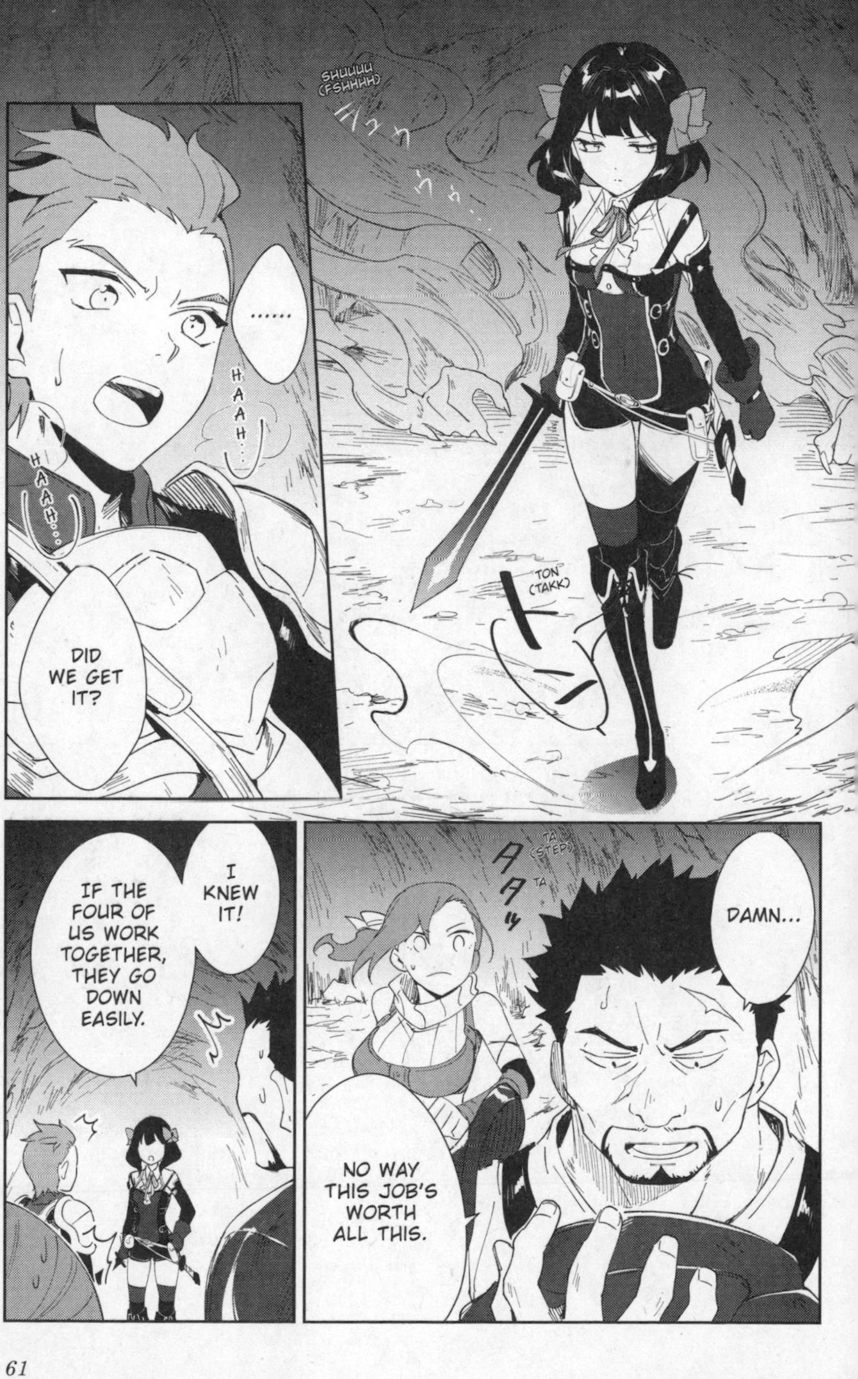
SHUUUU (FSHHHH)
TON (TAKK)
......
HAAH...
HAAH...
DID WE GET IT?
TA (STEP)
DAMN...
NO WAY THIS JOB'S WORTH ALL THIS.
I KNEW IT!
IF THE FOUR OF US WORK TOGETHER, THEY GO DOWN EASILY.

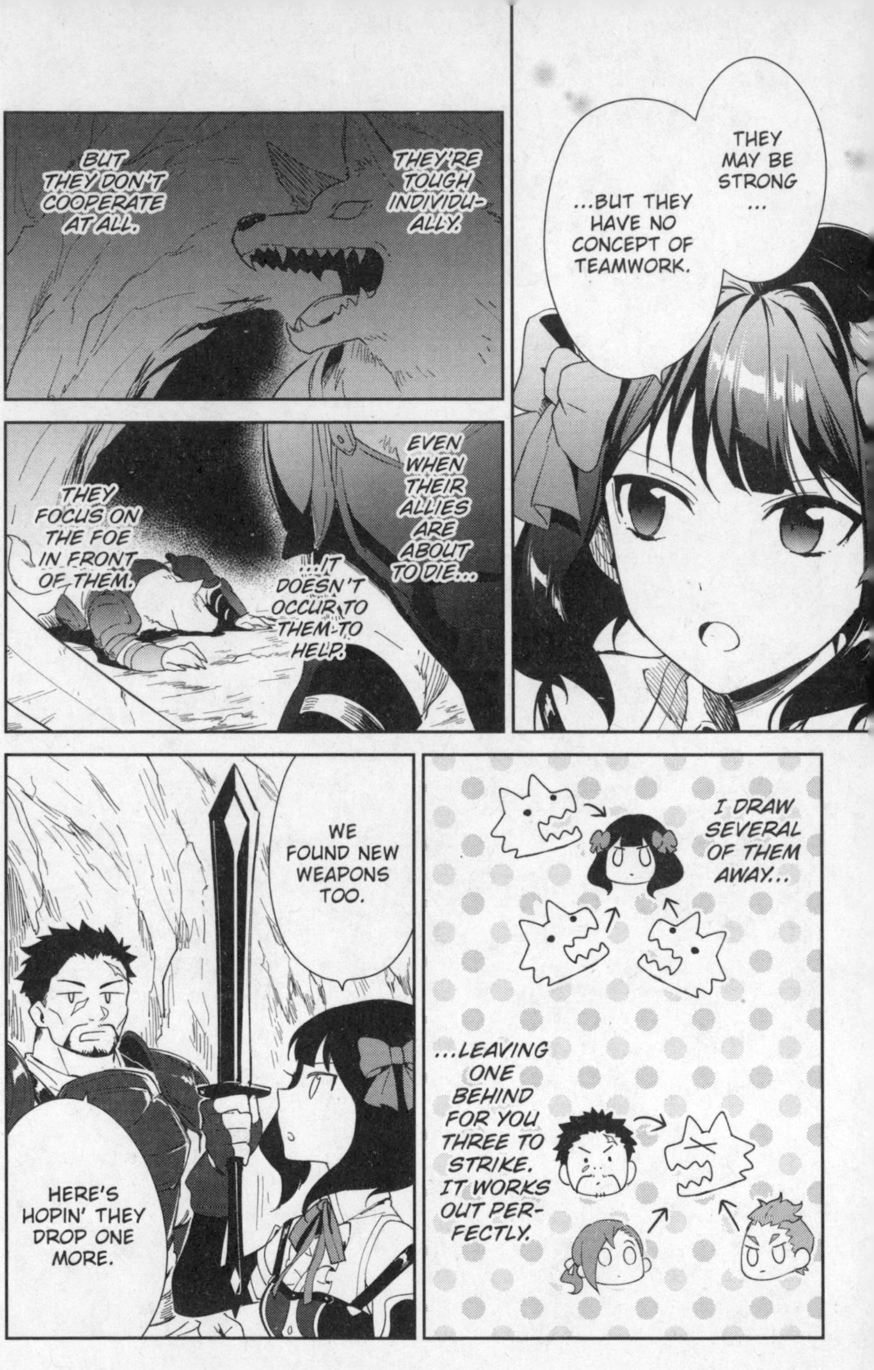
THEY MAY BE STRONG ...
...BUT THEY HAVE NO CONCEPT OF TEAMWORK.
THEY'RE TOUGH INDIVIDU-ALLY.
BUT THEY DON'T COOPERATE AT ALL.
EVEN WHEN THEIR ALLIES ARE ABOUT TO DIE...
...IT DOESN'T OCCUR TO THEM TO HELP.
THEY FOCUS ON THE FOE IN FRONT OF THEM.
I DRAW SEVERAL OF THEM AWAY...
...LEAVING ONE BEHIND FOR YOU THREE TO STRIKE. IT WORKS OUT PER-FECTLY.
WE FOUND NEW WEAPONS TOO.
HERE'S HOPIN' THEY DROP ONE MORE.

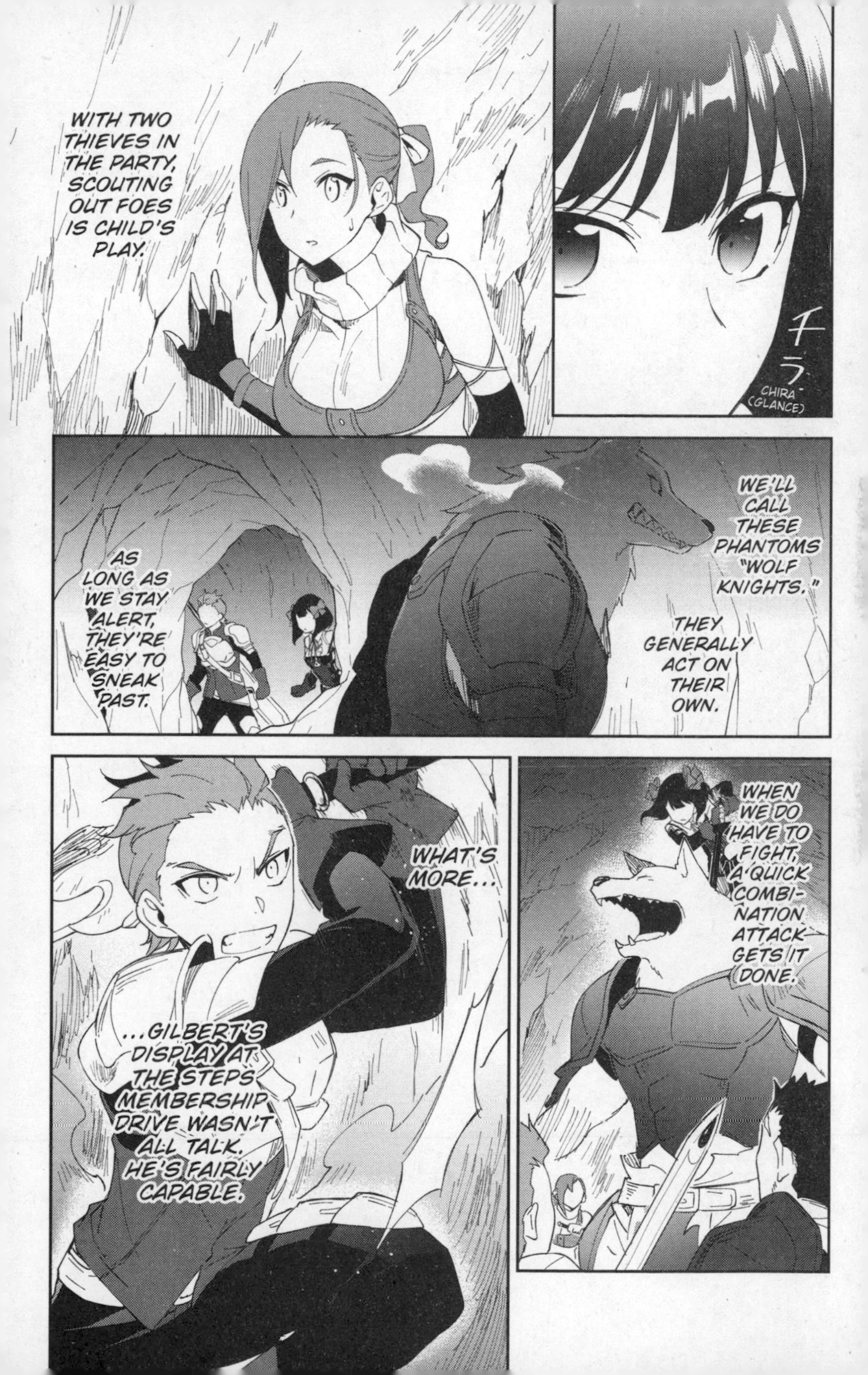
チラ
CHIRA (GLANCE)
WITH TWO THIEVES IN THE PARTY, SCOUTING OUT FOES IS CHILD'S PLAY.
WE'LL CALL THESE PHANTOMS "WOLF KNIGHTS."
THEY GENERALLY ACT ON THEIR OWN.
AS LONG AS WE STAY ALERT, THEY'RE EASY TO SNEAK PAST.
WHEN WE DO HAVE TO FIGHT, A QUICK COMBI-NATION ATTACK GETS IT DONE.
WHAT'S MORE...
...GILBERT'S DISPLAY AT THE STEPS MEMBERSHIP DRIVE WASN'T ALL TALK. HE'S FAIRLY CAPABLE.

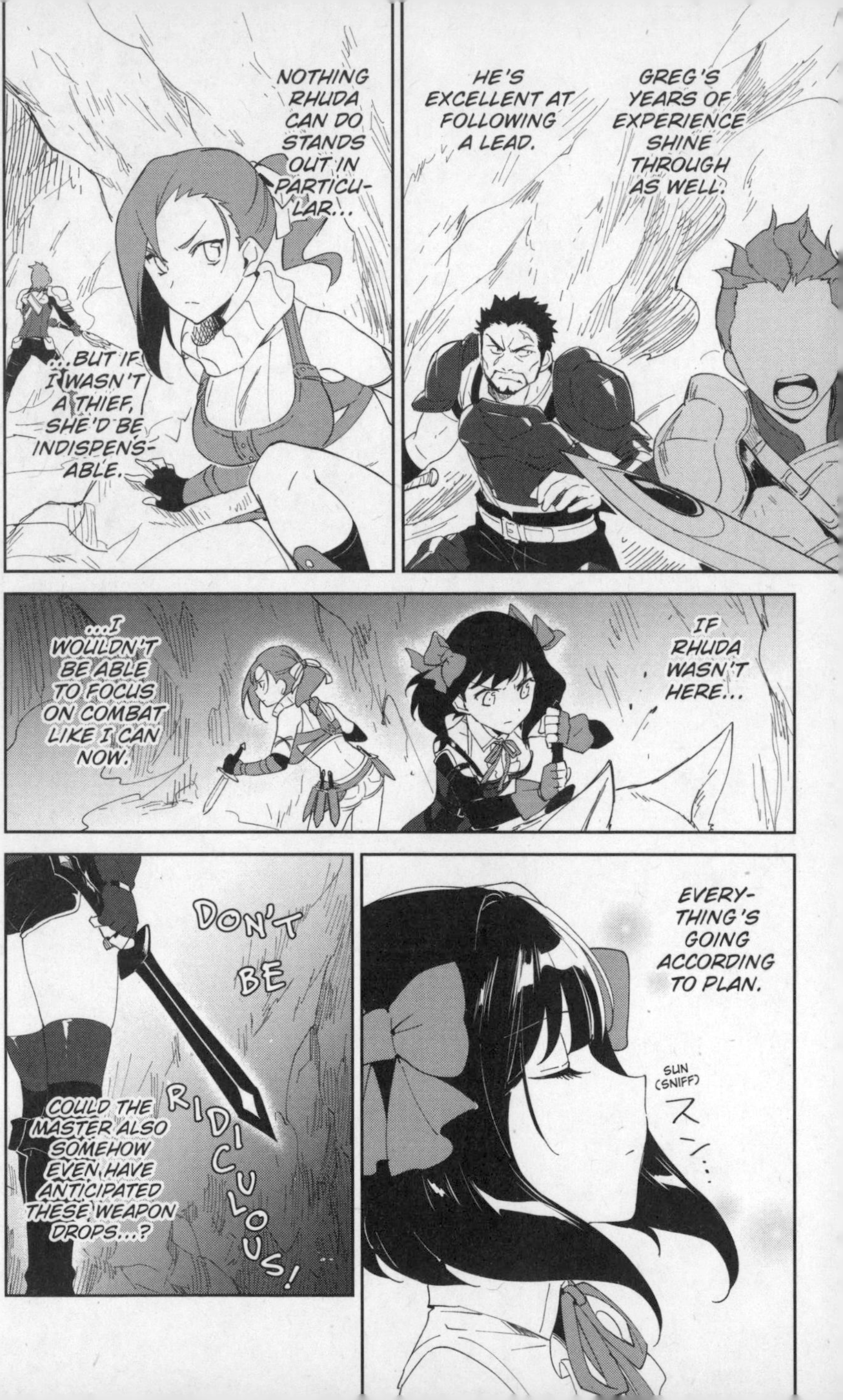
GREG'S YEARS OF EXPERIENCE SHINE THROUGH AS WELL.
HE'S EXCELLENT AT FOLLOWING A LEAD.
NOTHING RHUDA CAN DO STANDS OUT IN PARTICULAR...
...BUT IF I WASN'T A THIEF, SHE'D BE INDISPENSABLE.
IF RHUDA WASN'T HERE...
...I WOULDN'T BE ABLE TO FOCUS ON COMBAT LIKE I CAN NOW.
EVERYTHING'S GOING ACCORDING TO PLAN.
SUN (SNIFF)
ス~…
COULD THE MASTER ALSO SOMEHOW EVEN HAVE ANTICIPATED THESE WEAPON DROPS...?
DON'T BE RIDICULOUS!

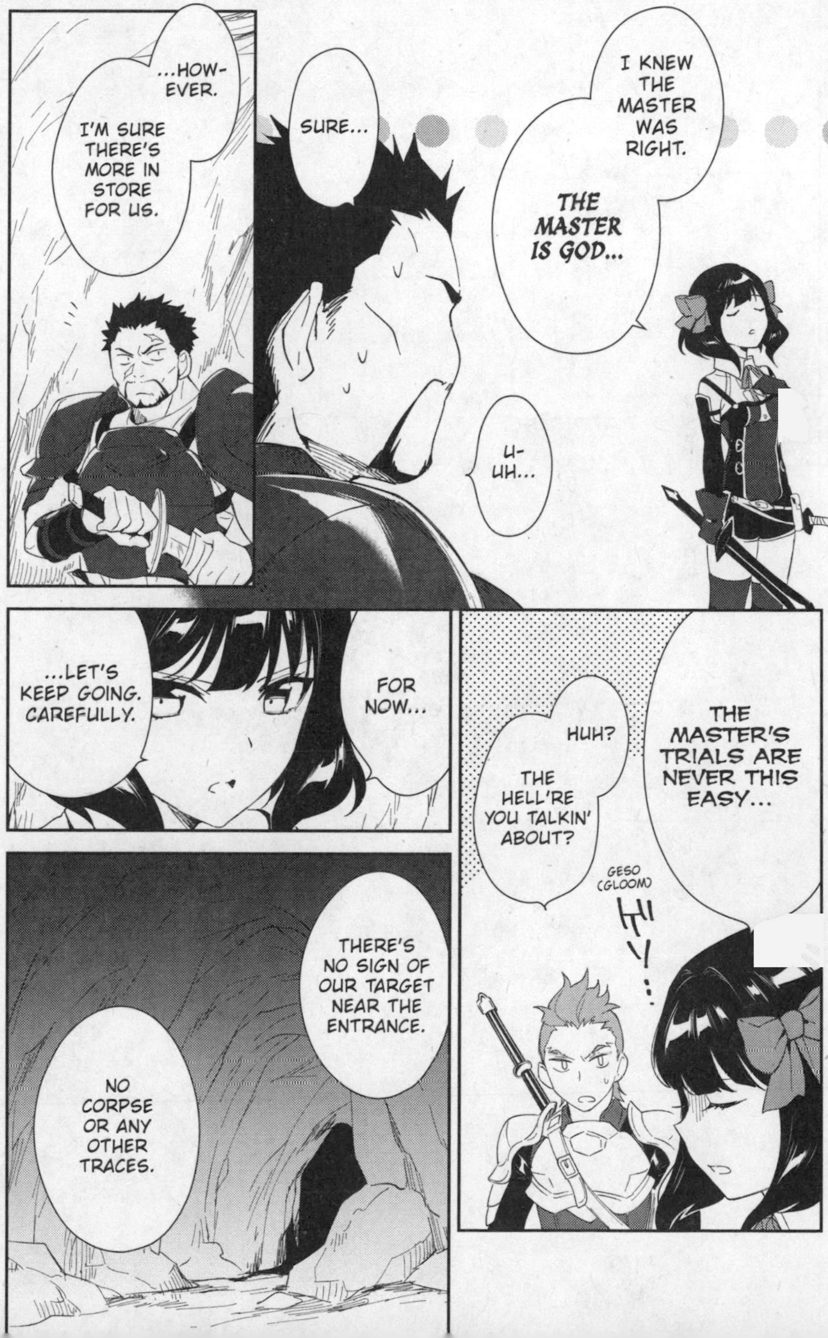
I KNEW THE MASTER WAS RIGHT.
THE MASTER IS GOD...
U-UH...
SURE...
...HOW-EVER.
I'M SURE THERE'S MORE IN STORE FOR US.
THE MASTER'S TRIALS ARE NEVER THIS EASY...
HUH?
THE HELL'RE YOU TALKIN' ABOUT?
GESO (GLOOM)
FOR NOW...
...LET'S KEEP GOING. CAREFULLY.
THERE'S NO SIGN OF OUR TARGET NEAR THE ENTRANCE.
NO CORPSE OR ANY OTHER TRACES.

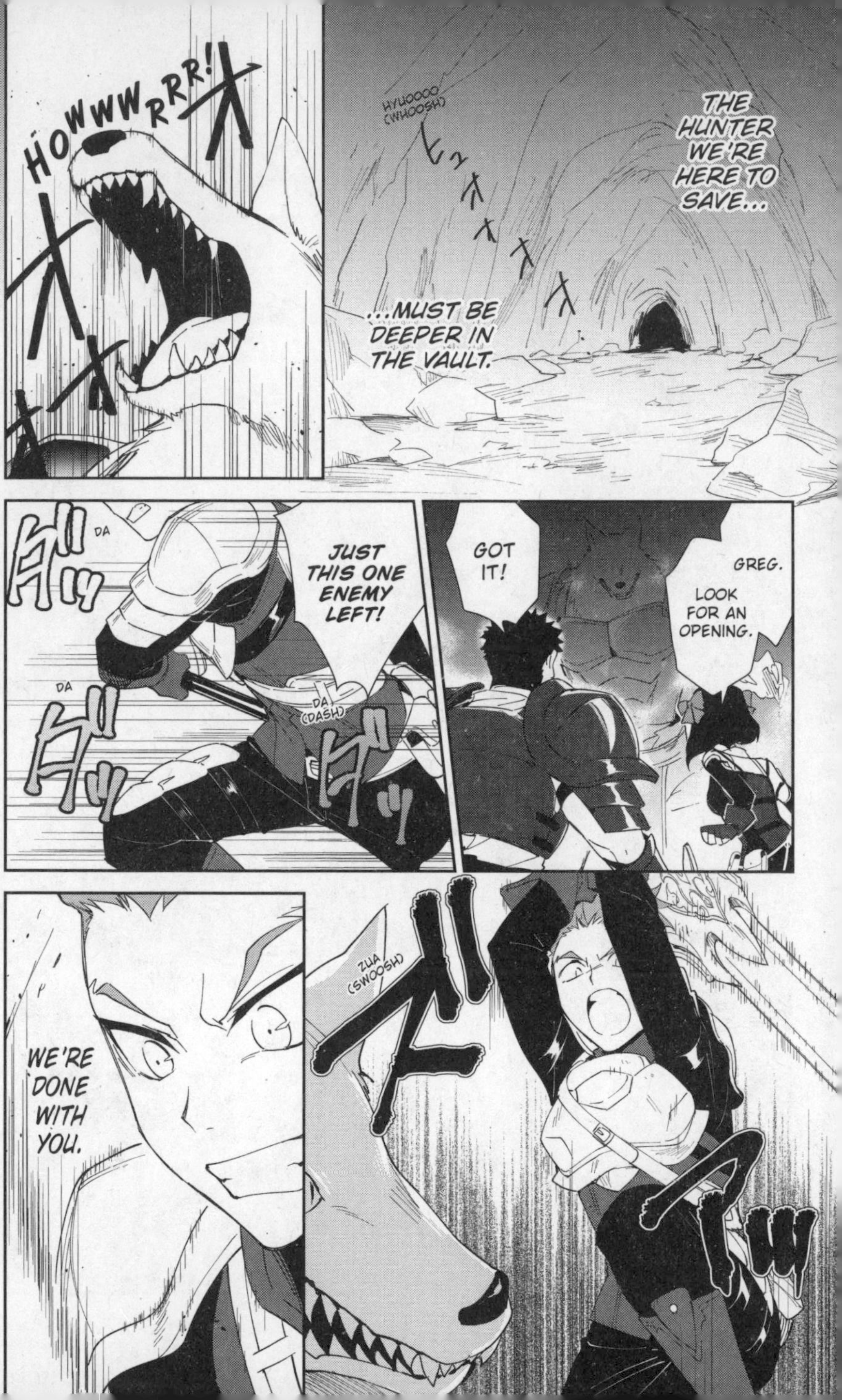
HYUOOOO (WHOOSH)
THE HUNTER WE'RE HERE TO SAVE...
...MUST BE DEEPER IN THE VAULT.
HOWWWRRR!
GREG.
LOOK FOR AN OPENING.
GOT IT!
JUST THIS ONE ENEMY LEFT!
DA (DASH)
DA
DA
ZUA (SWOOSH)
WE'RE DONE WITH YOU.

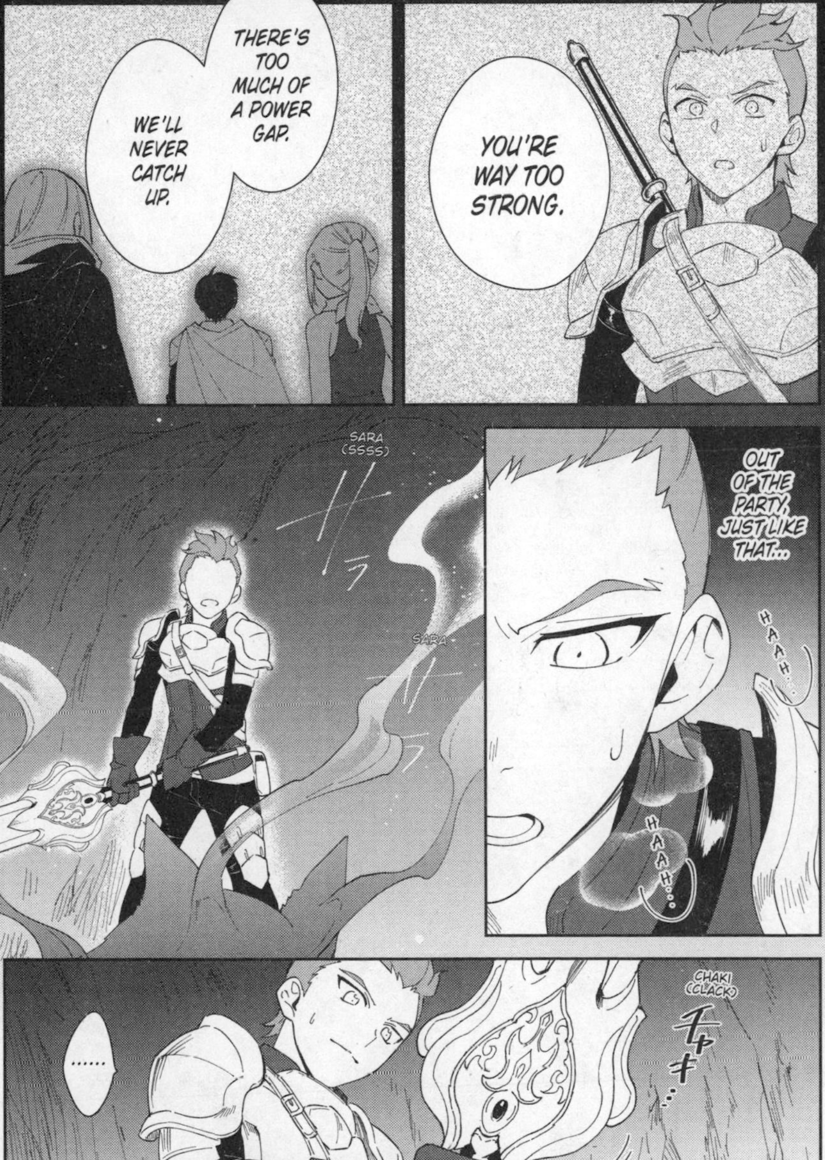
YOU'RE WAY TOO STRONG.
THERE'S TOO MUCH OF A POWER GAP.
WE'LL NEVER CATCH UP.
OUT OF THE PARTY, JUST LIKE THAT...
HAAAH...
HAAAH...
SARA (SSSS)
SARA
CHAKI (CLACK)
......

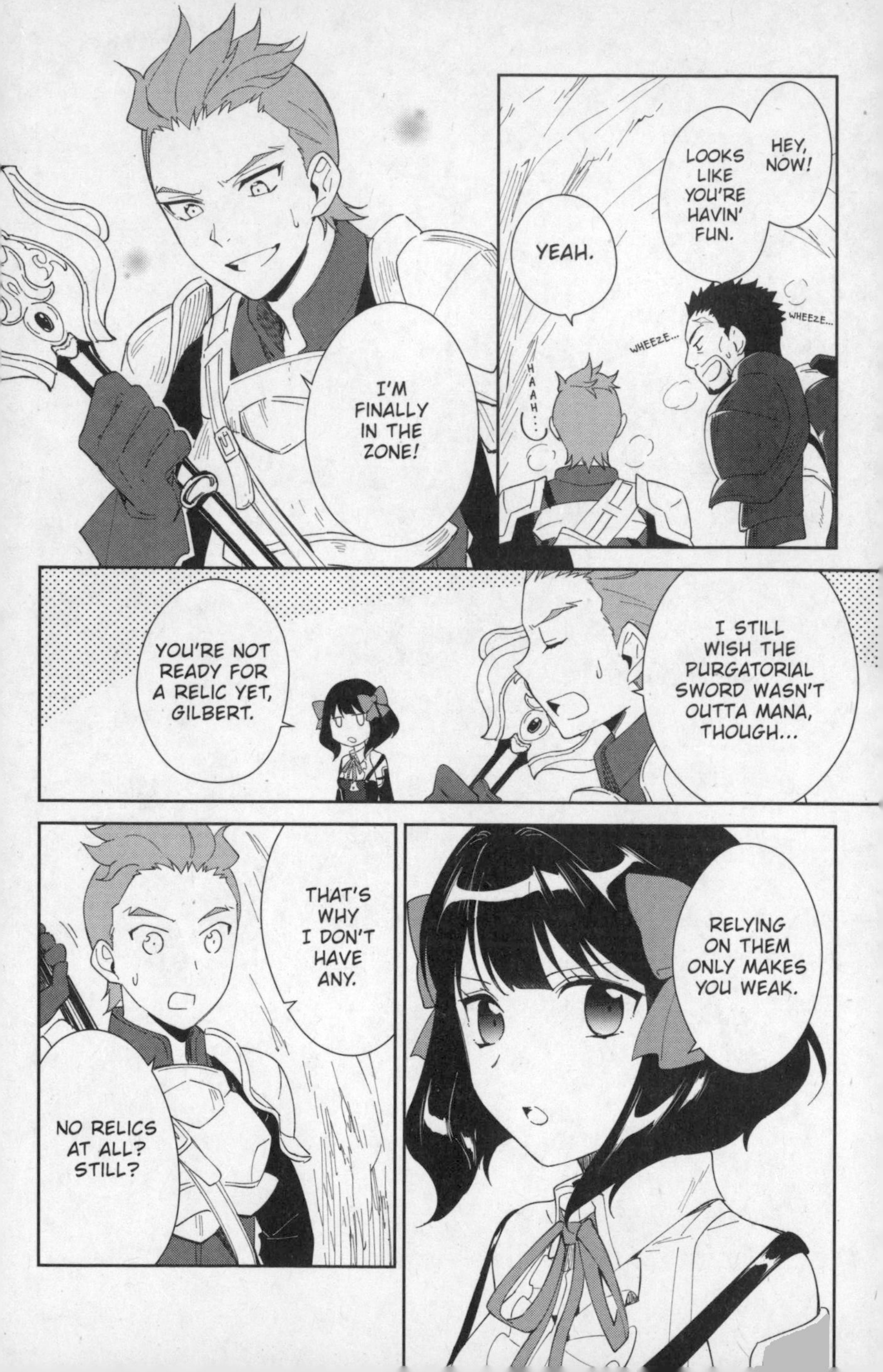
HEY, NOW!
LOOKS LIKE YOU'RE HAVIN' FUN.
YEAH.
WHEEZE...
WHEEZE...
HAAH...
I'M FINALLY IN THE ZONE!
I STILL WISH THE PURGATORIAL SWORD WASN'T OUTTA MANA, THOUGH...
YOU'RE NOT READY FOR A RELIC YET, GILBERT.
RELYING ON THEM ONLY MAKES YOU WEAK.
THAT'S WHY I DON'T HAVE ANY.
NO RELICS AT ALL? STILL?

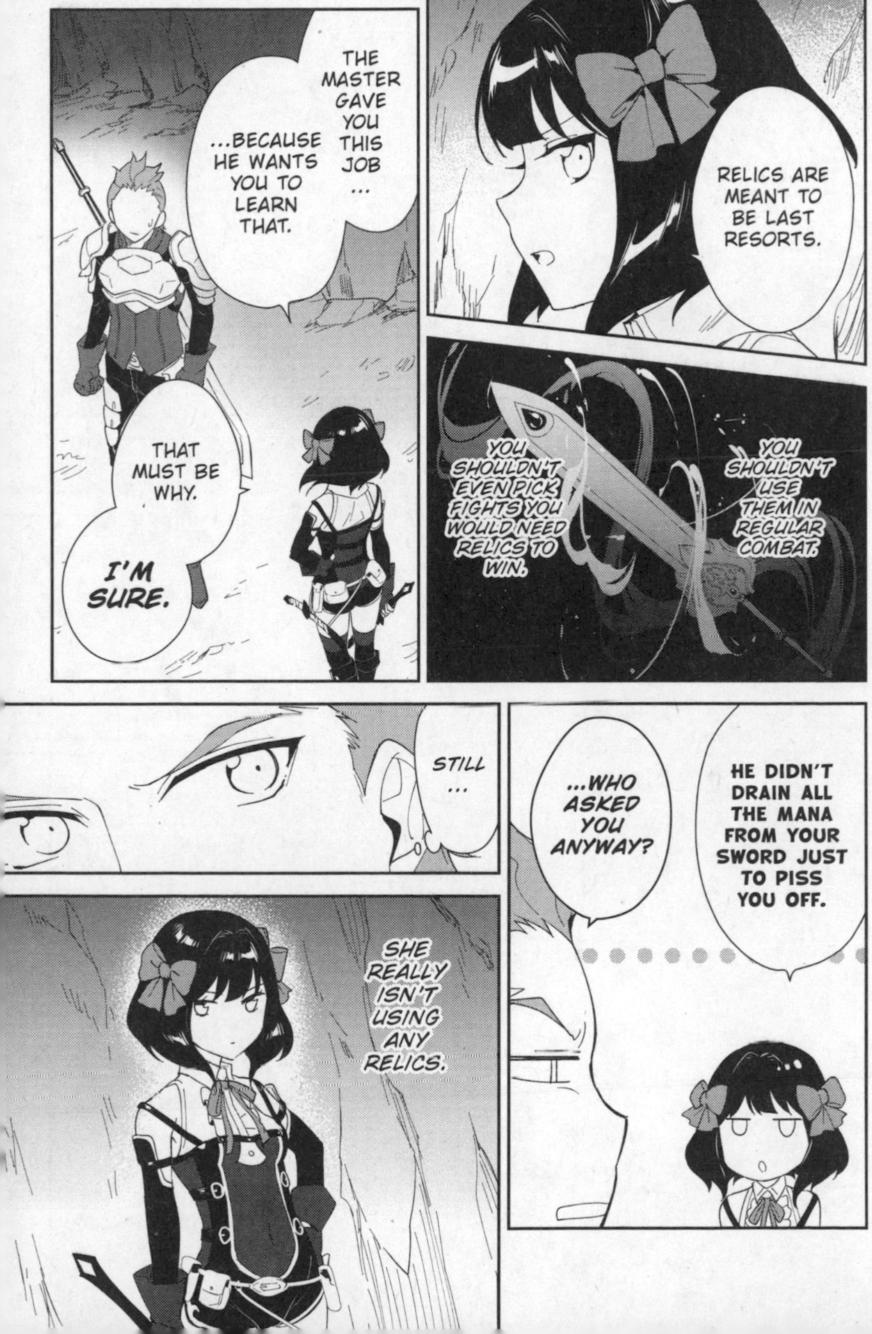
RELICS ARE MEANT TO BE LAST RESORTS.
YOU SHOULDN'T USE THEM IN REGULAR COMBAT.
YOU SHOULDN'T EVEN PICK FIGHTS YOU WOULD NEED RELICS TO WIN.
THE MASTER GAVE YOU THIS JOB ...
...BECAUSE HE WANTS YOU TO LEARN THAT.
THAT MUST BE WHY.
I'M SURE.
HE DIDN'T DRAIN ALL THE MANA FROM YOUR SWORD JUST TO PISS YOU OFF.
...WHO ASKED YOU ANYWAY?
STILL ...
SHE REALLY ISN'T USING ANY RELICS.

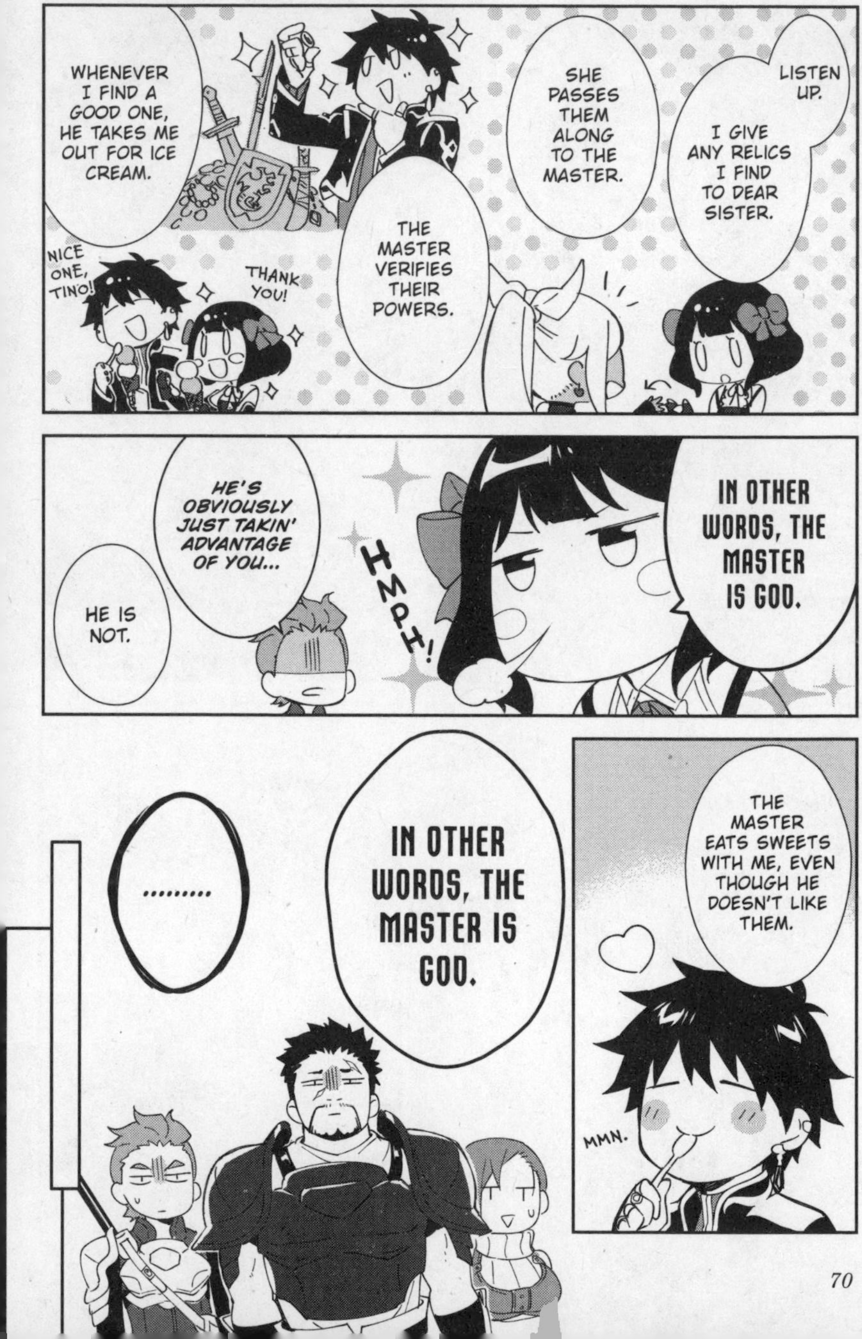
LISTEN UP.
I GIVE ANY RELICS I FIND TO DEAR SISTER.
SHE PASSES THEM ALONG TO THE MASTER.
THE MASTER VERIFIES THEIR POWERS.
WHENEVER I FIND A GOOD ONE, HE TAKES ME OUT FOR ICE CREAM.
NICE ONE, TINO!
THANK YOU!
IN OTHER WORDS, THE MASTER IS GOD.
HMPH!
HE'S OBVIOUSLY JUST TAKIN' ADVANTAGE OF YOU...
HE IS NOT.
THE MASTER EATS SWEETS WITH ME, EVEN THOUGH HE DOESN'T LIKE THEM.
MMN.
IN OTHER WORDS, THE MASTER IS GOD.
....

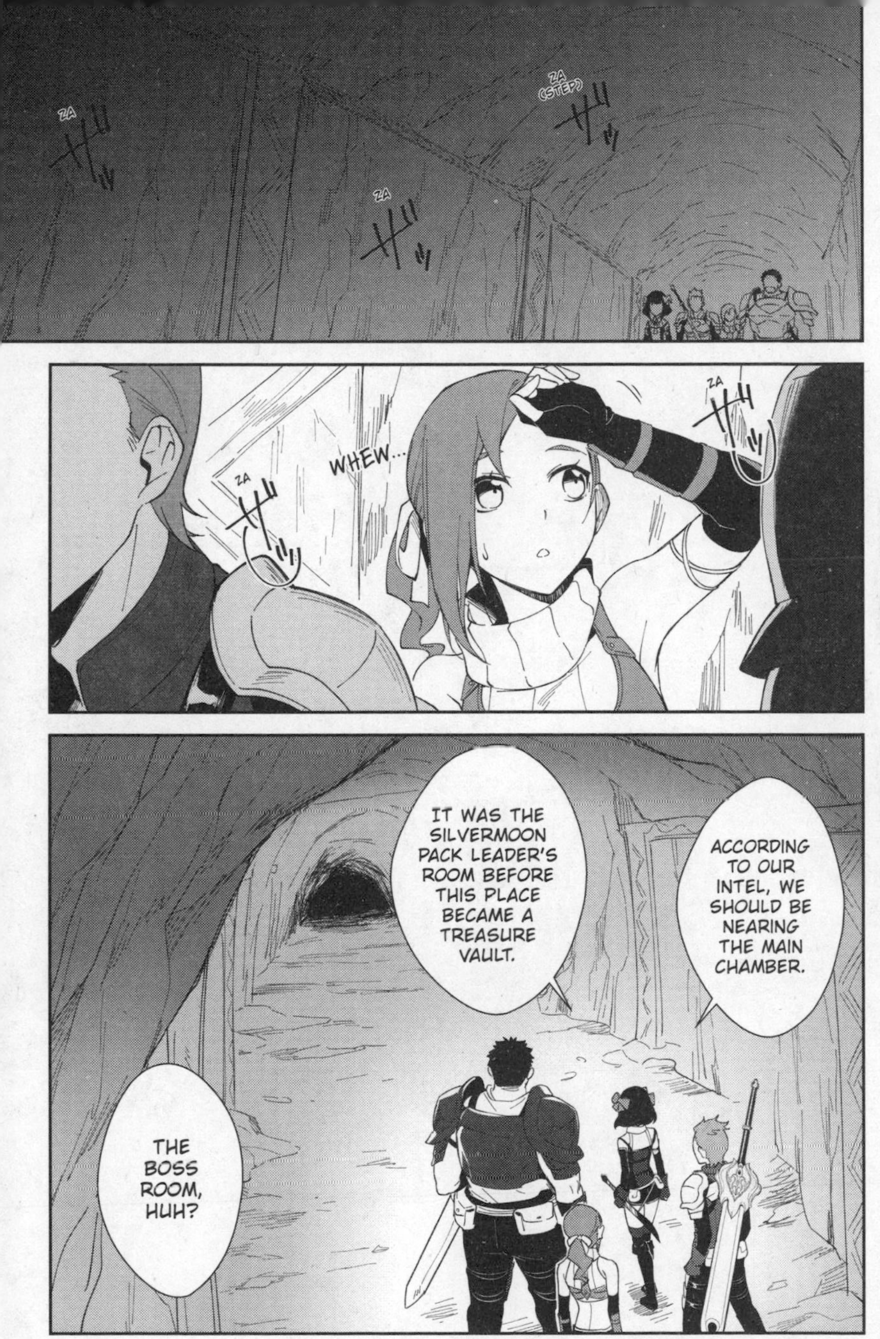
ZA (STEP)
ZA
ZA
ZA
WHEW...
ZA
ACCORDING TO OUR INTEL, WE SHOULD BE NEARING THE MAIN CHAMBER.
IT WAS THE SILVERMOON PACK LEADER'S ROOM BEFORE THIS PLACE BECAME A TREASURE VAULT.
THE BOSS ROOM, HUH?

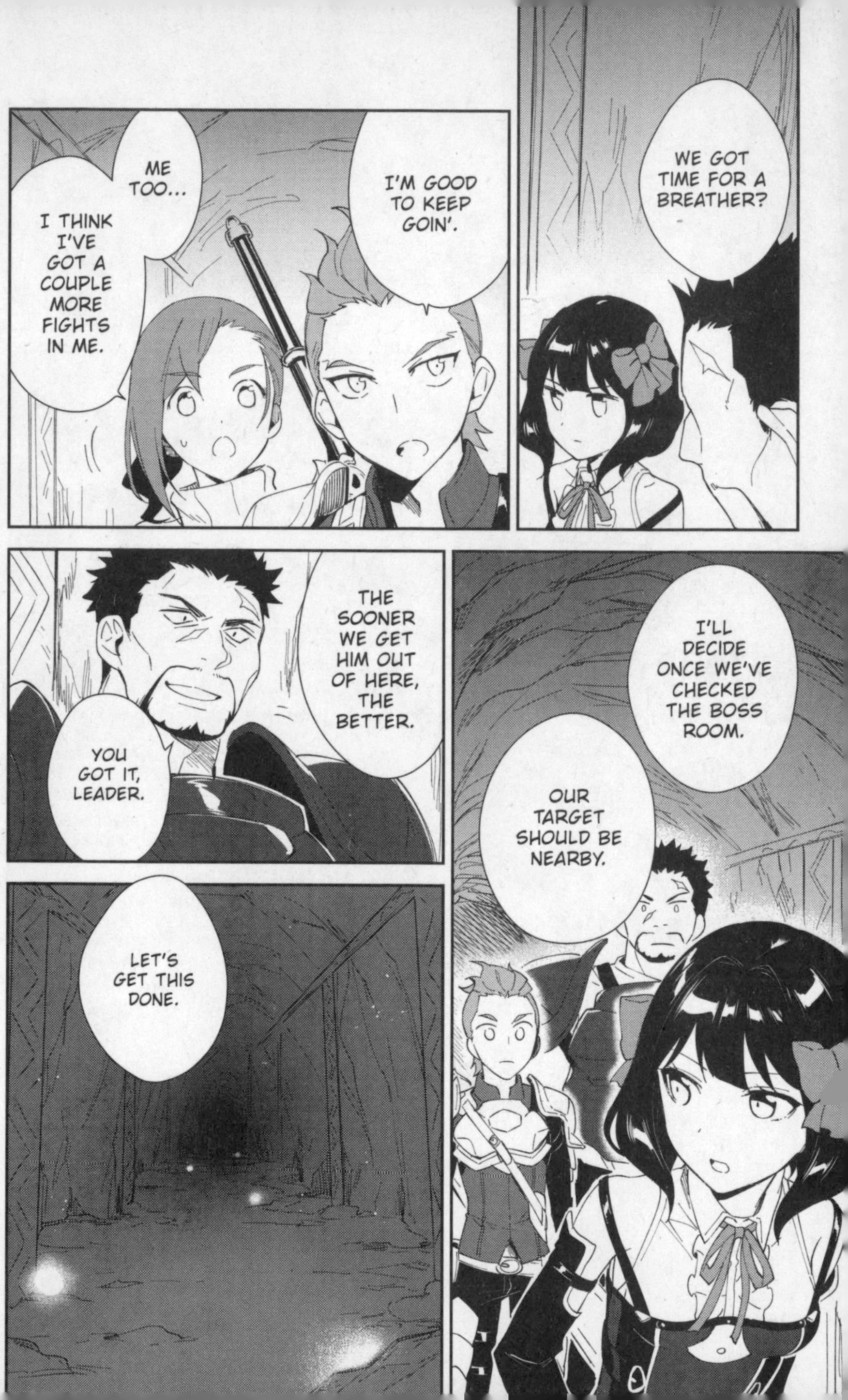
WE GOT TIME FOR A BREATHER?
I'M GOOD TO KEEP GOIN'.
ME TOO...
I THINK I'VE GOT A COUPLE MORE FIGHTS IN ME.
I'LL DECIDE ONCE WE'VE CHECKED THE BOSS ROOM.
OUR TARGET SHOULD BE NEARBY.
THE SOONER WE GET HIM OUT OF HERE, THE BETTER.
YOU GOT IT, LEADER.
LET'S GET THIS DONE.

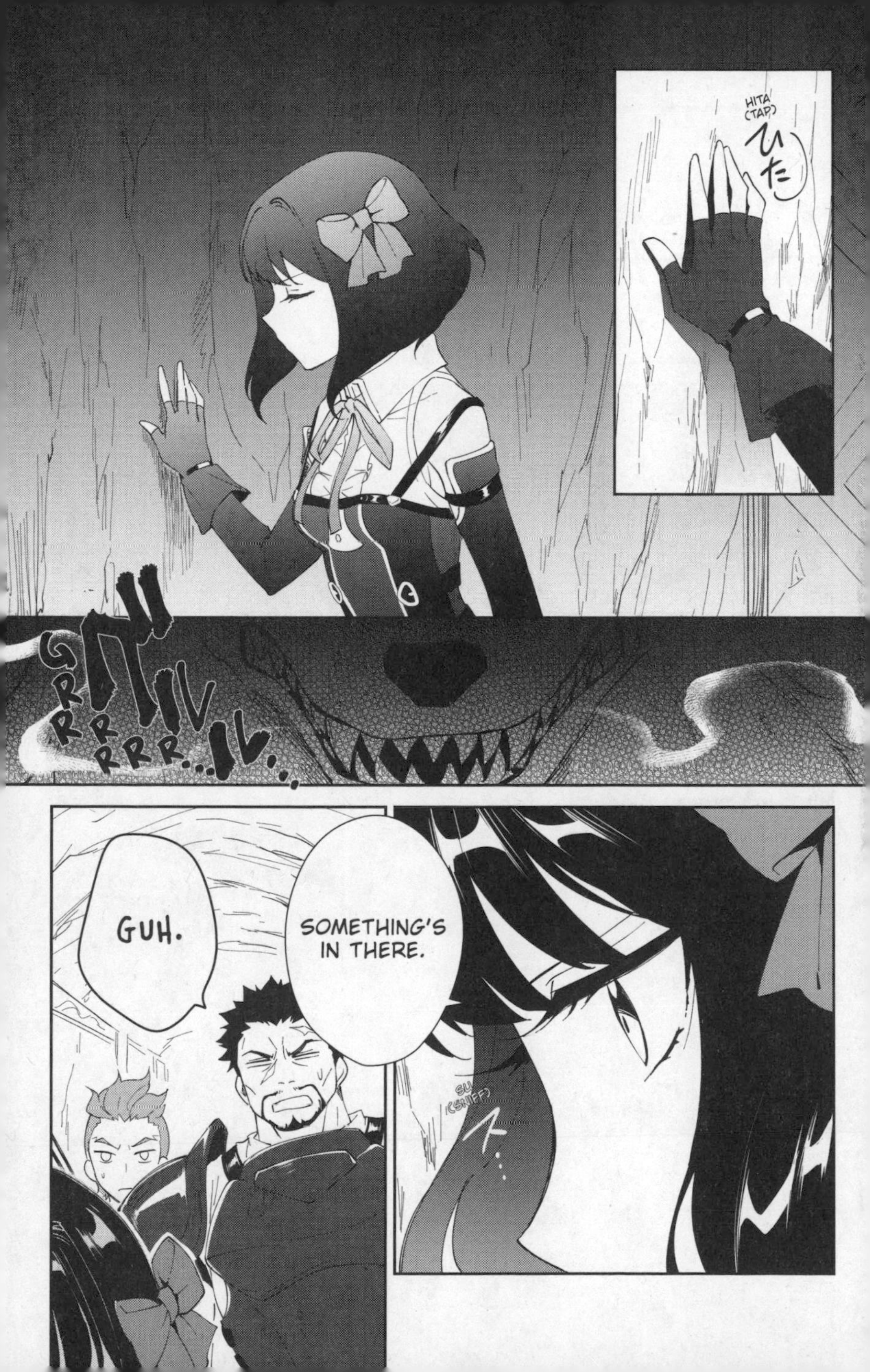
HITA (TAP)
ひた
GRRRRRRR...
SU (SNIFF)
SOMETHING'S IN THERE.
GUH.

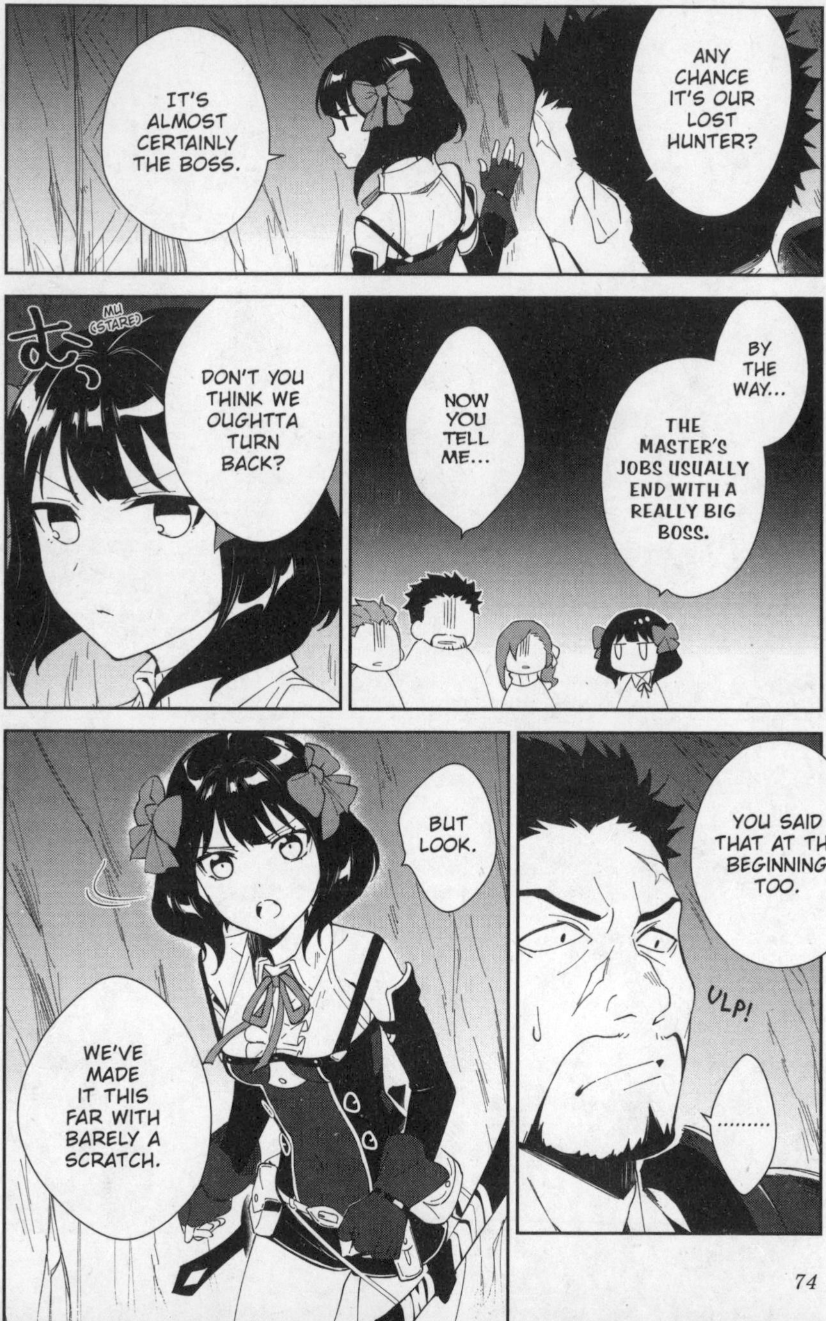
ANY CHANCE IT'S OUR LOST HUNTER?
IT'S ALMOST CERTAINLY THE BOSS.
BY THE WAY...
THE MASTER'S JOBS USUALLY END WITH A REALLY BIG BOSS.
NOW YOU TELL ME...
むっ
MU (STARE)
DON'T YOU THINK WE OUGHTTA TURN BACK?
YOU SAID THAT AT THE BEGINNING TOO.
ULP!
....
BUT LOOK.
WE'VE MADE IT THIS FAR WITH BARELY A SCRATCH.

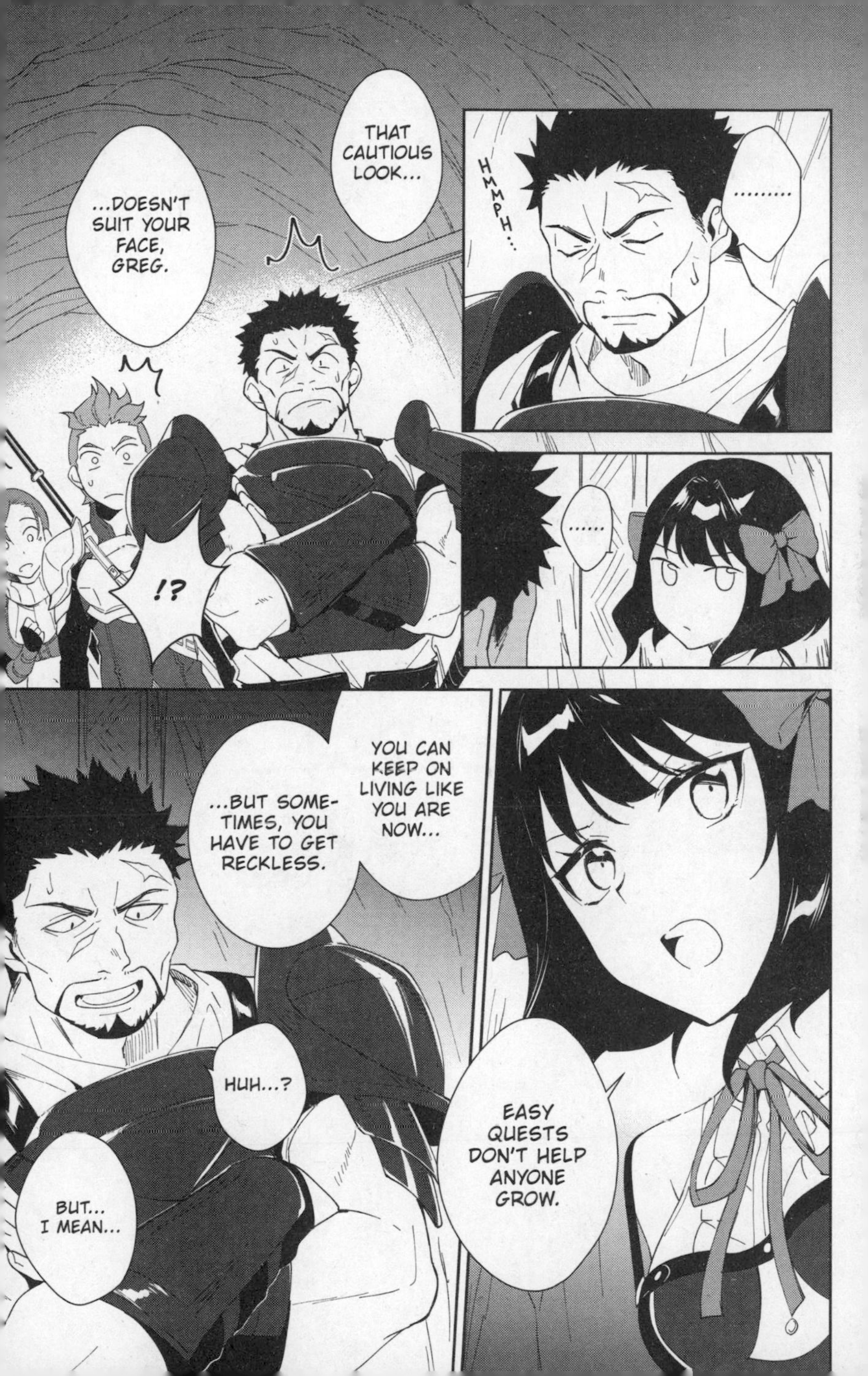
HMMPH...
....
......
THAT CAUTIOUS LOOK...
...DOESN'T SUIT YOUR FACE, GREG.
!?
EASY QUESTS DON'T HELP ANYONE GROW.
YOU CAN KEEP ON LIVING LIKE YOU ARE NOW...
...BUT SOME-TIMES, YOU HAVE TO GET RECKLESS.
HUH...?
BUT... I MEAN...

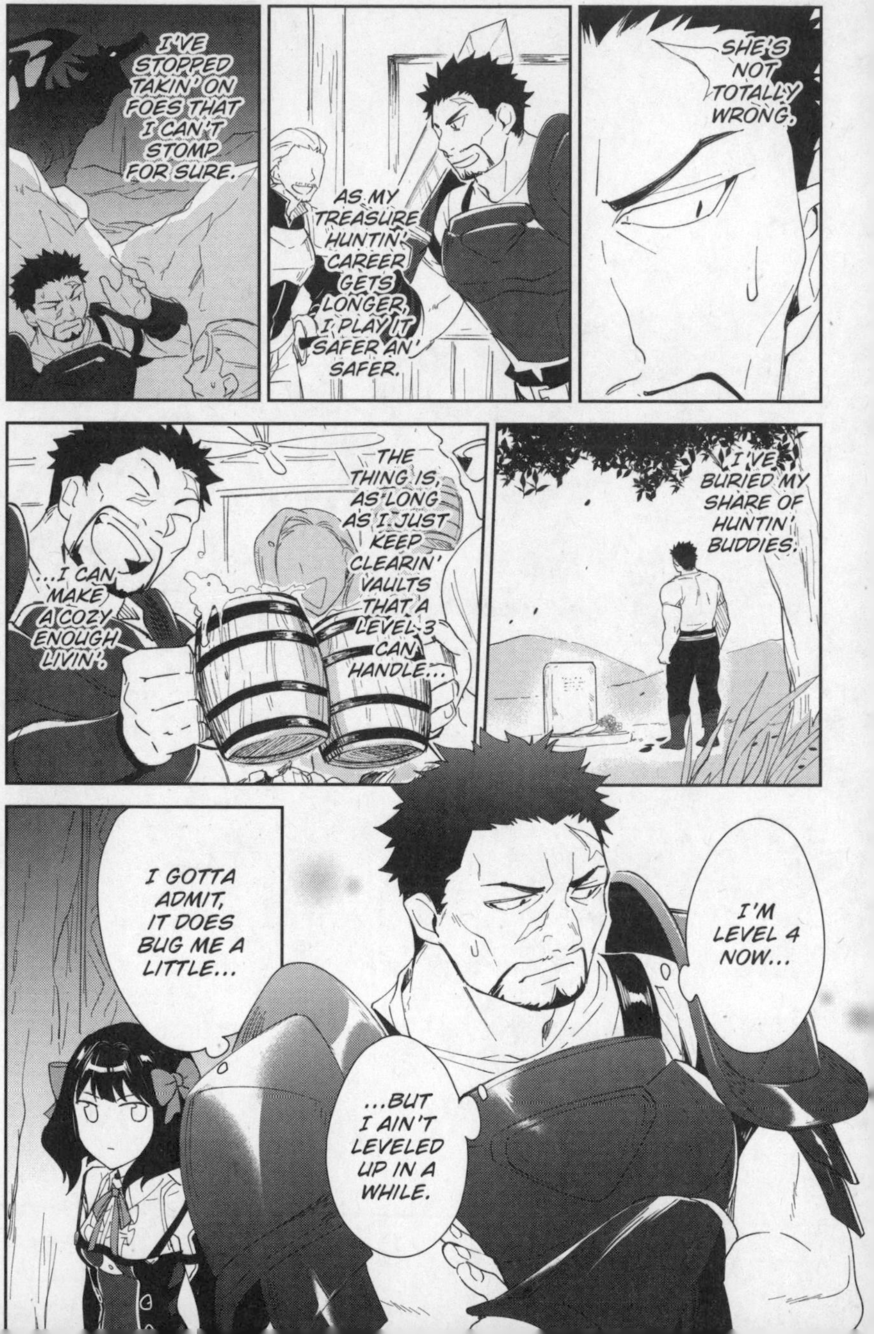
SHE'S NOT TOTALLY WRONG.
AS MY TREASURE HUNTIN' CAREER GETS LONGER, I PLAY IT SAFER AN' SAFER.
I'VE STOPPED TAKIN' ON FOES THAT I CAN'T STOMP FOR SURE.
I'VE BURIED MY SHARE OF HUNTIN' BUDDIES.
THE THING IS, AS LONG AS I JUST KEEP CLEARIN' VAULTS THAT A LEVEL 3 CAN HANDLE...
...I CAN MAKE A COZY ENOUGH LIVIN'.
I'M LEVEL 4 NOW...
I GOTTA ADMIT, IT DOES BUG ME A LITTLE...
...BUT I AIN'T LEVELED UP IN A WHILE.

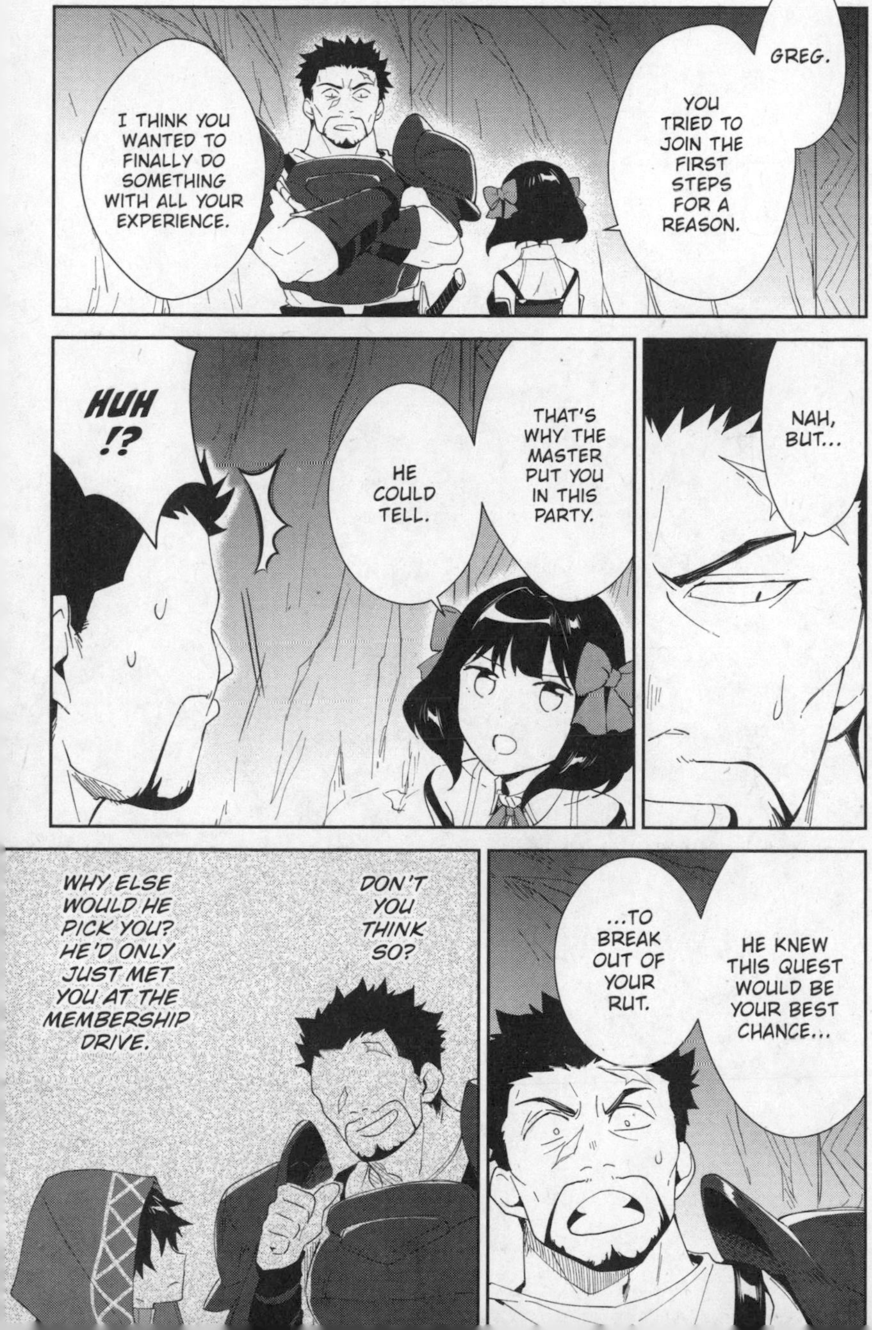
GREG.
YOU TRIED TO JOIN THE FIRST STEPS FOR A REASON.
I THINK YOU WANTED TO FINALLY DO SOMETHING WITH ALL YOUR EXPERIENCE.
NAH, BUT...
THAT'S WHY THE MASTER PUT YOU IN THIS PARTY.
HE COULD TELL.
HUH !?
HE KNEW THIS QUEST WOULD BE YOUR BEST CHANCE...
...TO BREAK OUT OF YOUR RUT.
DON'T YOU THINK SO?
WHY ELSE WOULD HE PICK YOU? HE'D ONLY JUST MET YOU AT THE MEMBERSHIP DRIVE.

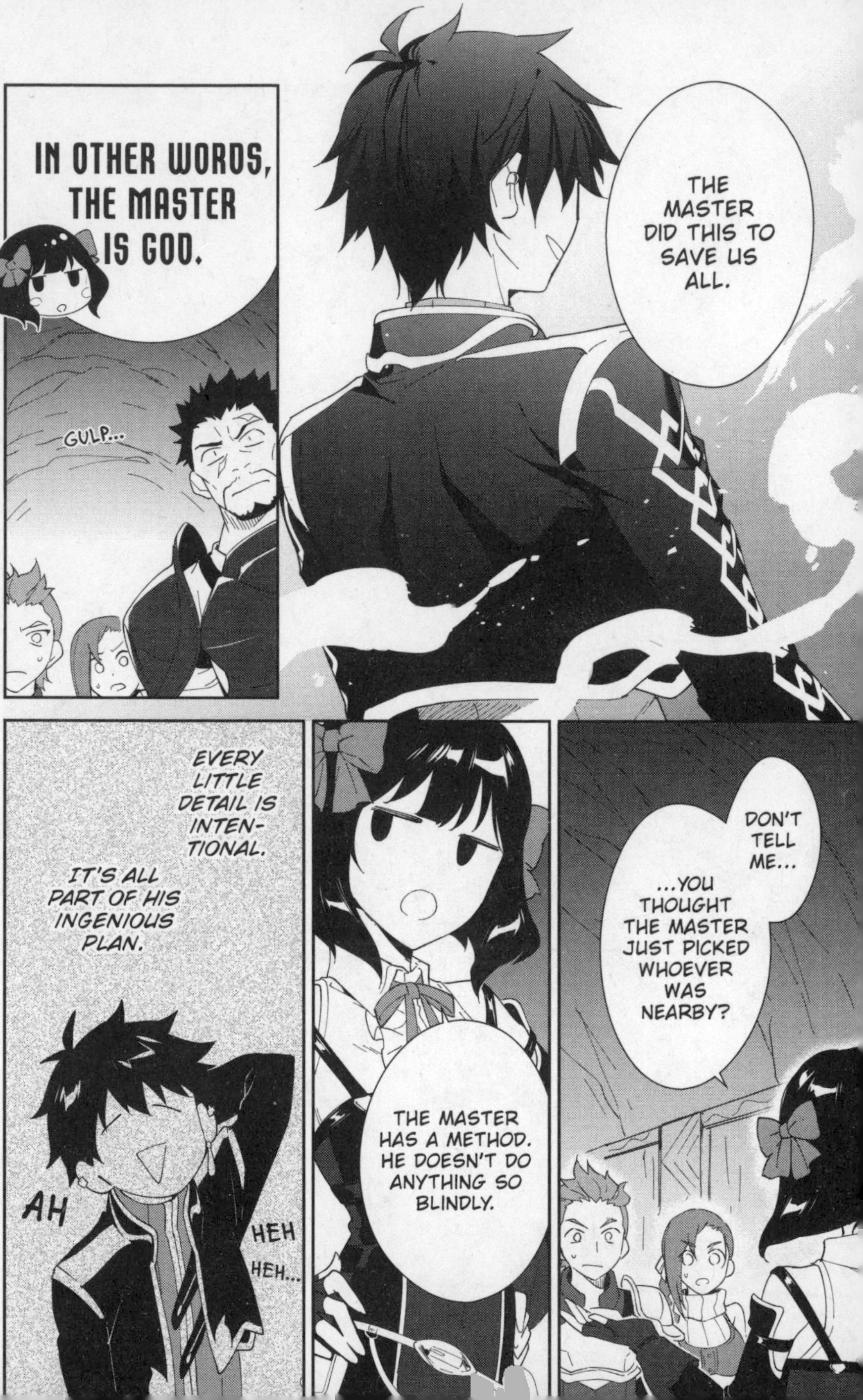
THE MASTER DID THIS TO SAVE US ALL.
IN OTHER WORDS, THE MASTER IS GOD.
GULP...
DON'T TELL ME...
...YOU THOUGHT THE MASTER JUST PICKED WHOEVER WAS NEARBY?
THE MASTER HAS A METHOD. HE DOESN'T DO ANYTHING SO BLINDLY.
EVERY LITTLE DETAIL IS INTEN-TIONAL.
IT'S ALL PART OF HIS INGENIOUS PLAN.
AH
HEH HEH...

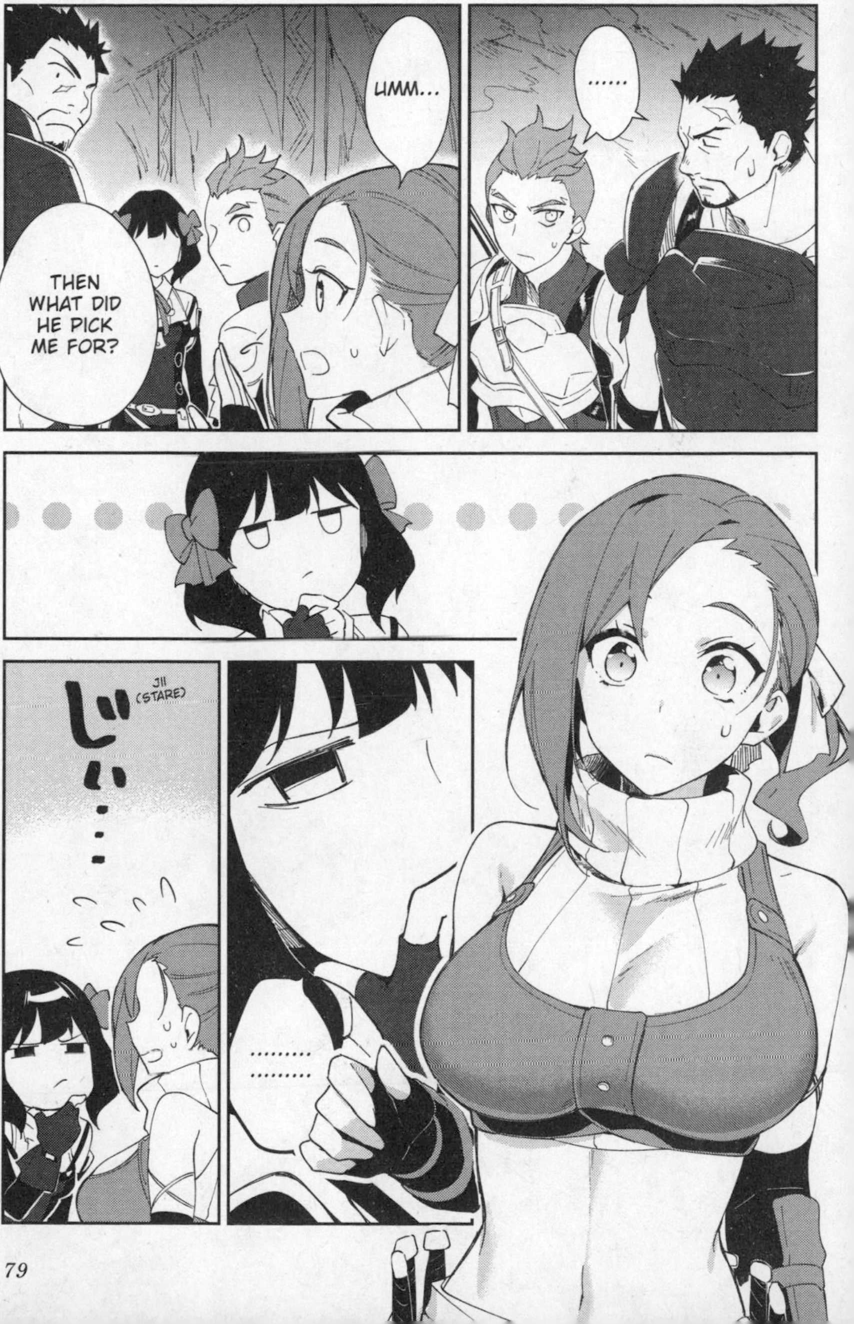
......
UMM...
THEN WHAT DID HE PICK ME FOR?
....
....
じぃ……
JII (STARE)

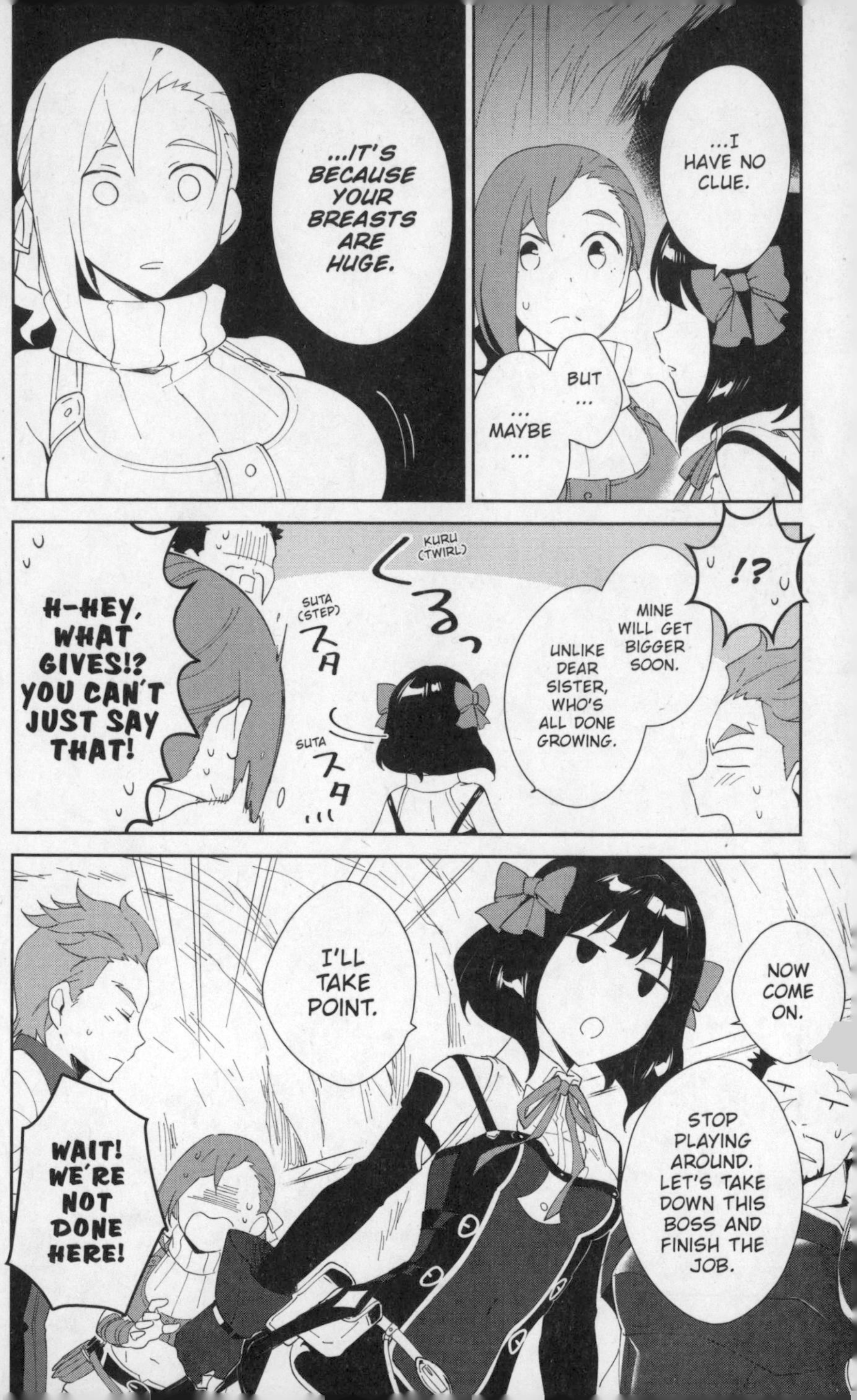
...I HAVE NO CLUE.
BUT ... ... MAYBE ...
...IT'S BECAUSE YOUR BREASTS ARE HUGE.
!?
MINE WILL GET BIGGER SOON.
UNLIKE DEAR SISTER, WHO'S ALL DONE GROWING.
KURU (TWIRL)
くるっ
SUTA (STEP)
スタ
SUTA
スタ
H-HEY, WHAT GIVES!? YOU CAN'T JUST SAY THAT!
NOW COME ON.
STOP PLAYING AROUND. LET'S TAKE DOWN THIS BOSS AND FINISH THE JOB.
I'LL TAKE POINT.
WAIT! WE'RE NOT DONE HERE!

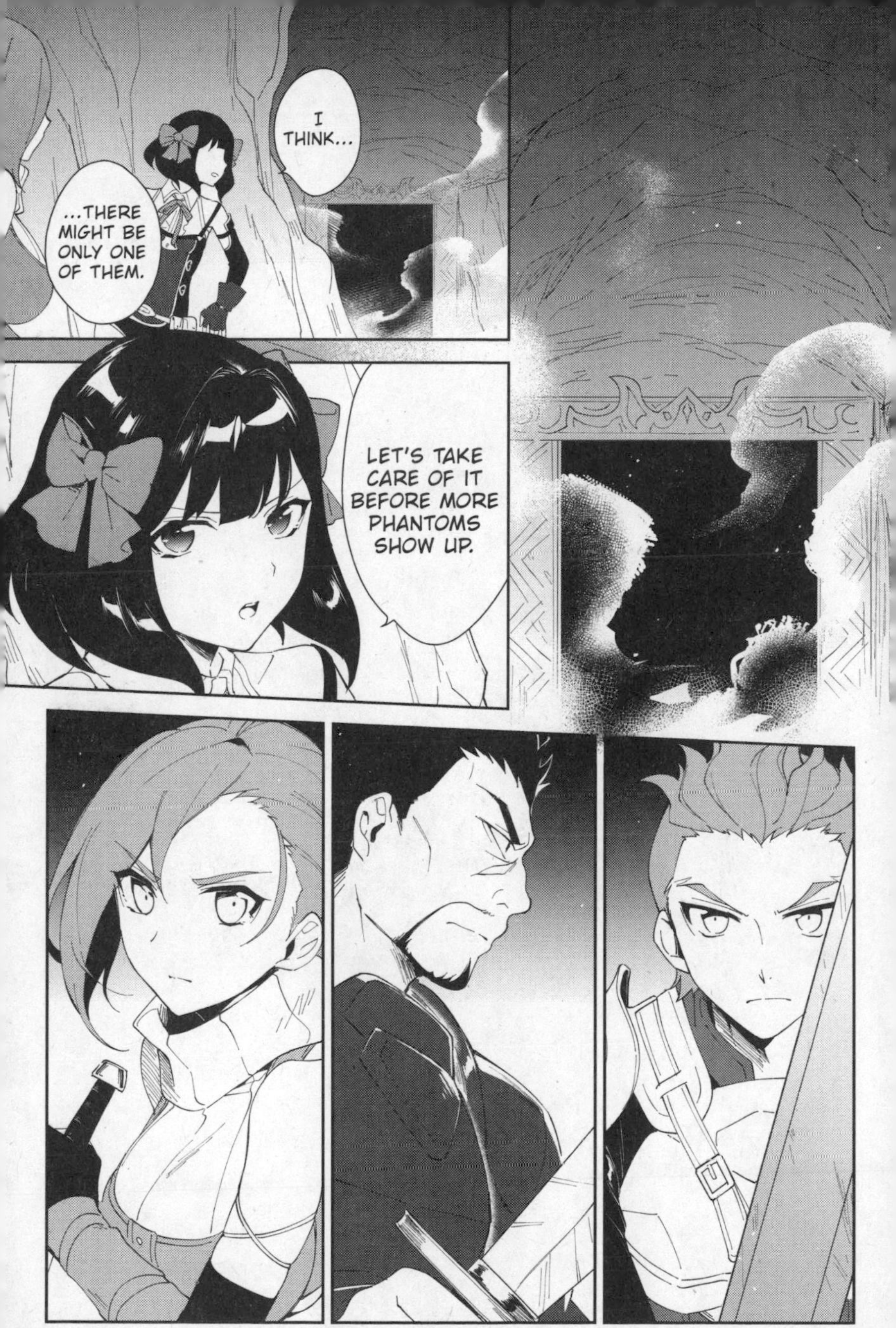
I THINK...
...THERE MIGHT BE ONLY ONE OF THEM.
LET'S TAKE CARE OF IT BEFORE MORE PHANTOMS SHOW UP.

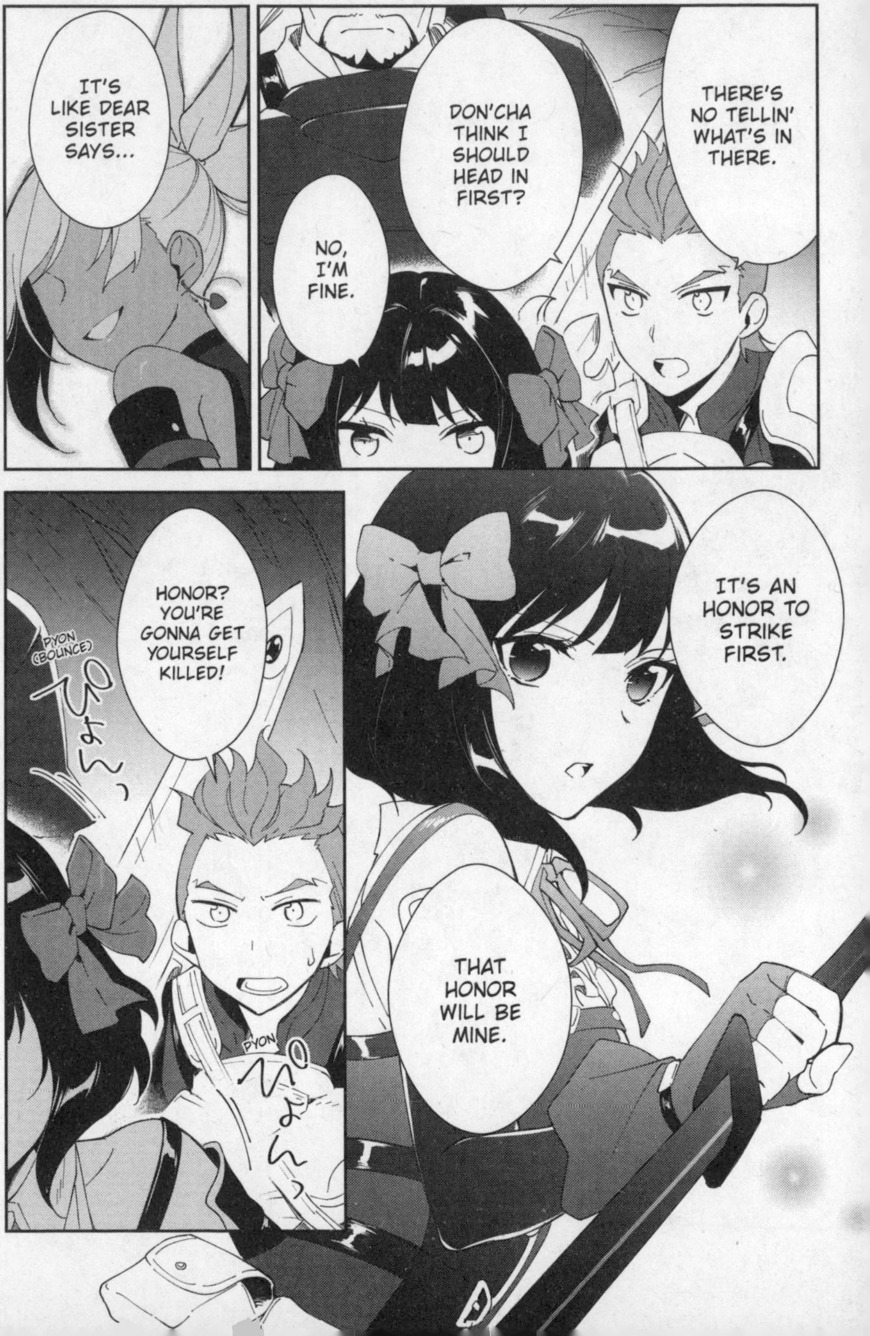
THERE'S NO TELLIN' WHAT'S IN THERE.
DON'CHA THINK I SHOULD HEAD IN FIRST?
NO, I'M FINE.
IT'S LIKE DEAR SISTER SAYS...
IT'S AN HONOR TO STRIKE FIRST.
THAT HONOR WILL BE MINE.
HONOR? YOU'RE GONNA GET YOURSELF KILLED!
PYON (BOUNCE)
ぴょんっ
PYON
ぴょんっ

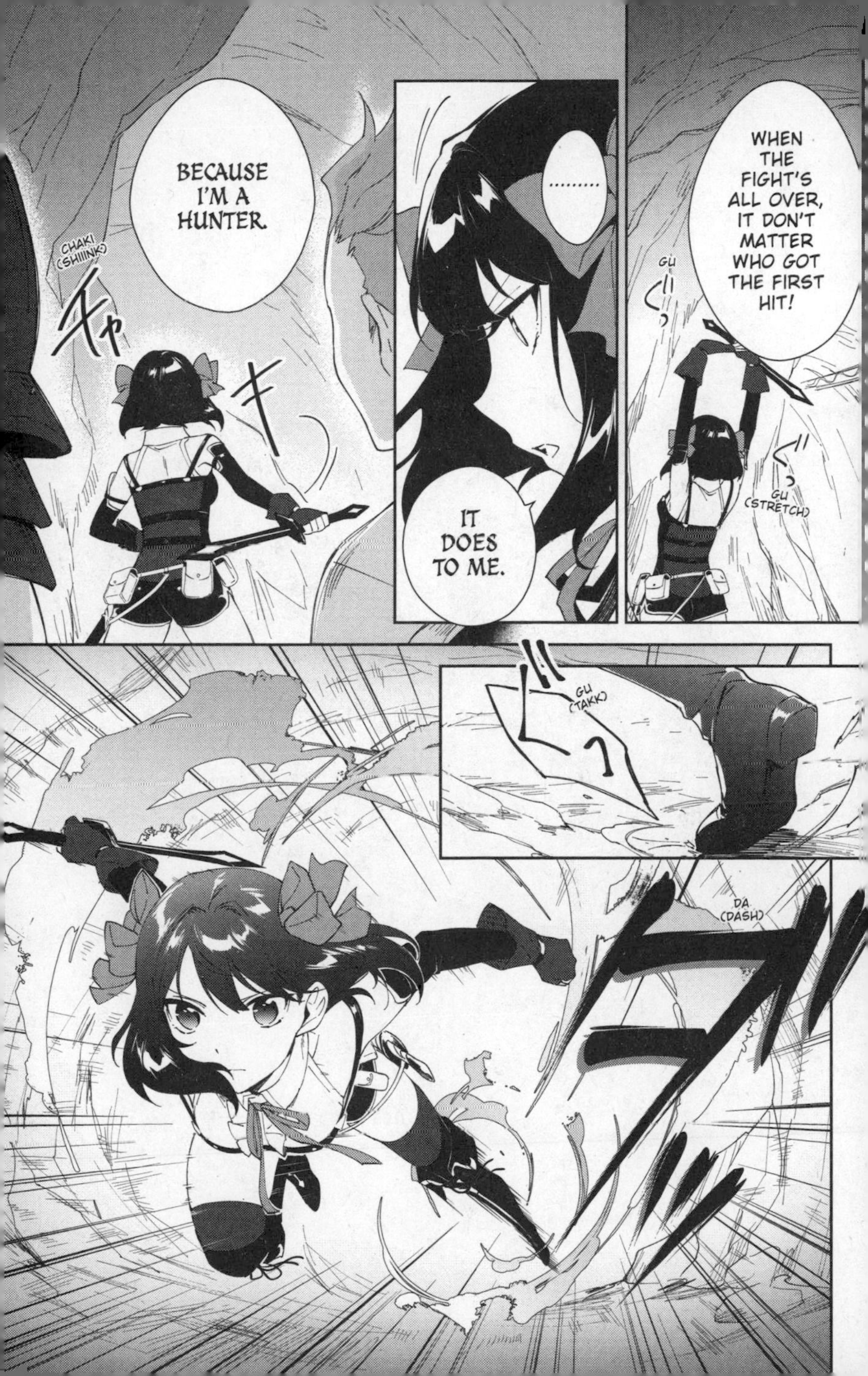
WHEN THE FIGHT'S ALL OVER, IT DON'T MATTER WHO GOT THE FIRST HIT!
GU
GU (STRETCH)
....
IT DOES TO ME.
BECAUSE I'M A HUNTER.
CHAKI (SHIIINK)
GU (TAKK)
DA (DASH)

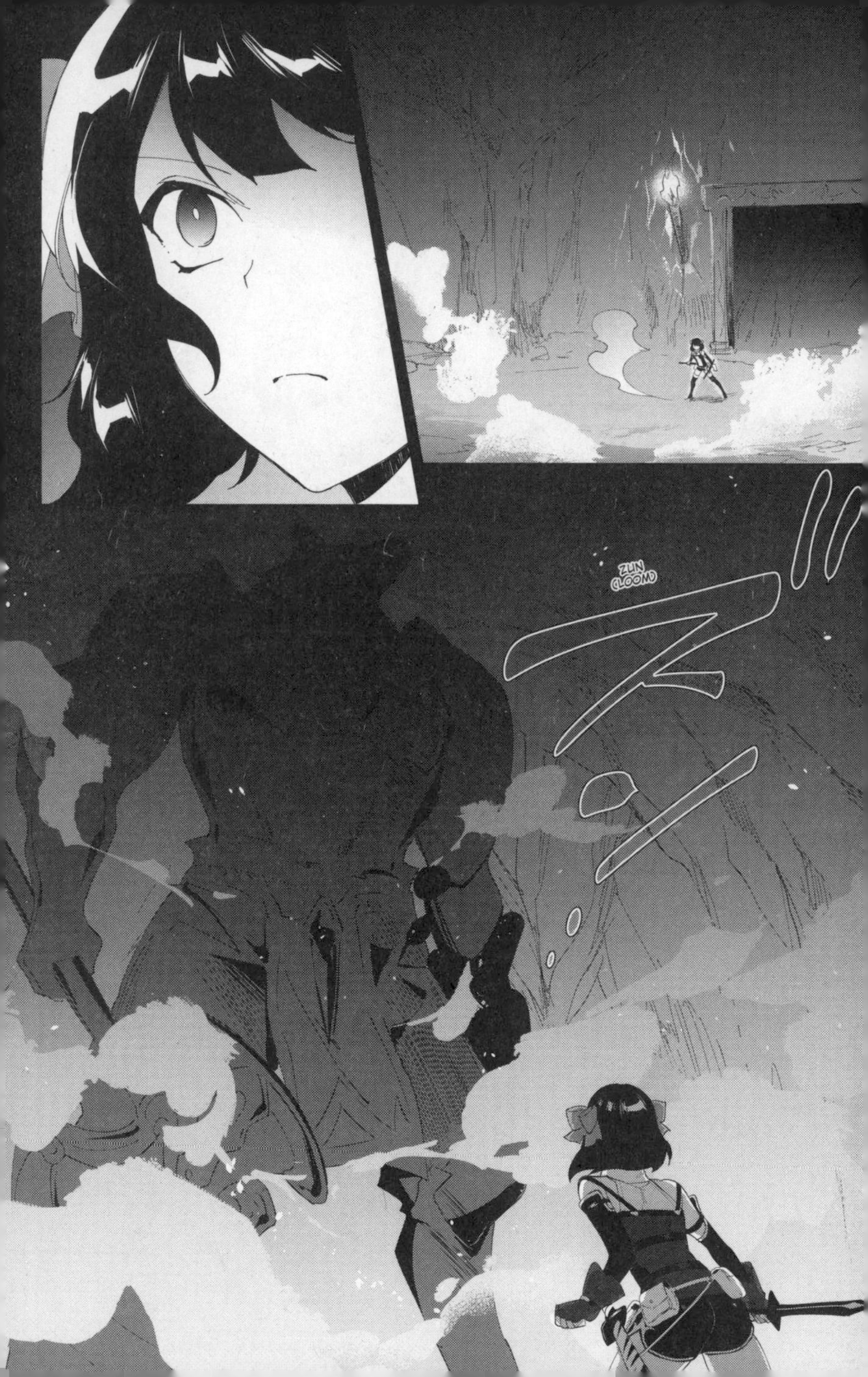
ZUN
(LOOM)

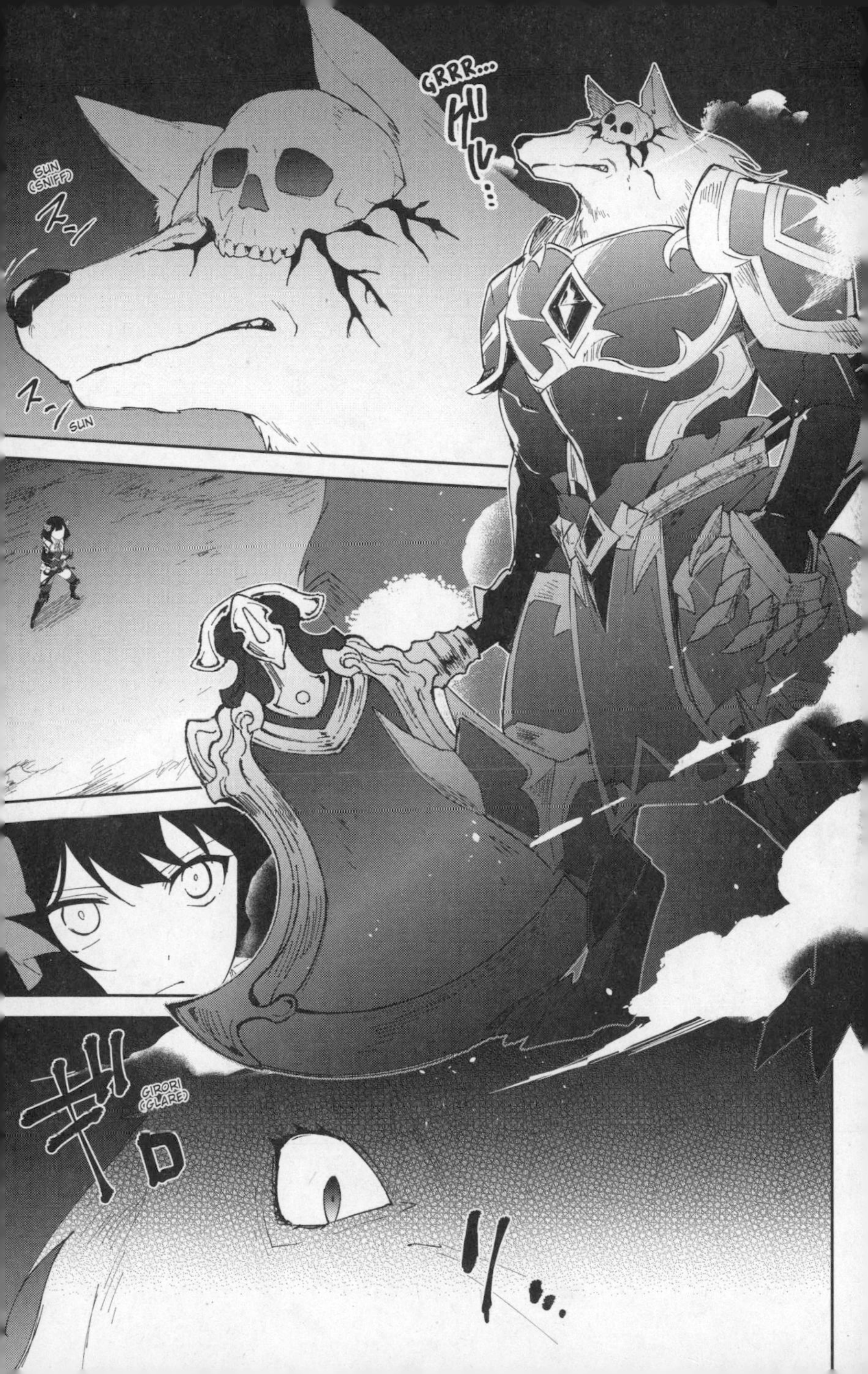
GRRR...
グルル…
SUN (SNIFF)
スン
スン
SUN
GIRORI (GLARE)
ギロッ…

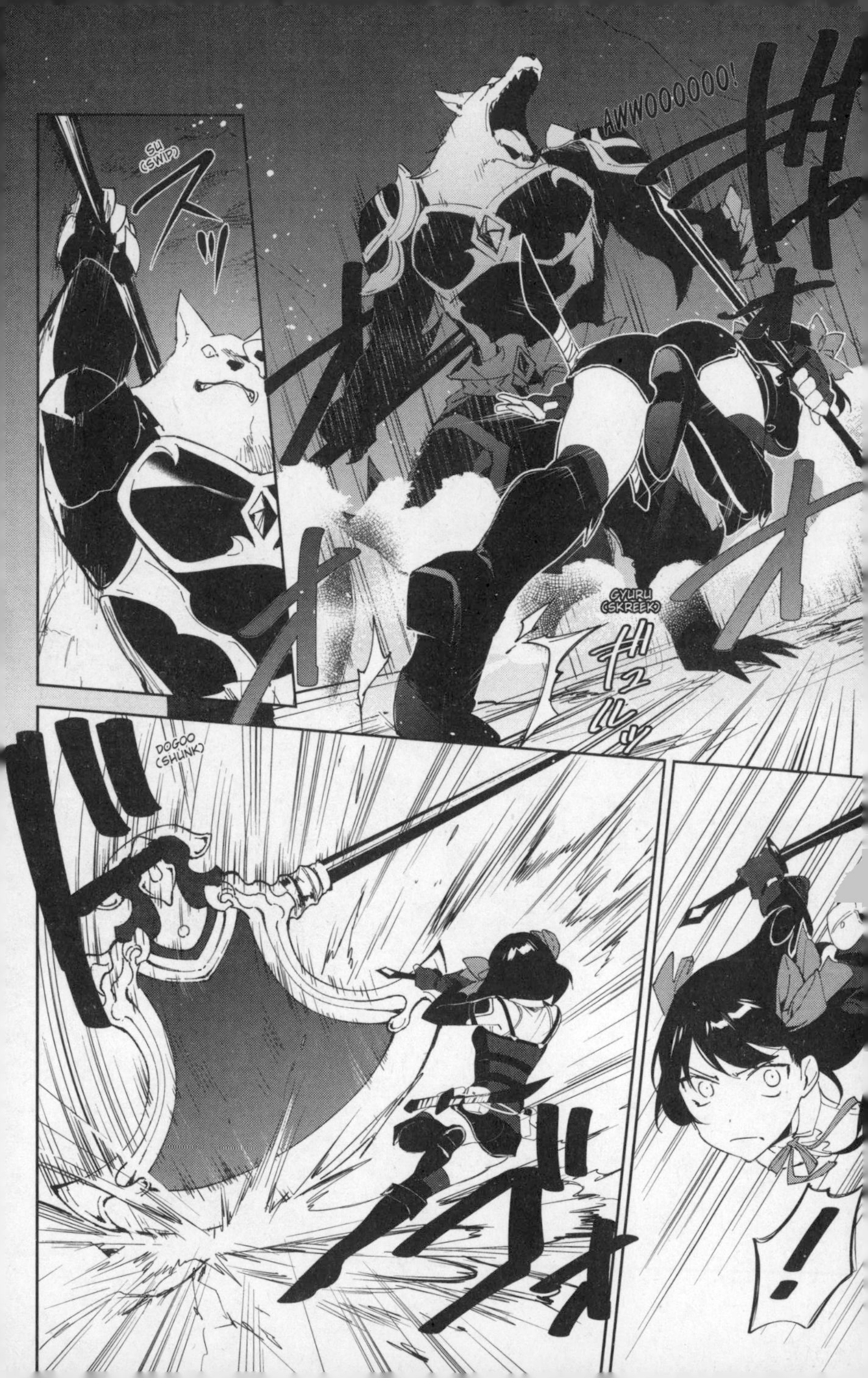
AWWOOOOOOO!
GYURU (SKREEK)
SU (SWIP)
!
DOGOO (SHUNK)

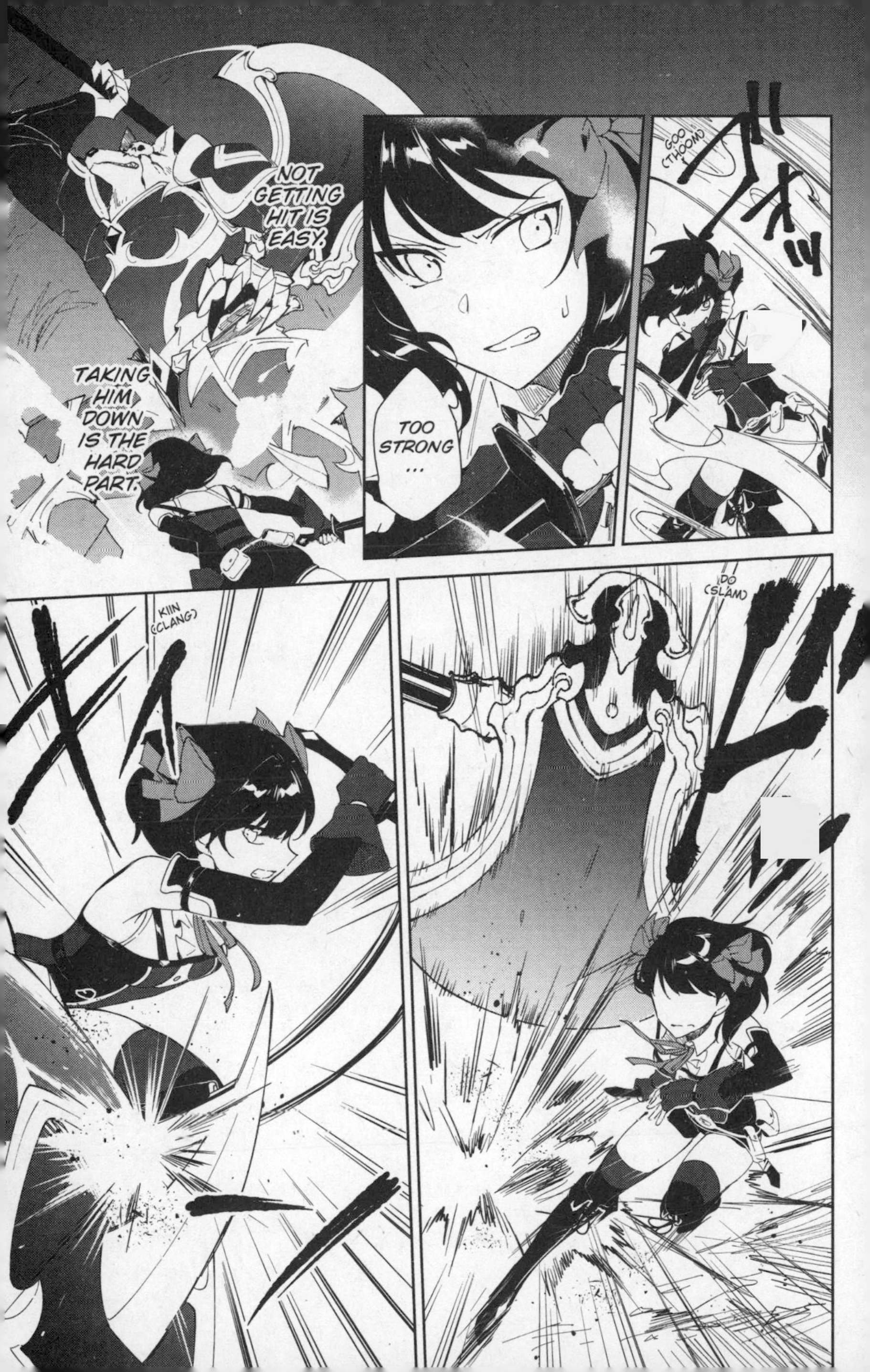
GOO (THOOM)
TOO STRONG...
NOT GETTING HIT IS EASY.
TAKING HIM DOWN IS THE HARD PART.
DO (SLAM)
KIIN (CLANG)

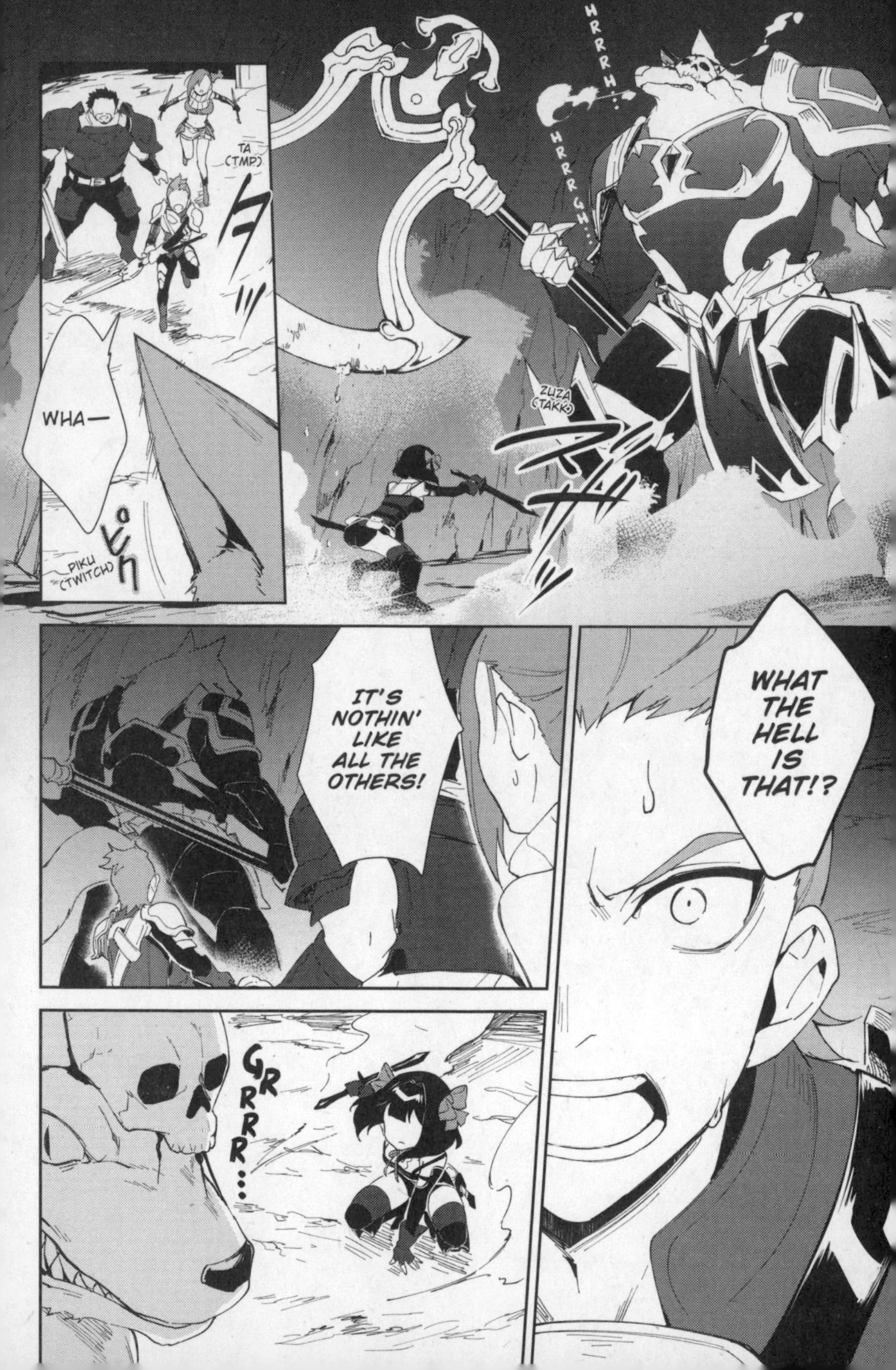
HRRRH...
HRRRGH...
ZUZA (TAKK)
TA (TMP)
WHA—
PIKU (TWITCH)
WHAT THE HELL IS THAT!?
IT'S NOTHIN' LIKE ALL THE OTHERS!
GRRRR...

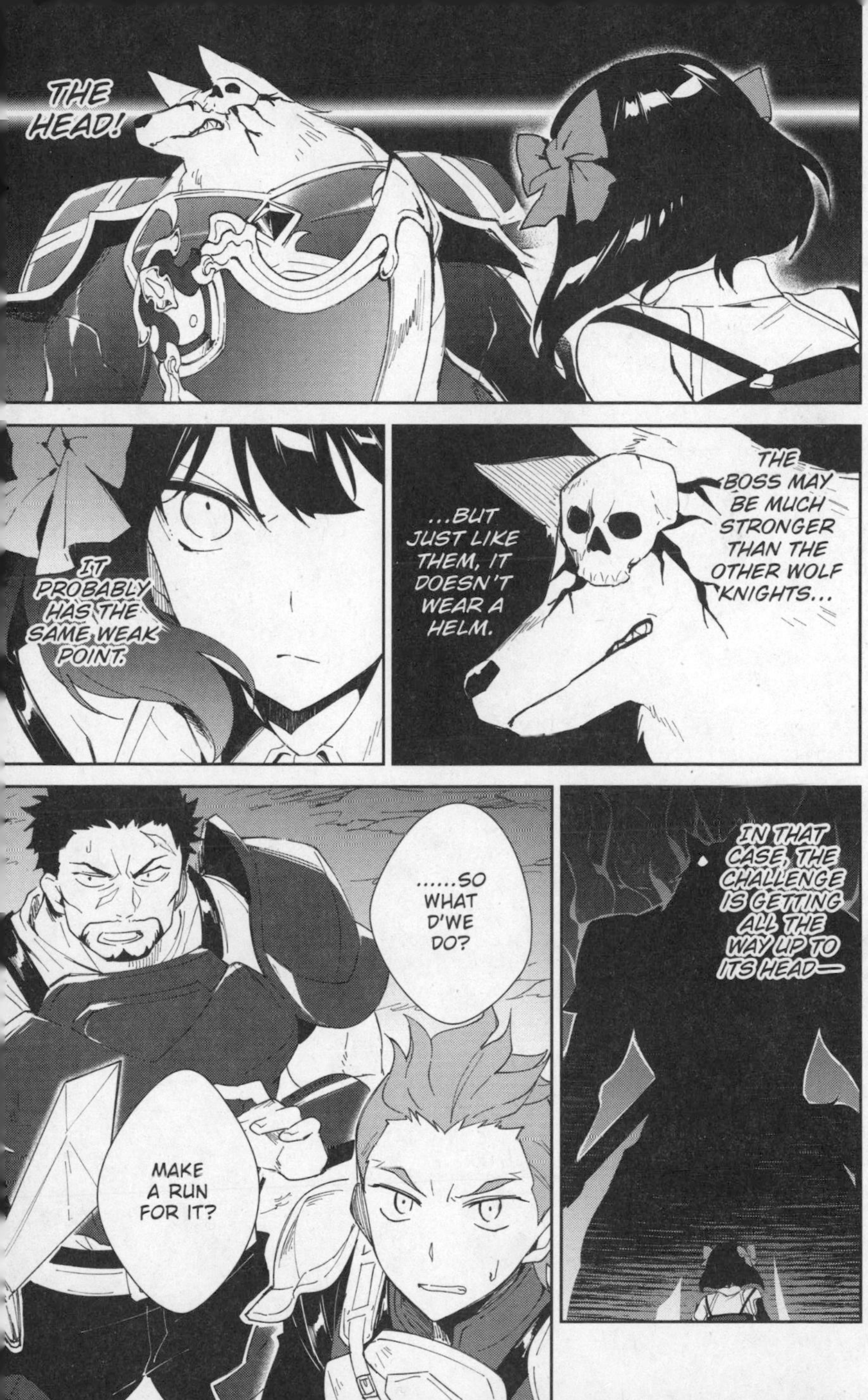
THE HEAD!
THE BOSS MAY BE MUCH STRONGER THAN THE OTHER WOLF KNIGHTS...
...BUT JUST LIKE THEM, IT DOESN'T WEAR A HELM.
IT PROBABLY HAS THE SAME WEAK POINT.
IN THAT CASE, THE CHALLENGE IS GETTING ALL THE WAY UP TO ITS HEAD—
......SO WHAT D'WE DO?
MAKE A RUN FOR IT?

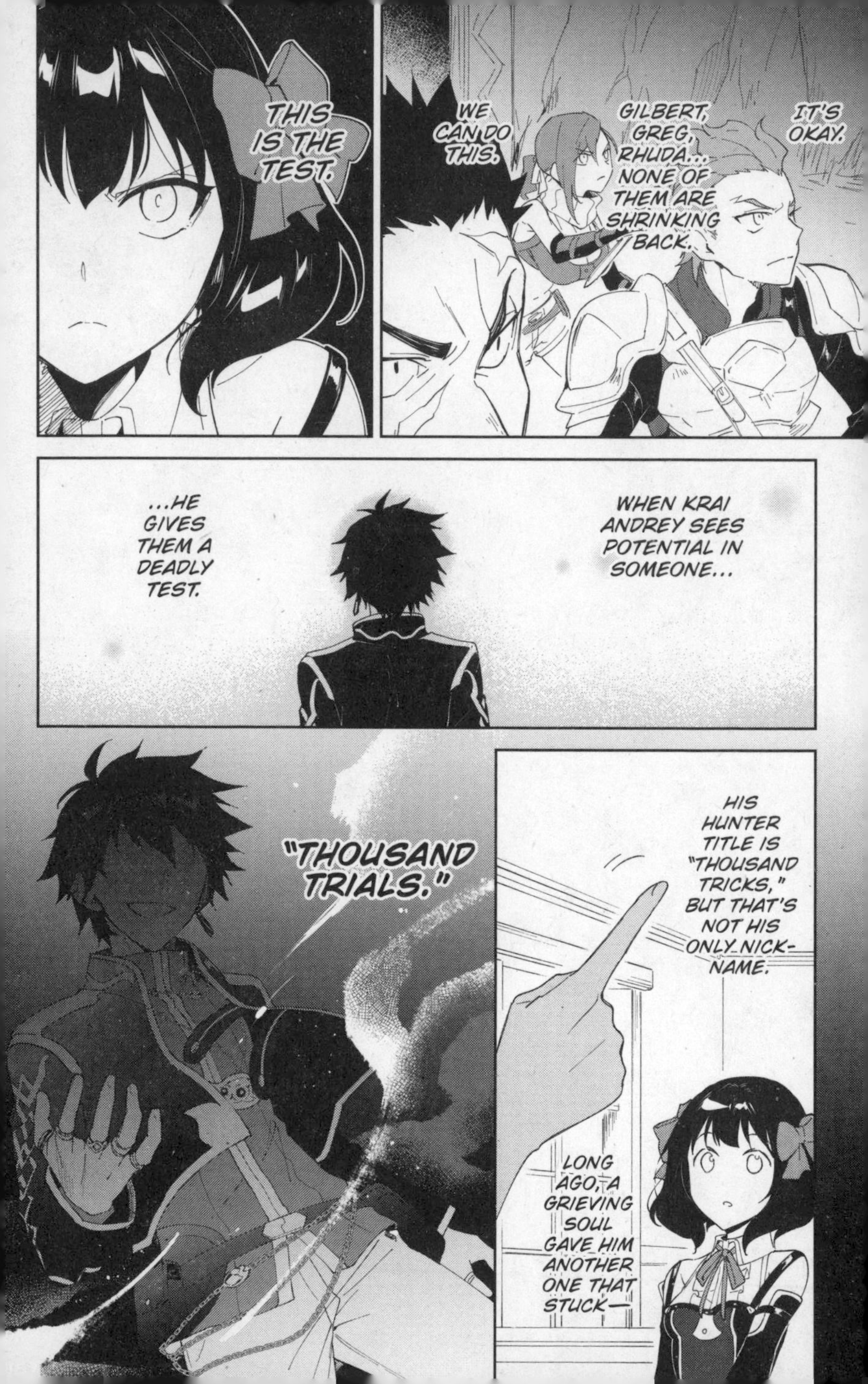
IT'S OKAY.
GILBERT, GREG, RHUDA... NONE OF THEM ARE SHRINKING BACK.
WE CAN DO THIS.
THIS IS THE TEST.
WHEN KRAI ANDREY SEES POTENTIAL IN SOMEONE...
...HE GIVES THEM A DEADLY TEST.
HIS HUNTER TITLE IS "THOUSAND TRICKS," BUT THAT'S NOT HIS ONLY NICK-NAME.
LONG AGO, A GRIEVING SOUL GAVE HIM ANOTHER ONE THAT STUCK—
"THOUSAND TRIALS."

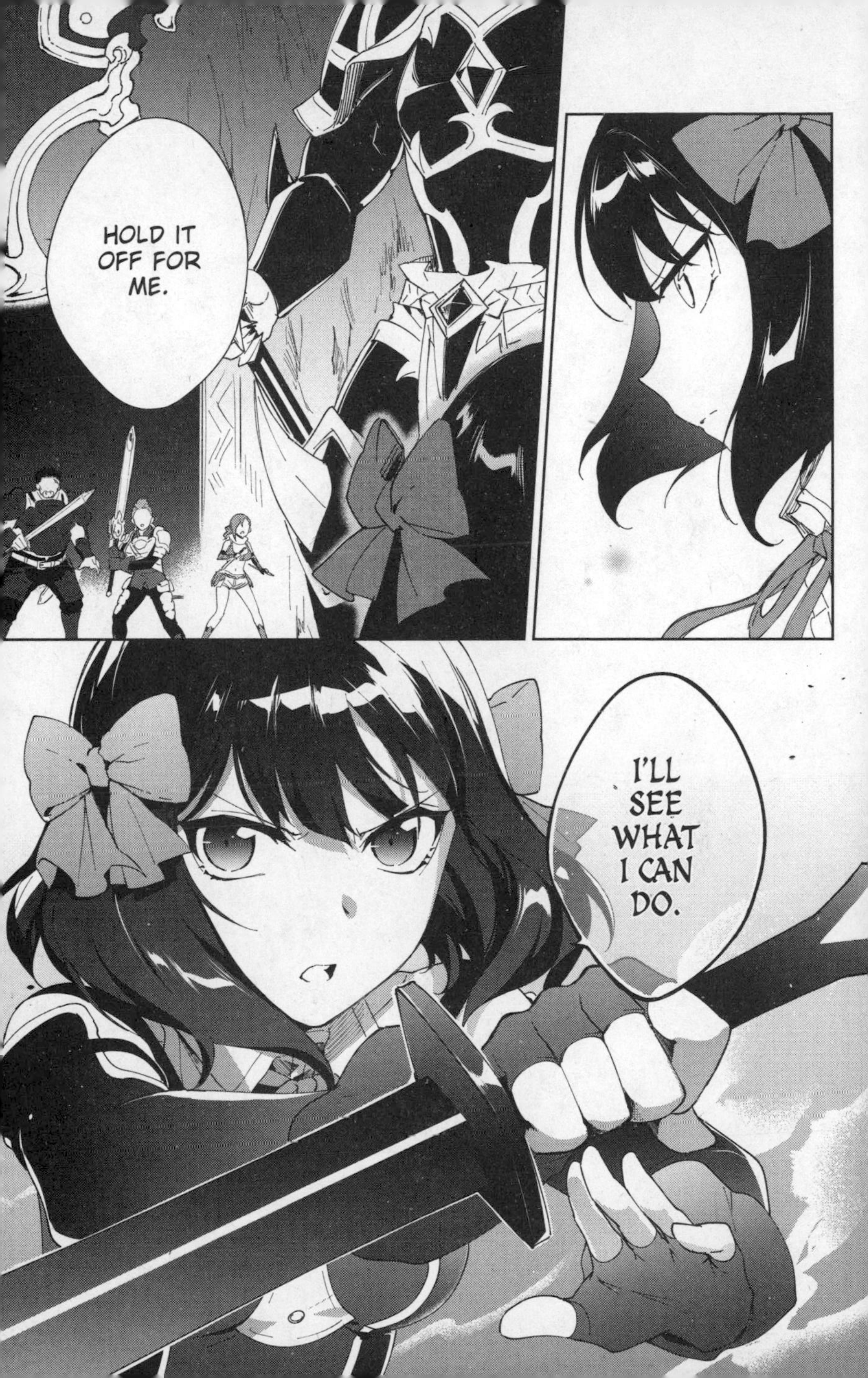
HOLD IT OFF FOR ME.
I'LL SEE WHAT I CAN DO.

LET THIS

Grieving Soul Retire

WOE IS THE WEAKLING WHO LEADS THE STRONGEST PARTY

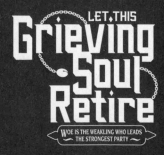

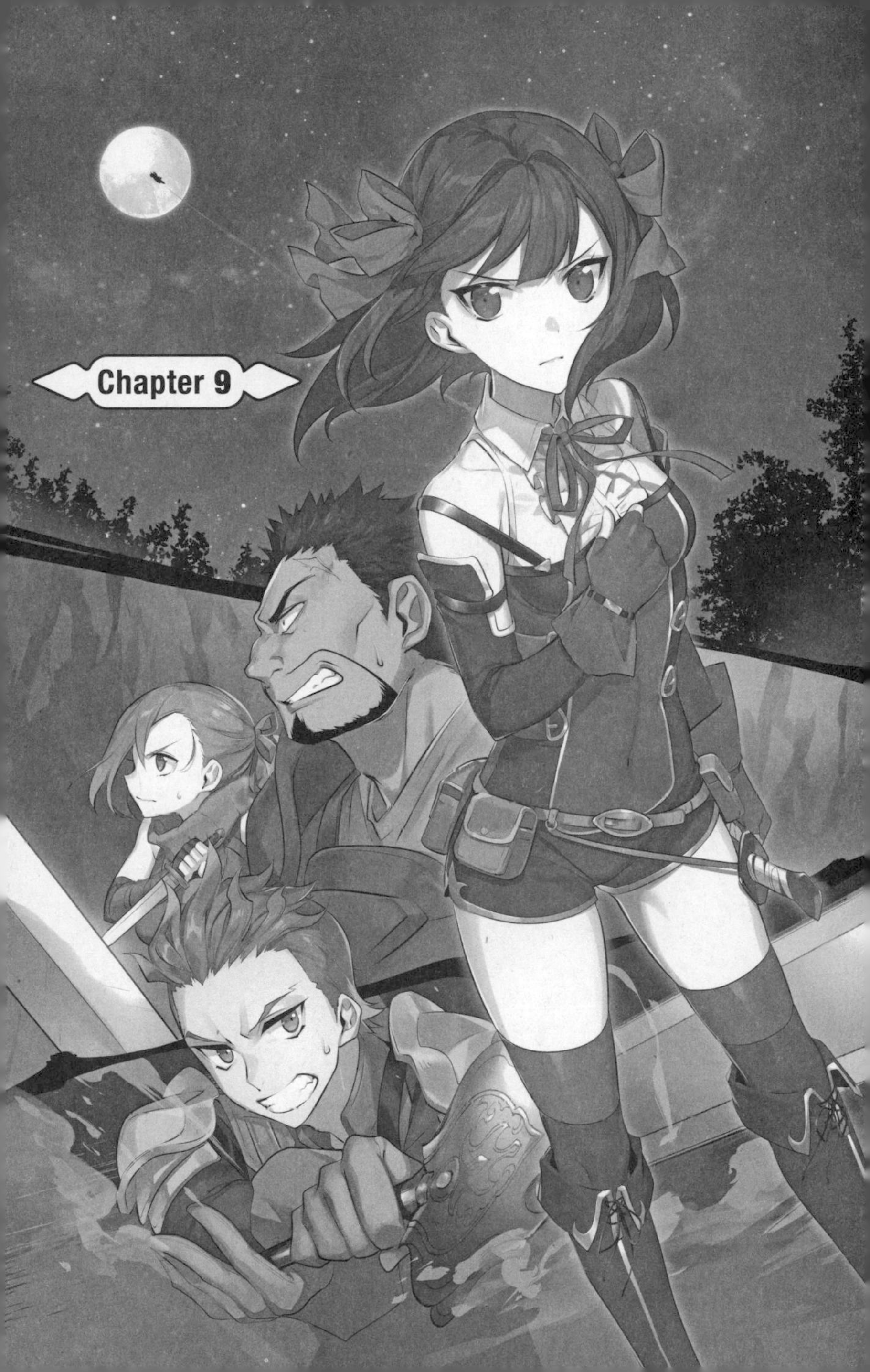
Chapter 9

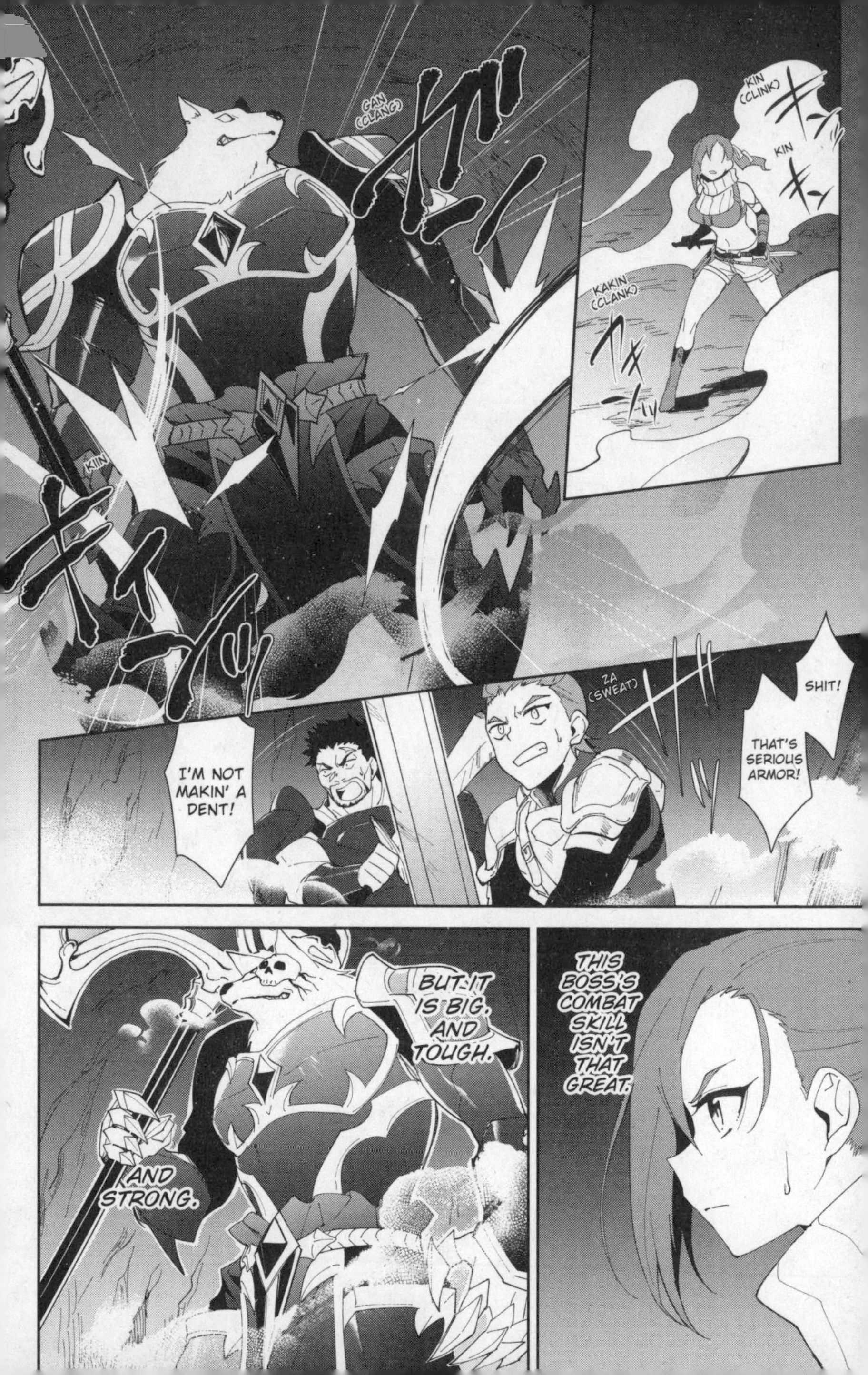
KIN (CLINK)
KIN
KAKIN (CLANK)
GAN (CLANG)
KIN
ZA (SWEAT)
SHIT!
THAT'S SERIOUS ARMOR!
I'M NOT MAKIN' A DENT!
THIS BOSS'S COMBAT SKILL ISN'T THAT GREAT.
BUT IT IS BIG. AND TOUGH.
AND STRONG.

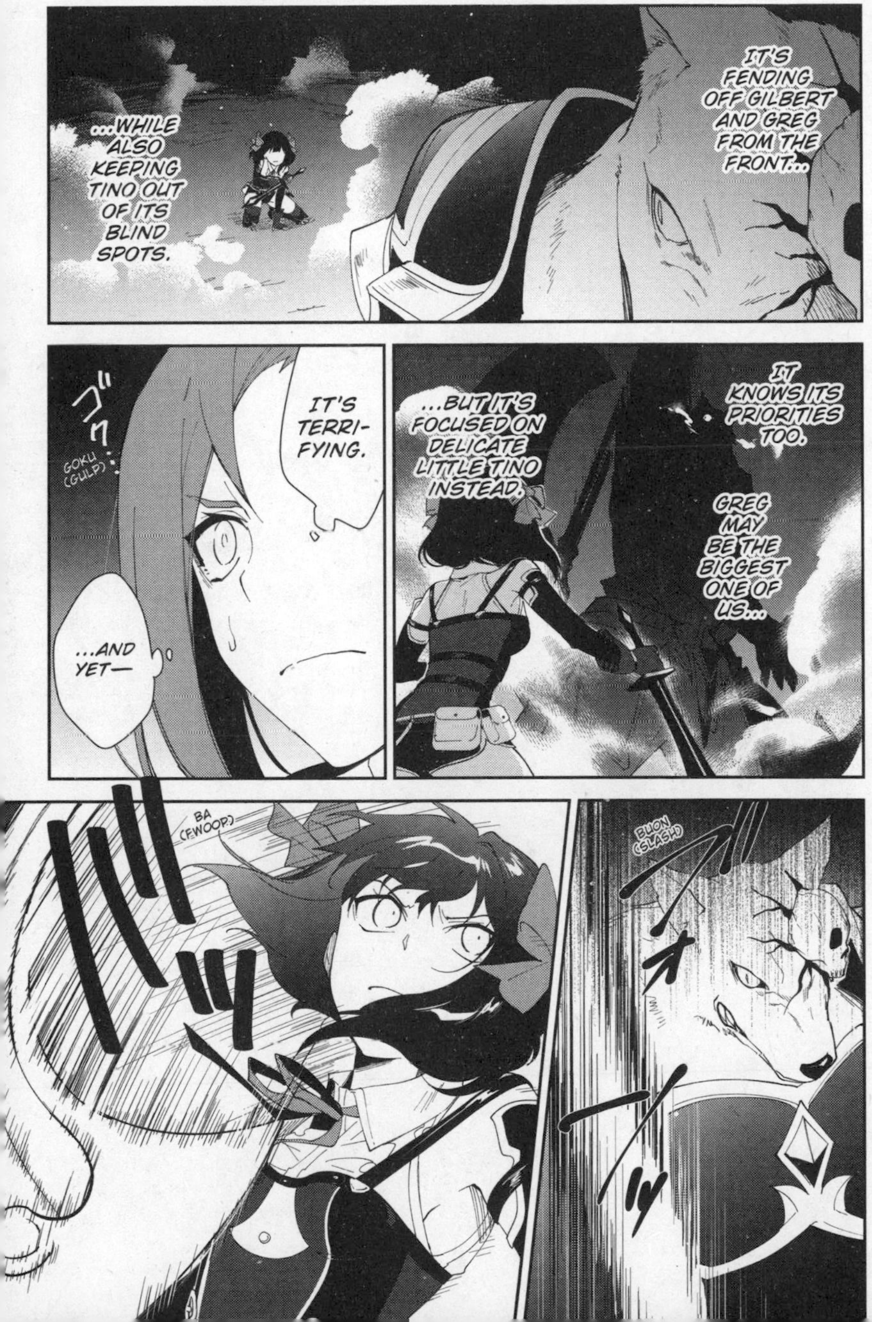
IT'S FENDING OFF GILBERT AND GREG FROM THE FRONT...
...WHILE ALSO KEEPING TINO OUT OF ITS BLIND SPOTS.
IT KNOWS ITS PRIORITIES TOO.
GREG MAY BE THE BIGGEST ONE OF US...
...BUT IT'S FOCUSED ON DELICATE LITTLE TINO INSTEAD.
ゴク
GOKU (GULP)
IT'S TERRIFYING.
...AND YET—
BUON (SLASH)
BA (F-WOOP)

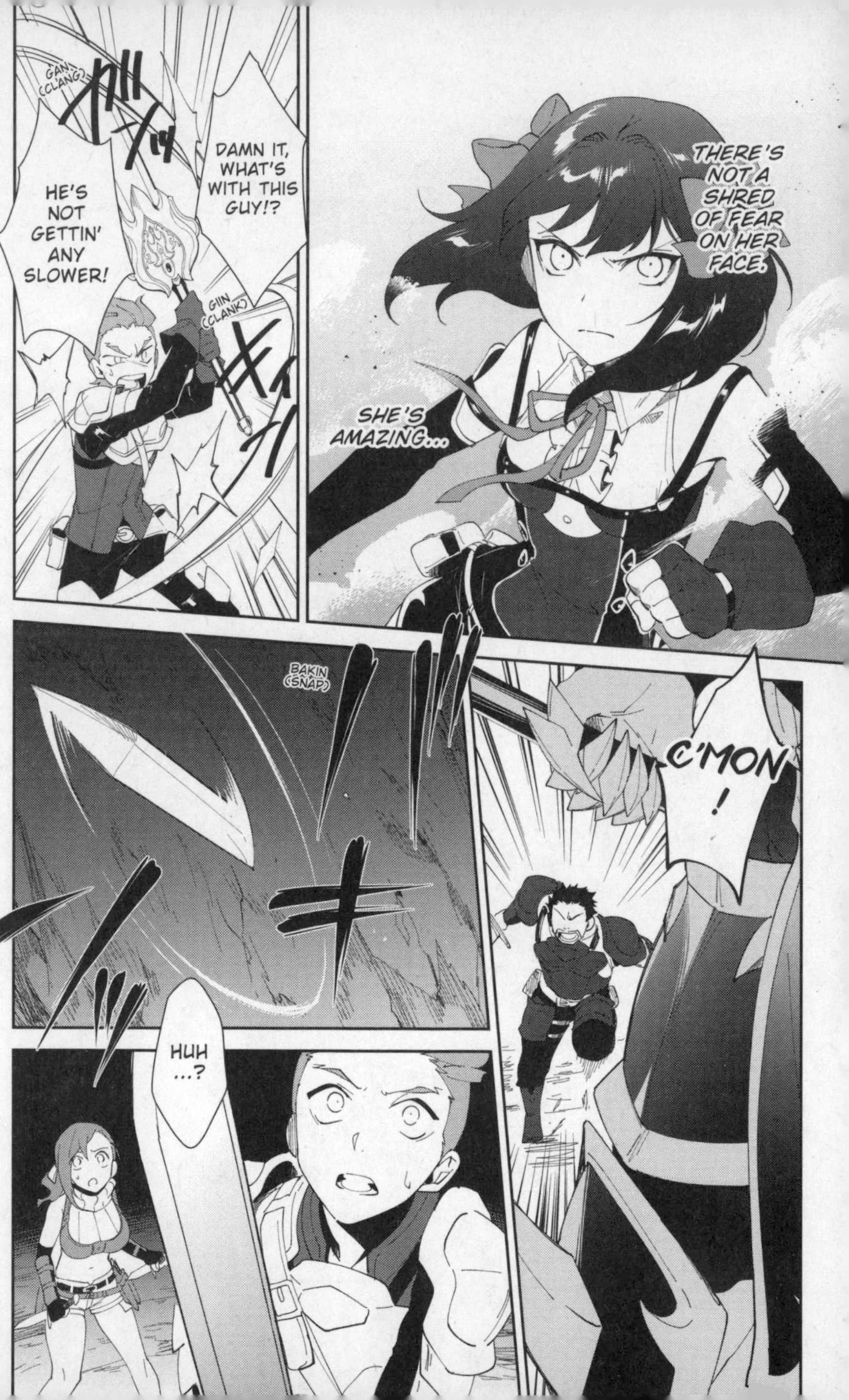
THERE'S NOT A SHRED OF FEAR ON HER FACE.
SHE'S AMAZING...
GAN (CLANG)
DAMN IT, WHAT'S WITH THIS GUY!?
HE'S NOT GETTIN' ANY SLOWER!
GIIN (CLANK)
C'MON!
BAKIN (SNAP)
HUH ...?

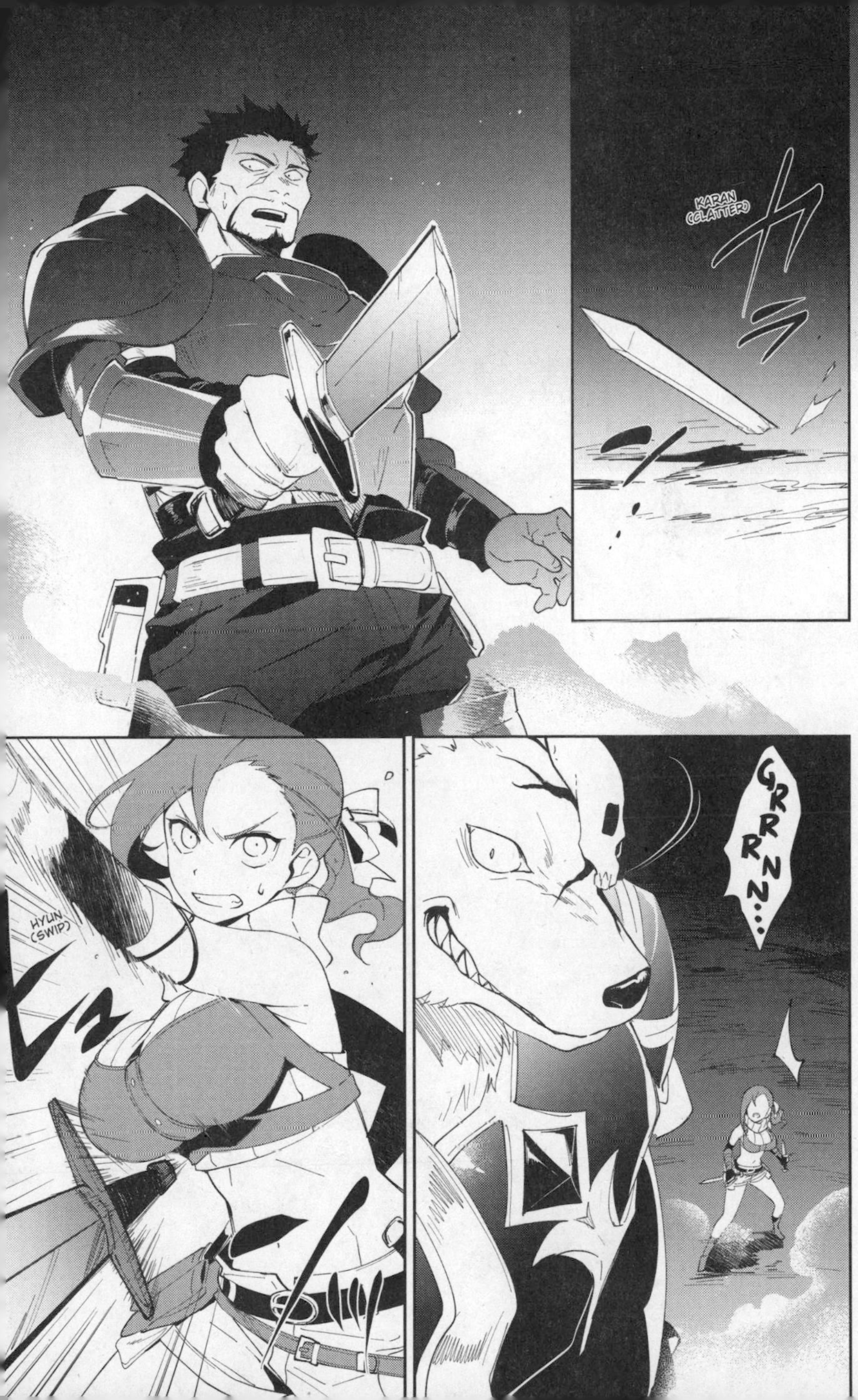
KARAN (CLATTER)
GRRRNN...
HYUN (SWIP)

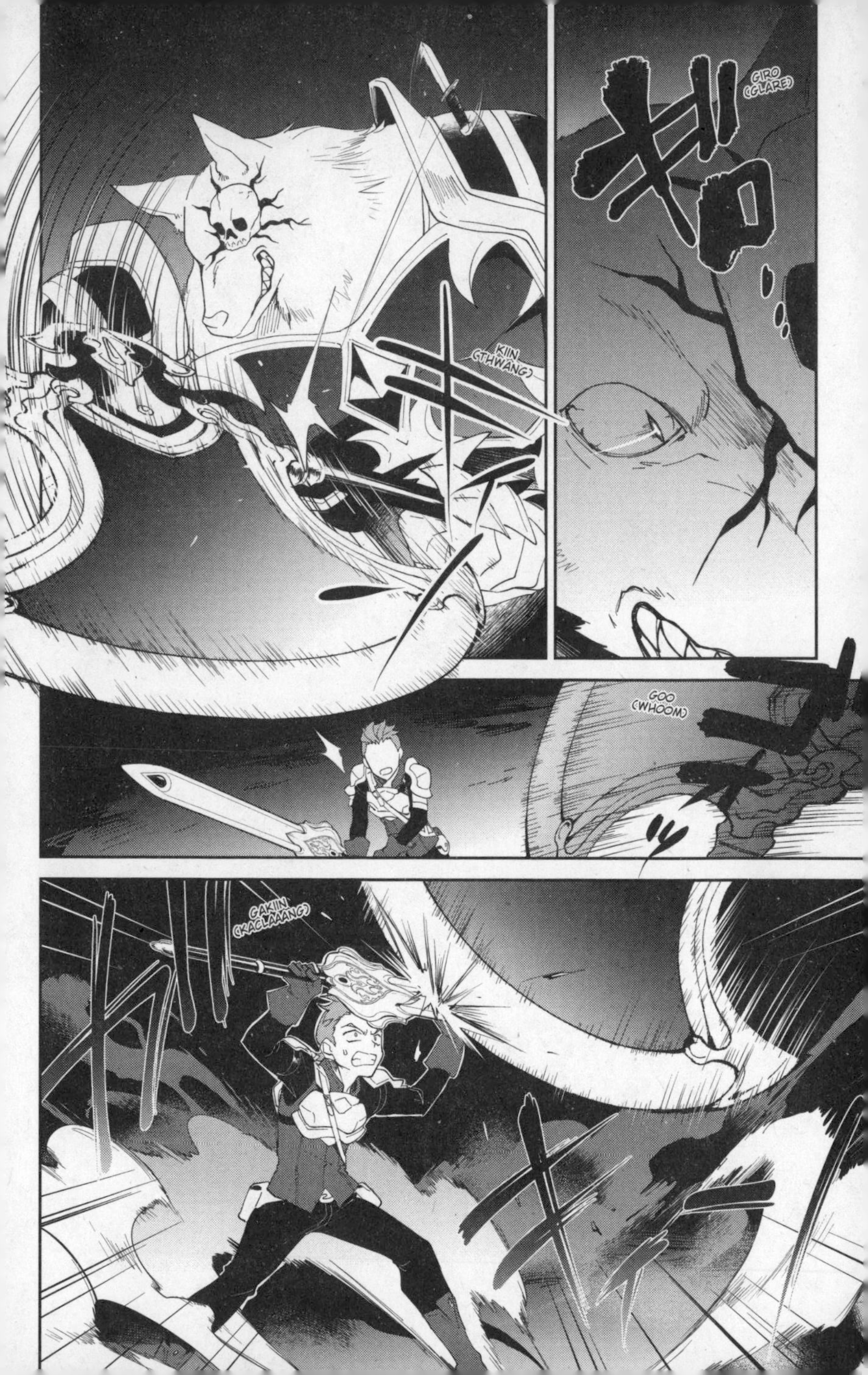
GIRO (GLARE)
KIIN (THWANG)
GOO (WHOOM)
GAKIIN (KACLAAANG)

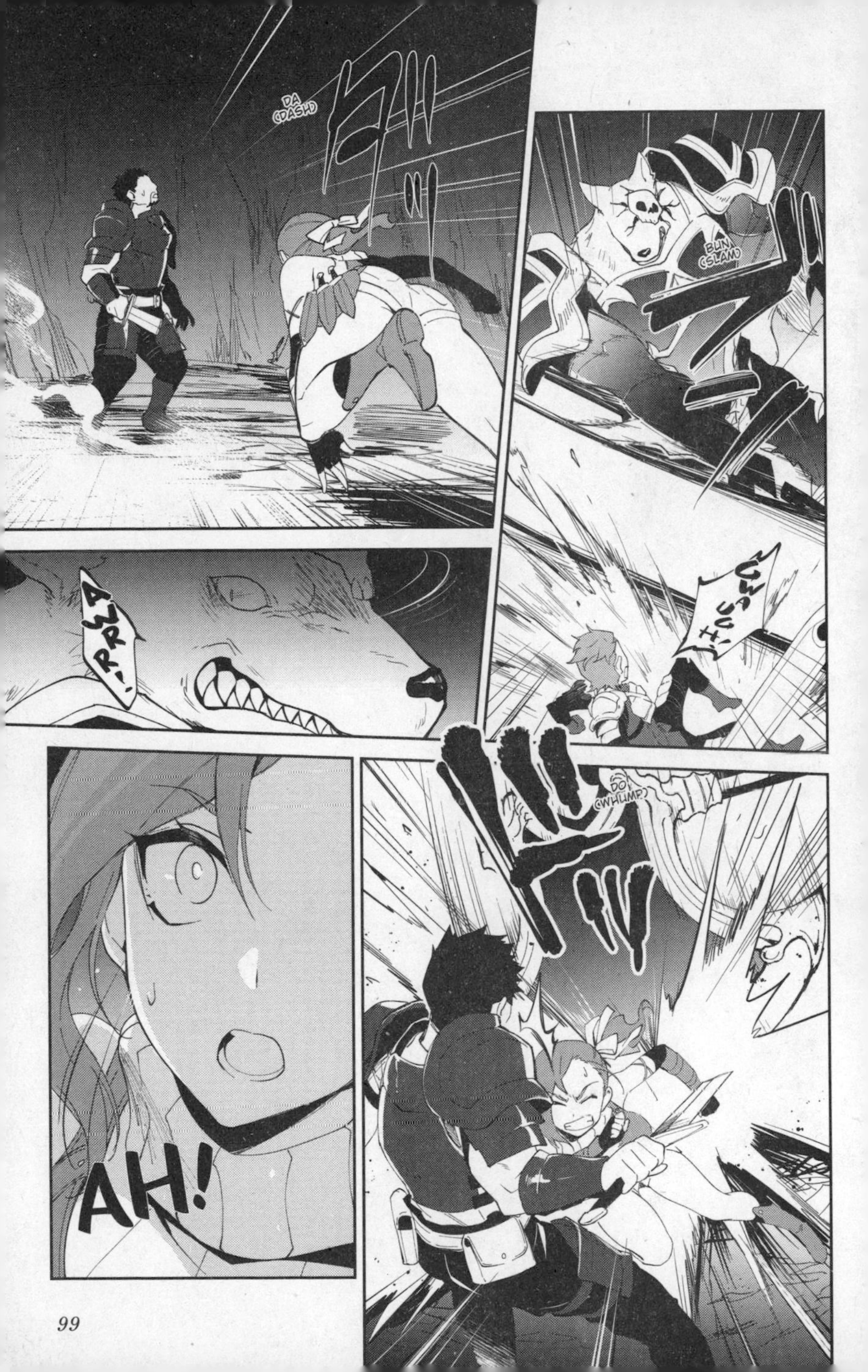
BUN
(SLAM)
DA
(DASH)
GWAUGH!
AWRR!
DO
(WHUMP)
AH!

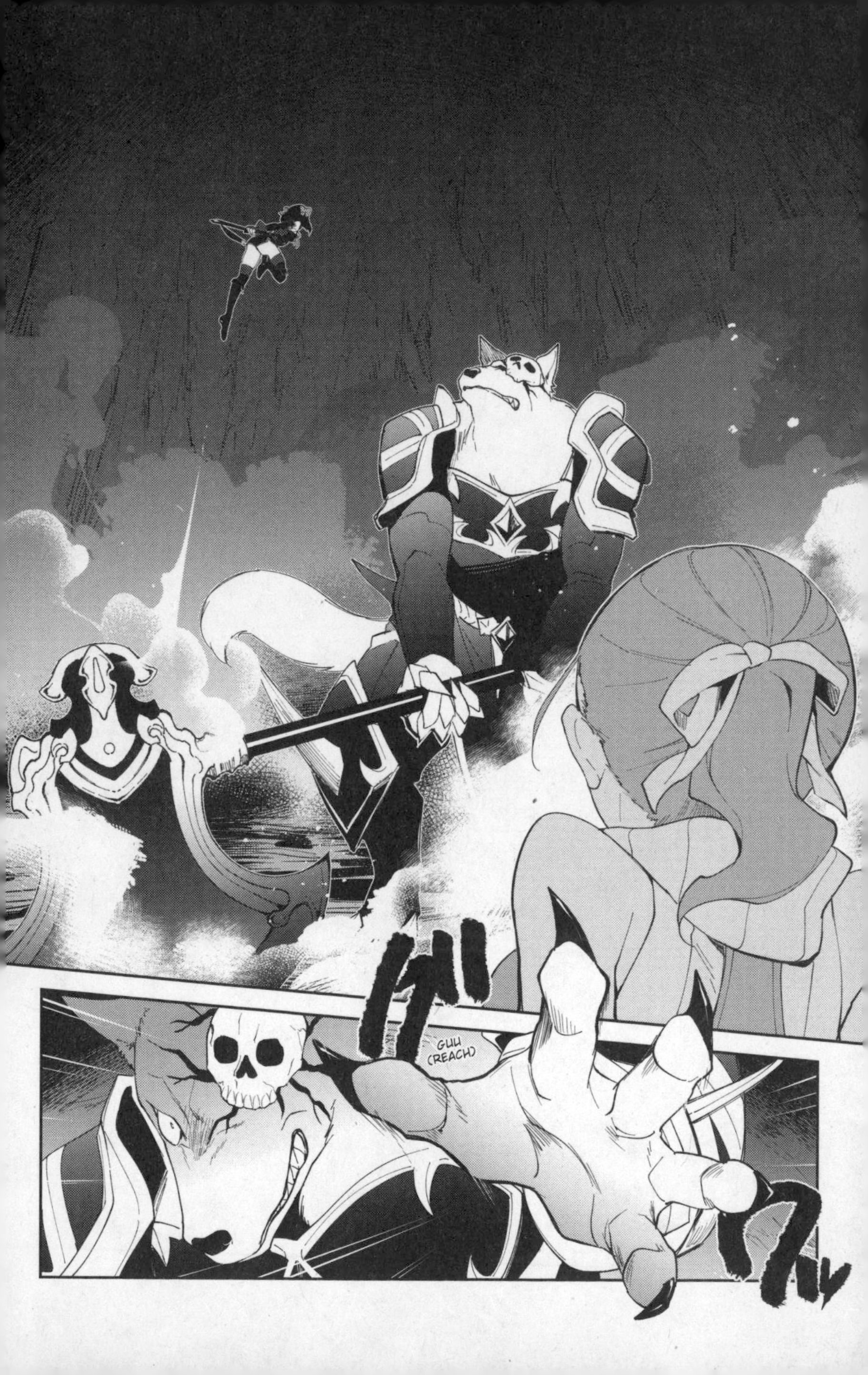
GULI
(REACH)

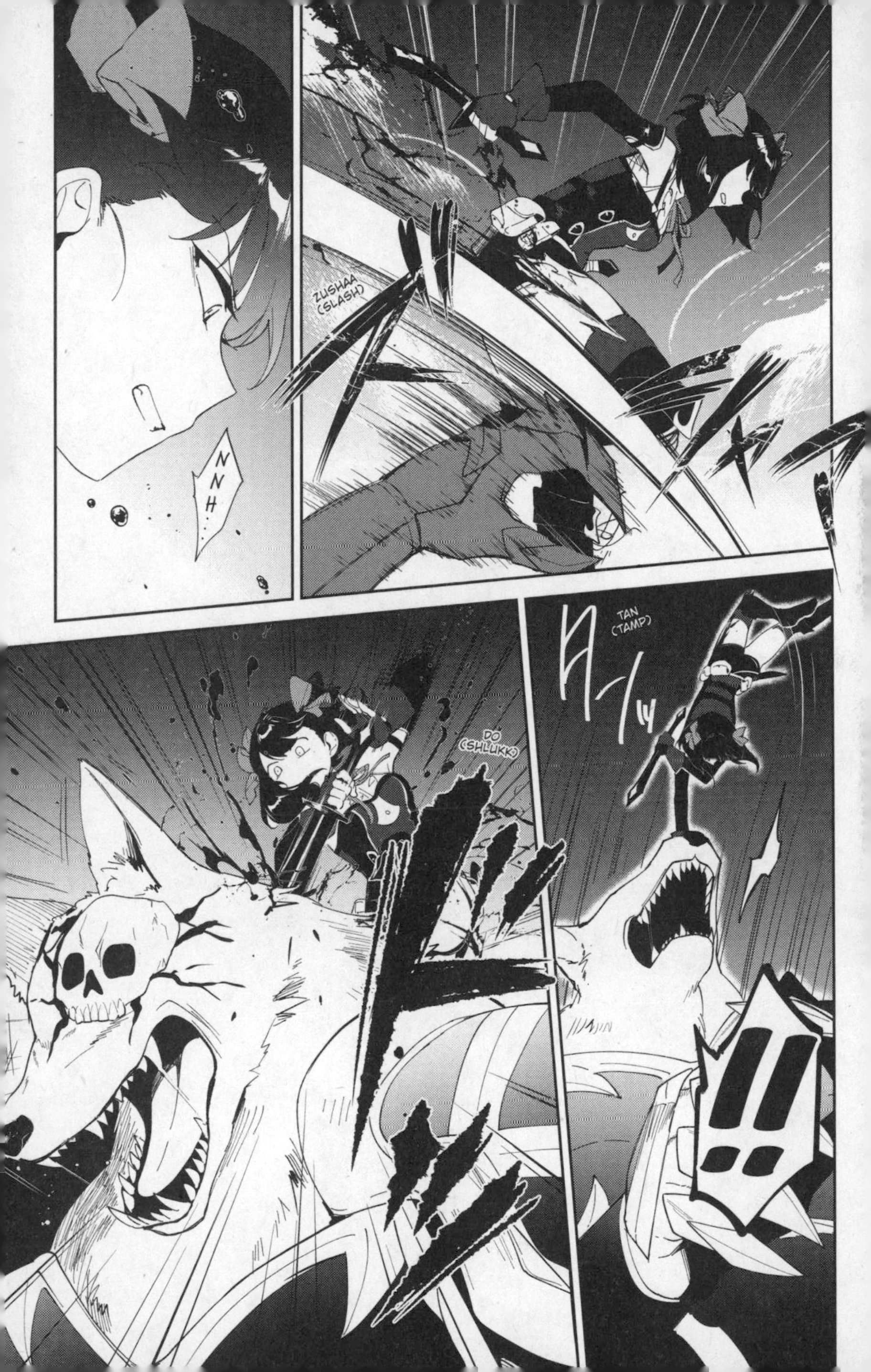
ZUSHAA (SLASH)
NNH..!
TAN (TAMP)
DO (SHLUKK)
!!

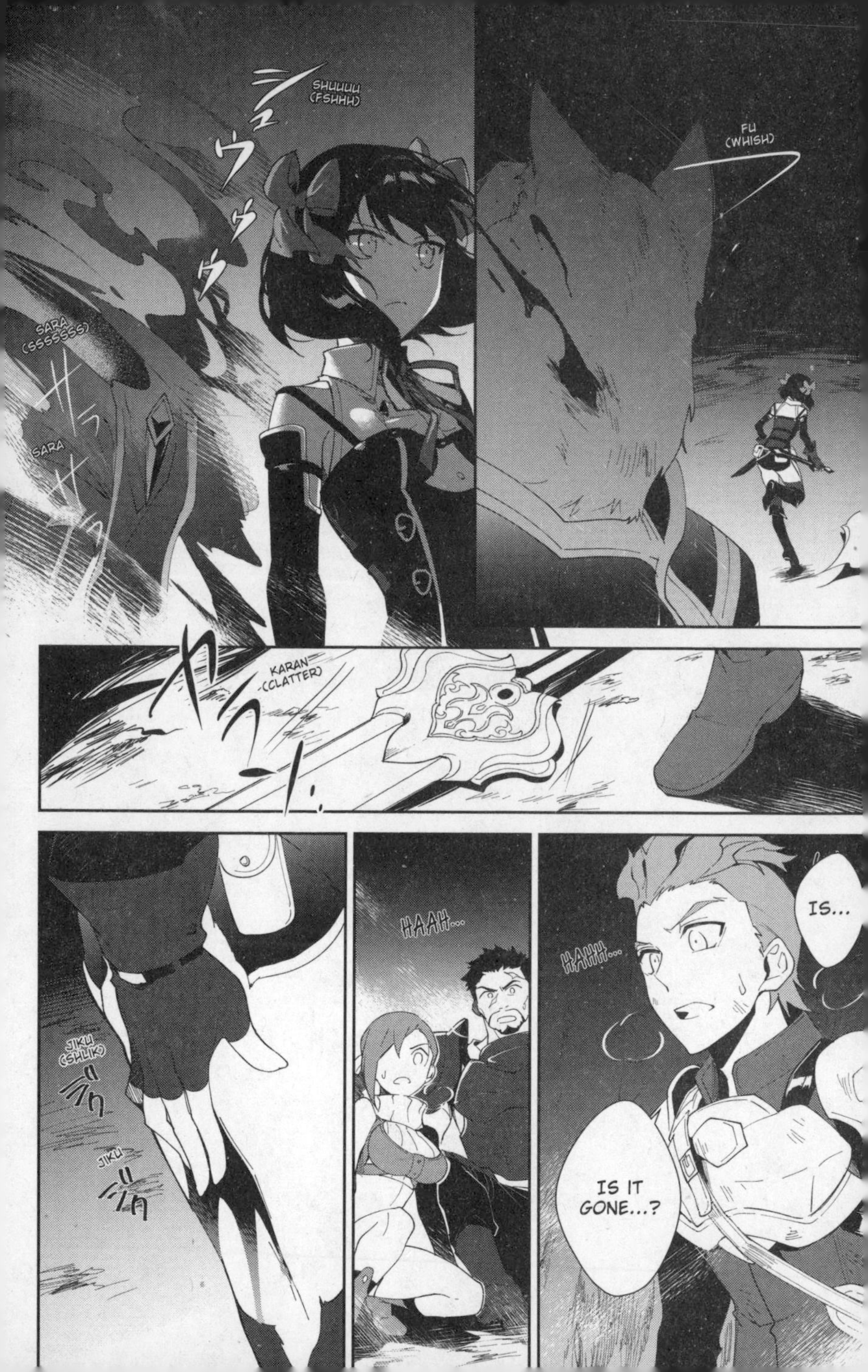
FU
(WHISH)
SHUUUU
(FSHHH)
SARA
(SSSSSSS)
SARA
KARAN
(CLATTER)
IS...
HAAH...
IS IT GONE...?
HAAH...
JIKU
(SHLIK)
JIKU

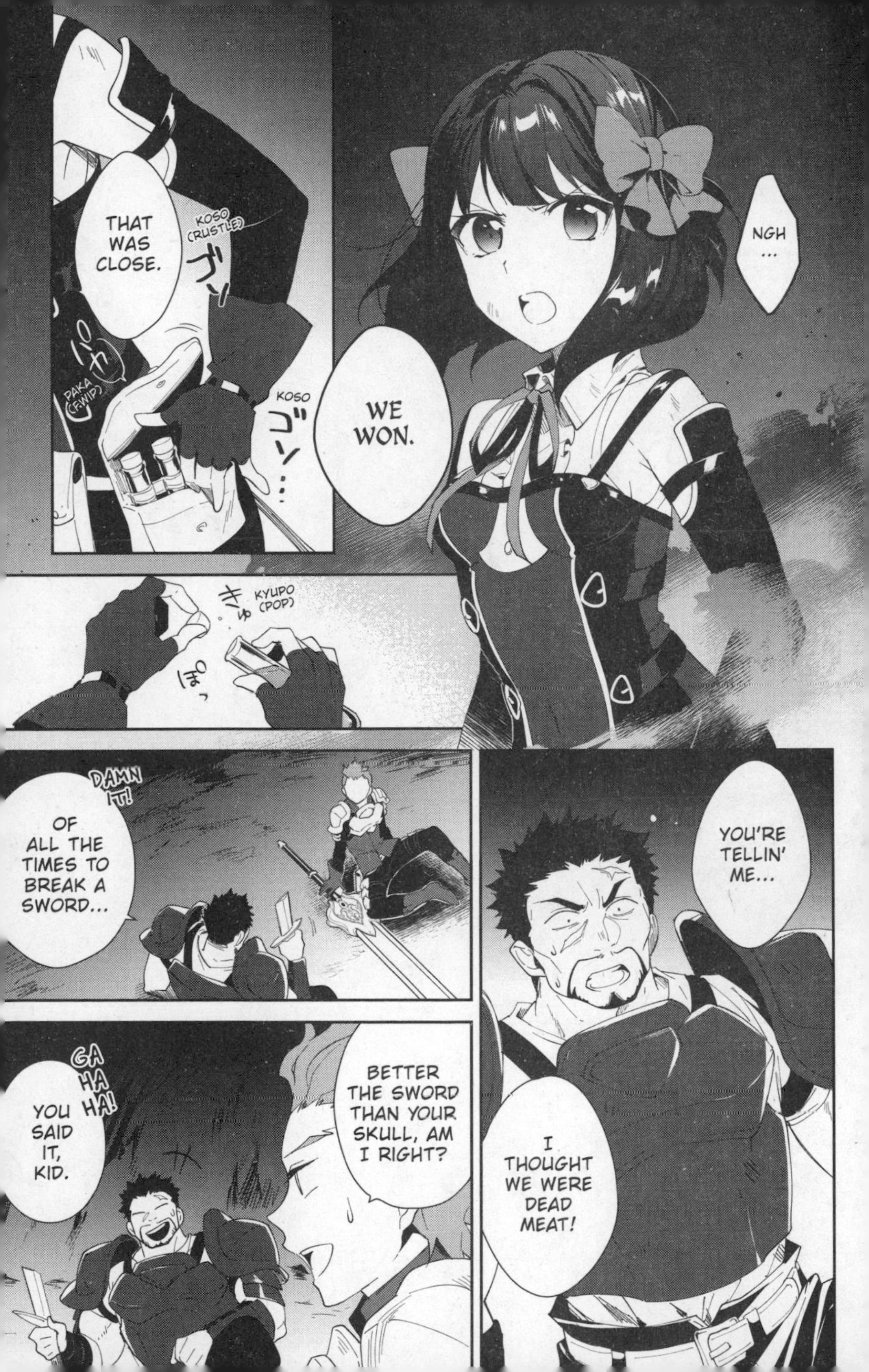
NGH...
WE WON.
THAT WAS CLOSE.
KOSO (RUSTLE)
ゴソ
PAKA (FWIP)
ぱか
KOSO
ゴソ…
KYUPO (POP)
きゅぽっ
YOU'RE TELLIN' ME...
I THOUGHT WE WERE DEAD MEAT!
DAMN IT!
OF ALL THE TIMES TO BREAK A SWORD...
BETTER THE SWORD THAN YOUR SKULL, AM I RIGHT?
GA HA HA!
YOU SAID IT, KID.

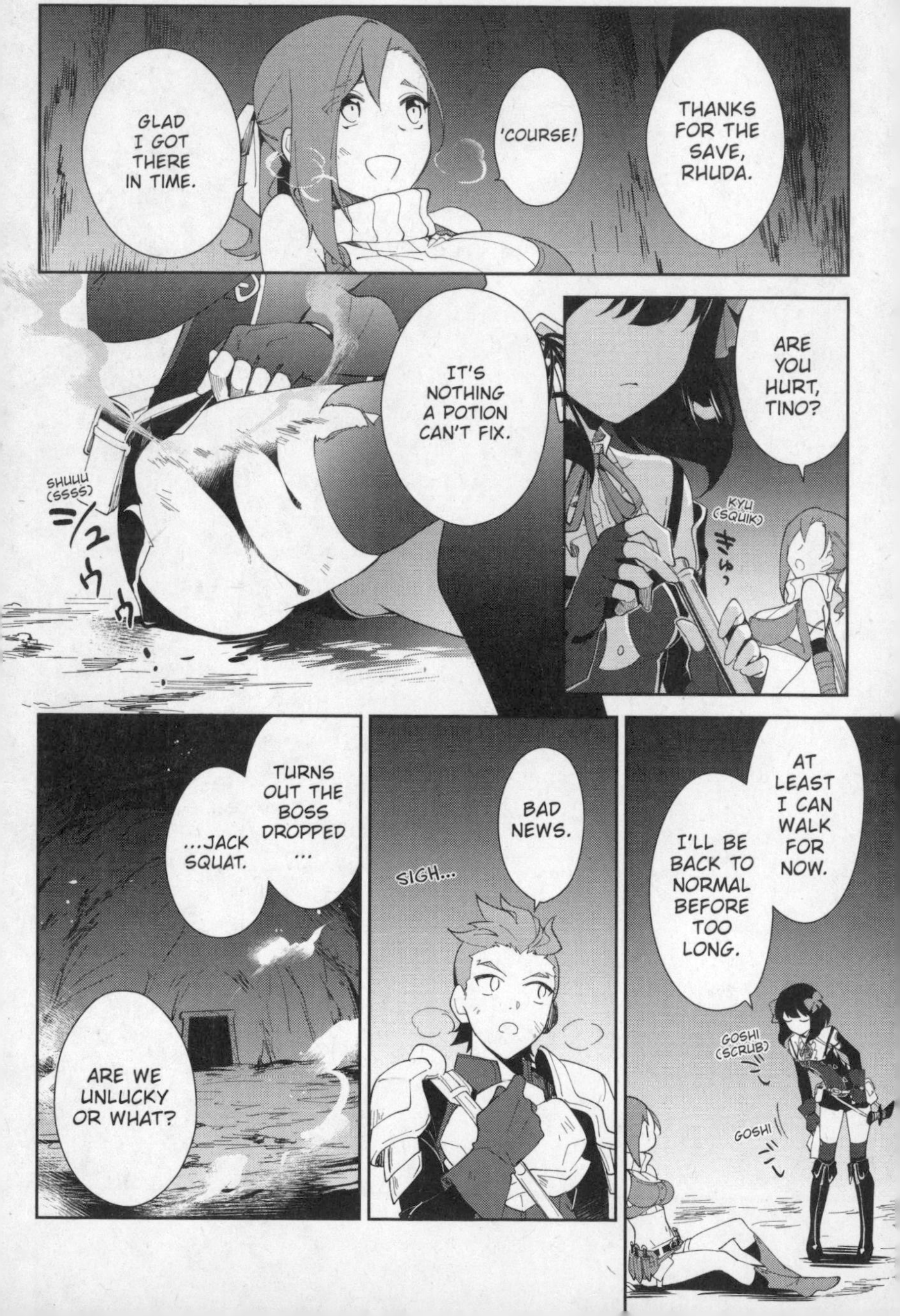
THANKS FOR THE SAVE, RHUDA.
'COURSE!
GLAD I GOT THERE IN TIME.
ARE YOU HURT, TINO?
KYU (SQUIK)
IT'S NOTHING A POTION CAN'T FIX.
SHUUU (SSSS)
AT LEAST I CAN WALK FOR NOW.
I'LL BE BACK TO NORMAL BEFORE TOO LONG.
GOSHI (SCRUB)
GOSHI
BAD NEWS.
SIGH...
TURNS OUT THE BOSS DROPPED ...
...JACK SQUAT.
ARE WE UNLUCKY OR WHAT?

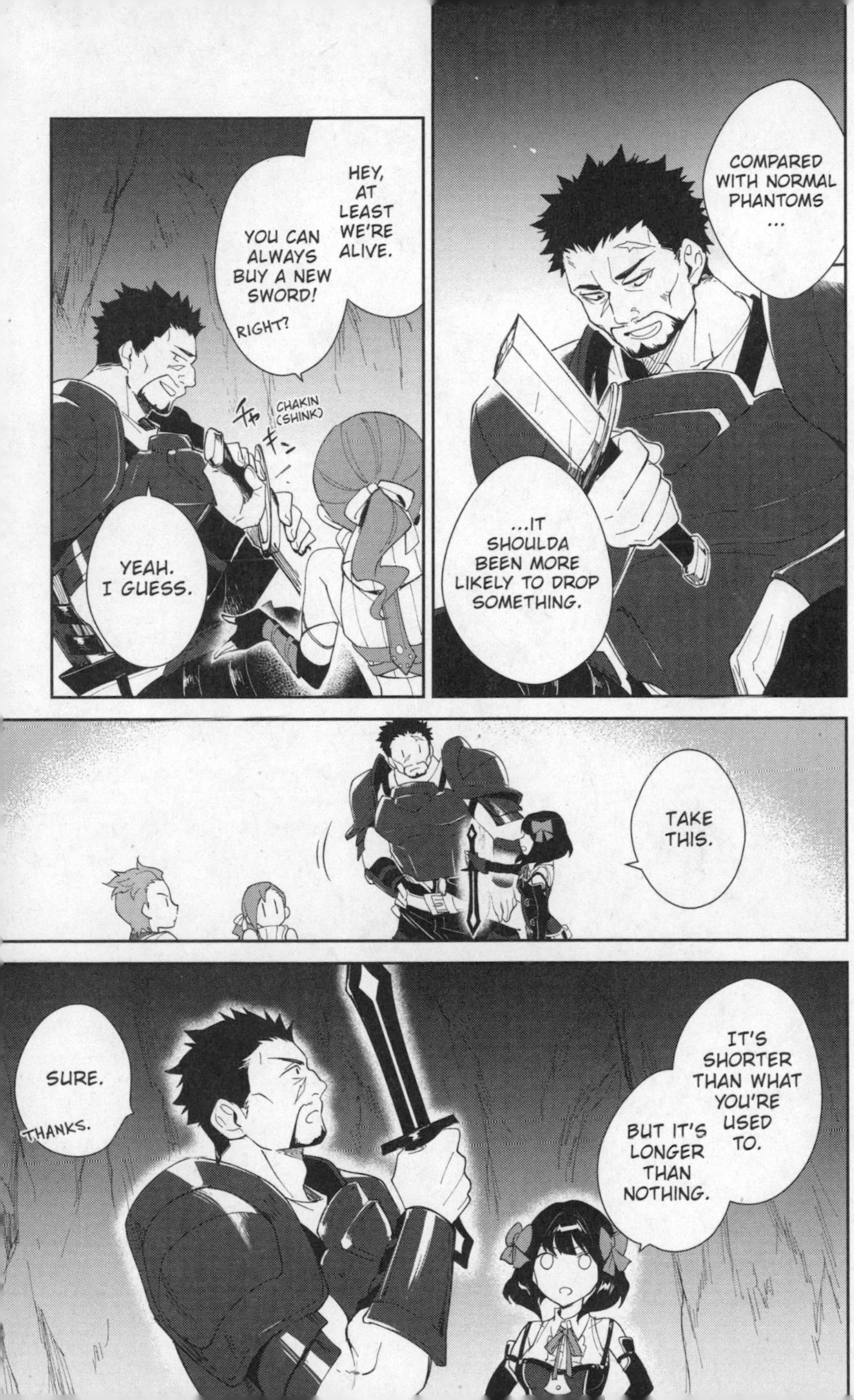
COMPARED WITH NORMAL PHANTOMS ...
...IT SHOULDA BEEN MORE LIKELY TO DROP SOMETHING.
HEY, AT LEAST WE'RE ALIVE.
YOU CAN ALWAYS BUY A NEW SWORD!
RIGHT?
CHAKIN (SHINK)
YEAH. I GUESS.
TAKE THIS.
IT'S SHORTER THAN WHAT YOU'RE USED TO.
BUT IT'S LONGER THAN NOTHING.
SURE.
THANKS.

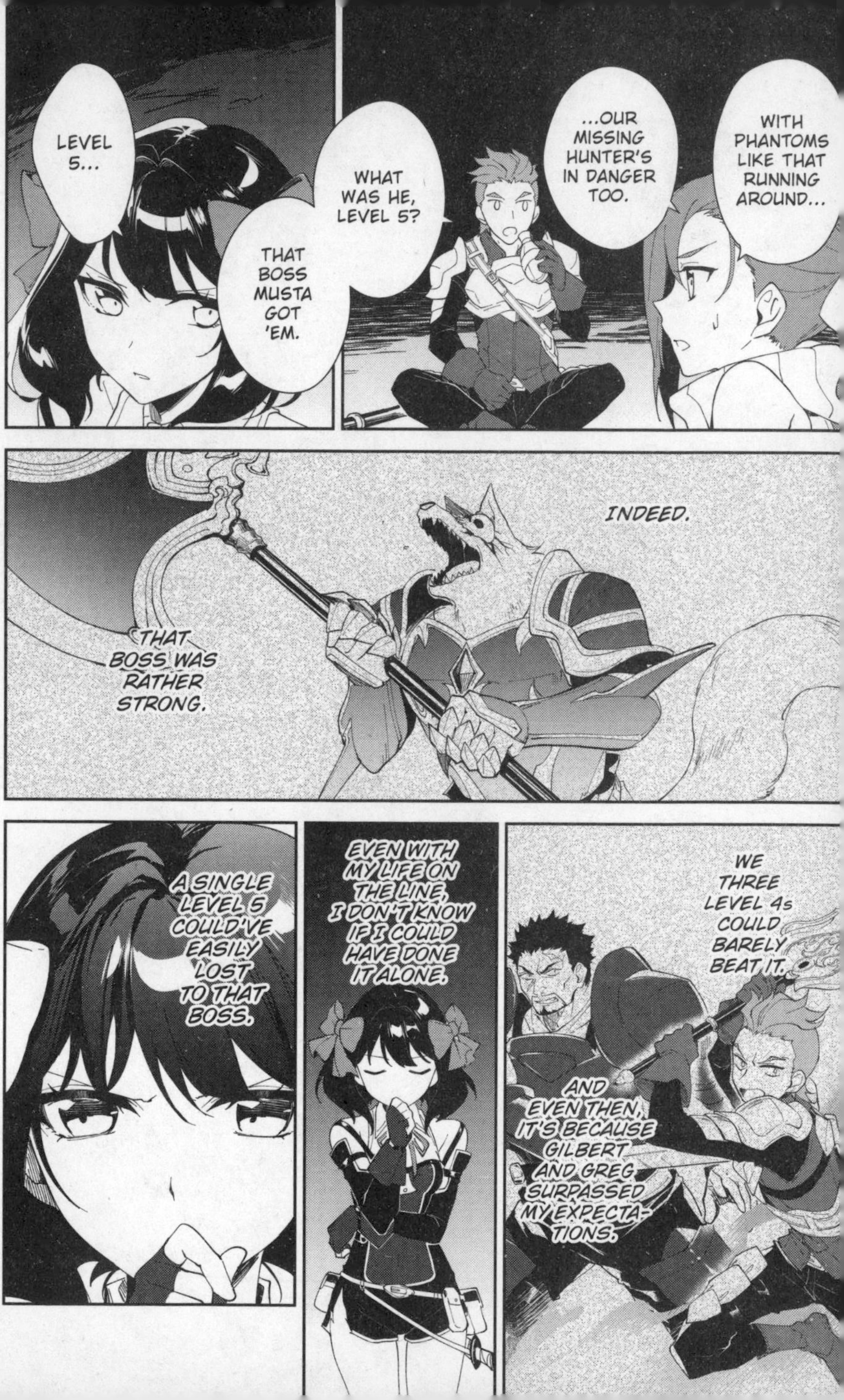
WITH PHANTOMS LIKE THAT RUNNING AROUND...
...OUR MISSING HUNTER'S IN DANGER TOO.
WHAT WAS HE, LEVEL 5?
THAT BOSS MUSTA GOT 'EM.
LEVEL 5...
INDEED.
THAT BOSS WAS RATHER STRONG.
WE THREE LEVEL 4s COULD BARELY BEAT IT.
AND EVEN THEN, IT'S BECAUSE GILBERT AND GREG SURPASSED MY EXPECTATIONS.
EVEN WITH MY LIFE ON THE LINE, I DON'T KNOW IF I COULD HAVE DONE IT ALONE.
A SINGLE LEVEL 5 COULD'VE EASILY LOST TO THAT BOSS.

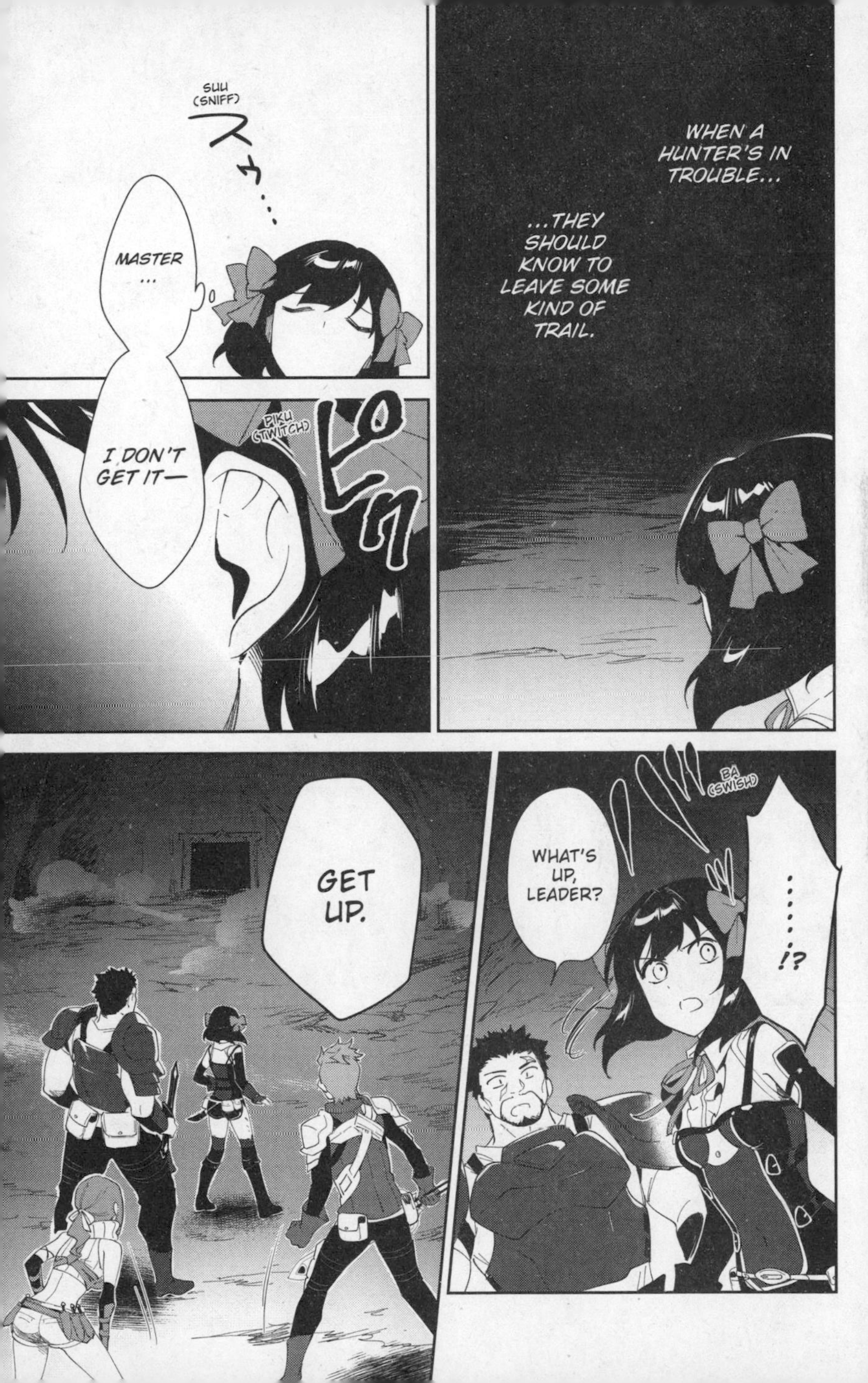
WHEN A HUNTER'S IN TROUBLE...
...THEY SHOULD KNOW TO LEAVE SOME KIND OF TRAIL.
SUU (SNIFF)
MASTER ...
PIKU (TWITCH)
I DON'T GET IT—
BA (SWISH)
......!?
WHAT'S UP, LEADER?
GET UP.

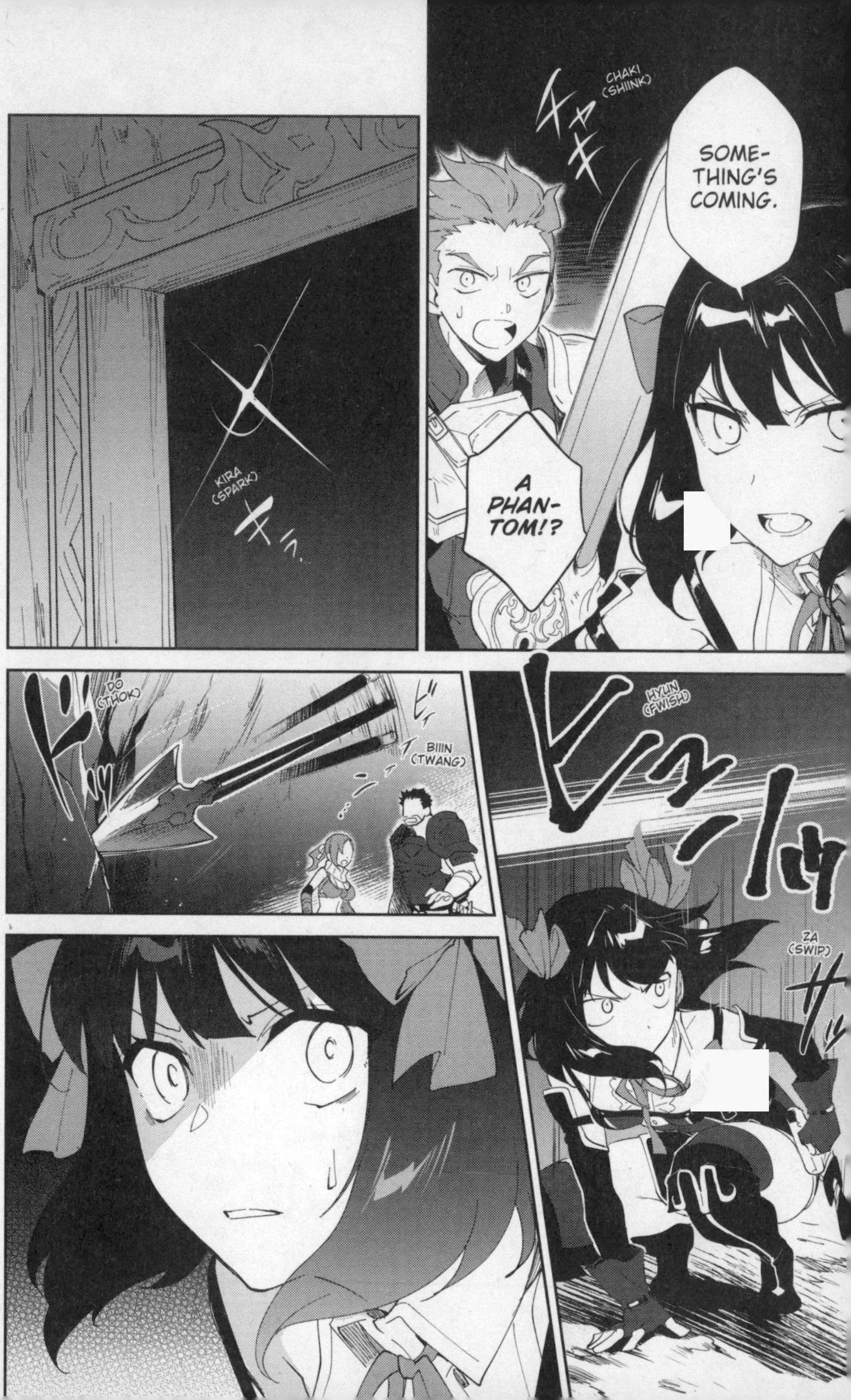
SOME-
THING'S
COMING.
CHAKI
(SHIINK)
A
PHAN-
TOM!?
KIRA
(SPARK)
HYUN
(FWISH)
ZA
(SWIP)
DO
(THOK)
BIIN
(TWANG)

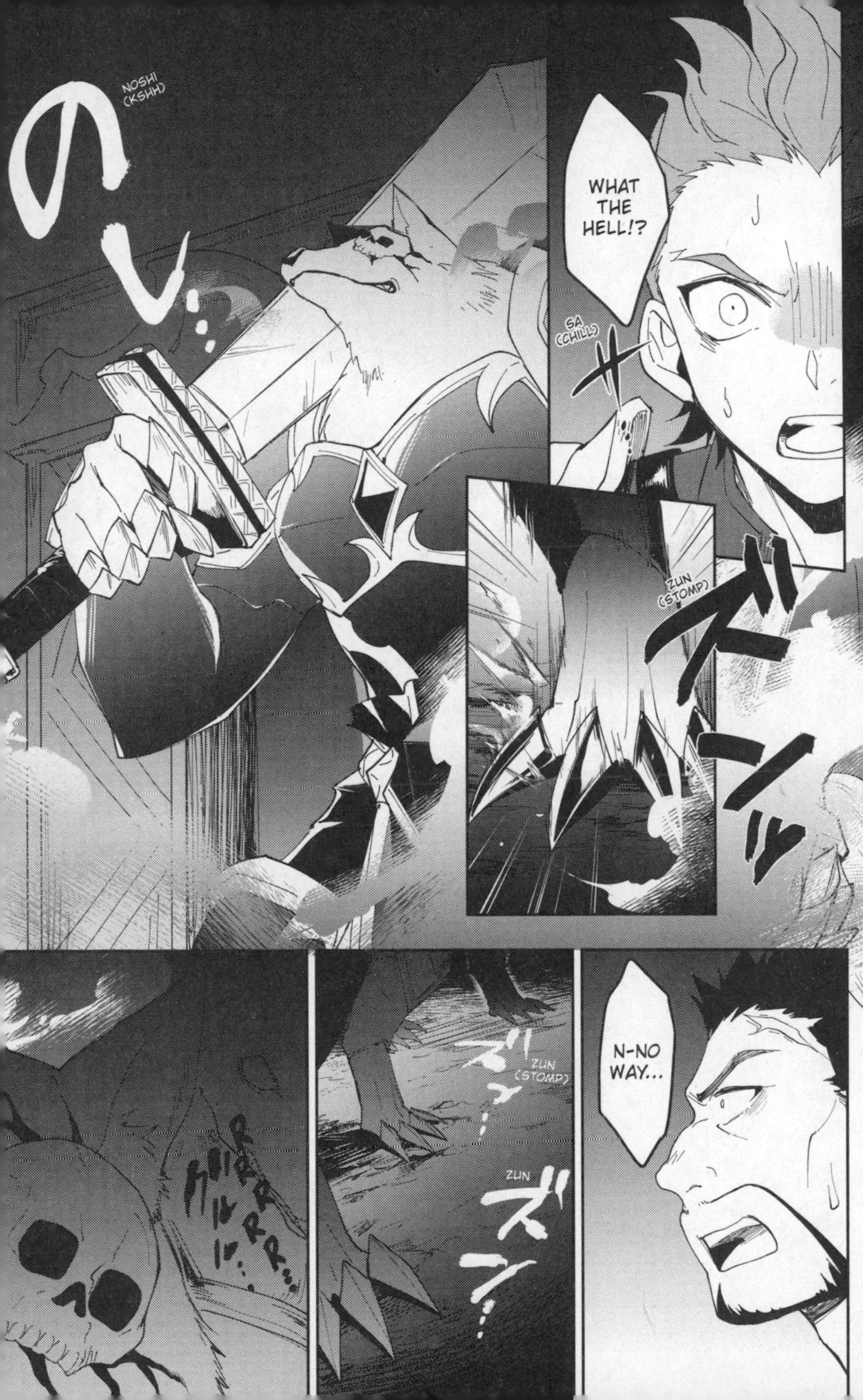
WHAT THE HELL!?
SA (CHILL)
ZUN (STOMP)
NOSHI (KSHH)
N-NO WAY...
ZUN (STOMP)
ZUN

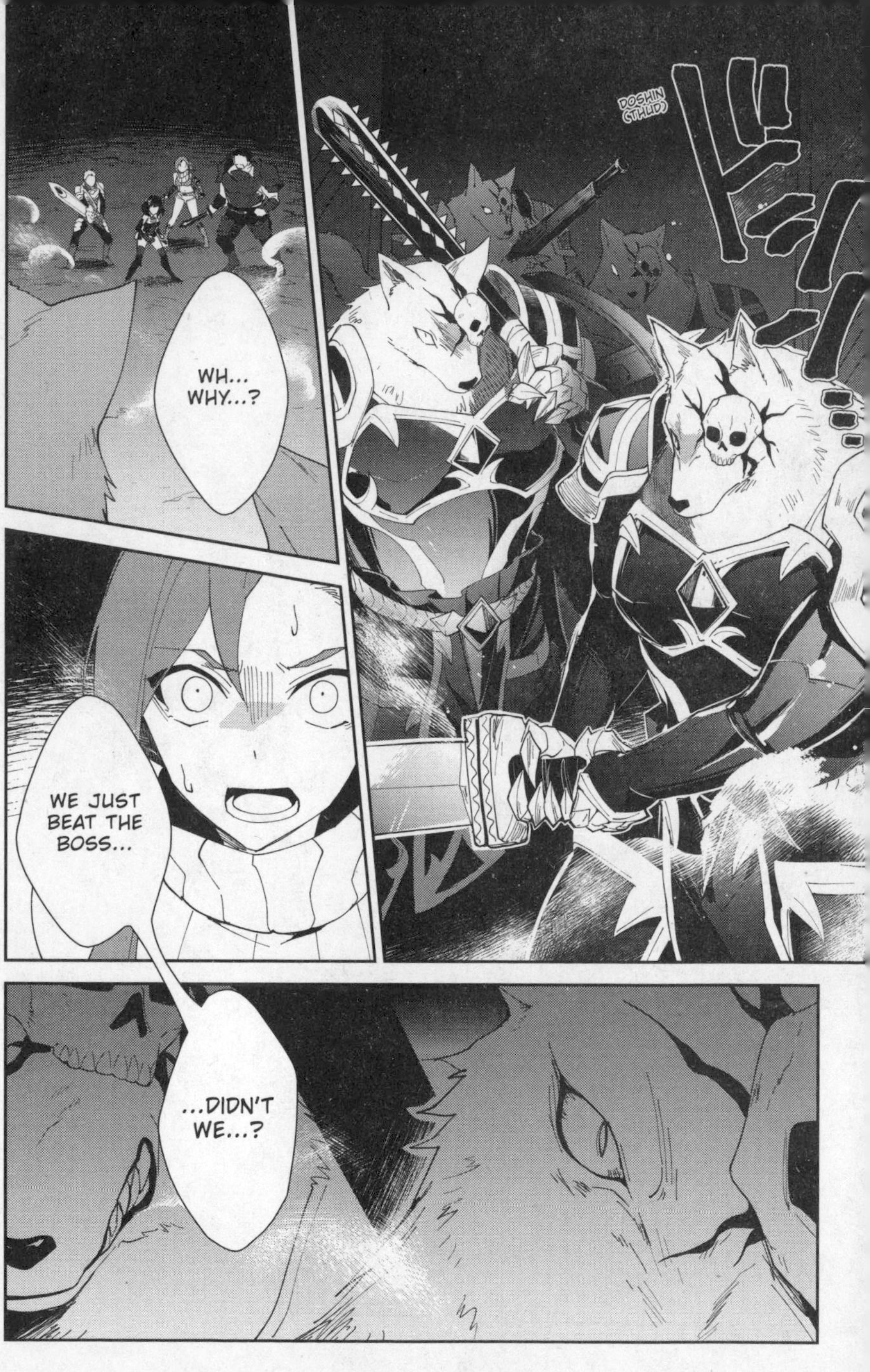
DOSHIN (THUD)
WH... WHY...?
WE JUST BEAT THE BOSS...
...DIDN'T WE...?

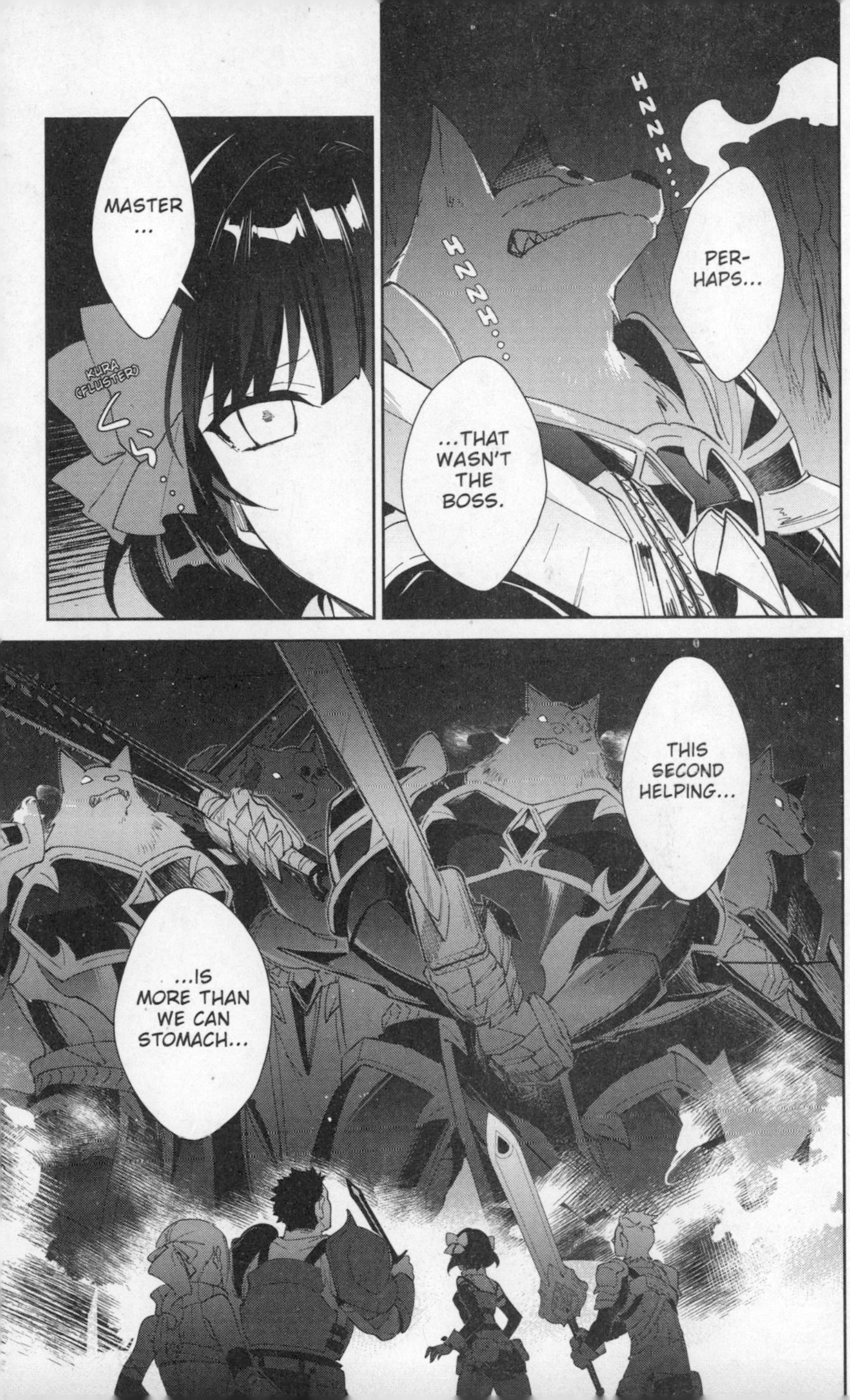
HNNH...
PER-HAPS...
HNNH...
...THAT WASN'T THE BOSS.
MASTER...
KURA (FLUSTER)
THIS SECOND HELPING...
...IS MORE THAN WE CAN STOMACH...

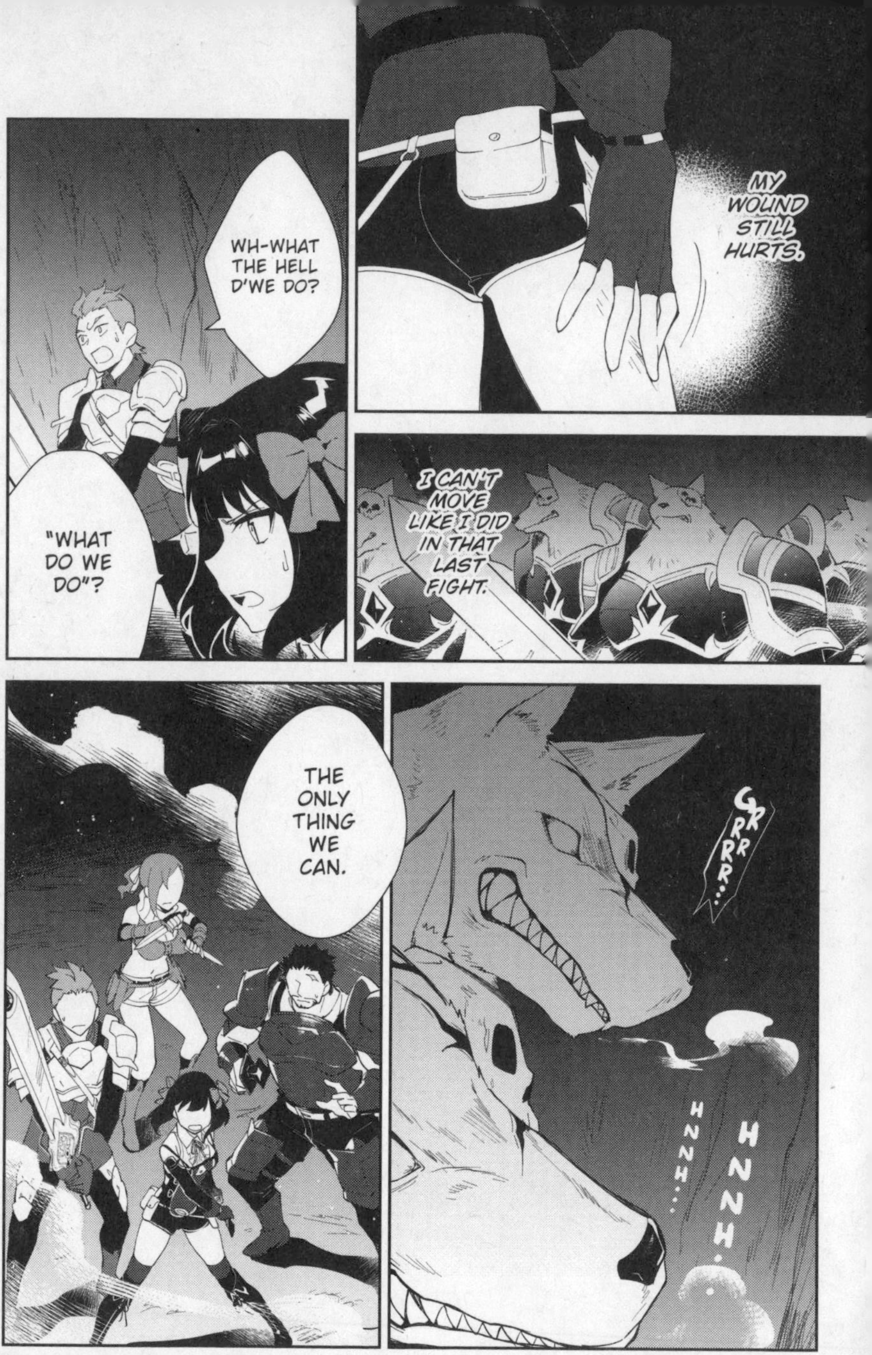
MY WOUND STILL HURTS.
I CAN'T MOVE LIKE I DID IN THAT LAST FIGHT.
WH-WHAT THE HELL D'WE DO?
"WHAT DO WE DO"?
GRRRR...
HNNH.
HNNH...
THE ONLY THING WE CAN.

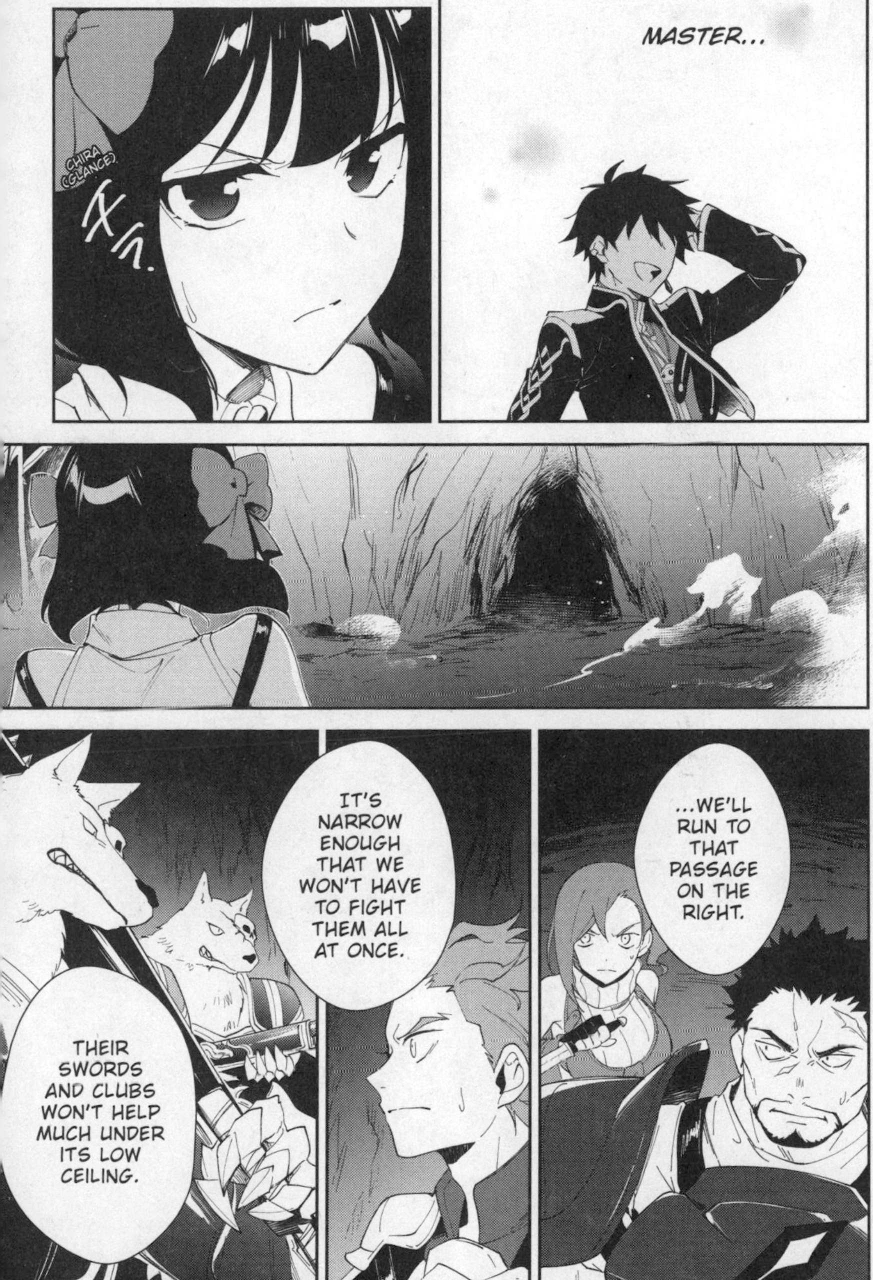
MASTER...
CHIRA (GLANCE)
...WE'LL RUN TO THAT PASSAGE ON THE RIGHT.
IT'S NARROW ENOUGH THAT WE WON'T HAVE TO FIGHT THEM ALL AT ONCE.
THEIR SWORDS AND CLUBS WON'T HELP MUCH UNDER ITS LOW CEILING.

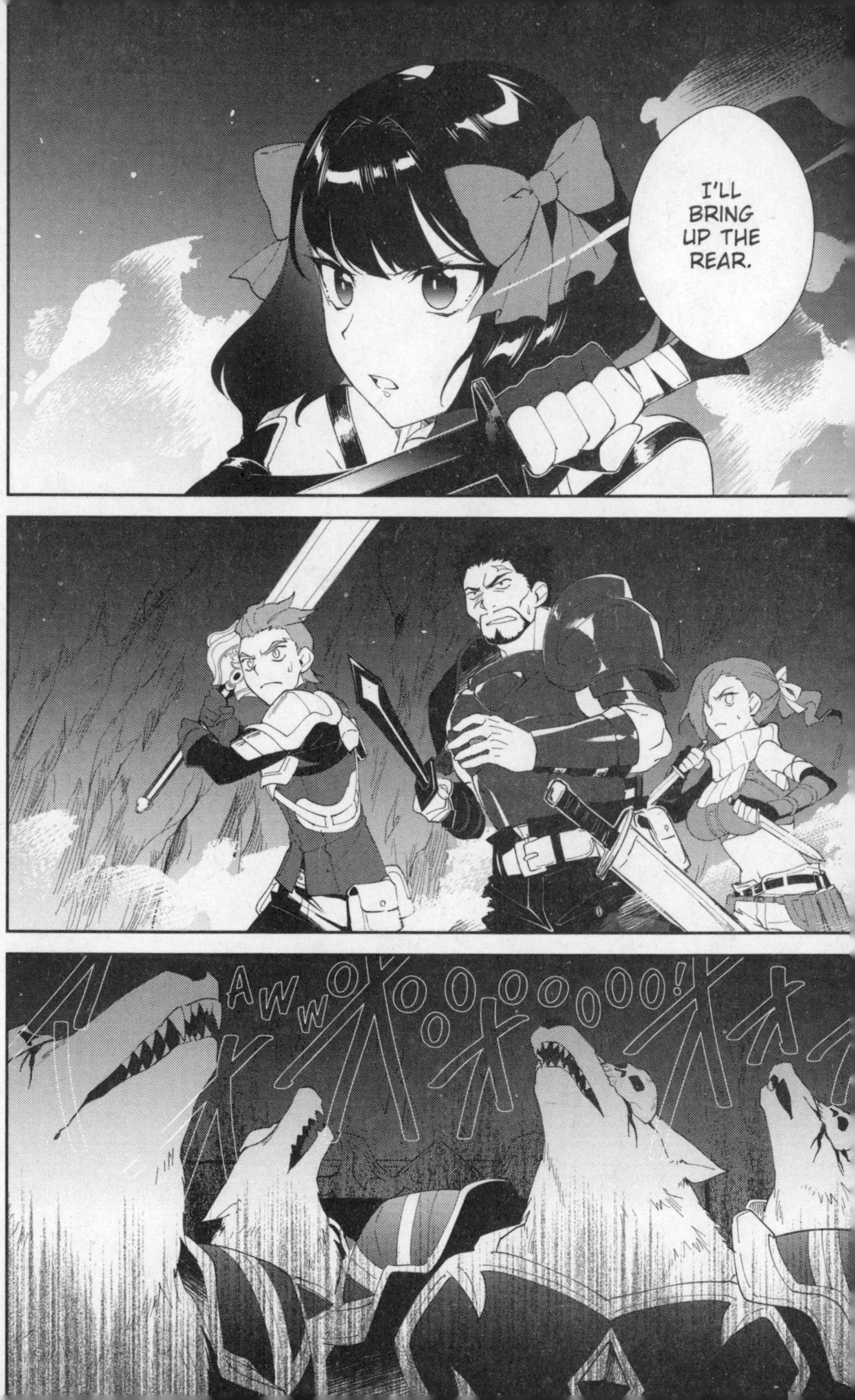
I'LL BRING UP THE REAR.
AWWOOOOOOOOO!

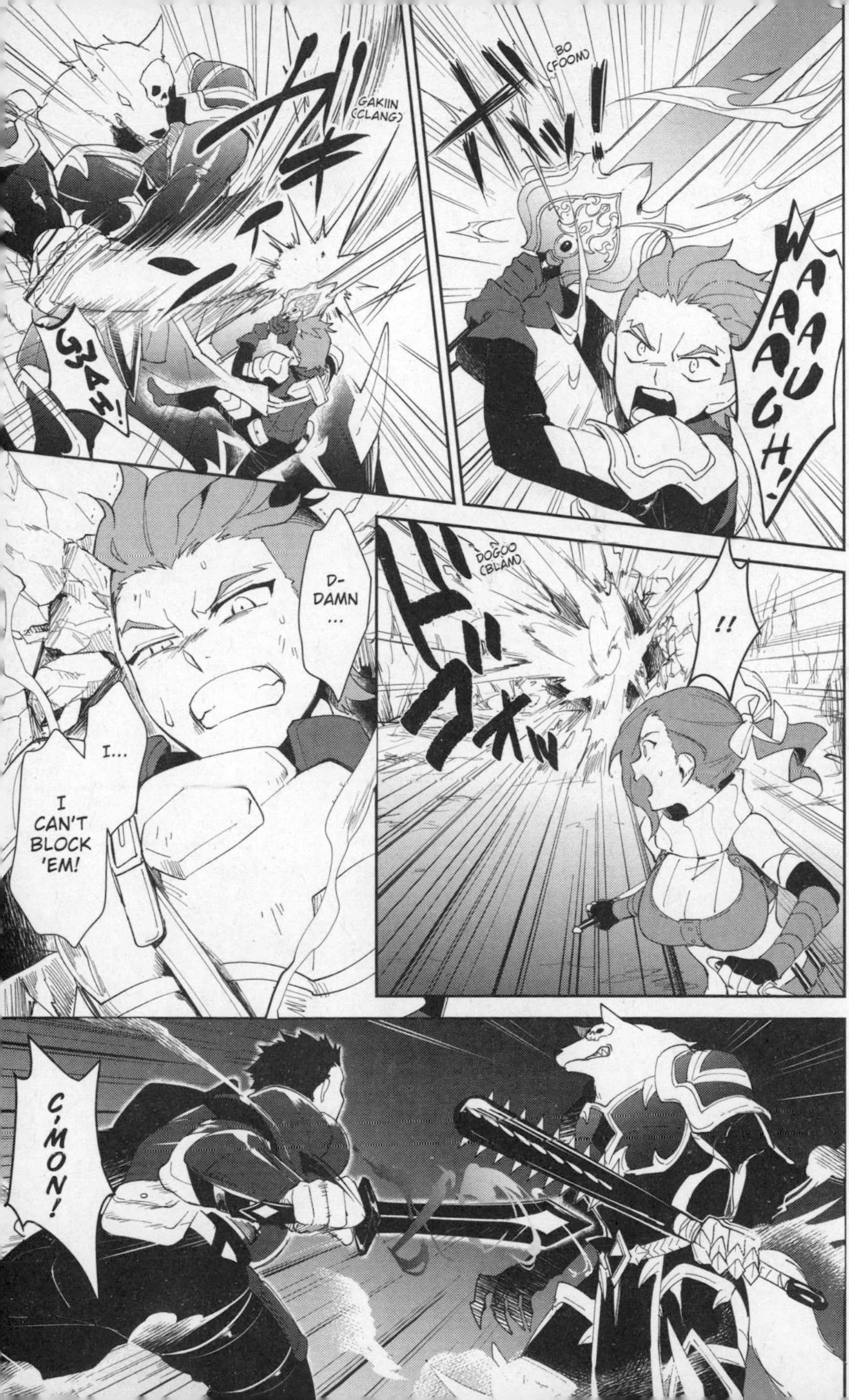
BO
(FOOM)
WAAAAAUGH!
GAKIIN
(CLANG)
GUAH!
DOGOO
(BLAM)
!!
D-DAMN...
I...
I CAN'T BLOCK 'EM!
C'MON!

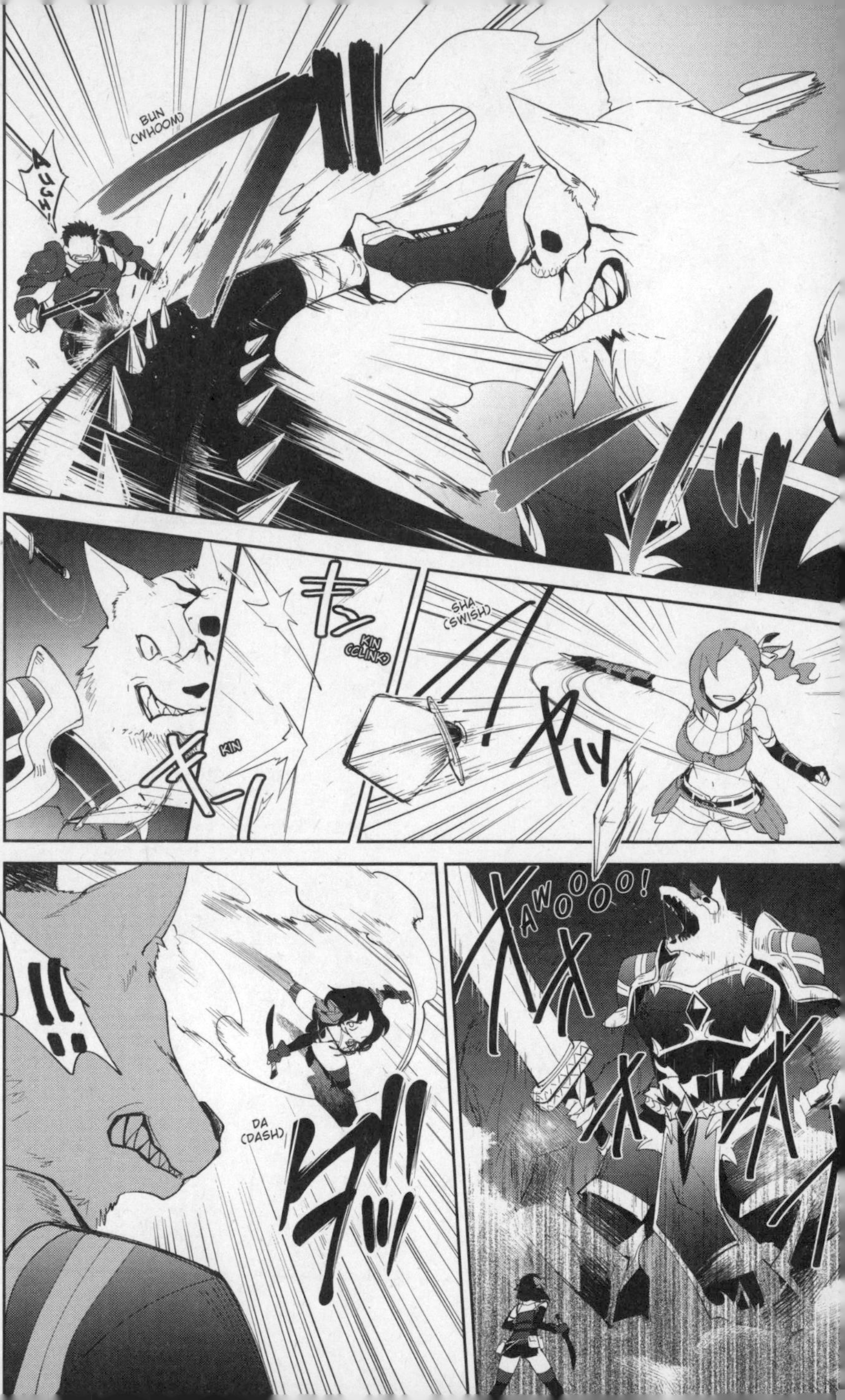
BUN (WHOOM)
AUGH!
SHA (SWISH)
KIN (CLINK)
KIN
AWOOOOO!
DA (DASH)

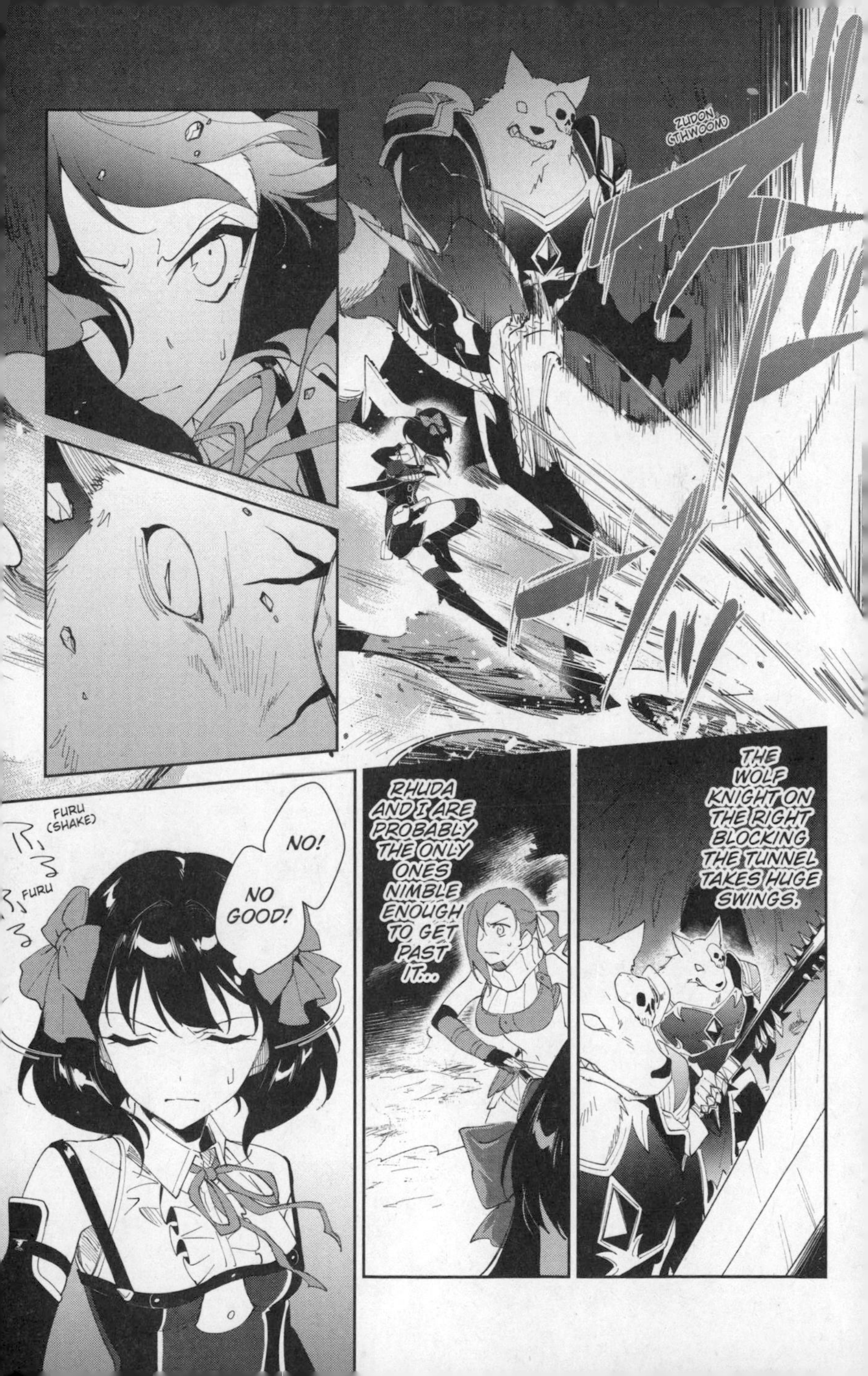
ZUDON (THWOOM)
THE WOLF KNIGHT ON THE RIGHT BLOCKING THE TUNNEL TAKES HUGE SWINGS.
RHUDA AND I ARE PROBABLY THE ONLY ONES NIMBLE ENOUGH TO GET PAST IT...
FURU (SHAKE)
FURU
NO!
NO GOOD!

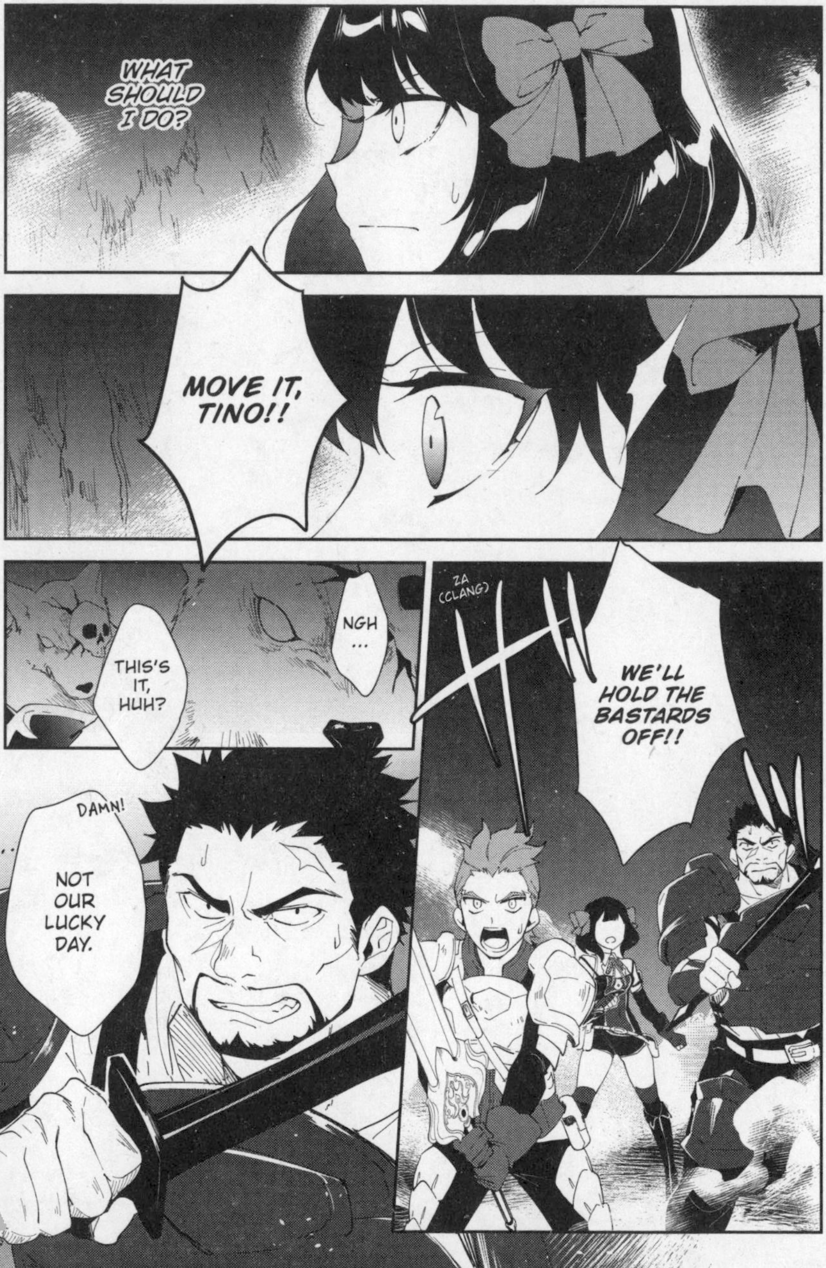
WHAT SHOULD I DO?
MOVE IT, TINO!!
ZA (CLANG)
WE'LL HOLD THE BASTARDS OFF!!
NGH...
THIS'S IT, HUH?
DAMN!
NOT OUR LUCKY DAY.

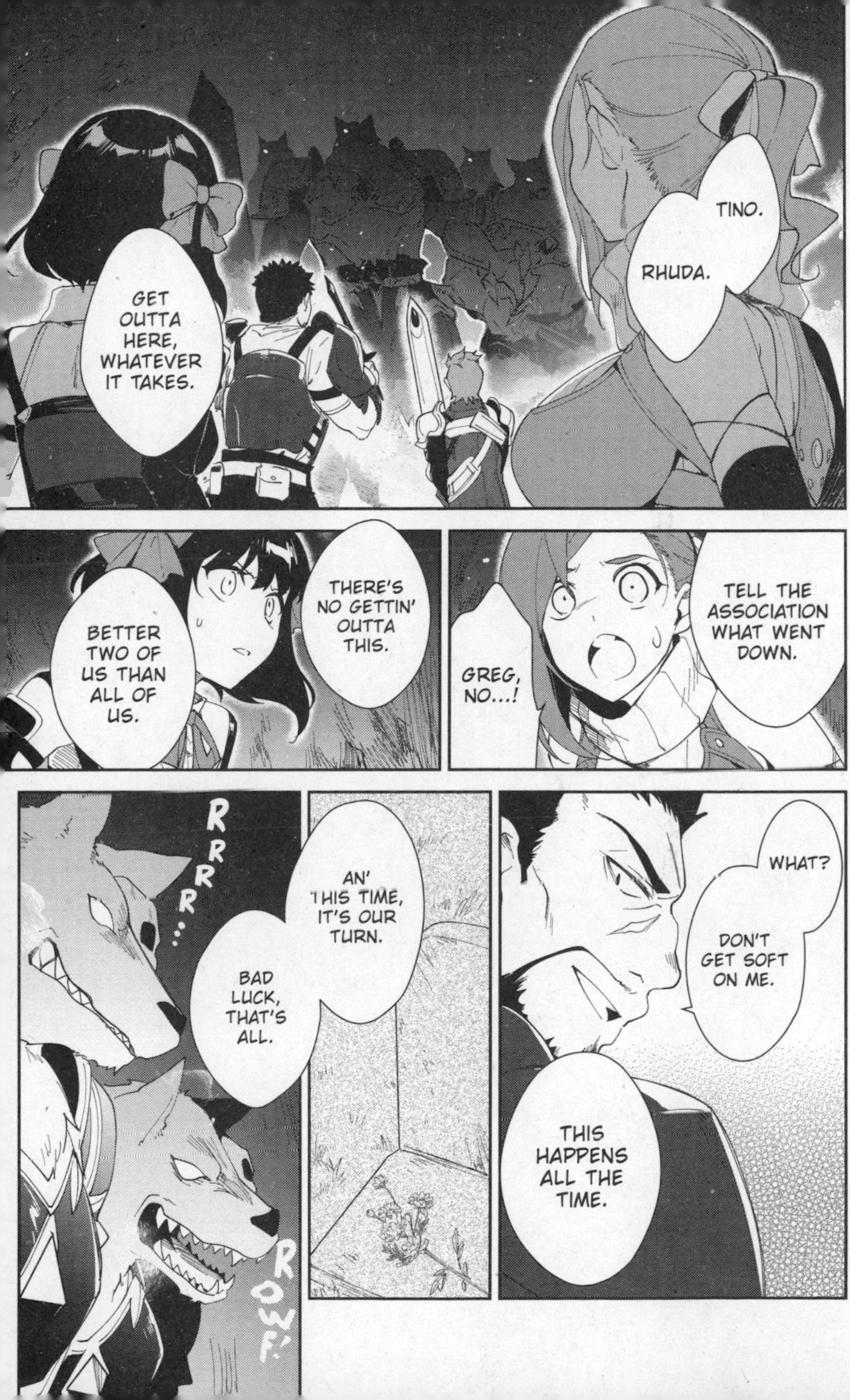
TINO.
RHUDA.
GET OUTTA HERE, WHATEVER IT TAKES.
TELL THE ASSOCIATION WHAT WENT DOWN.
GREG, NO...!
THERE'S NO GETTIN' OUTTA THIS.
BETTER TWO OF US THAN ALL OF US.
WHAT?
DON'T GET SOFT ON ME.
THIS HAPPENS ALL THE TIME.
AN' THIS TIME, IT'S OUR TURN.
BAD LUCK, THAT'S ALL.
RRRR...
ROWF!

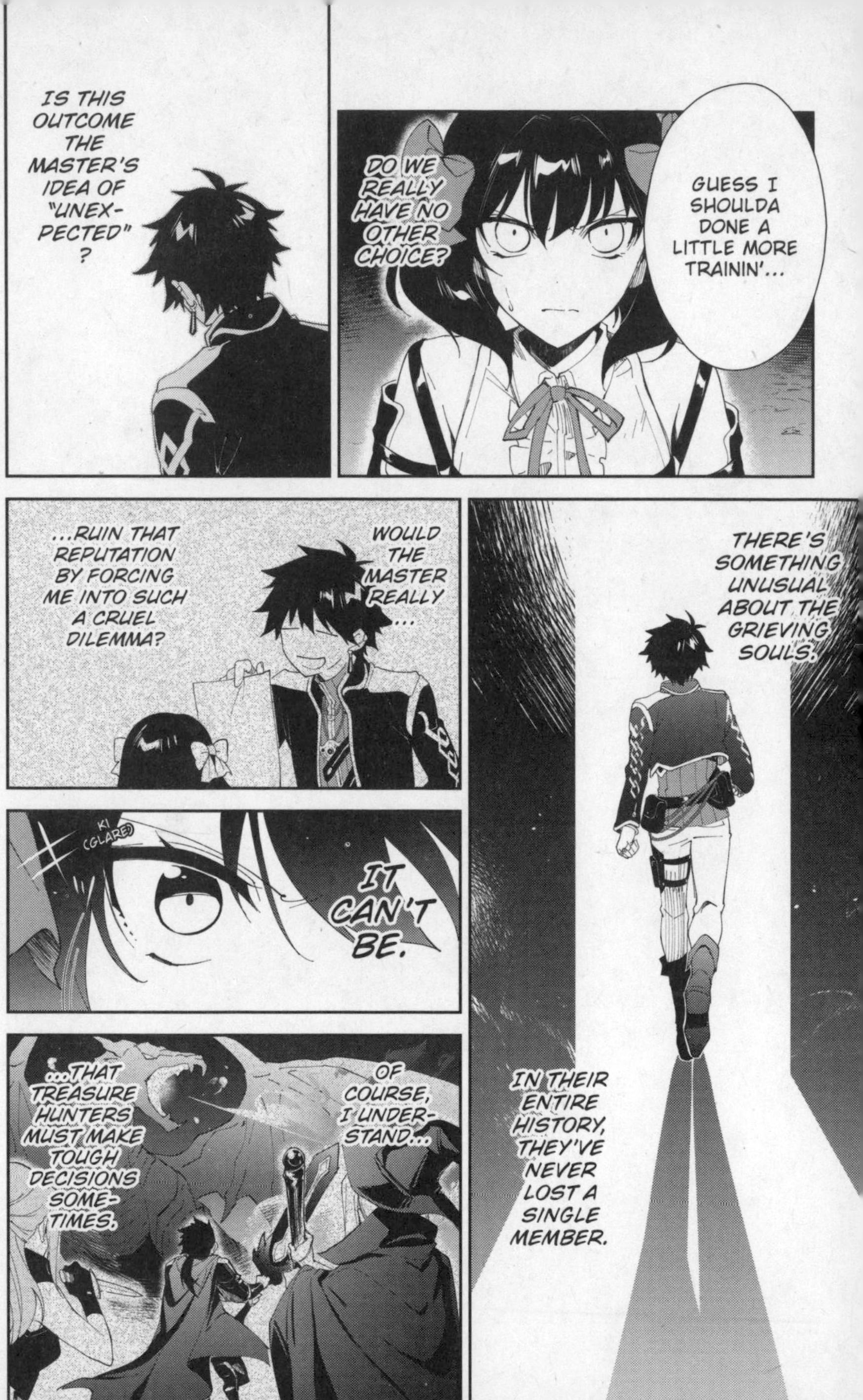
GUESS I SHOULDA DONE A LITTLE MORE TRAININ'...
DO WE REALLY HAVE NO OTHER CHOICE?
IS THIS OUTCOME THE MASTER'S IDEA OF "UNEXPECTED"?
THERE'S SOMETHING UNUSUAL ABOUT THE GRIEVING SOULS.
IN THEIR ENTIRE HISTORY, THEY'VE NEVER LOST A SINGLE MEMBER.
WOULD THE MASTER REALLY...
...RUIN THAT REPUTATION BY FORCING ME INTO SUCH A CRUEL DILEMMA?
KI (GLARE)
IT CAN'T BE.
OF COURSE, I UNDERSTAND...
...THAT TREASURE HUNTERS MUST MAKE TOUGH DECISIONS SOMETIMES.

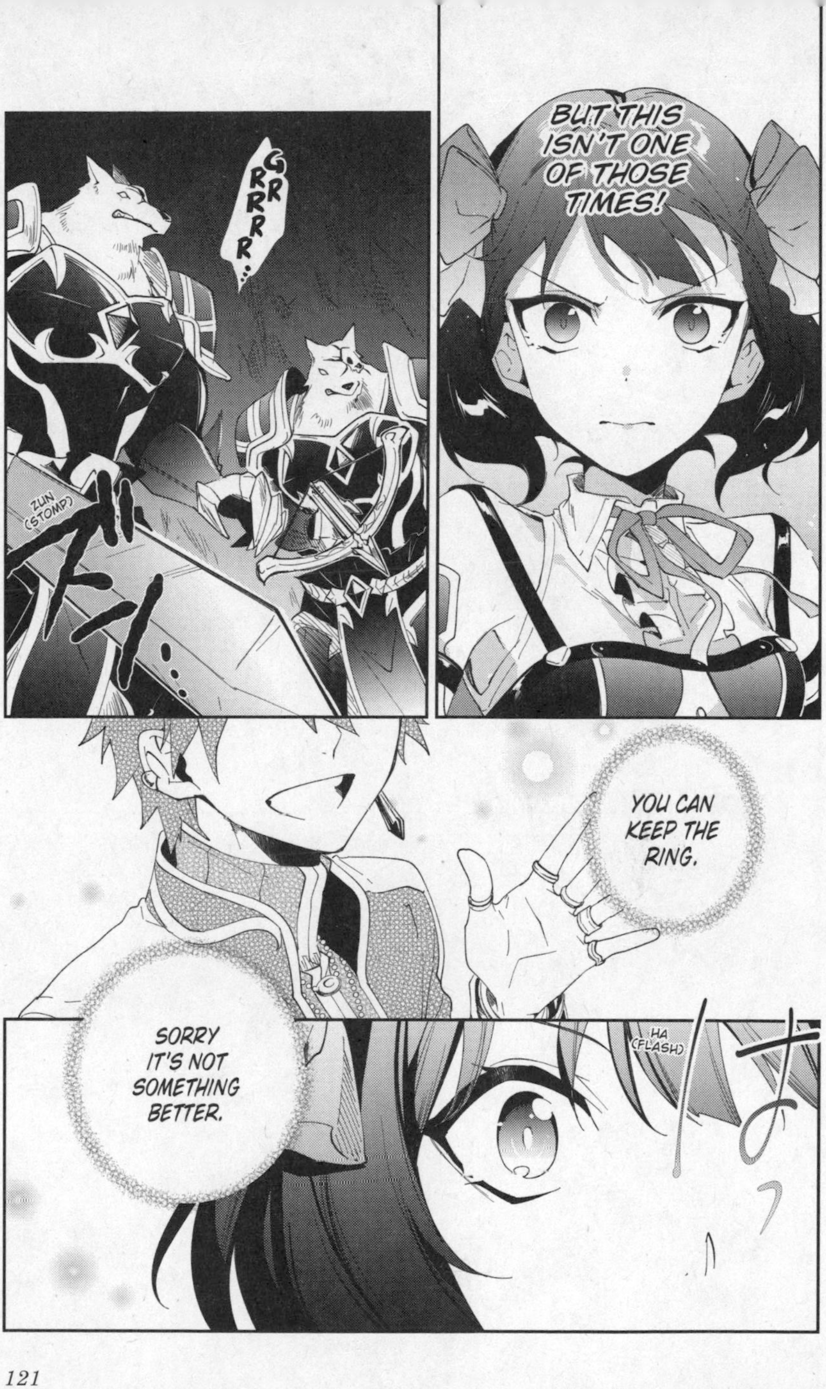
BUT THIS ISN'T ONE OF THOSE TIMES!
GRRRRR...
ZUN (STOMP)
YOU CAN KEEP THE RING.
SORRY IT'S NOT SOMETHING BETTER.
HA (FLASH)

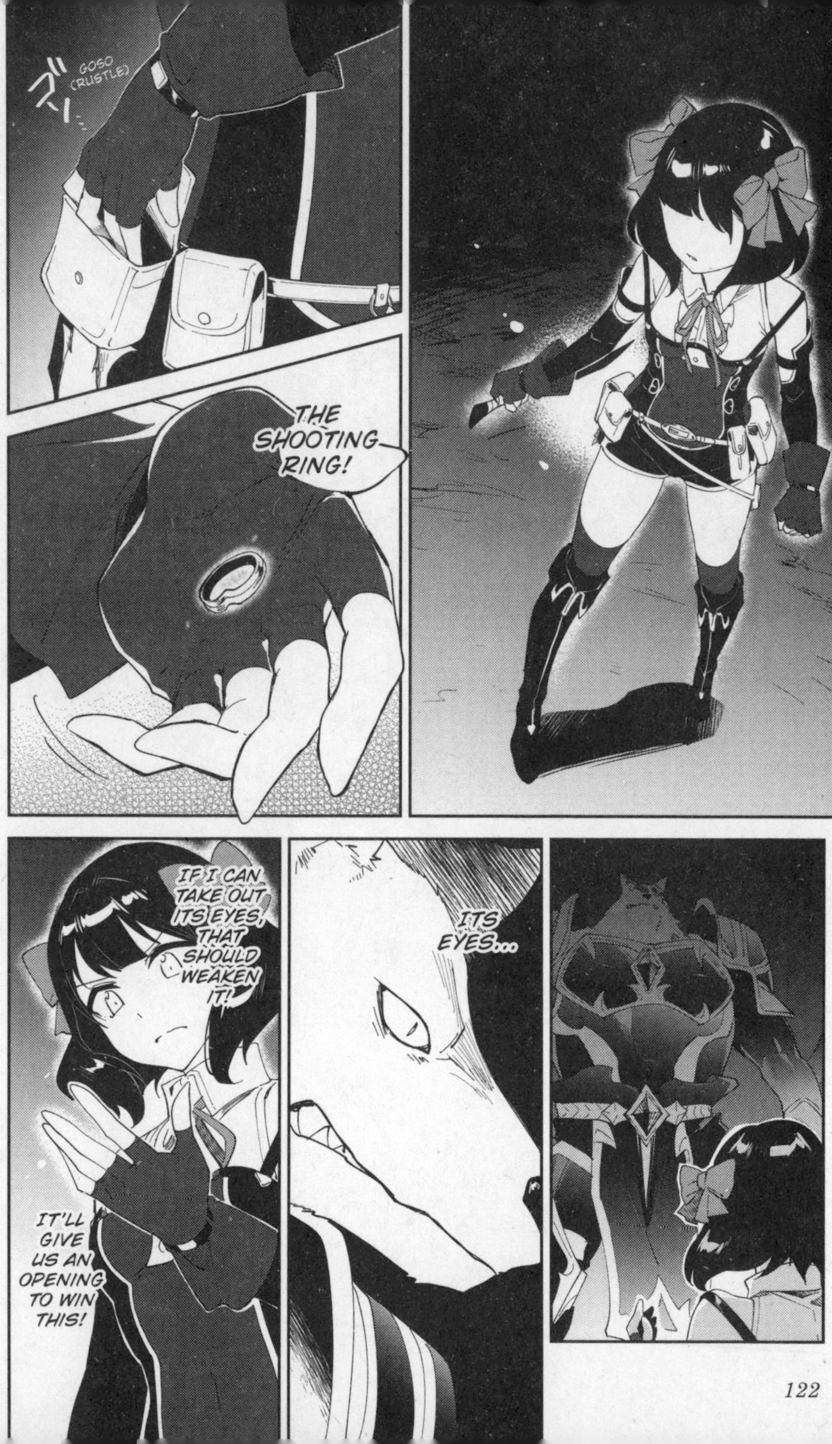
GOSO (RUSTLE)
THE SHOOTING RING!
ITS EYES...
IF I CAN TAKE OUT ITS EYES, THAT SHOULD WEAKEN IT!
IT'LL GIVE US AN OPENING TO WIN THIS!

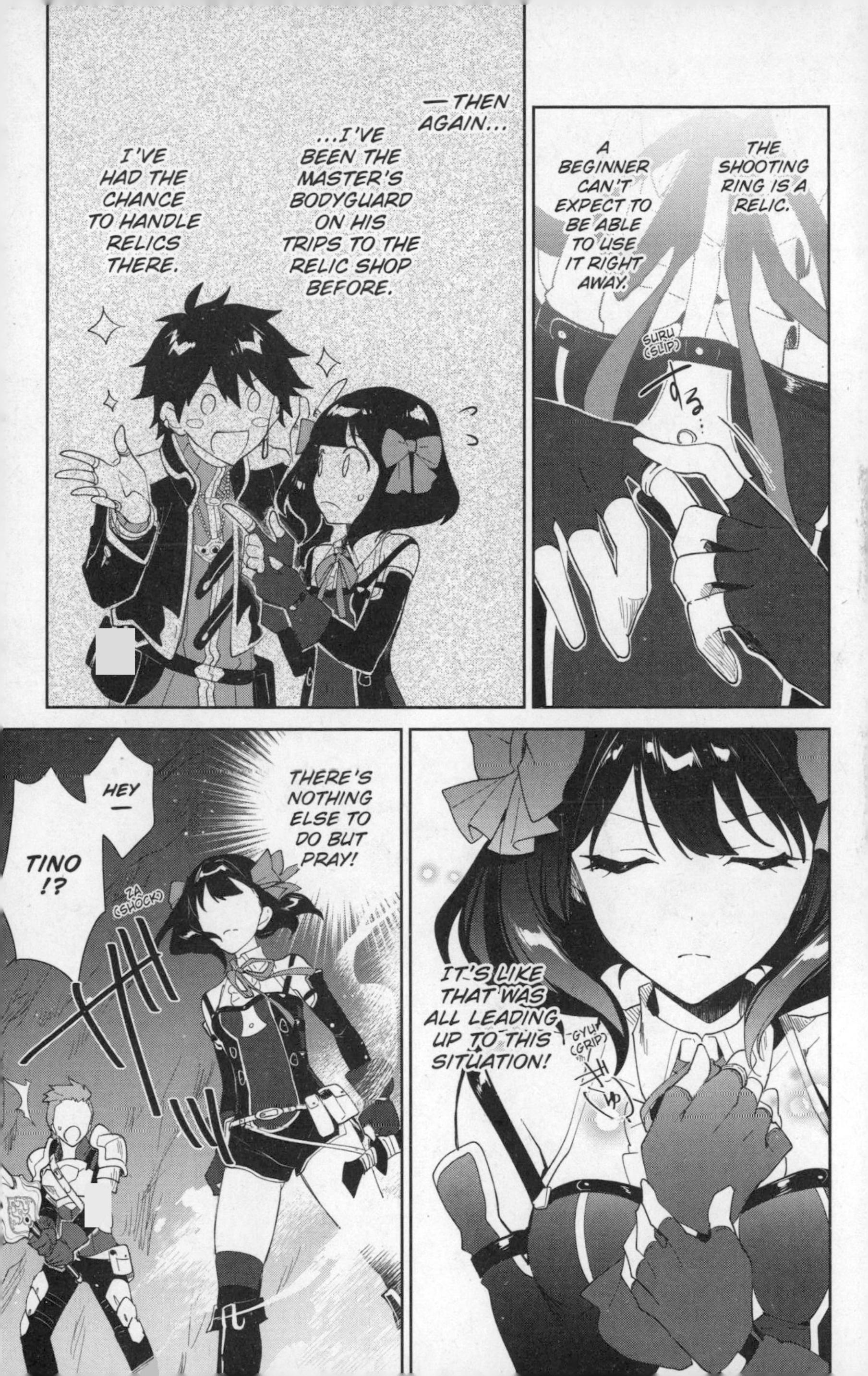
THE SHOOTING RING IS A RELIC.
A BEGINNER CAN'T EXPECT TO BE ABLE TO USE IT RIGHT AWAY.
SURU (SLIP)
—THEN AGAIN...
...I'VE BEEN THE MASTER'S BODYGUARD ON HIS TRIPS TO THE RELIC SHOP BEFORE.
I'VE HAD THE CHANCE TO HANDLE RELICS THERE.
IT'S LIKE THAT WAS ALL LEADING UP TO THIS SITUATION!
GYU (GRIP)
THERE'S NOTHING ELSE TO DO BUT PRAY!
HEY—
TINO!?
ZA (SHOCK)

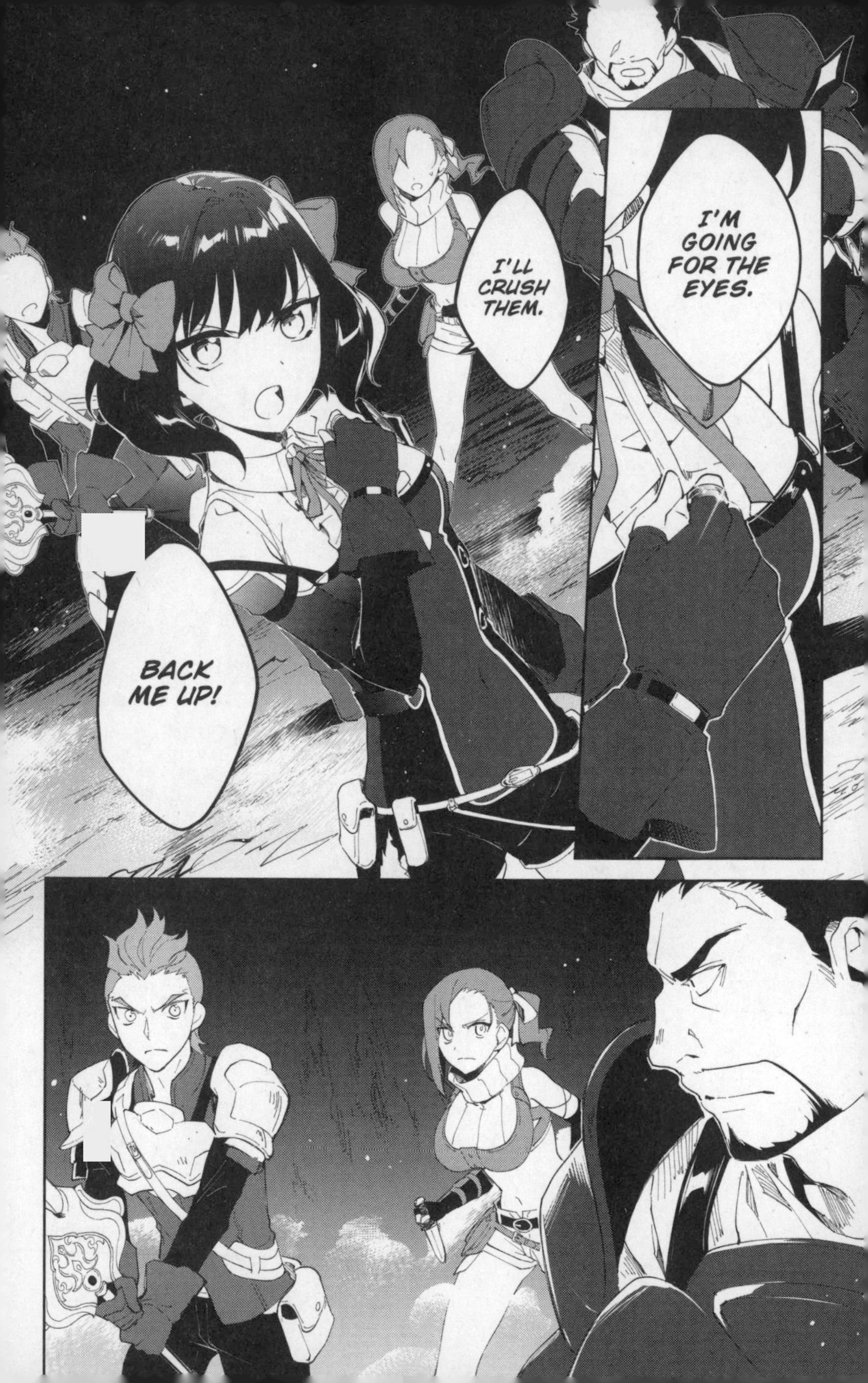
I'M GOING FOR THE EYES.
I'LL CRUSH THEM.
BACK ME UP!

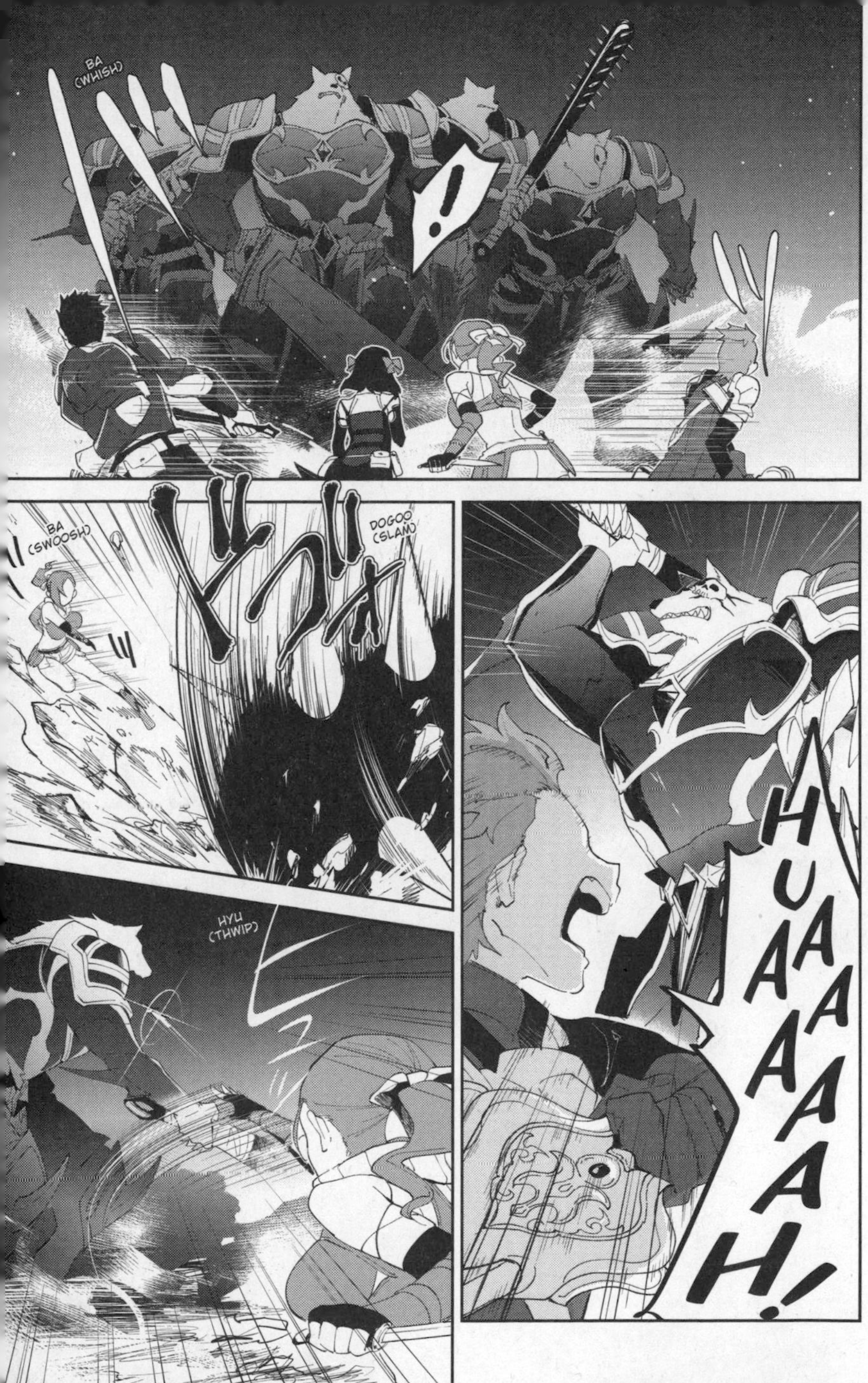
BA
(WHISH)
!
HUAAAAAAH!
DOGOO
(SLAM)
BA
(SWOOSH)
HYU
(THWIP)

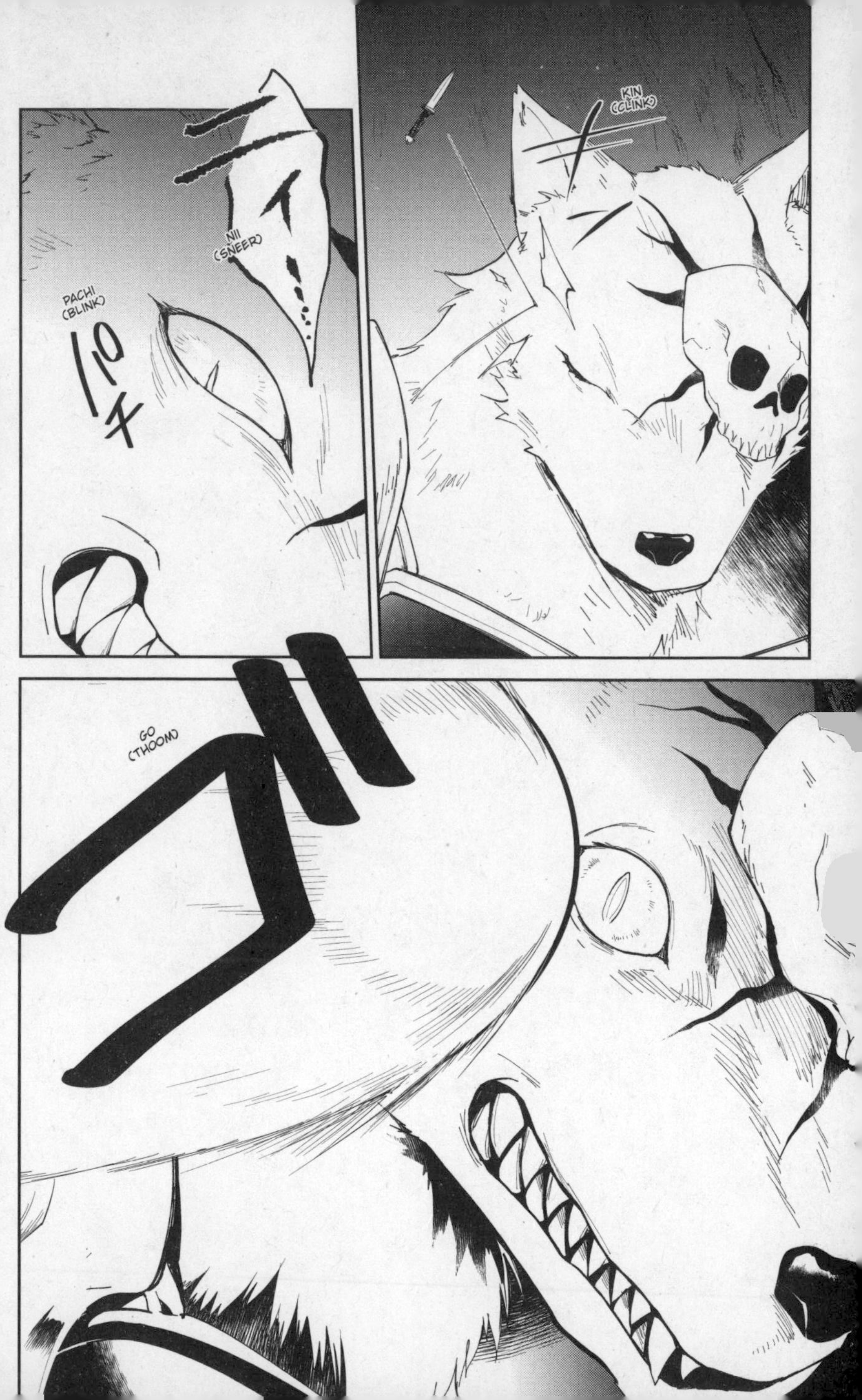
KIN (CLINK)
NII (SNEER)
PACHI (BLINK)
GO (THOOM)

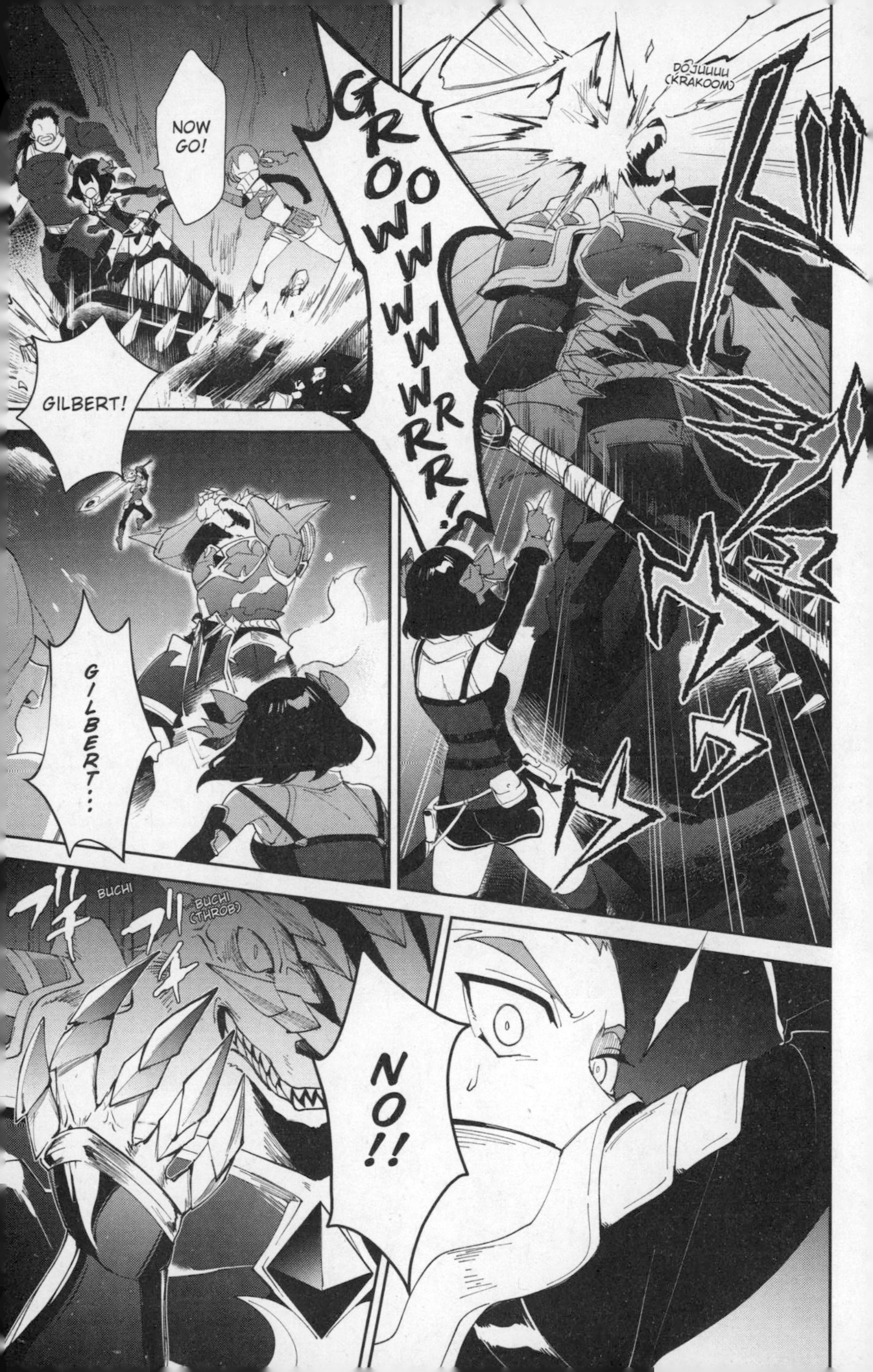
DOJUUUU (KRAKOOM)
GROOWWWWWRRR!
NOW GO!
GILBERT!
GILBERT...
NO!!
BUCHI
BUCHI (THROB)

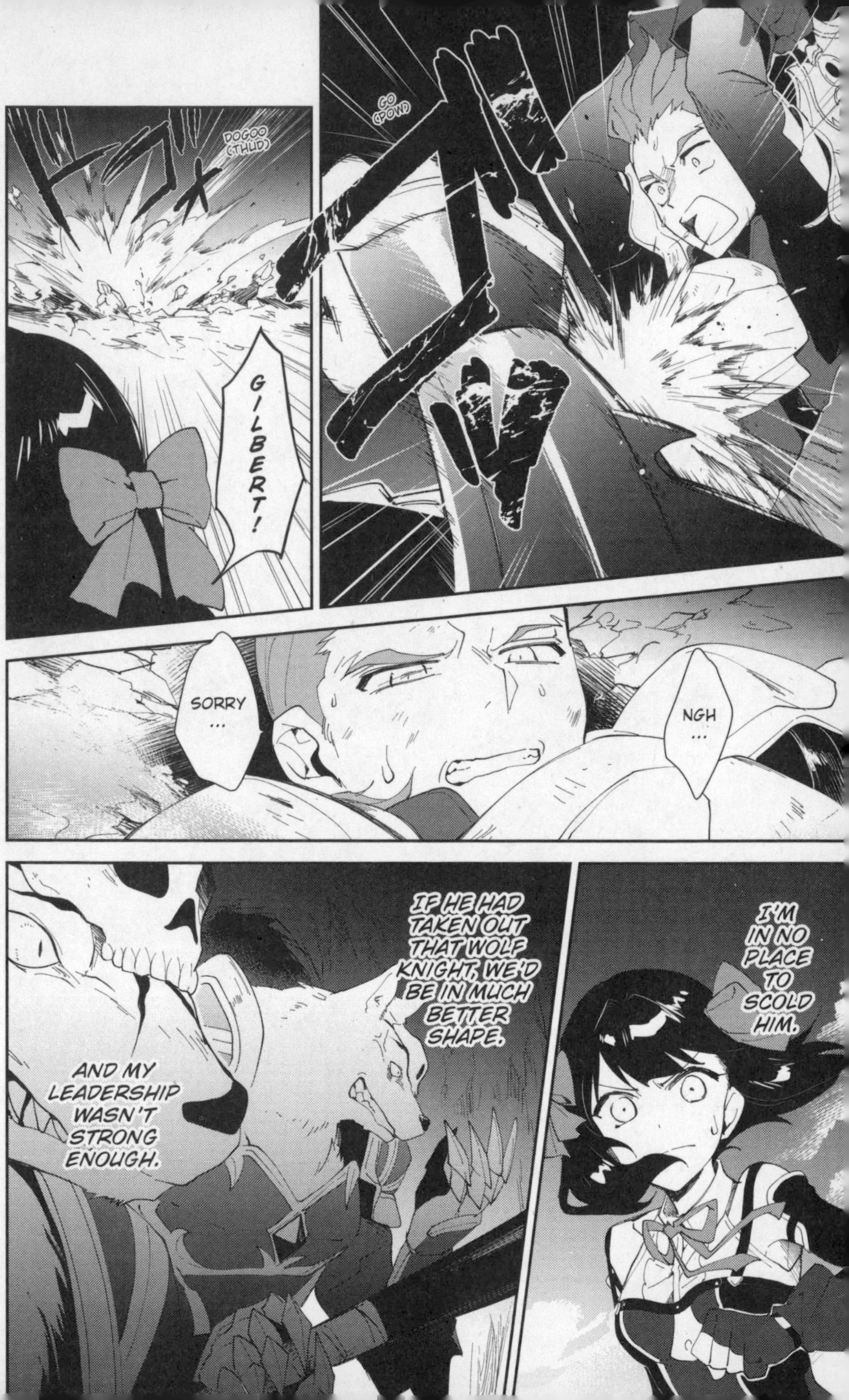
GO (POW)
DOGOO (THUD)
GILBERT!
NGH...
SORRY...
I'M IN NO PLACE TO SCOLD HIM.
IF HE HAD TAKEN OUT THAT WOLF KNIGHT, WE'D BE IN MUCH BETTER SHAPE.
AND MY LEADERSHIP WASN'T STRONG ENOUGH.

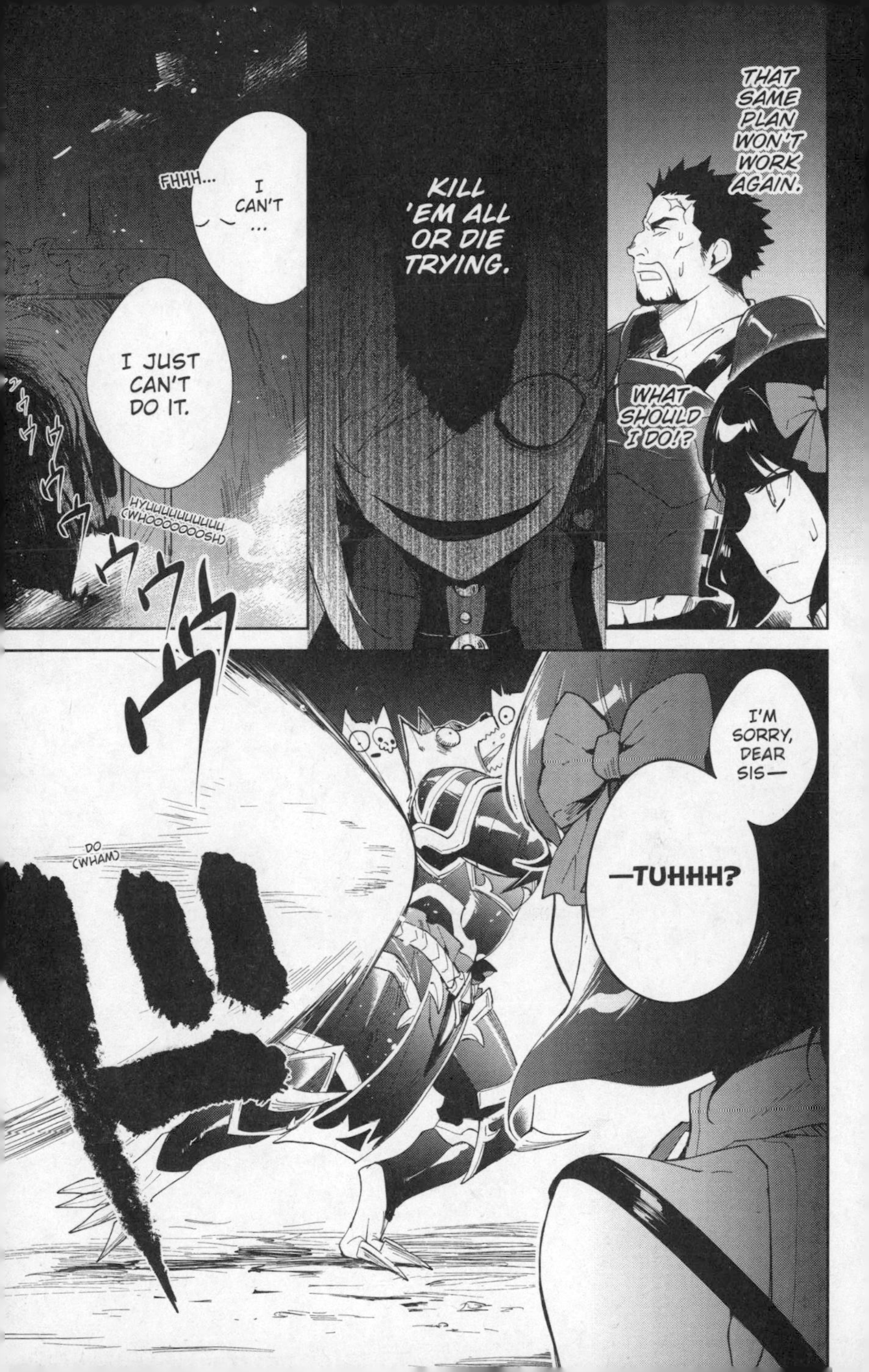
THAT SAME PLAN WON'T WORK AGAIN.
WHAT SHOULD I DO!?
KILL 'EM ALL OR DIE TRYING.
FHHH...
I CAN'T ...
I JUST CAN'T DO IT.
HYUUUUUUUUUU (WHOOOOOOOSH)
I'M SORRY, DEAR SIS—
—TUHHH?
DO (WHAM)

LET THIS
Grieving Soul
Retire

WOE IS THE WEAKLING WHO LEADS THE STRONGEST PARTY

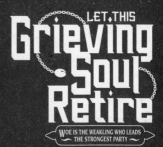

Chapter 10

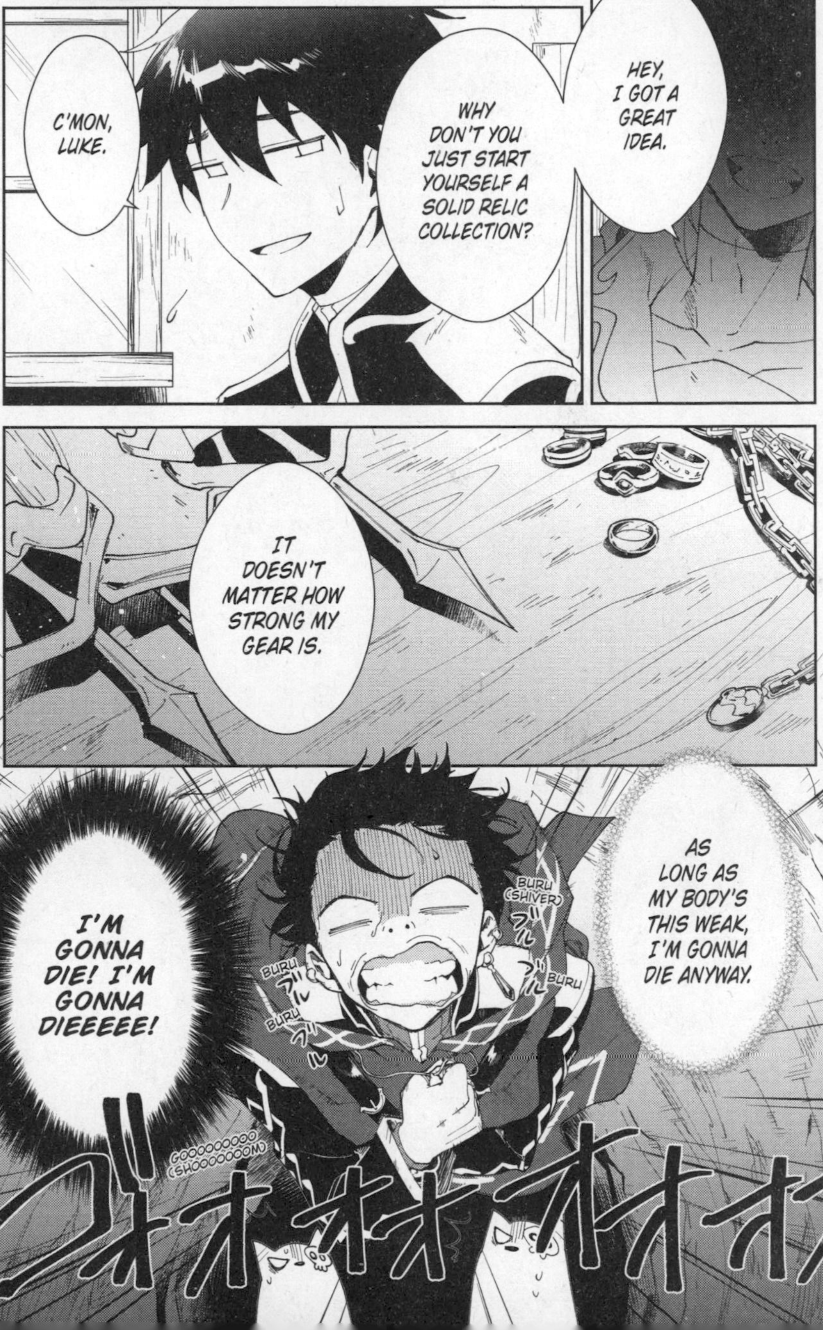
HEY, I GOT A GREAT IDEA.
WHY DON'T YOU JUST START YOURSELF A SOLID RELIC COLLECTION?
C'MON, LUKE.
IT DOESN'T MATTER HOW STRONG MY GEAR IS.
AS LONG AS MY BODY'S THIS WEAK, I'M GONNA DIE ANYWAY.
BURU (SHIVER)
BURU
BURU
BURU
I'M GONNA DIE! I'M GONNA DIEEEEEE!
GOOOOOOOOO (SHOOOOOOOOM)

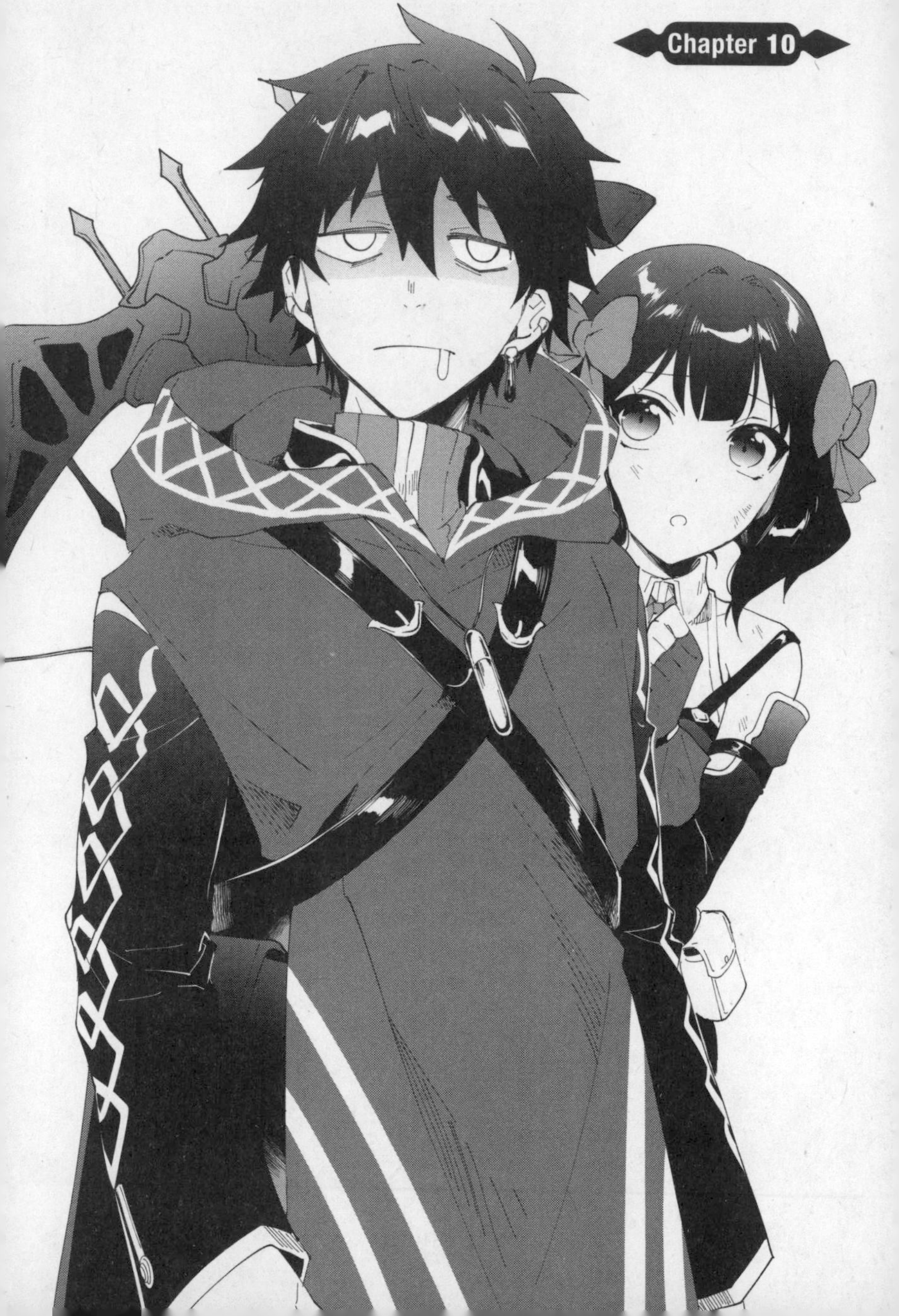
Chapter 10

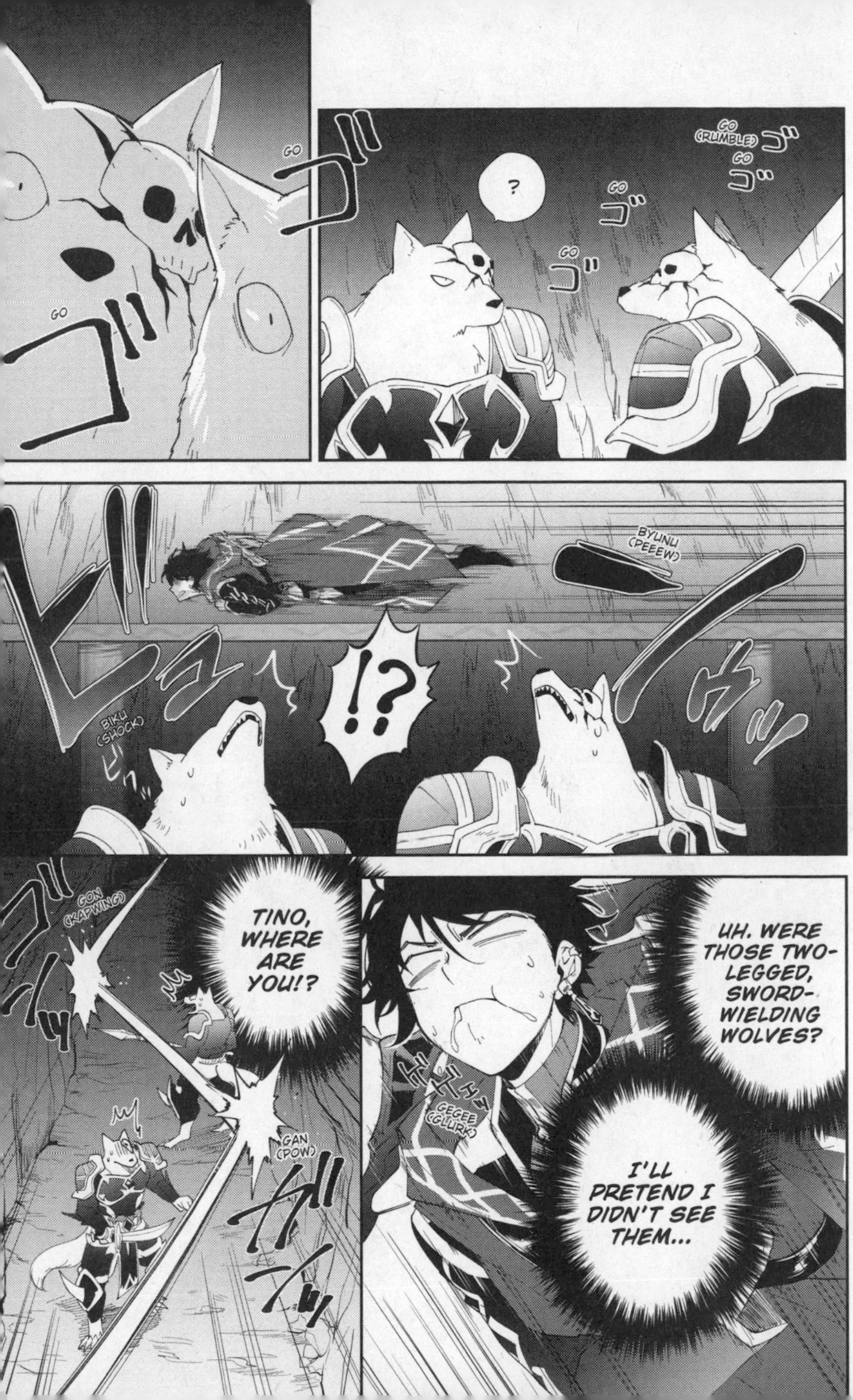
GO (RUMBLE)
GO
GO
GO
?
GO
GO
BYUNU (PEEEW)
!?
BIKU (SHOCK)
UH. WERE THOSE TWO-LEGGED, SWORD-WIELDING WOLVES?
GEGEE (GLURK)
I'LL PRETEND I DIDN'T SEE THEM...
GON (KAPWING)
TINO, WHERE ARE YOU!?
GAN (POW)

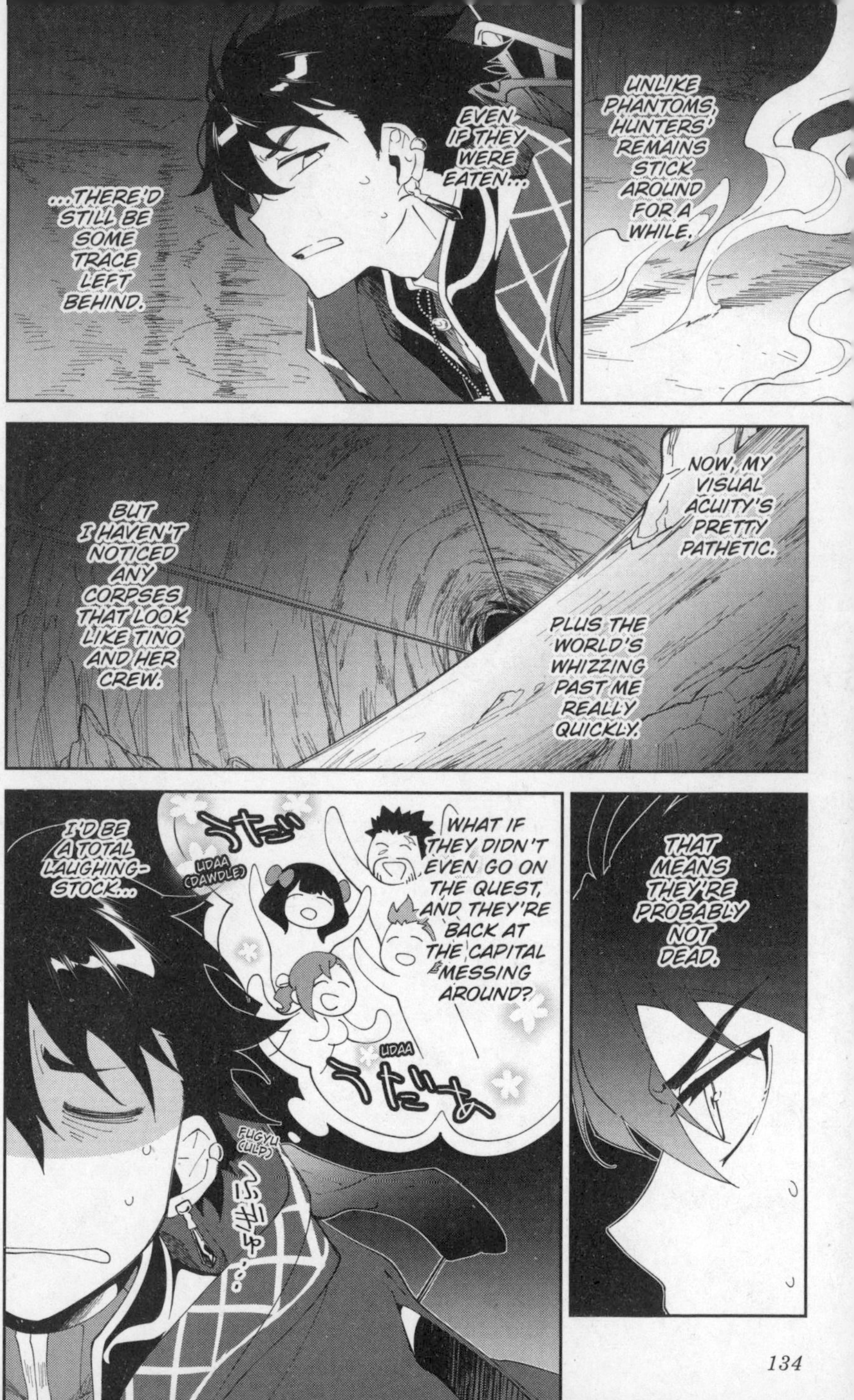
UNLIKE PHANTOMS, HUNTERS' REMAINS STICK AROUND FOR A WHILE.
EVEN IF THEY WERE EATEN...
...THERE'D STILL BE SOME TRACE LEFT BEHIND.
NOW, MY VISUAL ACUITY'S PRETTY PATHETIC.
PLUS THE WORLD'S WHIZZING PAST ME REALLY QUICKLY.
BUT I HAVEN'T NOTICED ANY CORPSES THAT LOOK LIKE TINO AND HER CREW.
THAT MEANS THEY'RE PROBABLY NOT DEAD.
WHAT IF THEY DIDN'T EVEN GO ON THE QUEST, AND THEY'RE BACK AT THE CAPITAL MESSING AROUND?
UDAA (DAWDLE)
I'D BE A TOTAL LAUGHING-STOCK...
UDAA
FUGYU (ULP)

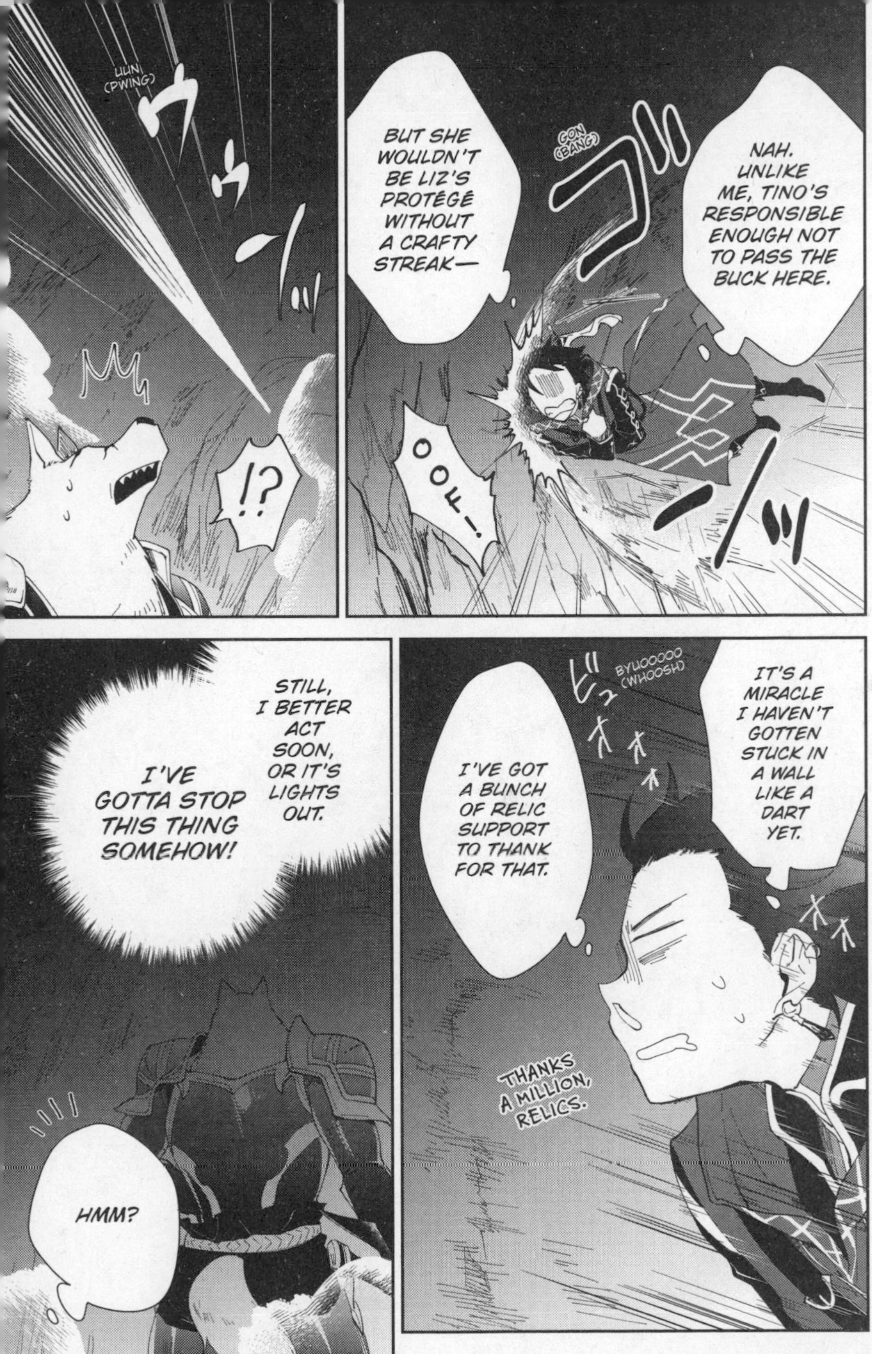
NAH. UNLIKE ME, TINO'S RESPONSIBLE ENOUGH NOT TO PASS THE BUCK HERE.
GON (BANG)
BUT SHE WOULDN'T BE LIZ'S PROTÉGÉ WITHOUT A CRAFTY STREAK—
OOF!
UUN (PWING)
!?
IT'S A MIRACLE I HAVEN'T GOTTEN STUCK IN A WALL LIKE A DART YET.
BYUOOOOO (WHOOSH)
I'VE GOT A BUNCH OF RELIC SUPPORT TO THANK FOR THAT.
THANKS A MILLION, RELICS.
STILL, I BETTER ACT SOON, OR IT'S LIGHTS OUT.
I'VE GOTTA STOP THIS THING SOMEHOW!
HMM?

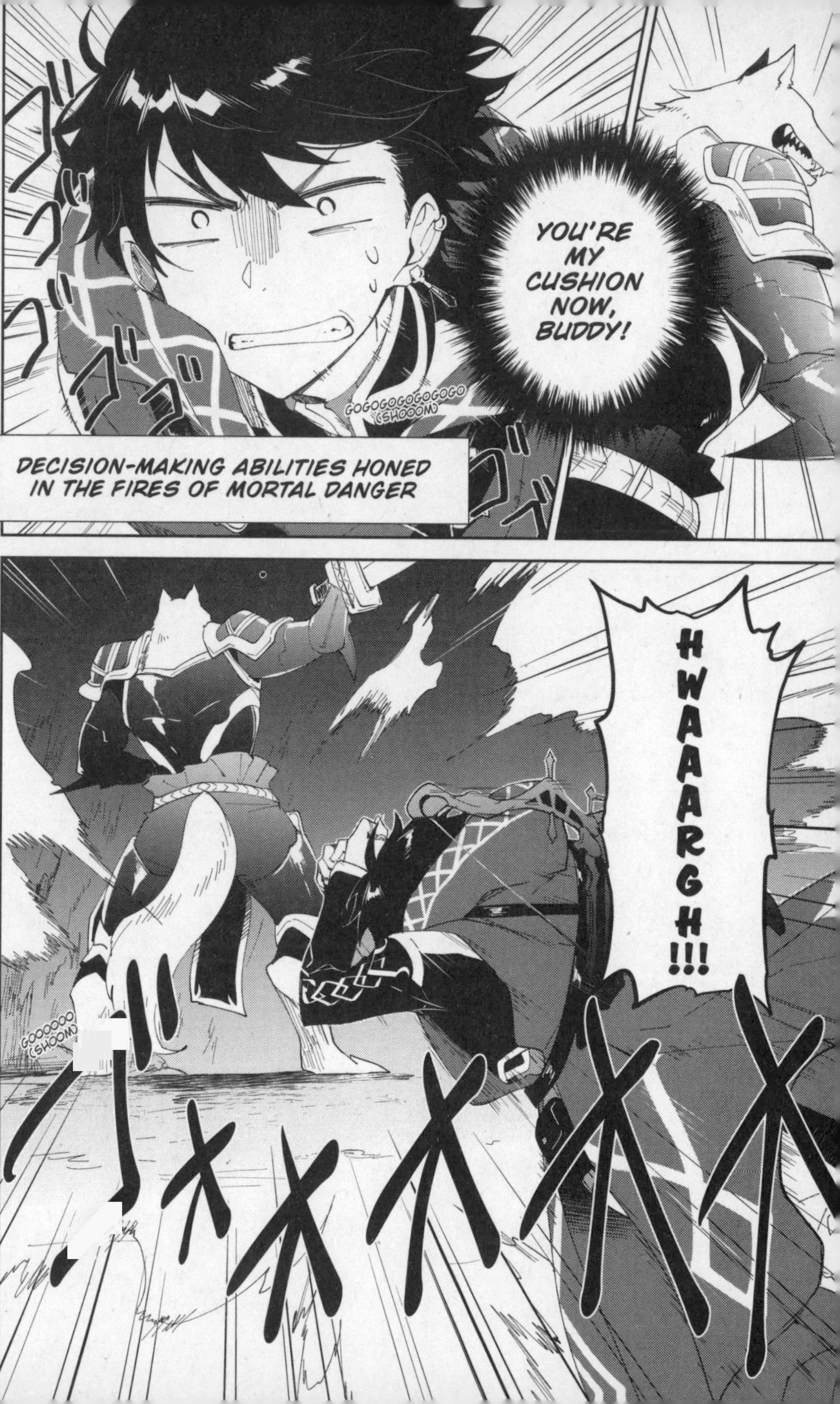
YOU'RE MY CUSHION NOW, BUDDY!
GOGOGOGOGOGOGO (SHOOOM)
DECISION-MAKING ABILITIES HONED IN THE FIRES OF MORTAL DANGER
HWAAARGH!!!
GOOOOOO (SHOOM)

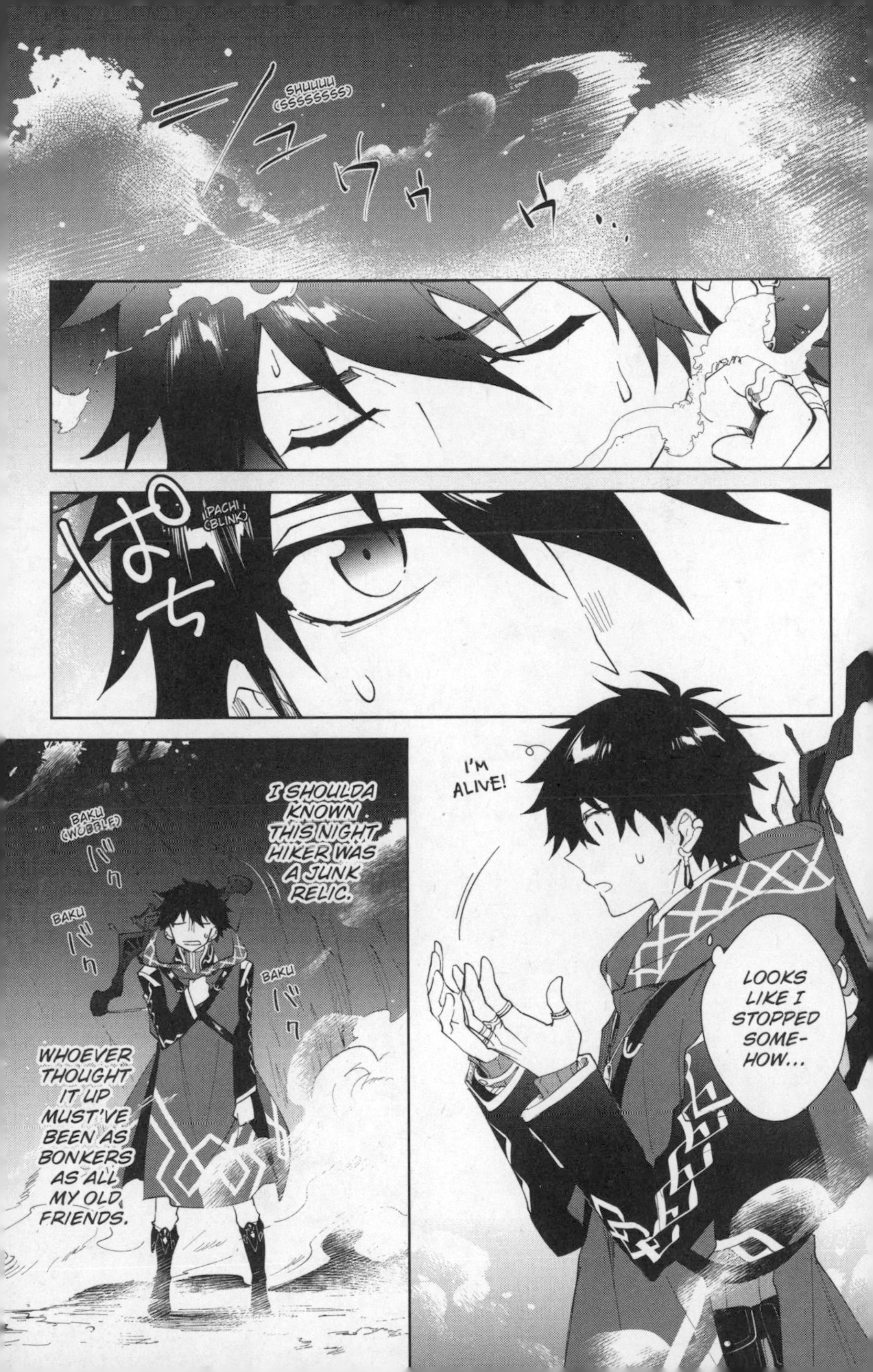
SHUUUU (SSSSSSSS)
PACHI (BLINK)
I'M ALIVE!
LOOKS LIKE I STOPPED SOME-HOW...
I SHOULDA KNOWN THIS NIGHT HIKER WAS A JUNK RELIC.
BAKU (WOBBLE)
BAKU
BAKU
WHOEVER THOUGHT IT UP MUST'VE BEEN AS BONKERS AS ALL MY OLD FRIENDS.

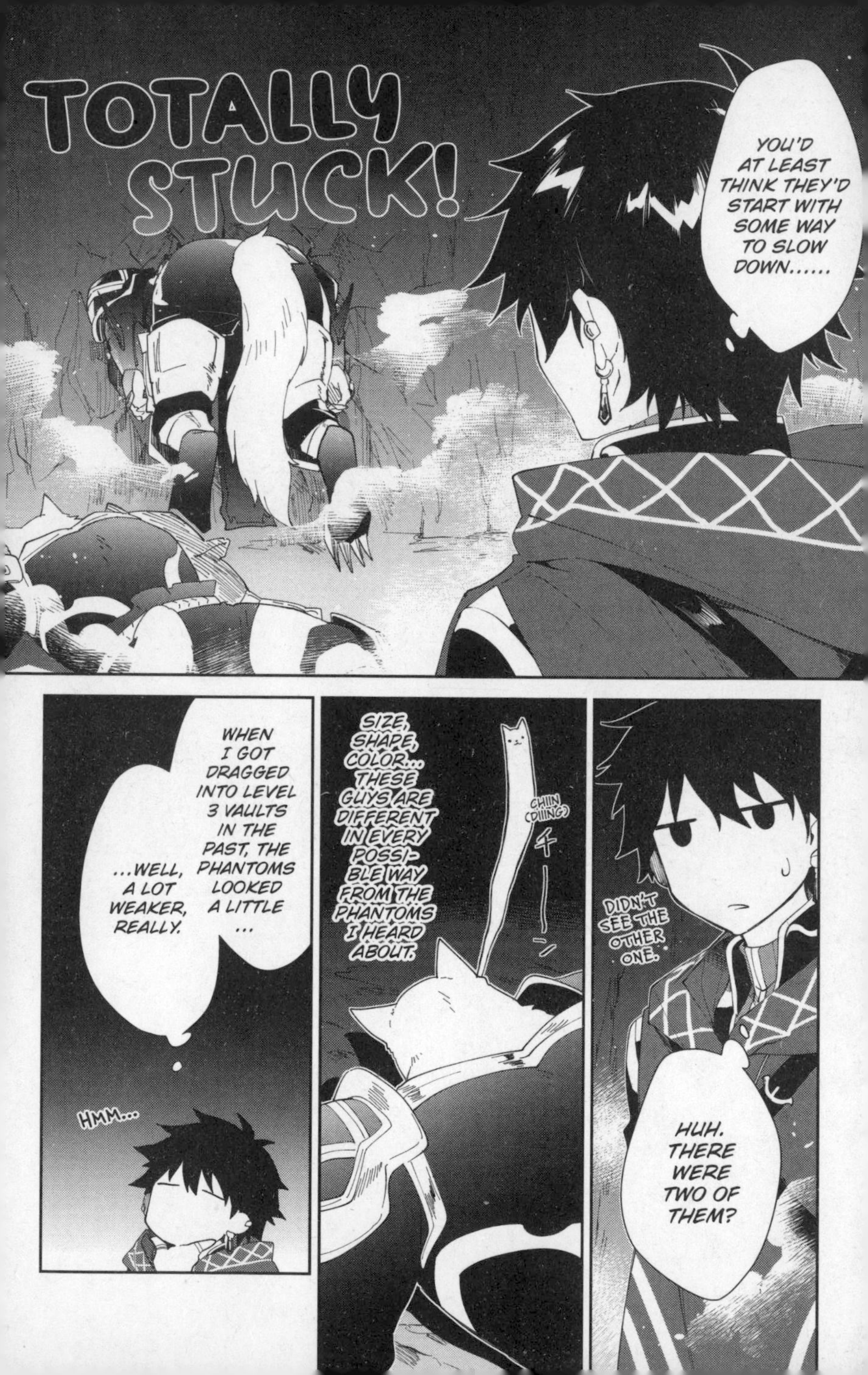
YOU'D AT LEAST THINK THEY'D START WITH SOME WAY TO SLOW DOWN......
TOTALLY STUCK!
DIDN'T SEE THE OTHER ONE.
HUH. THERE WERE TWO OF THEM?
SIZE, SHAPE, COLOR... THESE GUYS ARE DIFFERENT IN EVERY POSSI-BLE WAY FROM THE PHANTOMS I HEARD ABOUT.
CHIIN (DIIING)
WHEN I GOT DRAGGED INTO LEVEL 3 VAULTS IN THE PAST, THE PHANTOMS LOOKED A LITTLE ...
...WELL, A LOT WEAKER, REALLY.
HMM...

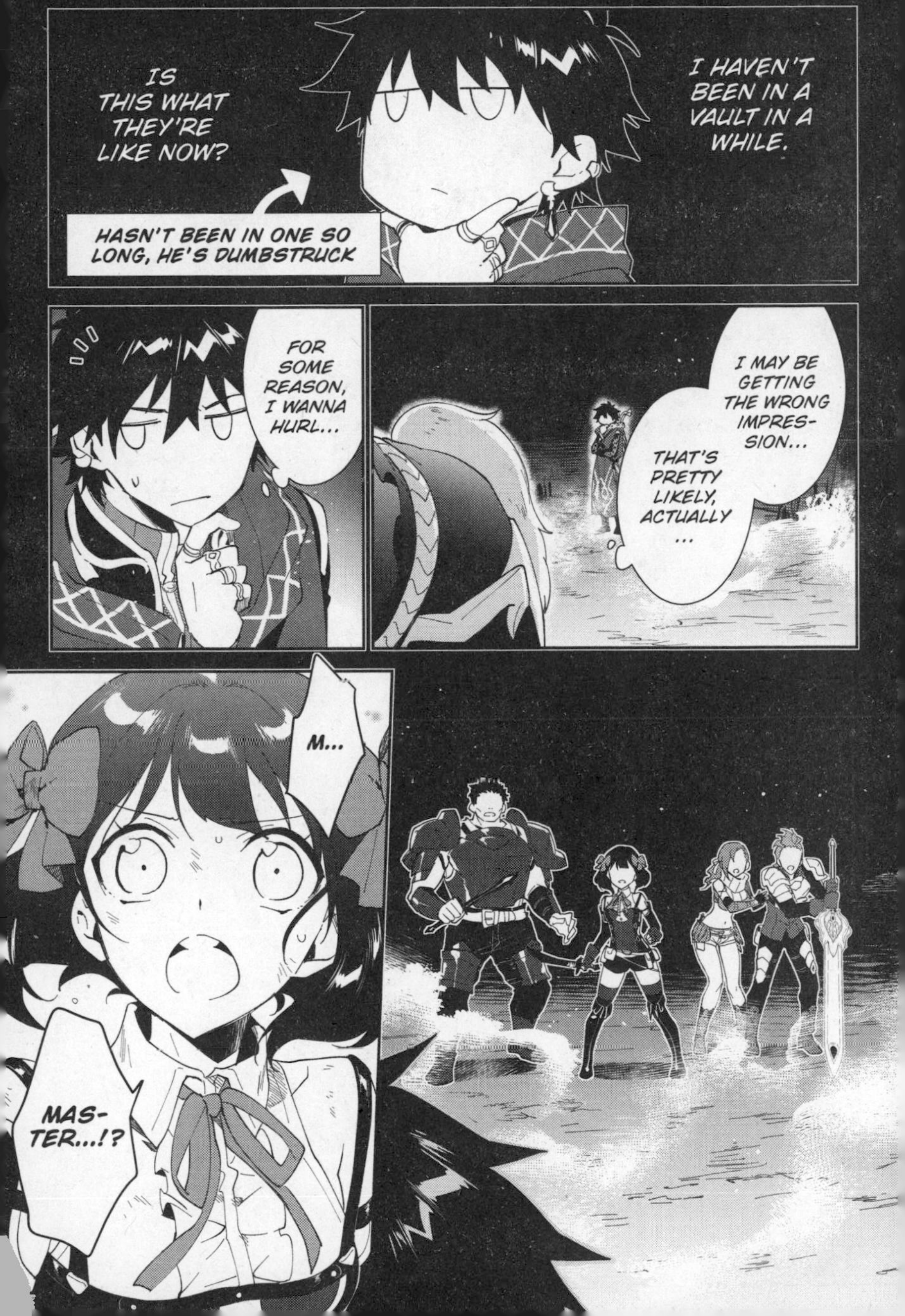
I HAVEN'T BEEN IN A VAULT IN A WHILE.
IS THIS WHAT THEY'RE LIKE NOW?
HASN'T BEEN IN ONE SO LONG, HE'S DUMBSTRUCK
I MAY BE GETTING THE WRONG IMPRES- SION...
THAT'S PRETTY LIKELY, ACTUALLY ...
FOR SOME REASON, I WANNA HURL...
M...
MAS- TER...!?

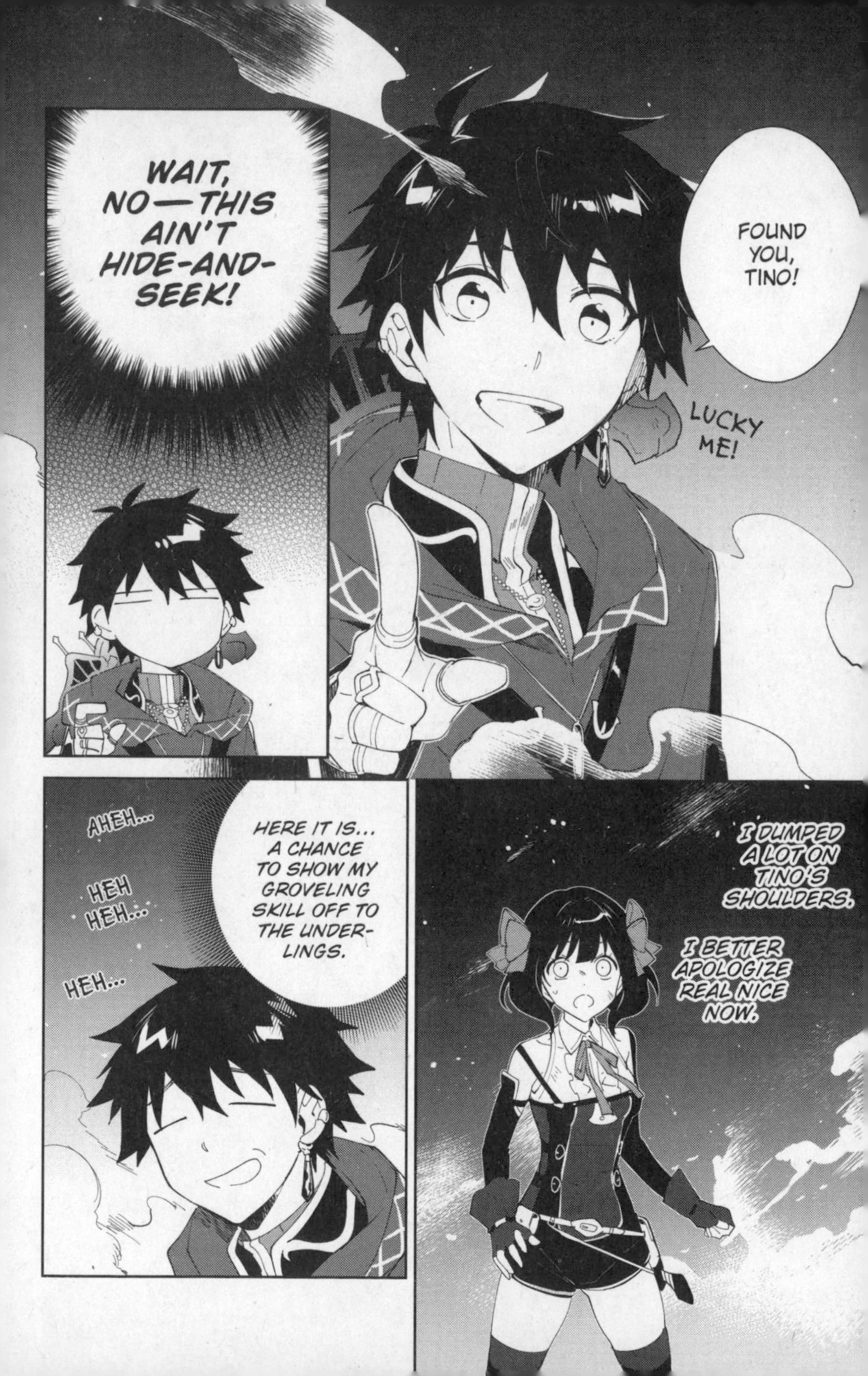
FOUND YOU, TINO!
LUCKY ME!
WAIT, NO—THIS AIN'T HIDE-AND-SEEK!
I DUMPED A LOT ON TINO'S SHOULDERS.
I BETTER APOLOGIZE REAL NICE NOW.
HERE IT IS... A CHANCE TO SHOW MY GROVELING SKILL OFF TO THE UNDER-LINGS.
AHEH...
HEH HEH...
HEH...

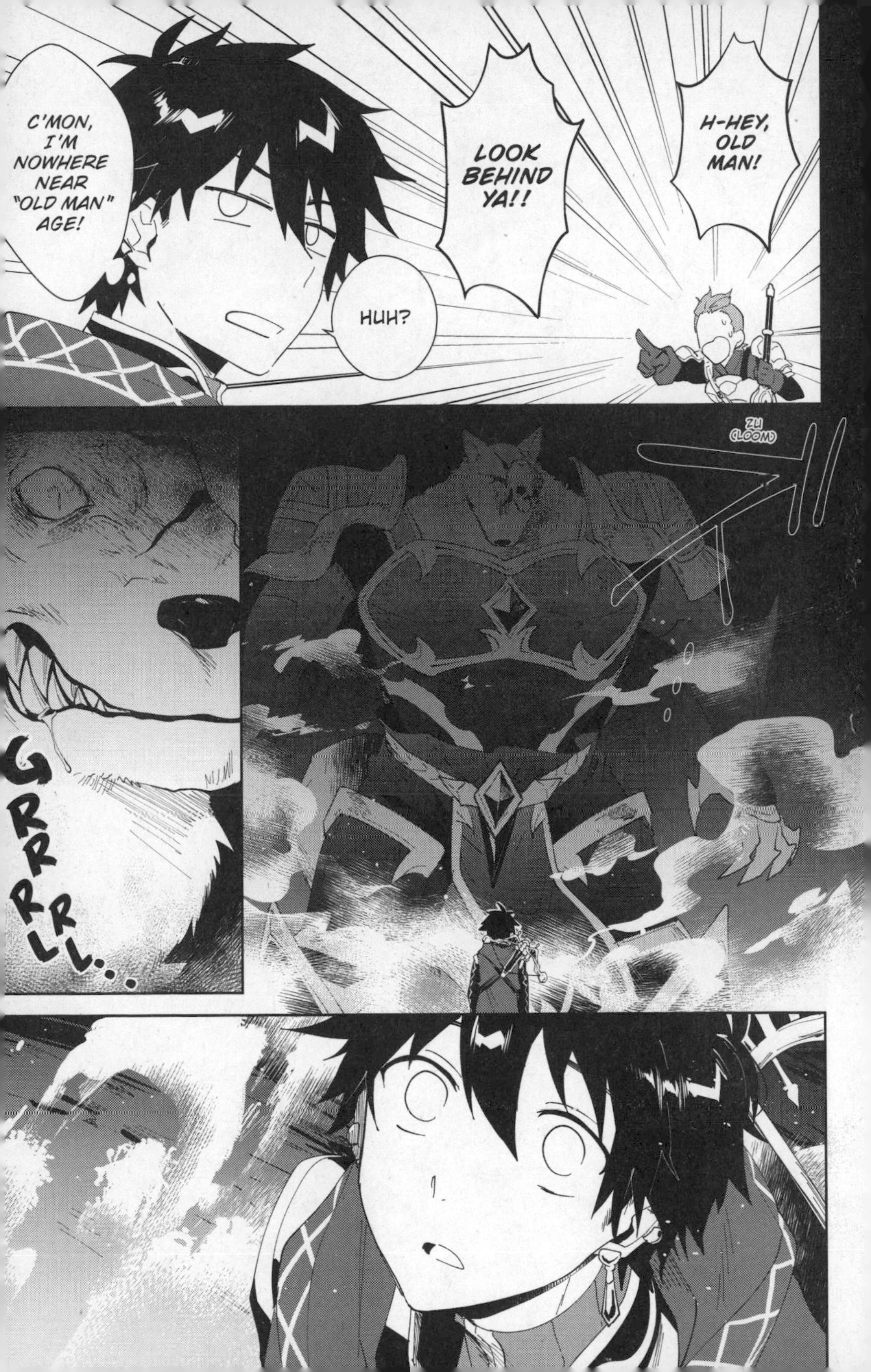
H-HEY, OLD MAN!
LOOK BEHIND YA!!
HUH?
C'MON, I'M NOWHERE NEAR "OLD MAN" AGE!
ZU (LOOM)
GRRRRRLL...

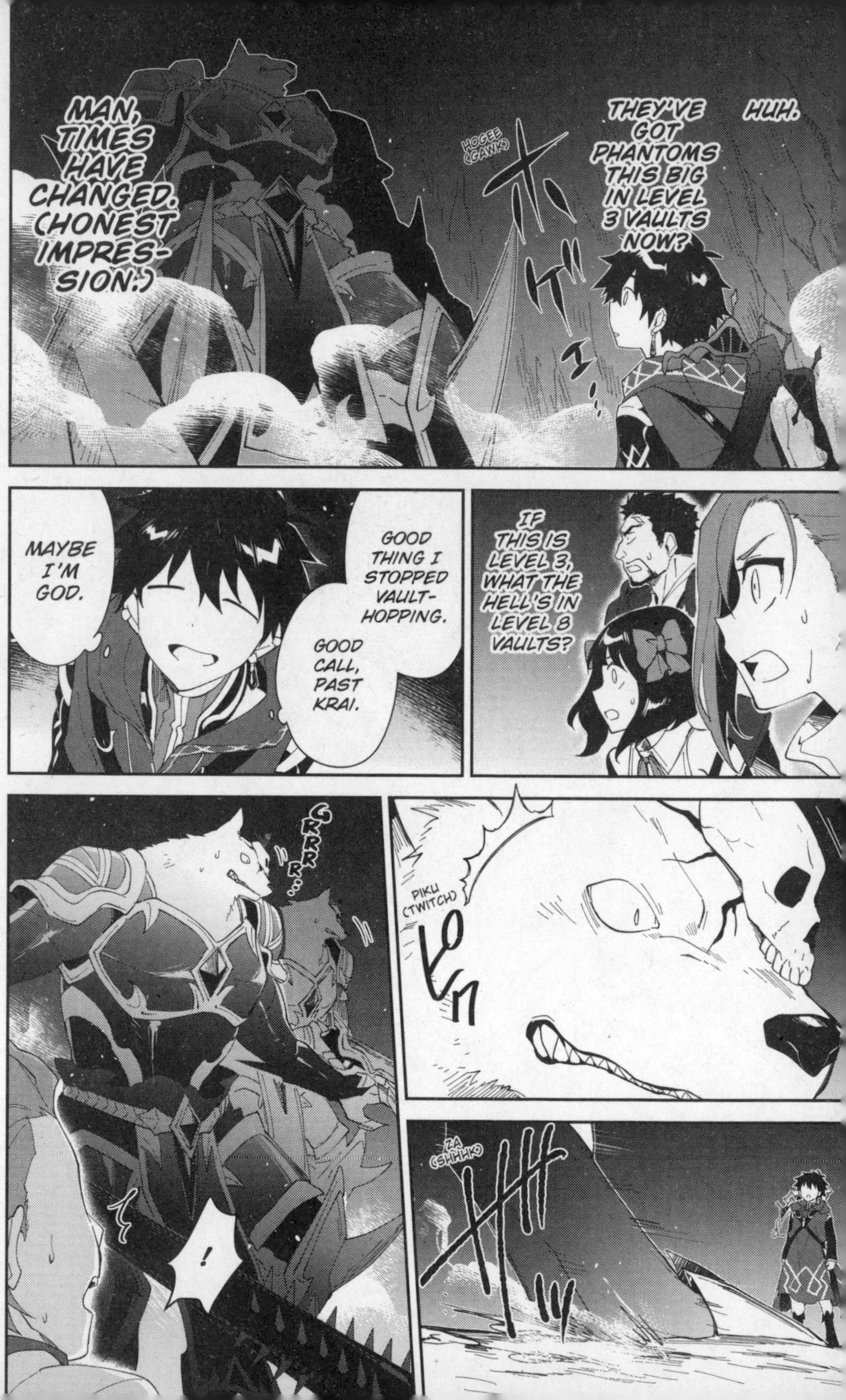
HUH.
THEY'VE GOT PHANTOMS THIS BIG IN LEVEL 3 VAULTS NOW?
HOGEE (GAWK)
MAN, TIMES HAVE CHANGED. (HONEST IMPRES-SION.)
IF THIS IS LEVEL 3, WHAT THE HELL'S IN LEVEL 8 VAULTS?
GOOD THING I STOPPED VAULT-HOPPING.
GOOD CALL, PAST KRAI.
MAYBE I'M GOD.
PIKU (TWITCH)
ZA (SHHHK)
GRRR...
!

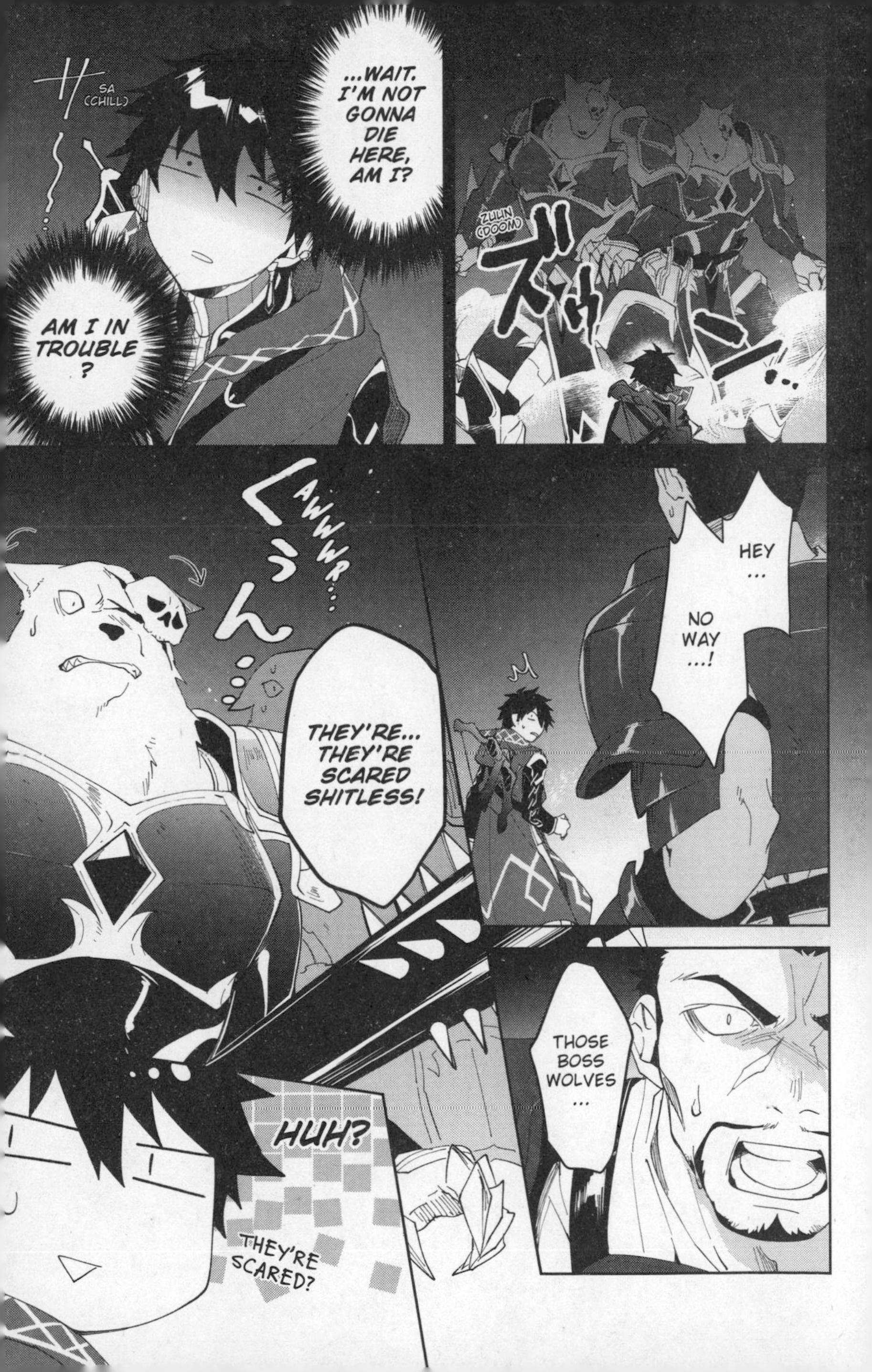
ZULIN (DOOM)
...WAIT. I'M NOT GONNA DIE HERE, AM I?
SA (CHILL)
AM I IN TROUBLE?
HEY...
NO WAY...!
AWWWR...
THEY'RE... THEY'RE SCARED SHITLESS!
THOSE BOSS WOLVES...
HUH?
THEY'RE SCARED?

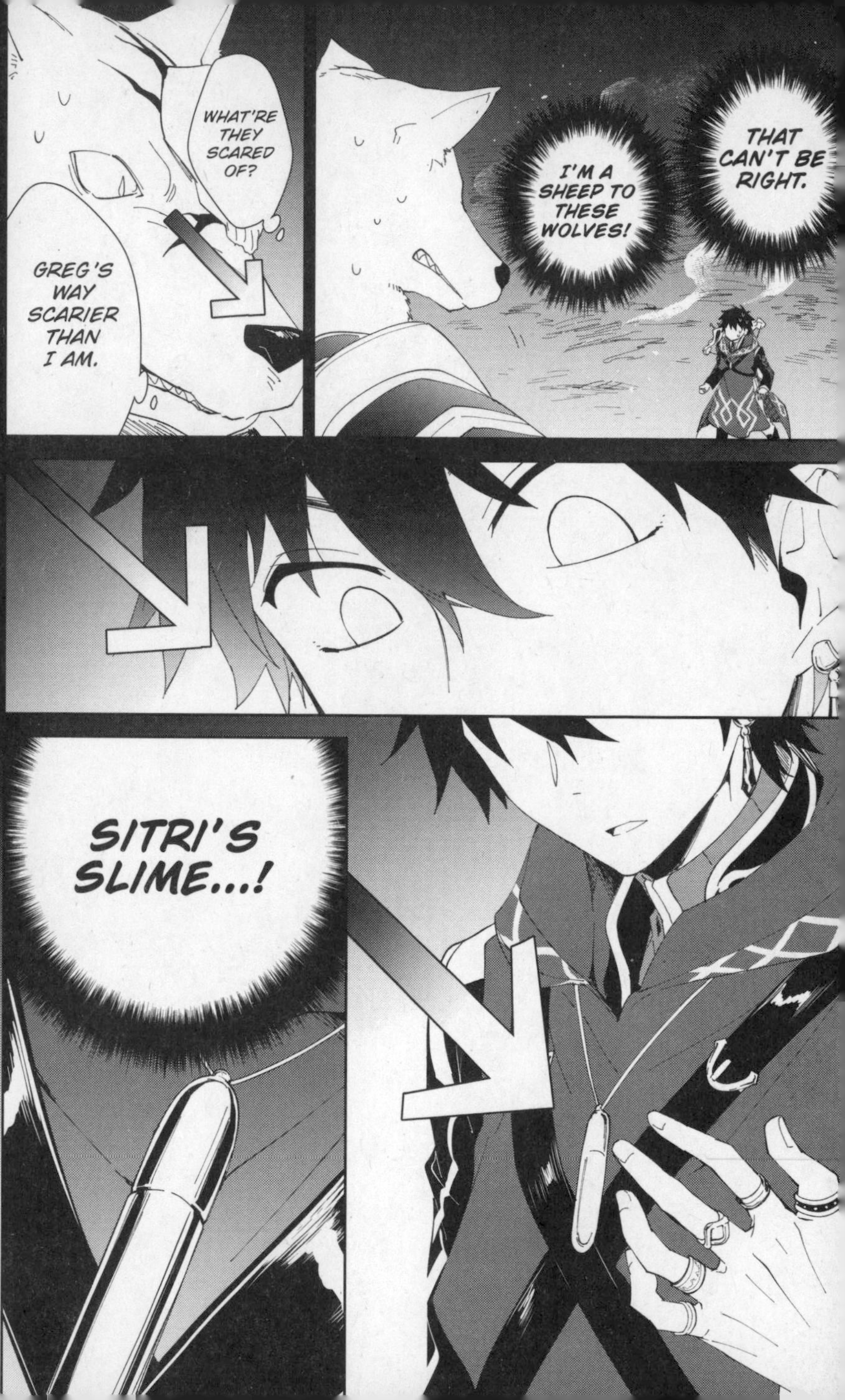
THAT CAN'T BE RIGHT.
I'M A SHEEP TO THESE WOLVES!
WHAT'RE THEY SCARED OF?
GREG'S WAY SCARIER THAN I AM.
SITRI'S SLIME...!

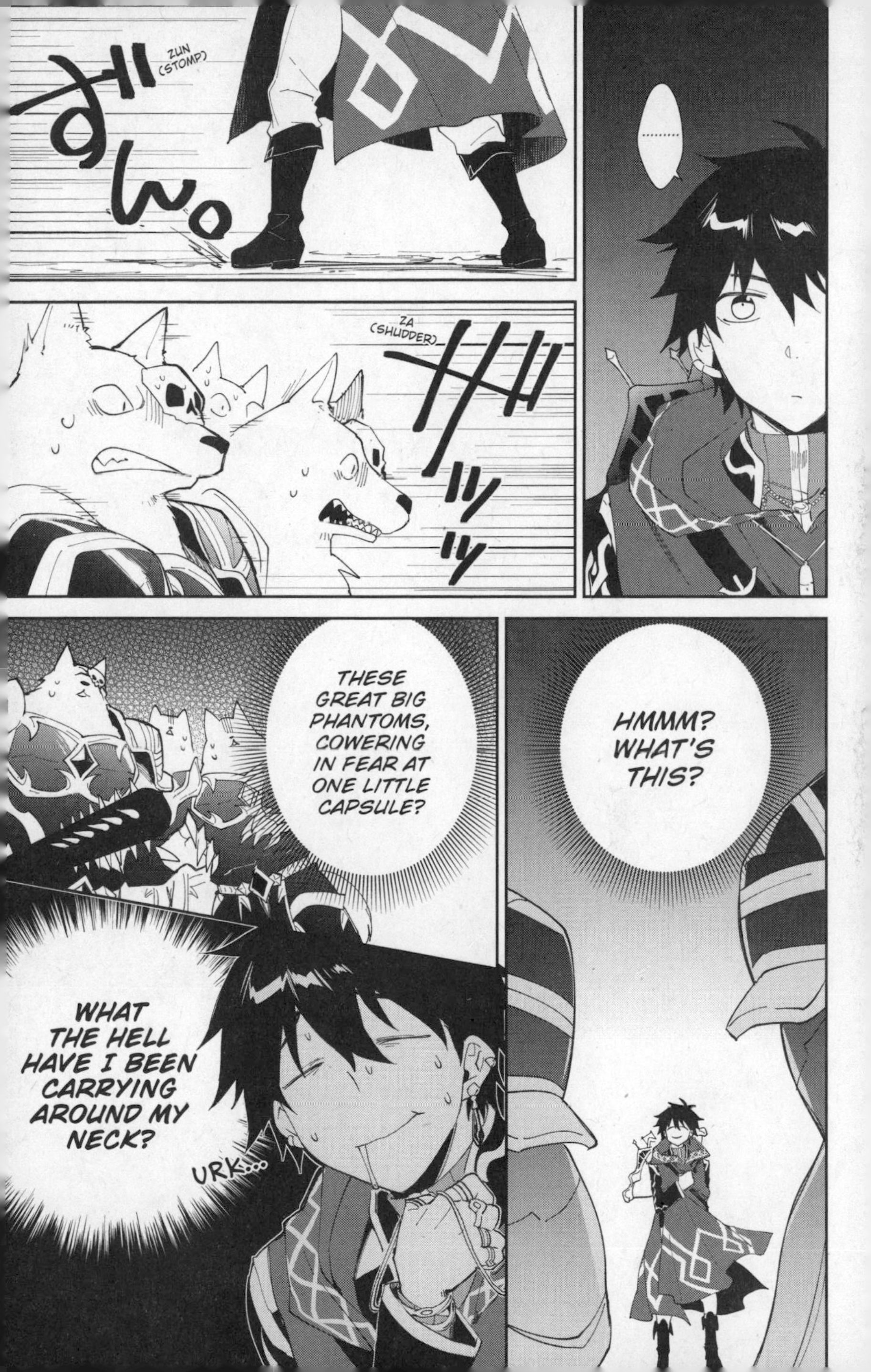

......
ZUN (STOMP)
ZA (SHUDDER)
HMMM? WHAT'S THIS?
THESE GREAT BIG PHANTOMS, COWERING IN FEAR AT ONE LITTLE CAPSULE?
WHAT THE HELL HAVE I BEEN CARRYING AROUND MY NECK?
URK...

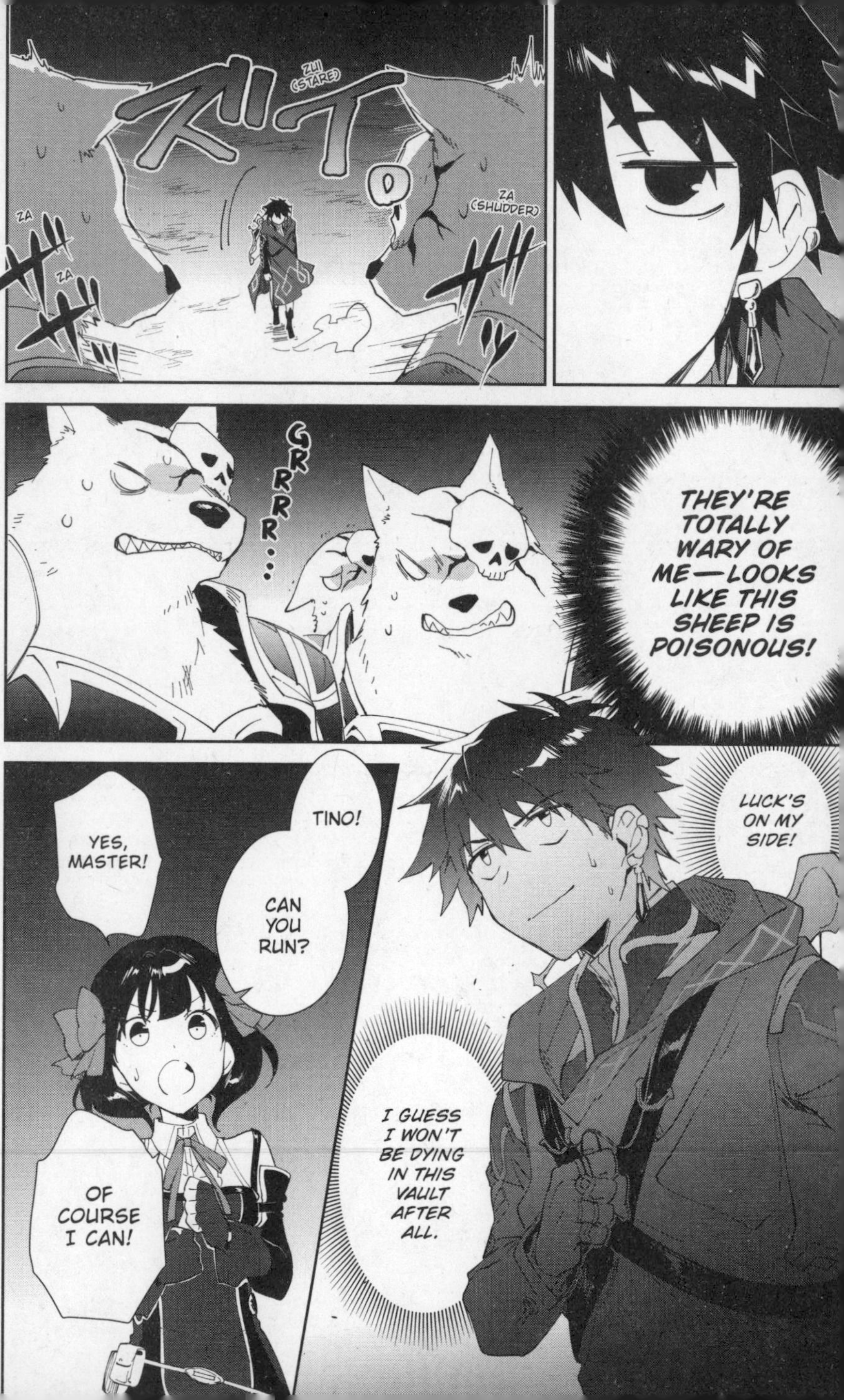
ZUI (STARE)
ZA (SHUDDER)
ZA
ZA
THEY'RE TOTALLY WARY OF ME—LOOKS LIKE THIS SHEEP IS POISONOUS!
GRRRR...
LUCK'S ON MY SIDE!
TINO!
CAN YOU RUN?
YES, MASTER!
I GUESS I WON'T BE DYING IN THIS VAULT AFTER ALL.
OF COURSE I CAN!

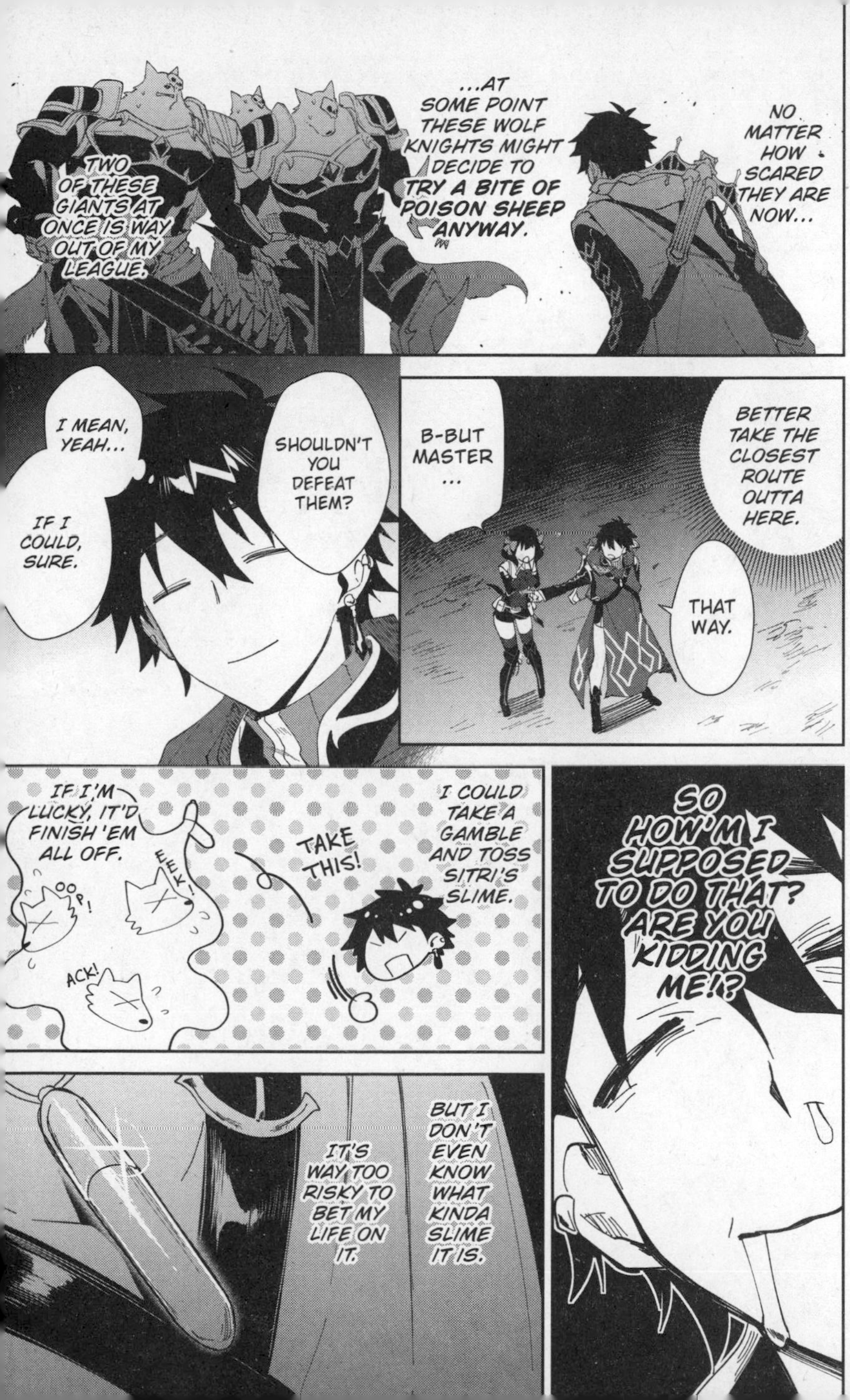
NO MATTER HOW SCARED THEY ARE NOW...
...AT SOME POINT THESE WOLF KNIGHTS MIGHT DECIDE TO TRY A BITE OF POISON SHEEP ANYWAY.
TWO OF THESE GIANTS AT ONCE IS WAY OUT OF MY LEAGUE.
BETTER TAKE THE CLOSEST ROUTE OUTTA HERE.
THAT WAY.
B-BUT MASTER...
SHOULDN'T YOU DEFEAT THEM?
I MEAN, YEAH...
IF I COULD, SURE.
SO HOW'M I SUPPOSED TO DO THAT? ARE YOU KIDDING ME!?
I COULD TAKE A GAMBLE AND TOSS SITRI'S SLIME.
TAKE THIS!
IF I'M LUCKY, IT'D FINISH 'EM ALL OFF.
EEEK!
OOP!
ACK!
BUT I DON'T EVEN KNOW WHAT KINDA SLIME IT IS.
IT'S WAY TOO RISKY TO BET MY LIFE ON IT.

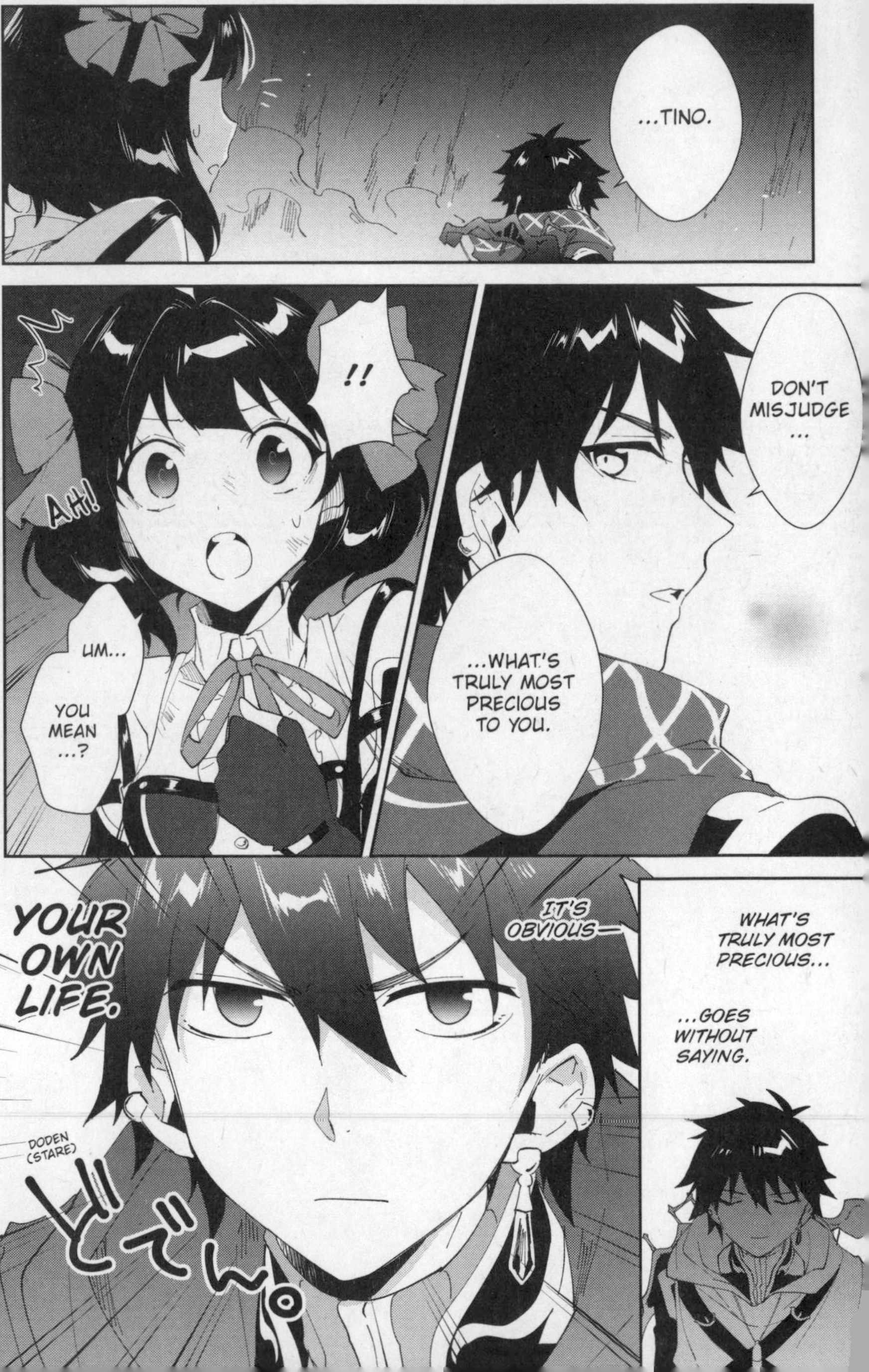
...TINO.
DON'T MISJUDGE ...
...WHAT'S TRULY MOST PRECIOUS TO YOU.
!!
AH!
UM...
YOU MEAN ...?
WHAT'S TRULY MOST PRECIOUS...
...GOES WITHOUT SAYING.
IT'S OBVIOUS—
YOUR OWN LIFE.
DODEN (STARE)
どでん。

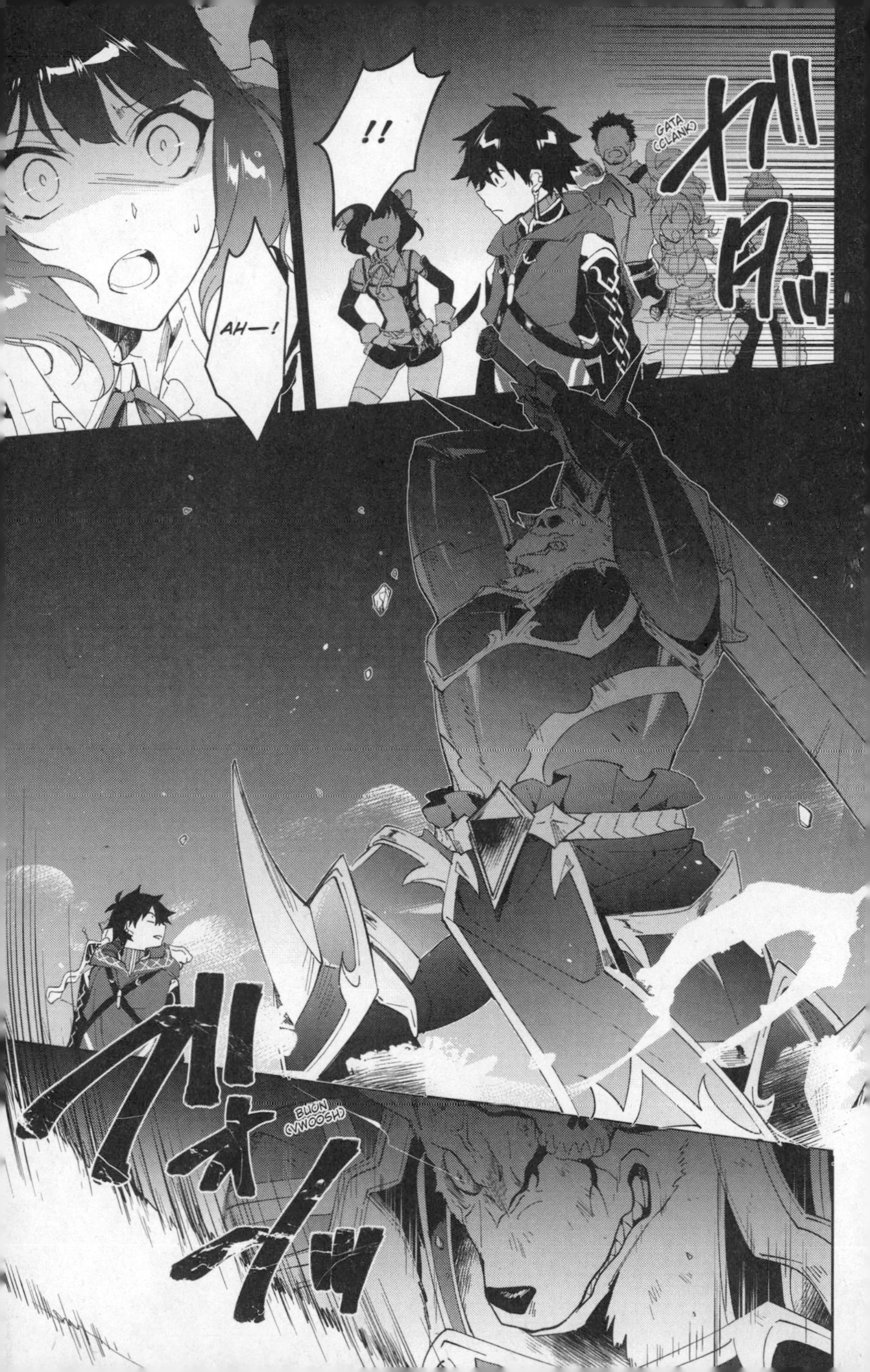
GATA (CLANK)
!!
AH—!
BUON (VWOOSH)

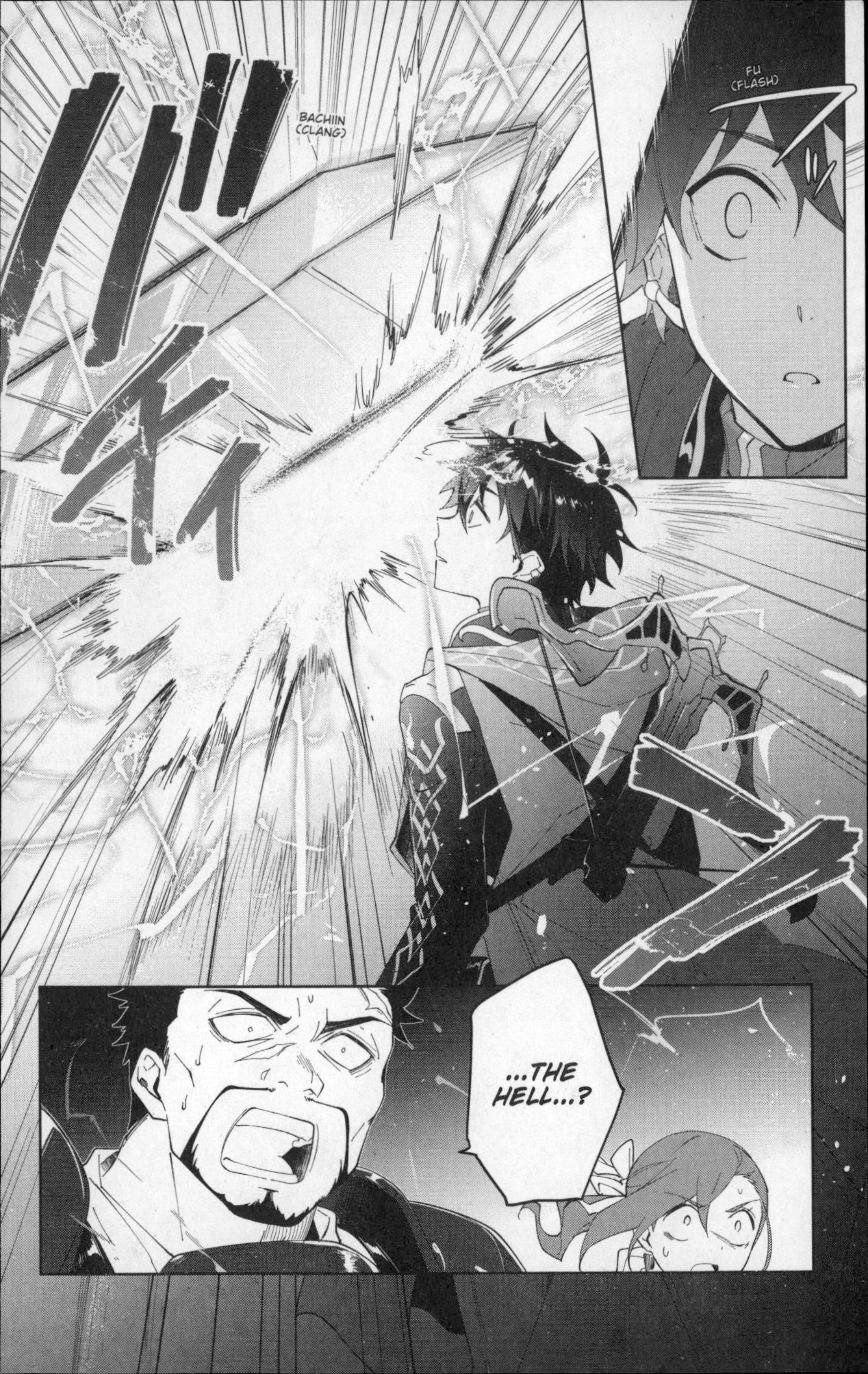
FU
(FLASH)
BACHIIN
(CLANG)
...THE HELL...?

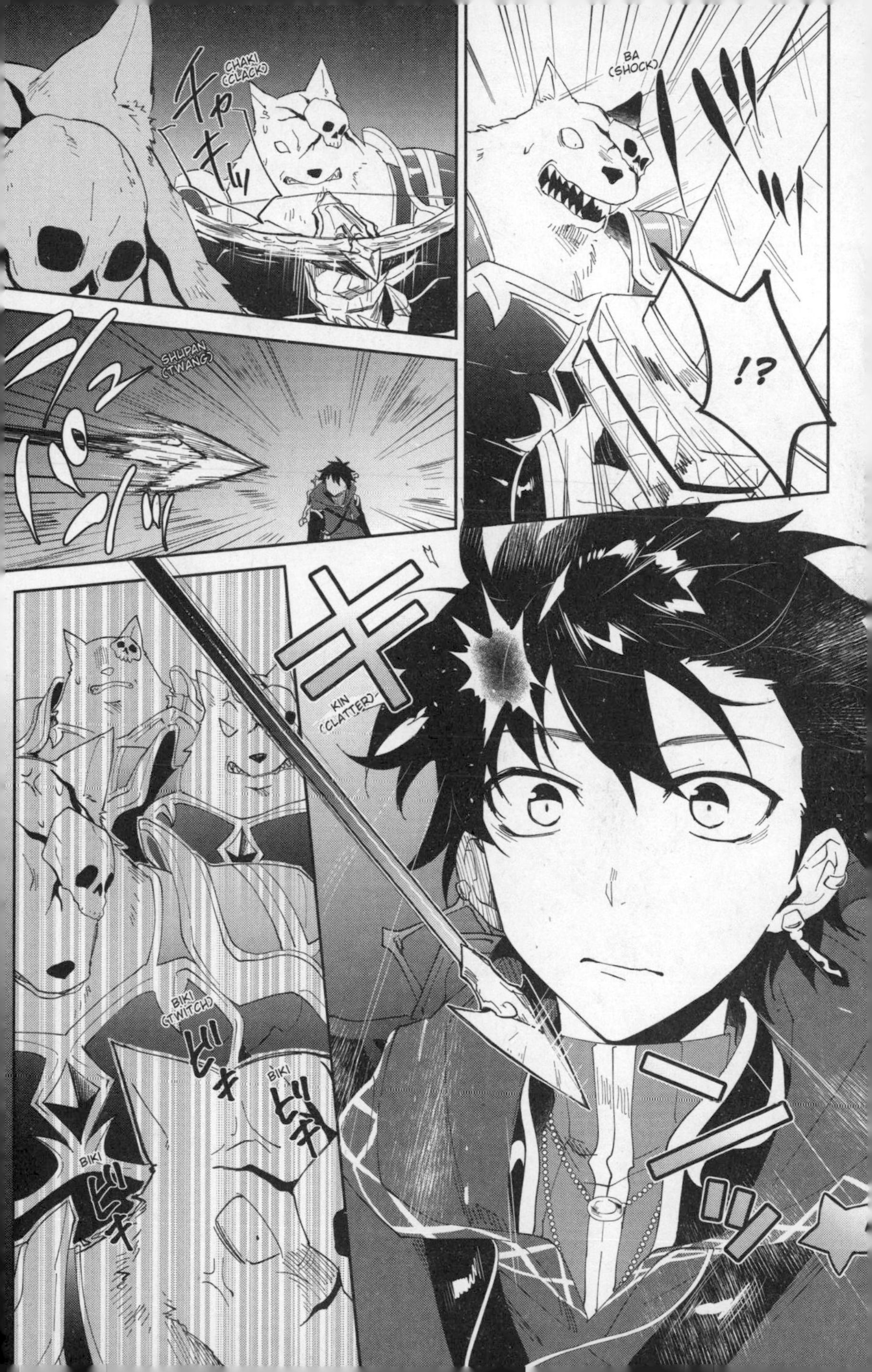
BA (SHOCK)
!?
CHAKI (CLACK)
SHUPAN (TWANG)
KIN (CLATTER)
BIKI (TWITCH)
BIKI
BIKI

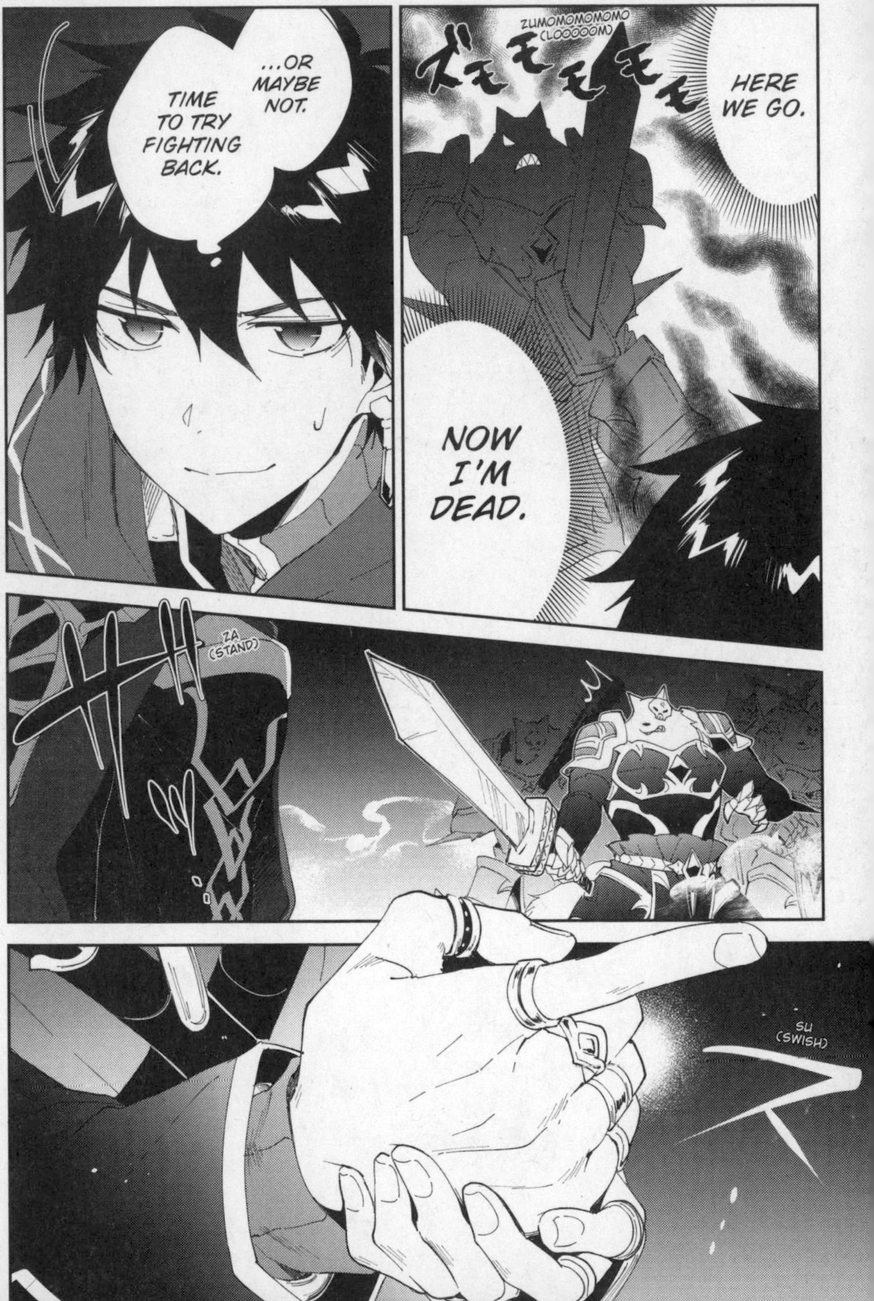
ZUMOMOMOMOMO (LOOOOOM)
HERE WE GO.
NOW I'M DEAD.
...OR MAYBE NOT.
TIME TO TRY FIGHTING BACK.
ZA (STAND)
SU (SWISH)

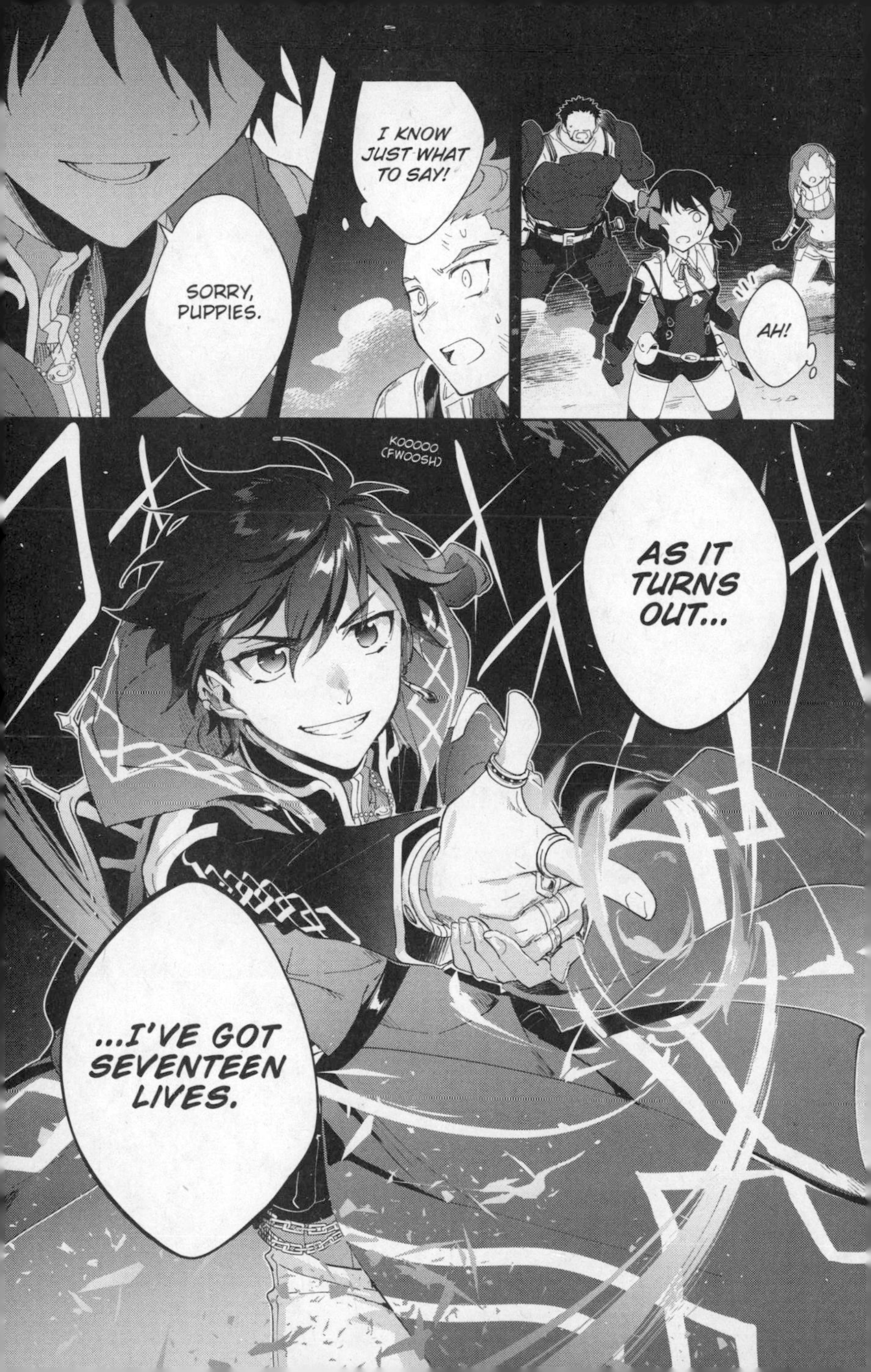
AH!
I KNOW JUST WHAT TO SAY!
SORRY, PUPPIES.
KOOOOO (FWOOSH)
AS IT TURNS OUT...
...I'VE GOT SEVENTEEN LIVES.

LET THIS
Grieving Soul Retire
WOE IS THE WEAKLING WHO LEADS THE STRONGEST PARTY

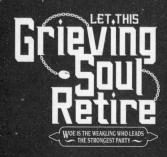

BONUS MANGA AFTERWORD!

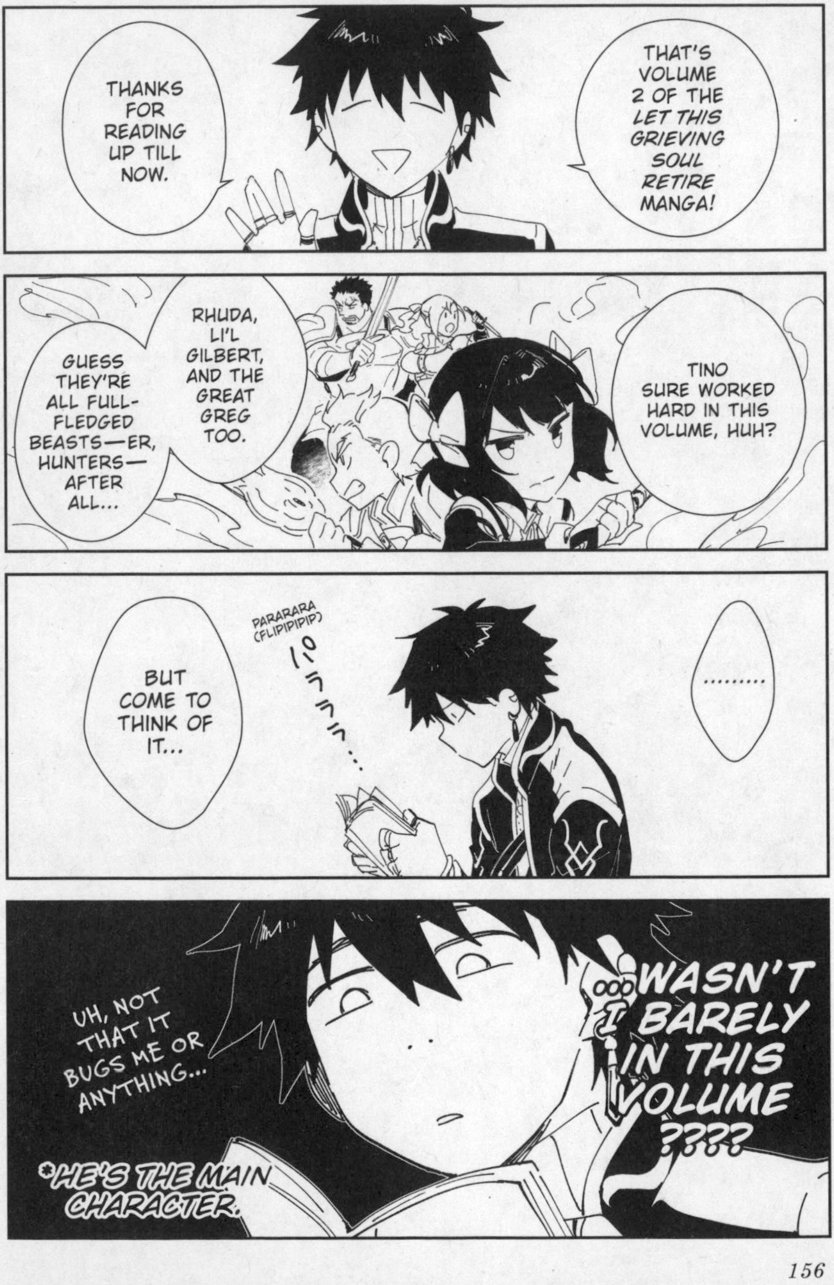

THAT'S VOLUME 2 OF THE *LET THIS GRIEVING SOUL RETIRE* MANGA!
THANKS FOR READING UP TILL NOW.
TINO SURE WORKED HARD IN THIS VOLUME, HUH?
RHUDA, LI'L GILBERT, AND THE GREAT GREG TOO.
GUESS THEY'RE ALL FULL-FLEDGED BEASTS—ER, HUNTERS—AFTER ALL...
....
PARARARA (FLIPIPIPIP)
パラララ…
BUT COME TO THINK OF IT...
WASN'T I BARELY IN THIS VOLUME????
UH, NOT THAT IT BUGS ME OR ANYTHING...
*HE'S THE MAIN CHARACTER.

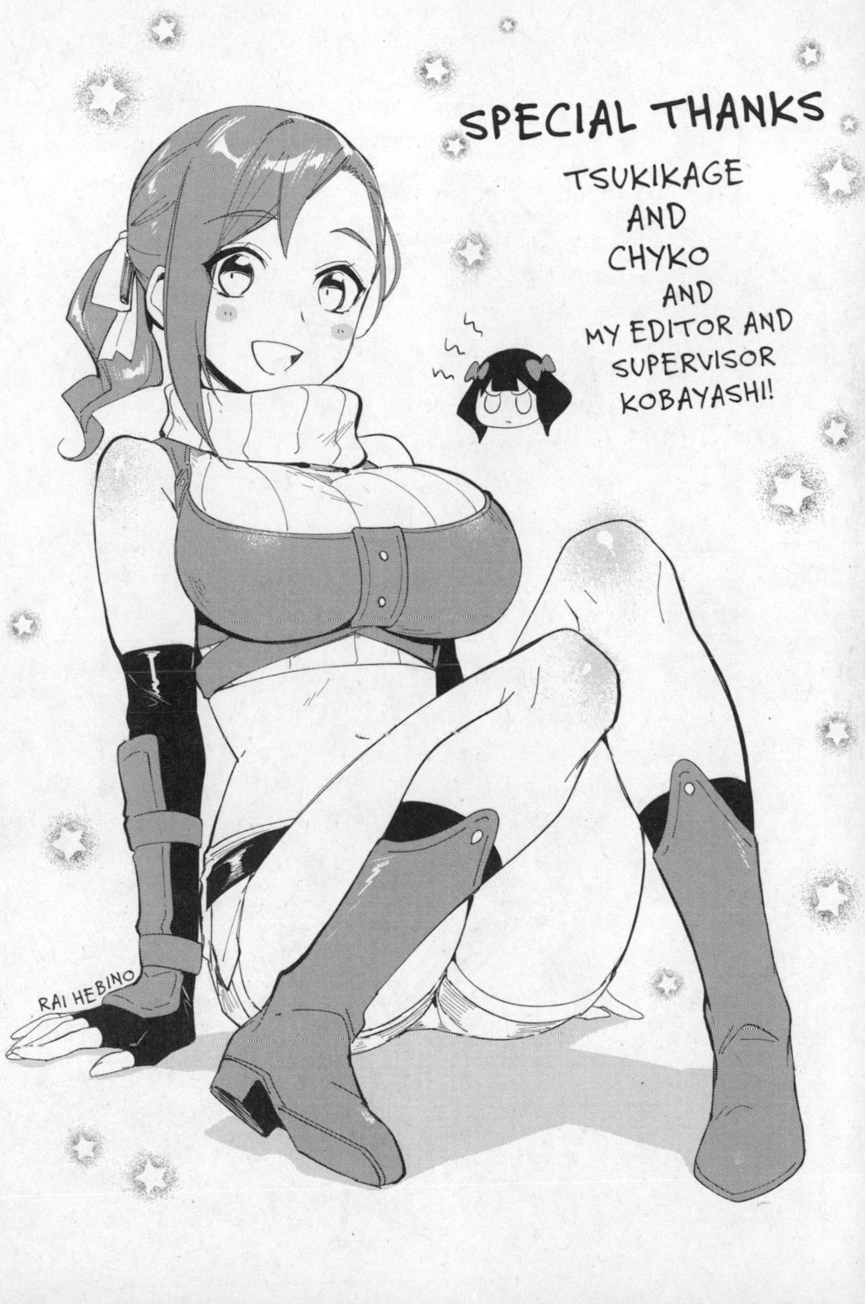
SPECIAL THANKS
TSUKIKAGE
AND
CHYKO
AND
MY EDITOR AND
SUPERVISOR
KOBAYASHI!
RAI HEBINO

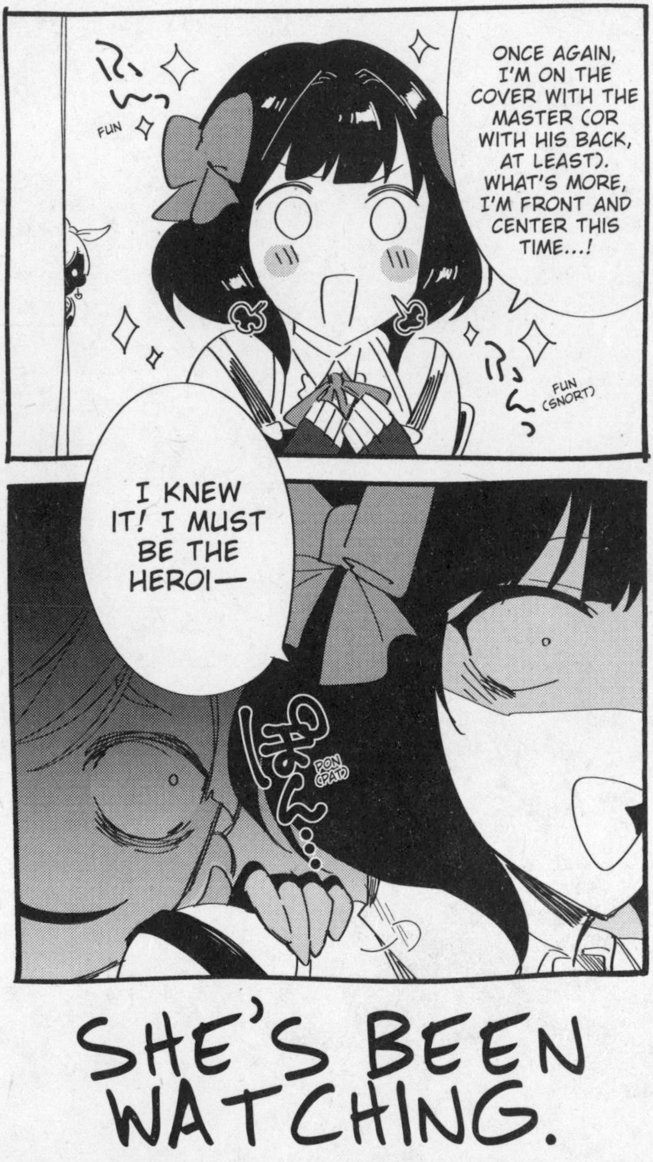
ONCE AGAIN, I'M ON THE COVER WITH THE MASTER (OR WITH HIS BACK, AT LEAST). WHAT'S MORE, I'M FRONT AND CENTER THIS TIME...!
FUN
FUN (SNORT)
I KNEW IT! I MUST BE THE HEROI—
PON (PAT)

SHE'S BEEN WATCHING.

Turn to the back of
the book for an
original short story by
Tsukikage, the author of
*Let This Grieving
Soul Retire*!

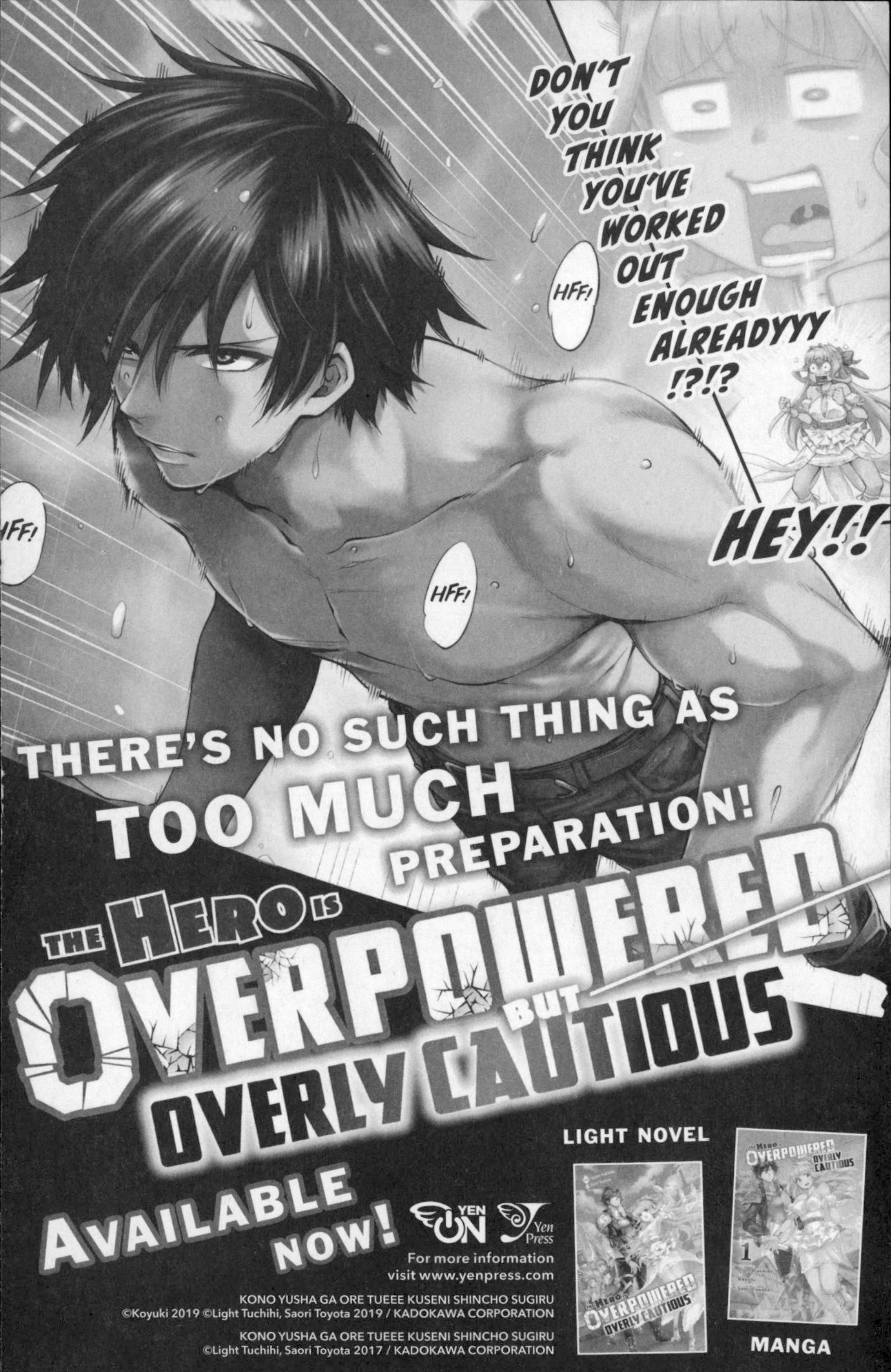
DON'T YOU THINK YOU'VE WORKED OUT ENOUGH ALREADYYY!?!?
HEY!!
HFF!
HFF!
HFF!
THERE'S NO SUCH THING AS TOO MUCH PREPARATION!
THE HERO IS OVERPOWERED BUT OVERLY CAUTIOUS
LIGHT NOVEL
MANGA
AVAILABLE NOW!
YEN ON
Yen Press
For more information visit www.yenpress.com
KONO YUSHA GA ORE TUEEE KUSENI SHINCHO SUGIRU
©Koyuki 2019 ©Light Tuchihi, Saori Toyota 2019 / KADOKAWA CORPORATION
KONO YUSHA GA ORE TUEEE KUSENI SHINCHO SUGIRU
©Light Tuchihi, Saori Toyota 2017 / KADOKAWA CORPORATION

COMBATANTS WILL BE DISPATCHED!

AVAILABLE WHEREVER BOOKS ARE SOLD!

LIGHT NOVEL
VOLUMES 1-6

MANGA
VOLUMES 1-5

©Natsume Akatsuki, Kakao • Lanthanum 2017
KADOKAWA CORPORATION
©Masaaki Kiasa 2018 ©Natsume Akatsuki, Kakao • Lanthanum 2018
KADOKAWA CORPORATION

Always bring a gun to a sword fight!

With world domination nearly in their grasp, the Supreme Leaders of the Kisaragi Corporation—an underground criminal group turned evil megacorp—have decided to try their hands at interstellar conquest. A quick dice roll nominates their chief operative, Combat Agent Six, to be the one to explore an alien planet...and the first thing he does when he gets there is change the sacred incantation for a holy ritual to the most embarrassing thing he can think of. But evil deeds are business as usual for Kisaragi operatives, so if Six wants a promotion and a raise, he'll have to work much harder than that! For starters, he'll have to do something about the other group of villains on the planet, who are calling themselves the "Demon Lord's Army" or whatever. After all, this world doesn't need two evil organizations!

For more information
visit www.yenpress.com

So I'm a Spider, So What?

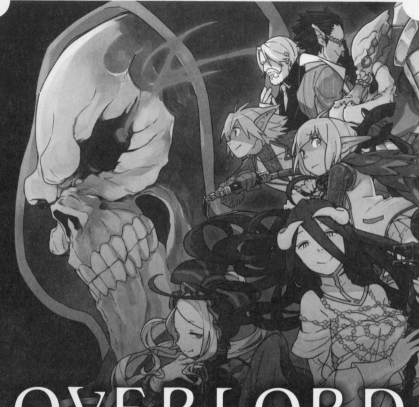

Rai Hebino

ORIGINAL STORY: Tsukikage

CHARACTER DESIGN: Chyko

TRANSLATION: John Neal

LETTERING: Chiho Christie

NAGEKI NO BOREI WA INTAI SHITAI ~SAIJAKU HUNTER NI YORU SAIKYO PARTY IKUSEIJUTSU~ Vol.2
©Rai Hebino/Tsukikage 2020
First published in Japan in 2020 by KADOKAWA CORPORATION, Tokyo.
English translation rights arranged with KADOKAWA CORPORATION, Tokyo, through TUTTLE-MORI AGENCY, INC., Tokyo.

Yen Press
150 West 30th Street, 19th Floor
New York, NY 10001

Visit us at yenpress.com • facebook.com/yenpress • twitter.com/yenpress
yenpress.tumblr.com • instagram.com/yenpress

First Yen Press Edition: March 2022

Yen Press is an imprint of Yen Press, LLC.
The Yen Press name and logo are trademarks of Yen Press, LLC.

The publisher is not responsible for websites (or their content) that are not owned by the publisher.

Library of Congress Control Number: 2021946317

ISBNs: 978-1-9753-3449-9 (paperback)
978-1-9753-3450-5 (ebook)

10 9 8 7 6 5 4 3 2 1

WOR

Printed in the United States of America

LET THIS

Grieving Soul Retire

WOE IS THE WEAKLING WHO LEADS THE STRONGEST PARTY

some problems of her own, really.

Ever since I became a clanmaster and hit level 8, I've had many more chances to consult with a lot more people.

I certainly don't expect to run into any less trouble from here on out, and being who I am, I'm sure I'll end up off-loading it on the members of the capital's top treasure-hunting clan.

But there's just one thing I want you to remember.

I may not be a very hard worker. I may be useless, and I may take every chance I get to take advantage of someone's goodwill. But despite all that, I've never acted out of anything like malice.

Who's Krai Andrey? Just a mildly incompetent, lazy relic lover. Careless, limp, and disappointing. In other words, just one completely average guy.

LET THIS Grieving Soul Retire

WOE IS THE WEAKLING WHO LEADS THE STRONGEST PARTY

and whenever I don't know what to do, I just follow whatever my conscience tells me. If I want to eat a bunch of sweets and still act like I'm a tough guy, that's fine. Honestly, everyone should be more like me and do whatever they want.

This world we live in is totally loaded with danger.

I'm easily the most incompetent level 8 hunter out there, and the laziest clanmaster, and the happiest party leader. Still, that's all pretty small stuff compared with the whole wide world.

I pray to the gods, but I don't believe in them. I feel like I'm destined for something—or maybe cursed would be more accurate—but I don't believe in fate, either. Whatever horrific disaster may strike, it's not my fault. It's not anyone's fault, of course.

If someone else did exactly the same thing I did, at exactly the same time, it wouldn't turn out any differently just because they weren't me. The hunters in the First Steps may call me "Thousand Trials," but I don't give out any tests or trials or anything, let alone a thousand. That's something they all decided on their own, out of some sense of valor.

Liz really puts Tino through the wringer for her training, and, well… I'll admit I feel a pang of guilt about that, being an old friend of Liz's and all. But still, Tino's only undergoing all that training because she herself wanted it, and listening to me doesn't go well for her anyway. Tino knows that everything I say and do tends to backfire, and yet she listens intently and follows along. You could probably say Tino's got with. I've basically lived my life like a log in a muddy stream, totally at the mercy of the current.

I've lost count of how many times I've tried to retire. Basically, any time any issue pops up at all, I shout that this is it, I'm retiring… But at this point, I'm stuck—like there's been a fence around me so long that I'll never be able to clear it.

That's right. I'm so pathetic that I can't even quit correctly.

At some point along the way, I'd earned myself a title. I started getting recognized as the leader of a hotshot young party. And no matter how big the skill gap between me and the others got, they never said a single thing about it.

I'd just been screwing around from the very start, but they've never complained. At this point, I figure they either have that holy, inexhaustible love befitting a saint—or a few screws loose in their heads.

Then, before I knew it, I'd found enlightenment.
And I stopped thinking.
People are always asking me what the hell I'm thinking. Well, the truth is I'm not thinking about anything at all. If nothing I do will end up going well, but doing nothing will only make things worse, there's no real point in thinking things through now, is there?

So I just do what I feel like. Whatever I want. That way, I can dodge any obstacles I see coming, could get to cut someone down; I passed Tino along as a protégé for the let's just say "hotheaded" Liz; I even had Sitri look for my own successor… Each and every one of those things ended up veering off in a completely different direction than I'd anticipated. If I had to score to the whole enterprise, I'd give myself about thirty points out of a hundred, tops.

Now, when you head into a treasure vault, there's a good chance that you'll run into a boss. If you're specifically there on an extermination quest, you can expect to face some sort of variant that's a step or two stronger than what you'd normally find. Plus, there's always a chance that you'll be traveling, going about your business, and then there you are, right in the middle of a rampaging horde of monsters. Or maybe it turns out you bear a resemblance to some heinous criminal with a huge bounty on his head, and you've got to deal with that.

You can play the lottery over and over again and never win and then take one step outside on a stormy day and get struck by lightning immediately. Case in point: If I spend all day lounging around in the clanmaster's room, boom, I'll get hit with a summons. No matter how much money comes flowing in, none of it gets saved. My childhood friends are out there getting hurt but steadily growing even stronger; meanwhile, I've completely lost any sense of how strong I am in the first place. That's the level I'm looking at.

I don't know anything that's going on to begin

So I was aware of my own weakness, but that's the funny thing: Because I was weak, I couldn't bring myself to say anything about it. And because Luke and the rest were so strong, they could easily absorb all the weakness I could manage. You know how they say when one door shuts, another opens? Or maybe it's more like how they say there's a lid for every pot. Doors, lids, whatever—either way, we made a miraculous accord.

Luke and the others would drag me along with them, and they'd never hesitate to strike in any random direction I pointed. Somehow, as a result, our party ended up being known as a real team of badasses.

We inspired fear and respect. We also earned the ire of plenty of criminals, and I ended up groveling for mercy for some reason or another along the line.

The hunter lifestyle brought me all sorts of problems, and while most of the specifics have faded into oblivion, if my memory holds correct, things went according to my assumptions exactly zero times.

Ask me to do it all over again, and I'd absolutely refuse. I don't think I could if I wanted to. Most of it hasn't even gone that well the first time around.

I tried to come across as calm and self-possessed. I gathered as much intel as I could before going on a quest. I put on airs like I was really hard-boiled. None of it worked; nothing I did went off without a hitch. I tried to disarm Luke, who'd take any chance he anything like that. I bet I'd simply be living another life as something other than a treasure hunter. And even then, even in that other life, Luke and the others would still be my friends.

I'm a normal guy, like you'd find pretty much anywhere. When I run into an obstacle I can't get past, I act like I'm struggling with it for a little while, and then I give up. I had no business getting verified as even just a level 1 hunter. Heroism was completely out of the question for a normal guy like me.

Five years of living and surviving as a treasure hunter hasn't changed that one bit.

I'm an incompetent who's aware of his own incompetence. I hate putting myself through rigorous training, and I can't bear to do hard work if there's no clear benefit to it.

Can I confess something to you? I don't want this position I've found myself in at all. Not at all. I never intended to raise my hunter level. Hell, the very first time I made a mistake, I tried to use it as an excuse to quit being a hunter. Luke managed to keep me from quitting, but by then, I'd already totally given up on the dream of becoming a hero.

I'm thoroughly mediocre, and I've got thoroughly mediocre ambitions to match. Status? Honor? Wealth? Power? I didn't need any of that. All I wanted was a fun life with just a touch of thrills every now and then.

until I made that fateful realization during our first exploration that I could finally say, "Sorry, guys. This is more than I can handle. I'm gonna sit this one out." I'm pretty sure that's because, to me, becoming a treasure hunter was just a way to keep playing our childish games for a while longer.

Luke and the others were different. They were making a serious attempt at becoming heroes. I don't think I ever did. I didn't notice it at the time, but that wasn't what I was aiming for.

Honestly, I have no idea how I managed to make it all the way to the end of our first real adventure together without soaking my pillow in tears, sobbing over how I'd never measure up to my rapidly improving friends. But eventually I did.

The night after that first treasure hunt, I finally felt that fatal sense of alienation from the friends who I'd known so long. Then, at last, I cried, absolutely distraught that I couldn't follow them where they were headed.

But now I get what was going on. I'm pretty sure that, back then, I was really just sad that we couldn't play together anymore.

Let's suppose Luke hadn't gone and said the crazy thing he said the next day: "Krai, if you haven't got a role, you should be our leader instead!" If he hadn't said that, and I'd gone on to leave the party, I wouldn't have fallen further into despair. I wouldn't have risen to the occasion and jumped to action, either. And I wouldn't have started hating Luke and the others or teachers (and they weren't all great teachers; there were some real morons mixed in there, too), and every single one of them told me, as mildly as they could, that I just didn't have the skills to cut it. At that point, I should've realized that I was in trouble.

But I stayed indecisive about the whole thing until I finally came of age and cleared my first treasure vault. In that instant, I knew what I had to do at last. Now, looking back on that little Krai Andrey and his indecision, I can't help but think about how horrifically carefree he was.

Even before those childhood friends of mine became full-fledged treasure hunters, you could already see glimpses of their excellent abilities. Even Sitri the alchemist—the late bloomer of the group, since we were out in the boonies where decent alchemy instructors are in short supply—managed to be well above average. Technique, know-how, strength—I watched as my friends steadily developed them all. They were hailed as prodigies, and all I could do was clap and cheer from the sidelines.

"Whoa! Nice going, Luke! You're the best swordsman in the world!" and all that. And I really was happy for them. But I was nothing like them; I was no child prodigy. I was just some loser kid.

Naturally, I could tell something was wrong. I even vaguely understood (though nothing seems vague about it now) that there was a gap in ability opening up between me and my friends. But I still didn't do anything with that understanding. It wasn't

Krai Andrey's Soliloquy

by Tsukikage

Let's just say, for the purpose of argument, that you asked me what the problem was.

I'd puzzle over it for a while, and then I'd tell you this: It's all problems and has been from the very start. In fact, my life's totally overflowing with problems—including the fact that nobody's ever asked me what the problem is, not even once, in the five years since I became a treasure hunter.

Back when I was young, I knew this guy named Exceed Zequence. Exceed was the most famous treasure hunter in the town where I grew up. (Not to oversell it—at the time, hunters there only ever got so famous.) Hearing his tales of heroism and adventure was what first sent my life down this dark path.

I had plenty of chances to notice what was going on. Plenty of chances to pick myself back up, too. I started my treasure hunter training along with my friends and my little sister. We had several different

Krai Andrey's Soliloquy

by Tsukikage